D0073168

THE ART OF PERSUASION
IN GREECE

THE ART OF
PERSUASION
IN GREECE

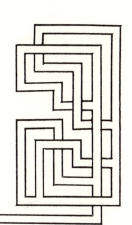

BY GEORGE KENNEDY

PRINCETON UNIVERSITY PRESS
PRINCETON, NEW JERSEY · 1963

Publication of this book
has been aided by
the Ford Foundation program
to support publication,
through university presses,
of work in the humanities
and social sciences

Printed in the United States of America
by Princeton University Press, Princeton, New Jersey

Sixth Printing, 1974

This book is intended to furnish teachers and students of Classics and of Speech with a history of Greek rhetoric. To date the only real claimant to that title has been Kroll's Pauly-Wissowa article, which has many virtues but is written in the typical manner of a German encyclopaedist and is now over twenty years old. My goal has been to be both comprehensive and selective and to plot a course between a broad survey of culture and a narrow history of technicalities. In this attempt the question arose as to how much discussion of the rhetorical techniques of literature should be included in a work concerned centrally with the development of rhetorical theory. I have resisted the temptation to indulge in rhetorical analyses of such poets as Euripides, Menander, and Callimachus but have found it impossible to omit such a discussion of the Attic orators. The reader should not expect to find here a detailed study of historical and legal aspects of the orators; the scholarship in that area is extensive. Certain important topics, the rhetorical theory of the laughable and the relation between rhetorical theory and the law, to name two, have been omitted in the belief that they are best treated as part of the history of Roman rhetoric. I have refrained from dealing with Roman rhetoric in itself because satisfactory treatment would require more than doubling the length of the book. The tradition is the same as that of Greece, but it should be viewed from the distinctive point of view of the Roman mind, Roman political institutions, and the Latin language. Thus, although Cicero will be mentioned many times in these pages, the book stops short of direct consideration of him or any other Roman rhetorician.

I have deliberately inserted much of the documentation from the ancient sources directly into the text: documentation should not be considered an apparatus incidentally tacked on to a scholarly discussion; it is the basis of the statements made and not only the fact of its existence, as indicated by the presence of a footnote number, but its nature should be before the reader's eye at all times.

A number of years ago the late Werner Jaeger, Sterling Dow, J. Peterson Elder, and Cedric H. Whitman encouraged me to study rhetoric, and I would like to record my gratitude to them for that as well as for other kindnesses. In 1960 I had the assistance of a Summer Research Grant of the Danforth Foundation. The staff of the Haverford College Library has been continually helpful. Finally, I am indebted to two anonymous readers provided by the Princeton University Press.

The book is dedicated to my good friend Paul Fenimore Cooper, Jr.

G.K.

Haverford College
December 1961

Contents

CONTENTS

CHAPTER FIVE

APPENDIX

The following works are repeatedly referred to by the author's name alone, followed by volume and page, section, or column number. When other works of these same authors are cited the full reference is given. For additional basic works on Greek rhetoric see chapter one, note 1, and chapter five, note 1.

Arnim — Hans von Arnim, *Leben und Werke des Dio von Prusa*, Berlin, 1898.

Barwick — Karl Barwick, "Die Gliederung der rhetorischen τέχνη," *Hermes* 57 (1922) 1-62.

Blass — Friedrich Blass, *Die attische Beredsamkeit*, 3 vols., Leipzig, vol. 1, second edition, 1887; vol. 2, first edition, 1874; vol. 3, part one, first edition, 1877, or, if specified, second edition, 1893; vol. 3, part two, first edition, 1880.

Bonner and Smith — Robert J. Bonner and Gertrude Smith, *The administration of justice from Homer to Aristotle*, 2 vols., Chicago, vol. 1, 1930; vol. 2, 1938.

Diels — Hermann Diels, *Die Fragmente der Vorsokratiker*, 3 vols., Berlin, seventh edition edited by Walther Kranz, 1954.

Halm — Carolus Halm, *Rhetores latini minores*, Leipzig, 1863.

Hunt — Everett Lee Hunt, "Plato and Aristotle on rhetoric and rhetoricians," *Studies in rhetoric and public speaking in honor of James Albert Winans*, New York, 1925, 3-60.

Jaeger — Werner Jaeger, *Demosthenes: the ori-*

gin and growth of his policy, Berkeley, 1938.

Jebb R. C. Jebb, The Attic orators, 2 vols., London, second edition, 1893.

Kroll W. Kroll, "Rhetorik," Paulys Real-Encyclopädie der classischen Altertumswissenschaft, Supplementband 7, Stuttgart, 1940.

Marrou H. I. Marrou (trans. by G. Lamb), A history of education in antiquity, London, 1956.

Navarre Octave Navarre, Essai sur la rhétorique grecque avant Aristote, Paris, 1900.

Norden Eduard Norden, Die antike Kunstprosa, 2 vols., continuous pagination, Leipzig and Berlin, fourth edition, 1923.

Radermacher Ludwig Radermacher, "Artium scriptores: Reste der voraristotelischen Rhetorik," Oesterreiches Akademie der Wissenschaften, Philosophisch-historische Klasse, Sitzungsberichte 227, Band 3, Vienna, 1951.

Solmsen Friedrich Solmsen, Die Entwicklung der aristotelischen Logik und Rhetorik (Neue philologische Untersuchungen 4), Berlin, 1929.

Spengel Leonardus Spengel, Rhetores graeci, 3 vols., Leipzig, vol. 1, part one, 1885; vol. 2, 1854; vol. 3, 1856.

Spengel-Hammer Caspar Hammer, Rhetores graeci ex recognitione Leonardi Spengel, Leipzig, 1894. This is the second edition of vol. 1, part two, of Spengel's work listed above.

Sudhaus Siegfried Sudhaus, Philodemi volumina rhetorica, 2 vols., Leipzig, vol. 1, 1892; vol. 2, 1896; supplementum 1895.

Untersteiner	Mario Untersteiner (trans. by Kathleen Freeman), *The sophists*, Oxford, 1954.
Walz	Christianus Walz, *Rhetores graeci*, 9 vols. (vol. 7 in two parts), London and elsewhere, 1832-1836.

Abbreviations of periodicals

AJP	*American journal of philology*
BPW	*Berliner philologische Wochenschrift* and its successor *Philologische Wochenschrift*
CJ	*Classical journal*
CP	*Classical philology*
CQ	*Classical quarterly*
CR	*Classical review*
CW	*Classical weekly* and its successor *Classical world*
HSCP	*Harvard studies in classical philology*
JKP	*Jahrbücher für klassische Philologie*
JP	*Journal of philology*
LEC	*Les études classiques*
Mn	*Mnemosyne*
NGG	*Nachrichten von der königlichen Gesellschaft der Wissenschaft zu Göttingen, Philologische-historische Klasse.*
QJS	*Quarterly journal of speech*
R-E	*Paulys Real-Encyclopädie der classischen Altertumswissenschaft*
REA	*Revue des études anciennes*
REG	*Revue des études grecques*
RhM	*Rheinisches Museum für Philologie*
SBB	*Preussische Akademie der Wissenschaften, Philosophisch-historische Klasse, Sitzungsberichte*
SBW	*Oesterreiches Akademie der Wissenschaften, Philosophisch-historische Klasse, Sitzungsberichte*
SM	*Speech monographs*
TAPA	*Transactions and proceedings of the American philological association*
WS	*Wiener Studien*

THE ART OF PERSUASION

IN GREECE

"We are freed from rhetoric only by study of its history."
PAUL SHOREY, TAPA 40 (1908) 185

CHAPTER ONE

Introduction: the nature of rhetoric[1]

One of the principal interests of the Greeks was rhetoric. Classicists admit the fact, deplore it, and forget it. After all, the Greeks condoned animal sacrifice, homosexuality, watered wine, and cock fights. But we will never understand the Greeks unless we understand what is peculiar about them. Because we know them best from their literature and because much of this was molded by rhetoric, we should make an effort to achieve a sympathetic comprehension of what they conceived that art to be. In its origin and intention rhetoric was natural and good: it produced clarity, vigor, and beauty, and it rose logically from the conditions and qualities of the classical mind.

Greek society relied on oral expression. Although literacy was clearly extensive in fifth- and fourth-century Athens, even then reading and writing, whether on stone, bronze, clay, wood, wax, or papyrus, was difficult and unnatural.

[1] Among general works on rhetoric are J. C. T. Ernesti, *Lexicon technologiae Graecorum rhetoricae*, Leipzig, 1795, announced for republication Hildesheim, 1962; A.-E. Chaignet, *La rhétorique et son histoire*, Paris, 1888; Charles Sears Baldwin, *Ancient rhetoric and poetic*, New York, 1924, republished Gloucester, Mass., 1959; W. Rhys Roberts, *Greek rhetoric and literary criticism*, New York, 1928; Kroll 1039-1138; Donald C. Bryant, "Aspects of the rhetorical tradition," QJS 36 (1950) 169 ff. and 326 ff. and "Rhetoric: its function," QJS 39 (1953) 401 ff.; M. L. Clarke, *Rhetoric at Rome*, London, 1953; Donald L. Clark, *Rhetoric in Greco-Roman education*, New York, 1957. For bibliography cf. Kroll; H. Ll. Hudson-Williams, "Greek orators and rhetoric," *Fifty years of classical scholarship* (ed. M. Platnauer), Oxford, 1954, 193 ff.; Charles S. Rayment, "A current survey of ancient rhetoric," CW 52 (1958) 75 ff. *L'année philologique: bibliographia critique et analytique de l'antiquité gréco-latine* (ed. J. Marouzeau), Paris, 1924—, annually contains a section "Rhétorique" as well as exhaustive listings under individual authors. SM carries annually in August "A bibliography of rhetoric and public address" (ed. James W. Cleary).

Both the mechanics of ancient civilization and its primary expression remained oral. The political system, for example, operated through the direct speech of the citizens among themselves and to their magistrates, and of the magistrates to their administrative assistants. Writing was used to record a vote, a law, a resolution, but rarely to achieve it in the first place. Political agitation was usually accomplished or defeated by word of mouth. The judicial system was similarly oral: verbal complaints were brought before magistrates, who held hearings; then the litigants pleaded their own cases in public before a jury of citizens. Documents were few. There were written business contracts, but they were negotiated and enforced by face-to-face argument rather than by prolonged correspondence. There were no newspapers, magazines, handbills, or circulars; information was spread orally. Entertainment was provided only to a limited extent by reading; informal conversation, the legitimate stage, or the sound of the human voice in some form constituted the commonest form of diversion. All literature was written to be heard, and even when reading to himself a Greek read aloud.

The oral nature of the society is evident in Greek literature, which flourished long before it was written down. The Homeric poems are undoubtedly the pinnacle of an oral tradition of epic verse that had sung of the deeds of the Trojan war and heroic Greece for generations, conforming extemporaneously to an exacting metrical form by the use of formulae and themes. Greek drama, both tragedy and comedy, grew out of the spontaneous oral traditions of festivals. The beginnings of philosophy are to be found in the traditional folk maxims and cosmologies which made the transition to writing in the poetry we attribute to Hesiod, and history reaches back to the beginnings of time through the tales told around a camp fire, the genealogies, real or fictitious, of famous families, and the advice imparted or the wonders reported by one traveler to another.

No less does oratory go back to the beginnings of civilization. The Greeks have always loved to talk and even wrangle, and have felt the force of their own words. They still feel it. Their earliest oratory must have had many of the characteristics evident in oral poetry. The techniques were learned by listening and imitation, but the power was achieved by an inspiration which carried the speaker on without conscious observance of rules. As he spoke he used ancestors of the commonplaces of later oratory—the topics, the traditional examples, the maxims which he had heard and used before—in the same way that the oral poet used his devices of repetition, and he did so without notes and without verbatim memorization.

The several classes of oral literature only gradually assumed written form.[2] According to Plato (*Phaedrus* 257d5 ff.) fifth-century politicians were afraid of being regarded as sophists if they published speeches. Even in the fourth century, perhaps four hundred years after the Phoenician alphabet had first been used for literary purposes in Greek, there is fear and suspicion of writing. Plato (*Phaedrus* 274c5 ff.) tells an elaborate story about the Egyptian god Theuth, who invented the alphabet and was told by the god Thamus that the invention was harmful, for instead of being an aid to memory the letters would destroy all memory. Plato goes on to object to writing because the words cannot explain and argue but always say the same thing. His view is not unique: there has been preserved a little work by Alcidamas, *On those writing written speeches or on the sophists*, which defends extemporaneity.[3]

Once oral literature became written, speech did not lose the special significance it had had, either in form or in sub-

[2] Cf. James A. Notopoulos. "Mnemosyne in oral literature," TAPA 69 (1938) 476 ff., and W. C. Greene, "The spoken and the written word," HSCP 60 (1951) 23 ff.

[3] Cf. Radermacher B.xxii.15; discussion and an English translation in LaRue Van Hook, "Alcidamas versus Isocrates," CW 12 (1919) 89 ff.

stance. Epic derives much of its vitality and realism from the direct discourse, varying in degree of formality but including complete speeches delivered in assemblies or small meetings, as well as addresses to troops or groups of men, personal appeals, and shrewd attempts to persuade, deceive, or beguile someone divine or human. The hymnic poetry does much the same, especially the *Hymn to Hermes,* where the day-old god defends himself with great verbal agility. Elegiac and lyric poems were occasionally composed in the form of addresses designed to persuade—Callinus to his countrymen and Sappho to Aphrodite are examples. True drama was first achieved when speech in the form of dialogue was added to speech in the form of exposition or chorus. The formal aspects of speech are clearly apparent in Greek drama, where the situation often is or resembles a trial.[4] The most striking example is Aeschylus' *Eumenides,* but speech matched against speech is a basic tool of all the tragedians. Modern drama sometimes makes use of a court room setting, but it rarely achieves a formality of speech in domestic circumstances equal to that in Greek plays. Historical writing, except for biography, has also largely abandoned the speeches which are a distinctive convention of ancient historians and their imitators. In the great writers the speeches are the expression of their imagination and fundamental convictions, in others they were a necessary adornment and opportunity for literary conceit. Ancient philosophy uses oratory both as example of logical method, as in the speeches of Gorgias, and for exposition of opposing doctrines, as in the dialogue. Ancient literary epistles are virtually private speeches. Greek oratory itself is an extensive field, including the sermon, the political pamphlet, the educational treatise, the funeral encomium, and the im-

---

[4] Cf. J. Duchemin, *L'ἀγων dans la tragédie grecque,* Paris, 1945. Good examples from the later fifth century are the trial of Polymestor in Euripides' *Hecuba* 1129 ff. and of Helen in the *Trojan women* 911 ff.

aginative exercise, as well as the more expected judicial and deliberative orations.

The significance of oratory is as great in substance as in form. Wherever persuasion is the end, rhetoric is present. This is most marked in formal speeches in epic or drama or history, but it can be found in passages not formally oratorical both in lyric and in philosophy. The philosopher in weighing the evidence, drawing the conclusion, and presenting a literate exposition is fulfilling much the same functions as the orator in court, and so is the historian, who has similar problems of witnesses, psychological credibility, narration of incident, ascription of motive, weighing of evidence, and estimation of justice, expediency, or honor. The Greek philosopher and dramatist share the concern of the historian and orator with justice and responsibility.

The significance of rhetoric and oratory in Greek and Roman intellectual life is further evident in education and criticism. It is not too much to say that rhetoric played the central role in ancient education.[5] In Hellenistic times it constituted the curriculum of what we would regard as secondary schools and acquired an important place in advanced education. Boys had already learned to read and write, had learned some arithmetic, and in Greece had had musical and gymnastic training when, at about the age of fourteen, they were sent to the school of the rhetorician for theoretical instruction in public speaking and for practical exercises. They might continue the latter for the rest of their lives. In the fifth and fourth century B.C. formal education rarely extended beyond elementary school, but instruction in public speaking was an important part of the teaching of the sophists; it was basic to the educational system of Isocrates; and it was even taught by Aristotle.

In view of the formal and substantival role of oratory in ancient literature it is not surprising that ancient literary

[5] Cf. Clark, op.cit. supra n. 1, and Marrou, esp. 194-205 and 284-291.

7

criticism is predominantly rhetorical. Oratory is often the center of interest, and, even in discussions ostensibly devoted to poetics, the organization, approach, standards, and terminology are largely borrowed from the rhetorical schools. The Greeks and Romans are thus shown to have been aware of the crucial part played by public speaking in their lives. This becomes all the more striking when one realizes that there was a general absence of developed criticism in antiquity. Neither Aristotle's *Poetics* nor the treatise *On the sublime,* which are the most perceptive surviving bits of literary criticism, come anywhere near describing the literary achievements of the Greeks, while the pedestrian *Ars poetica* of Horace is typical of the general failure of self-conscious analysis. Criticism of sculpture, painting, music, historiography, and choreography was also weak. Late in its history architecture found a Vitruvius, but otherwise public address is the only one of the creative arts of antiquity which has left a satisfactory discussion of its techniques and materials.

The Greek word for speech is *logos,* an ambiguous and sometimes mystical concept which may refer concretely to a word, words, or an entire oration, or may be used abstractly to indicate the meaning behind a word or expression or the power of thought and organization or the rational principle of the universe or the will of God. On the human level it involves man's thought and his function in society, and it further includes artistic creativity and the power of personality. In a passage echoed by many subsequent writers[6] Isocrates (*Nicocles* 5 ff. reproduced in *Antidosis* 253 ff.) sees in speech the basis of civilization:

"In most of our abilities we differ not at all from the animals; we are in fact behind many in swiftness and strength and other resources. But because there is born in

[6] A Latin counterpart is the even more eloquent encomium of Cicero, *De oratore* 1.30 ff.

us the power to persuade each other and to show ourselves whatever we wish, we not only have escaped from living as brutes, but also by coming together have founded cities and set up laws and invented arts, and speech has helped us attain practically all of the things we have devised. For it is speech that has made laws about justice and injustice and honor and disgrace, without which provisions we should not be able to live together. By speech we refute the wicked and praise the good. By speech we educate the ignorant and inform the wise. We regard the ability to speak properly as the best sign of intelligence, and truthful, legal, and just speech is the reflection of a good and trustworthy soul. With speech we contest about disputes and investigate what is unknown. We use the same arguments in public councils as we use in persuading private individuals. We call orators those who are able to discourse before a crowd and sages those who discourse best among themselves. If I must sum up on this subject, we shall find that nothing done with intelligence is done without speech, but speech is the marshal of all actions and of thoughts and those most use it who have the greatest wisdom."

Though a practical and a philosophic tradition may be discerned, and though there were temporary vagaries, the history of ancient rhetoric is largely that of the growth of a single, great, traditional theory to which many writers and teachers contributed. Quintilian, whose work sums up this tradition, after much weighing of the logical difficulties of earlier definitions (2.15) describes rhetoric as *bene dicendi scientia*, the science of speaking well. "Science" is a stronger term than many writers were willing to use, and "art" is the commoner word, but Quintilian's definition is otherwise satisfactory. Rhetoric in his sense involves both theory and practice. It will be more convenient, however, to use "oratory" in reference to actual speech and "rhetoric" as indicating the theory or technique of speaking.

According to this traditional theory in its developed form, all rhetoric is divided into five parts.[7] Invention (εὕρεσις, *inventio*) comes first and is concerned with the subject matter, with finding out the question at issue, which is called the *stasis* or *status*, and the appropriate arguments to use in proof or refutation. Proofs include, first, direct evidence, such as witnesses, contracts, and oaths; second, argumentation from the evidence or from historical examples on the basis of probability by means of epicheiremes, or rhetorical syllogisms; and finally more delicate means of persuasion such as the moral impression the speaker or his theme makes on the audience or judge and the pathos or emotion he is able to awaken by his verbal appeals, his gestures, or even such bald devices as the introduction of bloody swords, aged parents, and weeping children. Both logical arguments and emotional appeals were often commonplaces (κοινοὶ τόποι, *loci communes*) which the orator could use in more than one speech as needed. Three principal types of speech were recognized: deliberative or symbouleutic; judicial or dicanic, sometimes also called forensic; and epideictic or demonstrative. Since judicial oratory could more easily be reduced to rules than the other two, most treatments of rhetoric concentrate on speeches delivered in courts of law. Epideictic originally referred to demonstrations of merit or faults, but comes to include all oratory which is not deliberative or judicial; in late antiquity it is even used of other literary genres, including forms of poetry, so that all writing is embraced in the field of rhetoric. In classical Greece the most distinguished manifestations of epideictic were funeral and festival orations.

[7] The most thorough exposition of the system of ancient rhetoric, though with very little historical perspective, is Richard Volkmann, *Die Rhetorik der Griechen und Römer in systematischer Uebersicht*, Leipzig, 1885, announced for republication Hildesheim, 1963. The third edition, condensed by Caspar Hammer, constitutes part three of vol. 2 (Munich, 1890) of Iwan von Müller's *Handbuch der klassischen Altertumswissenschaft*.

The second part of rhetoric is arrangement (τάξις, *dispositio*). This was the first aspect of rhetoric to be treated systematically, and it furnished the basis for the earliest handbooks. Arrangement means the organization of a speech into parts, though the order in which arguments are presented, whether the strongest first or toward a climax, is sometimes discussed. The basic divisions of a speech recognized by the handbooks apply best to judicial oratory. These are 1) prooemium or introduction (προοίμιον, *exordium*), 2) narration (διήγησις, *narratio*), the exposition of the background and factual details, 3) proof (πίστις, *probatio*), and 4) epilogue or conclusion (ἐπίλογος, *peroratio*). Each part has its own function and characteristics: the prooemium, for example, aims at securing the interest and good will of the audience, and the speaker is advised to disclaim ability at speaking; the narration must be clear, brief, and persuasive, and it is often in a simpler style than other sections; the epilogue is often divided into a recapitulation, which is the essential logical function, and an emotional appeal to stir the audience. Many rhetoricians added other sections or subsections, but few of these are regularly to be found. A refutation or counter-refutation is sometimes necessary, but could be thought of as a part of the proof. Often at the beginning of the proof there is a distribution of headings to be discussed. Deliberative speeches usually have a prooemium, proof or main body, and epilogue, and only rarely a narration. The prooemium and epilogue employ the same techniques as those in judicial speeches. The proof often takes up such topics as expediency, possibility, justice, and honor. Epideictic had similar topics which the orator was instructed to take up one by one; for example, an encomium might involve praise of a man's country, ancestry, character, training, and conduct.

The third part of rhetoric is style (λέξις, *elocutio*). In fully developed rhetorical treatises the discussion is frequently organized around the four virtues of correctness, clarity,

11

ornamentation, and propriety. Ornamentation includes lists of tropes and figures, both of speech and of thought, and is thus concerned with diction or choice of words and the use of words in composition. Composition further includes periodic structure and prose rhythm. Styles are often classified into types, of which the threefold division—grand, middle, and plain—is the best known.

The fourth part of rhetoric is memory (μνήμη, *memoria*), which discusses mnemonic devices. The common system was to identify words or topics with physical objects and to imagine these against a well-known background.

The fifth part of rhetoric is delivery (ὑπόκρισις, *actio*). In the fully developed handbooks, rules for the control of the voice are given under this heading as well as elaborate instruction in the stance and the use of gestures by the orator.

The beginnings of this system of rhetorical theory are evident by the fourth century B.C. in Aristotle's *Rhetoric* and in the work known as the *Rhetorica ad Alexandrum*. The latter handbook is probably typical of the time; although it is preserved in the corpus of Aristotle, modern critics usually attribute it to Anaximenes of Lampsacus. Rhetoric underwent its greatest elaboration in the Hellenistic period, and the first complete handbook to show substantially the full theory is the *Rhetorica ad Herennium*, an anonymous first-century B.C. treatise once attributed to Cicero, whose early *De inventione* parallels part of it. Cicero's later works *De oratore* and *Orator*, as well as the *Partitiones oratoriae*, contain much of the traditional theory, as do writings of Dionysius of Halicarnassus and the elder Seneca. But it is in Quintilian's *Institutiones oratoriae* that rhetorical theory finds its most complete expression. From later antiquity there are numerous handbooks and essays;[8] the chief works in Greek are those by Hermogenes, who lived in the second

[8] These are to be found in Walz, Spengel, and Spengel-Hammer. On the Roman side cf. Halm.

half of the second century A.D., and introductions and commentaries to his works by later writers. Lost works like Theophrastus' *On style*, the writings of Hermagoras, and the works of Caecilius were as influential as many which have survived. They can be partially reconstructed from fragments. We would like to know more about the earliest writers on rhetoric, the sophists and speech writers of the late fifth century. Their works did not long survive, apparently because the discussions soon seemed meagre and because a survey made by Aristotle, the *Synagôgê technôn* or *Summary of the arts*, itself later lost, probably contained most of what was regarded as worth remembering (Cicero, *De inventione* 2.6).[9]

Thus, ancient rhetorical theory as exhibited in these works was a continuous, evolving tradition. Constantly revised and made more detailed, it remained unaltered in its essential features, the universal and accepted doctrine of the civilized speaking world. Universal and accepted, that is, save among a few philosophers who provoked a quarrel between rhetoric and philosophy, first in the early fourth and then again in the second century B.C.

Among the most significant thinkers of the fifth century B.C. were the traveling lecturers known as sophists. They were primarily teachers of political excellence whose aims were practical and immediate and whose investigations led in many instances to a philosophical relativism. Of these, Protagoras is the best example.[10] To him absolute truth was unknowable and perhaps nonexistent. Man is the measure and measurer of all things (e.g. Plato, *Theatetus* 152a1 ff.), and truth must be approximated in each individual time and place somewhat in the manner that the just is determined in a court of law. In this process rhetoric is useful and legitimate, for only when two sides are persuasively

---

[9] Cf. Leonardus Spengel, Συναγωγὴ τεχνῶν *sive artium scriptores*, Stuttgart, 1828, and Radermacher.

[10] Cf. Untersteiner 1-91 and Eric A. Havelock, *The liberal temper in Greek politics*, New Haven, 1957, 155 ff.

presented can the choice between them be clearly perceived and intelligently made. Similarly in political life no universal principles can be accepted. Courses of action must be determined between alternatives presented in persuasive fashion. Rhetoric thus becomes a necessary part of education and the basis of civic life. In the late fifth century this point of view received its fullest exploitation in the teaching of Gorgias: his philosophical relativism is seen in his famous thesis that nothing exists, if it did it could not be apprehended, and if it could be apprehended, that apprehension could not be communicated (e.g. Sextus Empiricus, *Against the professors* 7.65 ff.). His importance as a rhetorician is equally clear from the fact that Plato chose him as the butt of his invective against rhetoric.[11]

If, on the other hand, one were to argue that absolute truth both exists and is knowable, then certain principles, deducible from this truth, ought to guide activity. In this case rhetoric not only loses much of its importance, but becomes a potential danger because of its ability to present some other and erroneous course of action in an attractive way. Socrates apparently taught that truth was absolute and knowable and that a clear distinction should be made between dialectic, the question and answer method of obtaining the one correct answer, and rhetoric, which does not seem interested in the universal validity of the answer but only in its persuasiveness for the moment. This criticism Plato developed to such an extent that he is the most famous and most thorough-going of the enemies of rhetoric; the other Socratics do not seem to have felt an equally intense aversion.[12]

[11] Cf. Untersteiner 92-205 and G. B. Kerferd, "Gorgias on nature or that which is not," *Phronesis* 1 (1955) 3 ff. Gorgias is generally and logically regarded as a sophist, though Plato does not couple him with Protagoras, Prodicus, and Hippias; cf. E. R. Dodds, *Plato: Gorgias*, Oxford, 1959, 6 ff. Dodds hesitates to regard Gorgias as a serious thinker, but this seems over-cautious.

[12] On Plato's criticism of rhetoric cf. esp. Hunt 24 ff.; on the attitude of the other Socratics cf. Arnim 20.

The disagreement between Plato and the sophists over rhetoric was not simply an historical contingency, but reflects a fundamental cleavage between two irreconcilable ways of viewing the world. There have always been those, especially among philosophers and religious thinkers, who have emphasized goals and absolute standards and have talked much about truth, while there have been as many others to whom these concepts seem shadowy or imaginary and who find the only certain reality in the process of life and the present moment. In general, rhetoricians and orators, with certain distinguished exceptions, have held the latter view, which is the logical, if unconscious, basis of their common view of art as a response to a rhetorical challenge unconstrained by external principles. The difference is not only that between Plato and Gorgias, but between Demosthenes and Isocrates, Virgil and Ovid, Dante and Petrarch, and perhaps Milton and Shakespeare.

Plato's ideas on rhetoric are developed in the *Gorgias* and the *Phaedrus*. The former and earlier (about 387 B.C.) dialogue is the more bitter; the attack is directed principally against rhetoric as a part of education for political life. Plato denies that rhetoric is an art and defines it as a species of flattery, a sham counterpart of justice (463a6 ff.). It has no subject matter of its own, no truth to present, and is concerned solely with belief and illusion, not with knowledge (454b1 ff.). Gorgias, Polus, and Callicles are presented as progressively more and more practical politicians of the breed believing in expediency and force, historically best known to us from the pages of Thucydides; rhetoric was undoubtedly one of the tools of the pragmatic philosophy of such men as could carry on a Melian dialogue.

Plato's emotions are much involved in his rejection of rhetoric. Rhetoric is to him a word with associations of trickery, deceit, immorality, and superficiality. The trial and death of Socrates no doubt contributed to the intensity of his feeling. Because he is so prejudiced he appears to weight the scales in turn against rhetoric. He compares it to the art

15

of medicine and demands to know its subject matter. In the *Gorgias* he will not recognize that a man making use of rhetoric is at the same time making use of politics or medicine or some other art, just as is the dialectician. Plato damns the rhetorician for his bad statesmanship or bad diagnosis and refuses to discuss his rhetoric separately. Perhaps the fuzziness of Gorgias' thinking is not solely an invention of Plato; we do not know definitely. Plato makes Gorgias admit (460a3 f.) that he will have to teach his pupils subject matter, and he does not say that it would not be *qua* rhetorician that he would do so. Similarly Ion, in the dialogue of that name, does not understand, and Plato will not recognize, the relation of literary criticism to the subject matter of the work criticized. Protagoras (*Protagoras* 322d5 ff.) is allowed to distinguish between technical knowledge of a subject and moral and political knowledge, which are common to all. This is perhaps a step toward understanding the arts.

Although Plato denied that rhetoric as it existed was an art, he was, even in the *Gorgias*, prepared to admit the possibility of a true rhetoric (504d5 ff.), that is, of one which demonstrates absolute truth by means of true principles. This possibility he developed years later in the *Phaedrus*, where rhetoric is less roughly treated than in the *Gorgias* and where its true nature as a faculty of persuasion is at least considered (260d4 ff.). Plato believed, however, that the relation of rhetorical technique to subject matter is integral and essential, because the orator, in order to discover the probable, needs knowledge of the truth (259e4 ff.),[13] which can be obtained only by education in philosophy (261a4 f.), not by studying in the school of a rhetorician. A true rhetoric would aim at a true goal by means of

[13] Hunt 49 points out "a public so depraved as Plato felt all multitudes to be would never care so much for a resemblance to Truth as for a probability based upon consonance with its own interests and tasks."

sound logical and psychological means (271a4 ff.). Despite his mellowing, Plato does not appear to value rhetoric very highly; doubtless a philosopher could effect persuasion without effort.

Plato's criticisms of rhetoric were answered from two directions. Isocrates tried to provide a practical reply. In so doing he showed himself to be a follower of the traditions of the sophists. Education to Isocrates means education for political activity, that is, for the process of life (*Antidosis* 285); rhetoric is a primary tool (293). It may indeed be separated from dialectic, but not because the latter is concerned with absolute truth: it is nothing but hairsplitting, wrangling, and bickering (*Against the sophists* 1 ff.). Only the probable can be known (8), and this can best be presented by means of rhetoric. The whole practical study he describes as "philosophy" (*Antidosis* 270 ff.). The earlier speeches of Isocrates show some experimentation toward finding a proper subject for rhetoric, great and philosophical, superior to the trivia of the law courts and the politics of the assembly. He tried imparting some deeper significance to mythological subjects, he tried panhellenism, and he tried addresses of moral and political advice to individuals in the traditions of the gnomic poets. The panhellenic motif was the one which he found most satisfying, and, when he describes his own brand of oratory in the *Antidosis* (46 f.), it is this which he has in mind. It deals, he says, with the whole world of Hellas; its thoughts are lofty and original; its style is poetic, imaginative, and ornate.

Isocrates' answer to Plato is thus largely practical and seems to regard the issue as primarily an educational one. Isocrates and Plato were proprietors of competing educational establishments, each committed to his own system, apparently regarding education as a unity to be presented by a single teacher. It was no doubt painful to each to see the way the other's pupils were misled.

The theoretical refutation of Plato was to come from the friendlier but no less ruthless hand of Aristotle. Aristotle's ideas on rhetoric, as on other subjects, began with the teaching of Plato. In an early dialogue, the *Gryllos*, Aristotle apparently followed approximately the line of thought of Plato in the *Gorgias*, but by the time of the first chapter of the *Rhetoric*, which has been shown to have been written earlier than some other parts of the work, he has already revised his opinion and developed a psychological rhetoric out of Plato's hints in the *Phaedrus*. His development thus follows the general direction of Plato's own progress, but it continues much further. It is likely that Aristotle taught rhetoric in the Academy with Plato's approval before the latter's death, for the lectures were motivated by opposition to Isocrates, who was dead before Aristotle established his own school in Athens. According to Cicero (*De oratore* 3.141) Aristotle parodied a verse of the Philoctetes of Euripides in the words "it is shameful to keep silent and allow Isocrates to speak." Rhetoric, however, did not become a central concern of the philosophers; it was taught in the afternoon as a kind of supplementary subject (Philodemus, *Rhetoric* 6, col. 48, ii p. 50 Sudhaus; Quintilian 3.1.14).

Aristotle was practical enough to recognize the usefulness of rhetoric as a tool.[14] Those speaking the truth and doing so justly have, he thought (*Rhetoric* 1355a21 ff.), an obligation to be persuasive. They need rhetoric since the subjects under discussion are not known scientifically and thus are not capable of absolute demonstration. Further, a willingness to argue on both sides sometimes demonstrates the true nature of a case and in any event helps the orator to recognize the arguments, fair or unfair, of his opponent. Man has a right to defend himself with speech, which is more characteristic of the human race than is the use of

[14] On the difference in attitude of Plato and Aristotle cf. Hunt 44 ff.

the body. Some unfair uses may be made of rhetoric, but all good things including health, wealth, and strategy can be abused.

Whereas Plato had opposed rhetoric to dialectic, Aristotle compares the two: both have to do with things which are within the field of knowledge of all men and are not part of any specialized science. They do not differ in nature, but in subject and form: dialectic is primarily philosophical, rhetoric political; dialectic consists of question and answer, rhetoric of a set speech. Both can be reduced to a system and thus are properly called "arts." The first chapter of the *Rhetoric* (1355b8 ff.) concludes with a brief summary of Aristotle's opinion of the nature of rhetoric:

"It is clear, therefore, that rhetoric is not concerned with one distinct class of subjects, but is like dialectic and that it is useful and that its object is not persuasion, but the discovery of the available means of persuasion in each case, just as is true of all the other arts. For it is not the function of medicine to create health, but only to promote it as far as possible: it is possible even for those who cannot recover health to be treated properly. In addition, it is evident that the function of rhetoric is to recognize the persuasive and the apparently persuasive, just as it is the function of dialectic to discover both syllogism and apparent syllogism. Sophistry does not consist in the faculty of speaking, but in the moral purpose of the speaker."

Chapter two opens with the resulting definition of rhetoric as the faculty of discovering in each case the available means of persuasion.

Aristotle's remarks on the nature of rhetoric were in accord both with logic and with common sense. Despite the waning of political oratory, the need for rhetorical training was an accomplished fact in oral Greek society. Aristotle's defense was generally accepted, and opposition to rhetoric among philosophers, except the Epicureans, was slight during the following two hundred years. Not only the followers of Isocrates and the sophistic tradition but most philosophical schools, among them the Academy, included rhetoric in the curriculum. There was a general acceptance of the correspondence between rhetoric and dialectic. A system was evolved whereby instruction in fundamental rhetorical theory and practice in a graded set of exercises became the central concern of secondary education. The philosophical schools dealt with rhetorical scholarship from a broader point of view and directed advanced exercises.

Matters would probably have gone on peacefully had it not been for the appearance of a new educational crisis. The intensity of the dispute between rhetoric and philosophy in the time of Plato had been partly influenced by a concern with the best education for young men who sought to take a part in the life of a democratic state. Now in the second century B.C. education was affected by the new interest of the Romans in Greek culture. Professional rhetoricians began to offer programs of advanced instruction in rhetoric which bypassed the philosophers. These programs were probably intended to avoid the obscurities of philosophical disputation and to appeal to hardheaded Romans, but the rules and endless classifications which they offered the pupil to memorize were relatively useless in practice. Of the professionals by far the most famous was Hermagoras of Temnos. Hermagoras divided the subjects of rhetoric into two types: *hypotheses* and *theses*. An *hypothesis* was a particular subject involving specific people, places, and things, for example, "Did Brutus murder Caesar?" A case at law would be of this type. Contrasting with these *hypotheses* were *theses*, subjects of a general nature involving principles, but not specific facts, such as "Is it just to kill a tyrant?" These too were valuable exercises for a would-be orator, but it seemed to many philosophers that rhetoricians were intruding into such branches of philosophy as ethics, metaphysics, and politics without any systematic preparation. The philosophical schools had for some time practiced *theses* from their own points of view. The rhetoricians theoretically did not care which side of the case their pupils took or which side triumphed. They considered the question only as a problem with a rhetorical response, not as an exposition of a truth. Thus the philosophers saw in the advanced study of rhetoric a practical threat to their domination of higher education and the substitution of a system which was of great superficiality. Their objections were probably more justified than had been those of Plato, from whom, however, they drew many of their arguments.

A number of philosophers denounced and rejected completely the claims of the rhetoricians. The three philosophers who visited Rome in 155 B.C., Critolaus the Peripatetic, Carneades the Academic, and Diogenes of Babylon, the Stoic, were in varying degrees opponents of the rhetoricians. Cicero makes Crassus speak (*De oratore* 1.46) of the philosophers in Athens in the late second century "by all of whom the orator was with one voice driven from the government of states, excluded from all learning and knowledge of greater things, and pushed down and locked up in courts of justice and insignificant disputes as though in a mill."

The dispute between rhetoric and philosophy in the time of Aristotle had ended in a compromise in which philosophers accepted rhetoric as a means to a goal. The dispute between rhetoric and philosophy in the second century was never satisfactorily resolved, but rather faded away. Professional rhetoricians continued to teach their sterile systems and flourished. A number of philosophers developed a concept of oratory as it would be practiced by a true philosopher and gradually mitigated their objections to rhetoric itself. The old sophistic ideal of the well-trained man of public life devoted to action had never entirely disappeared. In the first century it reemerged among the Romans as an influential concept in intellectual history and kept this position to the end of antiquity. The most famous expression of the ideal is in Cicero's dialogue *De oratore* and especially the speeches of Crassus in books one and three thereof, where the author's own shadow extends over the portrait. Crassus is made to describe an ideal orator trained in rhetoric, philosophy, law, history, and, indeed, in all knowledge (1.45 ff.). He must be morally good and an active participant in public life, but he need have no specific moral or philosophical goal. The more practical process of rhetoric is substituted for the more theoretical goal of philosophy, but with a deeper basis of knowledge than could be derived solely from the study of rhetorical rules. Thus in a sense Cicero reverses the eloquent philosopher of the Greeks and substitutes a philosophical orator. There can be little question that this rhetorical ideal was more acceptable to the Romans than the figure of the sage. There is a suggestion of it in Cato's definition of the orator as *vir bonus, dicendi peritus* (Quintilian 12.1.1), and the dictators and demagogues of the late republic hardly sought for themselves the status of a philosopher king.

If the concept of the *bonus orator* was by nature not uncongenial to the Romans, it became increasingly familiar to them by constant training and practice. Roman education, after primary training at the hands of the *grammaticus*, was even more dominated by rhetoricians than was Greek. Athletics and music were almost ignored, and the other disciplines of the liberal arts were decidedly auxiliary to the one great training in speech, which was most characteristically developed in the declamation of *suasoriae* and *controversiae*. The practice of these exercises, even in Cicero's time and much more in the age of the elder Seneca, was not simply a schoolboy exercise but a social grace, cultivated by all educated people for their delight and amusement. The world was a rhetorician's world, its ideal an orator; speech became an artistic product to be admired apart from its content or significance. The logical conclusion of such a development was reached in the rhetorical poetry of the empire, where style eclipses subject as the poet poses for himself a series of rhetorical challenges, and in the educational system of Quintilian, where the training of the *bonus orator* from infancy to retirement is described in the greatest detail and contemporary philosophers, in accordance with Domitian's sentiments, are scorned and dismissed (1.*pr*.15 and 12.3.12).

Modern readers tend to sympathize with philosophy in its dispute with rhetoric. In the former discipline they see devotion to truth, intellectual honesty, depth of perception, consistency, and sincerity; in the latter, verbal dexterity, empty pomposity, triviality, moral ambivalence, and a desire to achieve arbitrary ends by any means. The picture is not quite so clear cut. Rhetorical theorists such as Aristotle, Cicero, and Quintilian are not unscrupulous tricksters with words; their recommendation makes the intellectual respectability of rhetoric at least worth considering. Furthermore, rhetoric was at times a greater liberalizing force in ancient intellectual life than was philosophy. It demonstrated that there were two sides to many if not all questions. The basic principle of humane law, that anyone, however clear the proof against him, has a right to present his case in the best light possible is an inheritance from Greek justice imposed by the debates of the sophists. "Even the wolf," the saying went, "is entitled to plead in his own defense" (Plato, *Phaedrus* 272c10). Similarly, in political debate there was in the best periods of ancient history a willingness to entertain the opinions of others when expounded with rhetorical effectiveness. At the very least rhetoric imparted vigor to ancient intellectual life; it has long been noted that oratory flourished most in the democracies and least under tyranny.

At the same time there were serious dangers inherent in rhetoric. It was dynamic, it was systematic, and it became traditional; all three of these factors worked an evil influence. In the fifth century B.C. only the first of these characteristics was evident, but the others came increasingly to the fore in succeeding centuries.

To begin with the danger issuing from the dynamic quality of rhetoric, it is clear that the power of oratory works upon an audience, but even more does it work upon a speaker. He can only too easily be led on, "inebriated with the exuberance of his own verbosity," as Disraeli said of Gladstone, to statements beyond what he intended and to an irresponsibility unsuspected at the beginning of his speech. This is no doubt what happened to Cleon in the debate about Pylos (Thucydides 4.27). The danger exists not only in extempore debate but also in rhetorical composition in the study, for the concern of the rhetorician is with process, with technique, with artistic excellence rather than with philosophical truth, political principle, or moral rectitude. Isocrates' vast discourses, elaborated over many years, are no less irresponsible and self-inflammatory than the remarks of Aeschines at Delphi which brought down a war upon the Amphissians (*Against Ctesiphon* 107 ff.). The good orator, good both in a moral and an artistic sense, must be aware of his power and must never forget his responsibility. No rhetoric can be better than the character of its orator, and sometimes it seduces him. A serious lack of moral responsibility becomes evident in some later Attic orators and persists in most of Latin oratory so that even Cicero could boast with some satisfaction of throwing dust in the eyes of a jury in defense of an unworthy client (Quintilian 2.17.21).

The systematic quality of rhetoric produced a similar result, for the rhetorician implied that his art could surmount all logical obstacles to effect persuasion of any position. Life and literature in such a view became a series of problems demanding the proper rhetorical response: there was a right and a wrong treatment of every case. Although the orator as a moral individual and not as a rhetorician had to judge whether or not to speak on behalf of a given cause or person, there was among lovers of discourse an intellectual, professional challenge in defending the indefensible or challenging the secure, in the classical phrase, in making the worse seem the better cause. How many ancient politicians made their initial fame by a sudden attack upon a man whose greatness seemed unquestioned! In rhetorical theory the trend toward systemization produced a body of rules and exercises which were more and more abstracted from practical needs, increasingly detailed and complex, and thus less and less able to produce the eloquence which was their goal.

Finally, the traditional quality of rhetoric discouraged novelty in thought, style, and treatment by implying as time went on that all the answers were known and that the problems now discussed by orators had been perfectly treated in the past. Later rivals of Demosthenes and Cicero were not given much to hope for in the way of successful imitation. New oratorical forms, varied diction, a new set of examples met with no encouragement and thus found no opportunity to develop into forms which were artistically as good as what had been done. This attitude toward oratory begat a similar point of view toward other literary genres and perhaps toward political reform, all of which contributed to the general intellectual pessimism of Hellenistic and Roman times.

Now that the limits of the subject have been marked out and some of its significance suggested we may return to the beginning to study the evolution of rhetoric in greater detail.

CHAPTER TWO

Techniques of Persuasion in Greek
Literature before 400 B.C.

According to the tradition preserved in many ancient writers[1] the art of rhetoric was invented in the second quarter of the fifth century B.C. in Syracuse in Sicily. As a result of the overthrow of the Syracusan tyrants much litigation had arisen, and either Tisias or Corax or both undertook to teach a technique of judicial rhetoric to those unaccustomed to public speaking. It was thought by later writers that rhetoric was brought to Athens by the famous sophist Gorgias, who came on an embassy from Leontini to request Athenian help in 427 (Diodorus Siculus 12.53.2) and that it developed there as part of the sophistic movement. Sophistry was a practical kind of philosophy which taught the techniques of civic life, of which rhetoric was clearly one, and which in the case of some thinkers deepened into a more complete system of knowledge. The practical aspect was, however, always the more important: the sophists thought of themselves as training statesmen not philosophers (Plato, *Protagoras* 318d5 ff. and *Republic* 600c2 ff.); their theoretical positions, insofar as they assumed any, were based on facts observed in the operations of the Greek states. Thus their logic reflected the process of determining truth as seen in the law courts and their view of man's function was based on the observed need for skill in public address. In other words, sophistry was in large part a product of rhetoric, which was by far the older force and in the end the more vital one. Rhetoric was in no real sense an invention of the sophists, but their speculations

[1] The references to the beginnings of rhetoric are collected by Radermacher. For further discussion of Corax, Tisias, and Gorgias cf. chapter three. The influence of Empedocles on early rhetoric, mentioned in some sources, is unascertainable and may be ignored.

helped crystallize its theories and show its significance. Despite tradition it is not true that Gorgias played the outstanding role in the early history of rhetoric. He was only one of the more striking personalities.

The circumstances which made the later fifth and most of the fourth centuries a golden age in the history of rhetoric and oratory are fundamentally a complex series of interrelationships between new ideas and old traditions in literature, philosophy, and all Greek culture. We must remember that oratory was one of the oldest and most active of Greek traditions, but one which was not self-conscious until the fifth century. The immediate cause of the greatly increased consciousness of rhetorical techniques in fifth-century Athens was the application of the democratic process on a large scale to judicial procedure. Although our information is incomplete, it seems that until the time of Ephialtes (462 B.C.) most legal cases in Athens were heard either before single magistrates or before the Areopagus, which might be regarded as a large professional board since its members were all ex-magistrates whose oratorical standards were austere (Aristotle, *Rhetoric* 1354a23). There existed one popular court, the Heliaea, whose functions were probably restricted to authorizing penalties in excess of those which magistrates were allowed by statute to impose. It is possible also that the political assembly had jurisdiction over capital charges. Subsequent to 462 the jurisdiction of magistrates was restricted to preliminary examinations and the Areopagus lost all of its jurisdiction except in homicide cases and in certain religious matters like suits involving the sacred olive trees (Plutarch, *Cimon* 15.2).[2] In place of the magistrates and Areopagus large popular juries called *dikastêria* were chosen. A body of 6,000 was used as a pool from which individual panels of 201 or more jurors were chosen by lot for each case. These juries had complete jurisdiction to determine

---

[2] Cf. C. Hignett, A *history of the Athenian constitution*, Oxford, 1952, 198 ff. and 216 ff.

both law and fact, and the presiding official was simply a chairman with no power of control or instruction.[3] Such juries affected greatly the nature of trials. Previously, as seen in the trial scene in Aeschylus' *Eumenides,* the basic procedure had been an almost informal altercation between litigants in reply to questions of the judge. It was, however, obviously impossible for the large juries personally to direct such an examination in an orderly way and contrary to the entire new theory of democratic courts for the procedure to be conducted by anybody else. There was not even a public prosecutor, since what we would think of as criminal cases were usually instigated and prosecuted by an interested private citizen. The procedure substituted was a presentation of the case by the litigants themselves, each in a single set speech with sometimes a single opportunity for rebuttal. This imposed on each litigant, and potentially on each Athenian citizen, a need to be an effective public speaker, to be able to organize a long speech and deliver it clearly and effectively. The popular and unprofessional nature of the jury much relaxed the need for logical, relevant treatment of points of law and increased opportunities for irrelevant, but brilliant digressions and emotional appeal.[4] It is a direct result of these conditions that all early handbooks of rhetoric were devoted to expounding the techniques of judicial oratory to prospective litigants.

Corresponding to this judicial development, the political history of the fifth century illustrates the widening base of the government. More and more people with less and less political background took an active part in the operations of Athens. There was thus a need for techniques of political oratory which could be easily learned, a need met largely by the teaching of the sophists. Wilamowitz[5] believed that

---

[3] Cf. Bonner and Smith 1, 223 ff.

[4] The Athenians recognize this principle in their debate with the Melians, Thucydides 5.85. Cf. also Aristotle, *Rhetoric* 1414a8 ff.

[5] U. von Wilamowitz-Moellendorf, *Aristoteles und Athens* 1,

the origin of Attic literary prose was to be found in the political strife between oligarchs and democrats in the fifth century. It may be going too far to see there the origin of prose, which had after all Ionian antecedents, but democracy had some influence in that it increased the number of speakers and the size of the audience. It is clear that democracy was as much a major influence on interest in rhetorical *methods* in deliberative oratory as it was in judicial oratory. The relationship between rhetoric and democracy can also perhaps be seen in Rome. Oratory had flourished for a century when Latin teachers of rhetoric appeared at the beginning of the first century B.C. The senatorial party, regarding them as a sign of democratic progress, tried to silence them (Suetonius, *De rhetoribus* 1). Similarly, under the Thirty Tyrants in Athens the teachers of rhetoric were briefly ordered to desist (Xenophon, *Memorabilia* 1.2.31). The power of the word, once it had been consciously realized in rhetorical theory, was multiplied. It was the means of achieving safety and success for the individual and of discovering the expedient for the commonwealth. Confidence in debate was a characteristic of Greek democracy until the tragedies of the Peloponnesian war overtook Athens.[6] Coincident with this self-consciousness of political and judicial eloquence and the development of rhetorical theory, epideictic oratory came into prominence, first perhaps in the form of funeral orations (λόγοι ἐπιτάφιοι) which in the early fifth century replaced the poetic laments (θρῆνοι), then in the oratory of the sophists, finally in a form of display—oratory for the sake of oratory.

Berlin, 1893, 169 ff. Cf. also Friedrich Solmsen, *Antiphonstudien* (*Neue philologische Untersuchungen* 8) Berlin, 1931, 2 ff.

[6] Cf. Thucydides 2.40.2 and 3.82.3 and John H. Finley, Jr., "Euripides and Thucydides," HSCP 49 (1938) 41 ff. The question of the value of debate seems to have influenced the discussion between Creon and Haemon in Sophocles' *Antigone* 724 ff.

Four signs mark the awakening of the rhetorical consciousness in Greece. They correspond to three parts of
developed rhetoric: invention, arrangement, and style. The
first sign is the new rationalism of proofs and arguments.
Writers of the later fifth century delight in the gymnastics
of argument, although some of their proofs are more apparent than real. The usual system was to prove that a
course of action, a future action in the case of a deliberative
speech, a past action in the case of a judicial speech, was or
was not expedient, just, possible, honorable, or the like.
Most of these abstractions were in the process of being
defined or redefined in the fifth century. Particularly do we
encounter interest in the nature of justice and its relation
to written law (the theme of Sophocles' *Antigone*, for
example) or in the nature of expediency (familiar from
Thucydides and many plays of Euripides). In the demonstration of expediency or justice the fifth-century orator
made use of another abstract concept, that of probability.
The assumption that men generally tend to act in a rational,
predictable way is hereby used to prove the way in which
a particular man or state will act or has acted on a particular
occasion. Plato (*Phaedrus* 267a6 f.) attributes argument
from probability to Tisias and Gorgias, who, he says, realized
how much more "honored" were probabilities than the
truth, which may itself be improbable. They may well have
explicitly discussed use of the argument. Probability was,
however, certainly known in Athens before the arrival of
Gorgias in 427. To take only one example, in *Oedipus the
king*, 583 ff. (probably produced in 429), Creon seeks to
prove that he has no motives to replace Oedipus as king.
His arguments are clearly derived from probability: is it
probable that he would plot against the king when he now
enjoys all the benefits without any of the cares of office?
A certain standard of human nature is accepted, and the
proposed action is compared to it. This passage is imitated

and a similar argument advanced by Euripides a few years later in the *Hippolytus* (1013 ff.).[7]

Argument from probability makes use of a concept of man's nature which relates its developed use to the age of the sophists. It is sophistic also in its ambivalent nature. We have already said that both Protagoras and Gorgias denied that absolute truth can be known. Something can be said on both sides of every question, and perhaps absolute truth does not even exist. So thought many of the sophists. Such an epistemology, itself a product of rhetoric, has a special use for argument from probability, which would be logically excluded from a philosophy claiming to be scientific and exact, for only too often is it possible to demonstrate the probability of exact opposites. The first *Tetralogy* of Antiphon (esp. 1.B.3) illustrates this, as does the classic example of argument from probability adduced by Aristotle (*Rhetoric* 1402a17 ff., cf. Plato, *Phaedrus* 273b3 ff.): if a weak man is accused of assault his defense will be that it is not probable that he would attack a stronger man. But if he is likely to be guilty, if he is himself the stronger, he may argue that the crime is still not probable for the very reason that it was bound to appear so. The strong man, knowing this, would have desisted from his intent. There is thus both a simple and a relative argument from probability, and the argument itself becomes a two-edged sword. This is the way, par excellence, to make the worse seem the better cause, as all rhetoricians are accused by their opponents of doing. In fact, however, behind the techniques lies a wise and sound principle. Justice, even if it exists in the absolute, is not always obvious and cases cannot be judged only on appearances and common sense. The belief that everyone is entitled to present his conduct in the best possible light and

---

[7] Argument from probability occurs in earlier works of Euripides, cf. *Phoenix* fr.811. Cf. J. T. Lees, Δικανικὸς λόγος in *Euripides*, Lincoln, Neb., 1891. The earliest Greek examples of argument from probability will be discussed later in this chapter.

31

that even an "obvious" criminal is entitled to have his day in court is the foundation of real justice.

Once learned, the application of argument from probability was extensive. The technique was developed by Aristotle into a complete system of rhetorical demonstration through the use of the two formal devices of enthymeme and example. It achieved persuasion with a minimum of effort on the part of the orator and had about it two characteristics which appealed to the Greeks, verbal agility and seeming dependence on a law of nature that given certain facts predictable results follow. This was a comforting thought in a world long ruled by arbitrary powers and now just beginning to find justice in the authority of Zeus, to predict the regular occurrence of astronomical phenomena, and to observe a pattern in social and political history. Furthermore, in practice probability appeared safer than witnesses who were only too easily corrupted, for probabilities could not be bought.

The second sign of the birth of rhetoric was the new interest in dividing speeches into parts, each with a special function. This interest no doubt reflects the beginning of a fondness for definition and classification which became stronger among the Greeks. The simple pattern of beginning, middle, and end, required for any artistic unity, was gradually refined into a series of parts adapted to the typical judicial dispute. This was effected especially by the separation of the narrative from the proof, needed for clear presentation of background to the jury, and by the addition of an epilogue, needed to recapitulate the most important points and to convey emotional conviction.[8] In the next chapter we will examine the early rhetorical handbooks which without exception were organized around and mostly

---

[8] Cf. B. A. VanGroningen, *La composition littéraire archaïque grecque*, Amsterdam, 1958, 233 ff. This book contains a good treatment of the function of the epilogue but does not recognize the historical importance of the narration in judicial oratory.

concerned with the separate parts into which a speech should be divided.

The third sign of rhetorical consciousness is interest in what we may call the new prose styles.[9] There were at least three: that associated with Gorgias, the distinguishing characteristic of which is imitation of poetic devices (Aristotle, *Rhetoric* 1404a24); that associated with Thrasymachus, characterized by a rhythmic structure; and the more general and earlier style lacking these particular qualities, but identified by a marked love of antithesis, that is, by a balanced contrast of words or ideas. This is a prominent feature of the earliest work of Antiphon.[10] It is mimicked by Plato in the *Protagoras* (337a1 ff.) as a characteristic of the great sophist, and Finley argues convincingly that its presence in the orations of the early books of Thucydides represents the actual style of the speakers.[11] It is almost an obsession in the early plays of Euripides. In Sophocles it is most noticeable in the *Antigone* (probably produced in 441 B.C.).[12]

Attempts have been mistakenly made to associate the beginnings of the antithetical style with specific writers. Diels[13] and Norden,[14] for example, pointed out inclination to antithesis in the fragments of such pre-Socratic philosophers as Empedocles, Democritus, and Heraclitus, with whom some of the sophists are said to have studied. But precedents could as well be found in Hesiod, Theognis, and other poets whom the sophists certainly studied and for whose didactic poetry they sought to substitute a poetic

---

[9] Cf. Norden 15 ff.

[10] Cf. John E. Hollingworth, *Antithesis in the Attic orators from Antiphon to Isaeus*, Menasha, Wis., 1915, and Grover C. Kenyan, *Antithesis in the speeches of the Greek historians*, Chicago, 1941.

[11] John H. Finley, Jr., "The origins of Thucydides' style," HSCP 50 (1939) 82 ff.

[12] Cf. Finley, *op.cit.* supra n. 11, 53 ff.

[13] Hermann Diels, "Gorgias und Empedocles," SBB (1884) 1.343 ff.

[14] Cf. Norden 16 ff.

prose.[15] The habit of antithesis was deeply ingrained in the Greek character, as is evident from the μὲν . . . δέ construction, from the fondness of the Greeks for contrasting figures like Prometheus and Epimetheus, and from the structure of most Greek art and literature. Aristotle says (*Rhetoric* 1410a20 ff.) that the antithetical style is pleasing because contraries are easily understood and even more so when placed side by side; antithesis thus resembles a syllogism, for a refutative syllogism is a bringing together of contraries. As we have seen, to many sophists such a confrontation of opposites is the fundamental process of reasoning, and it seems safe to conclude that some of the popularity of antithesis in the fifth century was its compatibility to contemporary logic. Perhaps one should go further and regard stylistic antithesis as the source of sophistic logic in the same way that judicial procedure may be the source of sophistic epistemology. The little sophistic treatise known as the *Dissoi logoi*, literally *Two-fold speeches* (Diels 90), furnishes a good example of the significance seen in antithesis by the sophists and the relativism to which it led.

In a democratic state words could change history. They performed the functions of gold, of divine intervention, and of massed armies of men. Surely the word was a remarkable thing. It deserved special and intense study, and this it received in the new science of philology—the fourth sign of rhetorical consciousness. A number of the sophists engaged in linguistic studies. Protagoras, for example, compiled an *Orthoepeia* which appears to have been a list of "proper" words as distinct from metaphors.[16] Such studies

[15] Cf. Navarre 92 ff.; Karl Reich, *Einfluss der griechischen Poesie auf Gorgias* 2, Würzburg, 1909, 4 ff.; Ben Edwin Perry, "The early Greek capacity for viewing things separately," TAPA 68 (1937) 403 ff., esp. 425; Werner Jaeger (trans. by G. Highet), *Paideia* 1, New York, 1939, 294 ff.

[16] Hermias, cf. Radermacher B.iii.5, says that the work of Protagoras was a κυριολεξία, or lexicon of words in their proper meaning,

were the basis of a developed sense of style and were, no doubt, important elements in refining the more obvious devices of the new prose. Prodicus of Ceos similarly studied definitions.[17] Some of the sophistic work was grammatical, such as Protagoras' studies of gender and mood.[18] Interest in etymologies is evident from Plato's *Cratylus*: apparently at least two schools existed, one insisting that language is a matter of convention, another that there is an absolute truth or falsehood in the meanings of words.[19] The distinction is clearly parallel to the absolute and relative epistemology of the various thinkers. This philological development was further colored by the sophists' concern with education, a principal portion of which was the study of literature and especially poetry.[20]

When study of rhetoric began in the fifth century B.C. much of what was said was merely a theorizing of conventional practice. Techniques of rhetorical theory are already evident in the speeches of the Homeric poems to such a degree that later antiquity found formal rhetoric everywhere in Homer and on the basis of *Iliad*, 15.283 f., even conjured up a picture of practice declamations among the Homeric

and that Protagoras aimed at words in their proper sense rather than speech through comparisons and epithets. Cf. Hunt 10 ff.

[17] Cf. Radermacher B.vii.6-10; Finley, *op.cit.* supra n. 6, 44 n. 3; Hermann Mayer, *Prodikos von Keos und die Anfänge der Synonymik bei den Griechen*, Paderborn, 1913; Hunt 8 f.

[18] Cf. Radermacher B.iii.6-14.

[19] Convention seems to have been supported by Democritus, nature by Heraclitus; cf. Laurenz Lersch, *Die Sprachphilosophie der Alten*, Bonn, 1838, 10 ff.; W. Nestle, *Herodots Verhältnis zur Philosophie und Sophistik*, Stuttgart, 1908, 10 f.; J. van Ijzeren, "De *Cratylo* Heracliteo et de Platonis *Cratylo*," MN 49 (1921) 174 ff.; R. Philippson, "Platons *Kratylos* und Demokrit," BPW 49 (1929) 923 ff.; Louis Méridier, *Platon* 5.2 (Budé), Paris, 1931; A. Pagliaro, "Il *Cratilo* di Platone," *Dionisio* 15 (1952) 178 ff.; A. Guzzo, "La problematica del *Cratilo*," *Filosofia* 7 (1956) 609 ff.

[20] Cf. C. P. Gunning, *De sophistis Graecae praeceptoribus*, Amsterdam, 1915, 44 ff. On sophistic study of literature cf. Plato's *Protagoras* 339a1 ff. and Isocrates' *Antidosis* 266.

heroes.[21] Speech in the epic is generally treated as an irrational power, seen in the ability to move an audience and in its effect on a speaker himself, and is thus inspiration, a gift of the gods.[22] But it is difficult to believe that there did not exist in all periods certain critical principles, generally, if tacitly, accepted. The fact that Phoenix in the *Iliad* (9.442 f.) claims to have been sent to teach Achilles to be a speaker of words and a doer of deeds is an indication of the existence of some kind of rhetorical training. Perhaps this was mainly a process of listening to older speakers and, like an oral bard, acquiring formulae, themes, maxims, and stock topics such as myths and historical examples, perhaps also denunciations and oaths, all of which are the ancestors of the commonplaces of later oratory. Oratory in the Homeric poems is always represented as extemporaneous and as fitted together out of words or groups of words known to the speaker. Thus, even Thersites knows many words in his mind, though they are disordered (*Iliad* 2.213), while Achilles is ready and cunning of speech (22.281). Menelaus spoke fluently, but with few words, and Odysseus was unprepossessing in stance, but his words flew like flakes of snow (3.212 ff.). Later antiquity (e.g. Aulus Gellius 6.14.7) regarded Menelaus as an example of the plain style, Odysseus of the grand style, and the honey-sweet speech of Nestor (1.249) as the model of the middle style.

Homeric oratory is weakest in the construction of logical argument.[23] The closest approaches to rational proof in the

[21] Cf. Quintilian 2.17.8. On Homeric rhetoric cf. the works cited infra n. 22-23; Radermacher A.ii-iv; George A. Kennedy, "The ancient dispute over rhetoric in Homer," AJP 78 (1957) 23 ff.; Fritz Wehrli, *Zur Geschichte der allegorischen Deutung Homers in Altertum*, Borna-Leipzig, 1928.

[22] Cf. Friedrich Solmsen, "The gift of speech in Homer and Hesiod," TAPA 85 (1954) 1 ff.

[23] Cf. Maurice Croiset, *De publicae eloquentiae principiis apud Graecos in Homericis carminibus*, Montpellier, 1874, ch. 2, and Marcel Delaunois, "Comment parlent les héros d'Homère," LEC 20 (1952) 80 ff.

Iliad are short bits, such as Achilles' "proof" that he should have been allowed to keep Briseis since Menelaus had so loved *his* wife that the whole war was undertaken to recover her (9.377 ff.), and occasional considerations reminiscent of the general topics developed by the sophists. In general, persuasion is effected by what Aristotle would call non-artistic arguments, that is, by something corresponding to direct evidence not invented by the speaker. A good example is the speech of Odysseus to Achilles on the embassy in *Iliad* nine. The speech is well arranged rhetorically and seeks to persuade Achilles that he should arise and save the Achaeans, for it is what his father advised (the words are directly quoted) and he will be rewarded with prizes from Agamemnon, which are listed in full. These prizes are the considerations principally intended to persuade Achilles and as such take the place of arguments.

The *Iliad* is, of course, not altogether lacking in artistic persuasion: Odysseus did not make up the quotation from Achilles' father, but he does make use of the emotional appeal inherent in the quotation as a means of appealing to Achilles. Aristotle later was to classify pathos as a second form of artistic proof. An even better example is the pathos on which Priam relies in his appeal to Achilles for the body of Hector in book twenty-four.

Aristotle's third form of artistic proof is ethos, or character. This is often illustrated in Homer where, as Croiset noted,[24] the speaker relies heavily on his personal authority and the impression he gives, as does Agamemnon in his debate with Achilles in book one. Thus also Athena increases the poise and dignity of Telemachus in *Odyssey* 2.12, to make up for his youthfulness. Later rhetoricians did not forget the importance of weight of character in effecting persuasion.

Another form of argument is that supplied by historical example. Of this by far the best illustration is the Meleager

[24] *op.cit.* supra n. 23, 9.

story, told by Phoenix in book nine of the *Iliad* (529-599). It is important to notice the length of this story. In telling it the poet relishes it for its own sake and forgets for the moment why he tells, for he is not obsessed with logical proof; he is a poet rather than an orator and is more concerned with the past than with the present. Historical example is a regular feature of later oratory. Herodotus, as we shall see, uses extended examples in much the same way as does the poet of *Iliad* nine, but otherwise the example is introduced only to be dropped immediately, for its rhetorical function is support of some fact, possibility, or probability, and the practical orator has not the time for poetry or even history.

The ordinary structure of an Homeric speech is a spirited introduction followed by some suggestion, request, demand, or threat. There is occasionally some narrative (e.g. Achilles to Thetis, *Iliad* 1.365 ff.) but never a full epilogue either of recapitulation or of emotional appeal. The emotional impact of a speech is usually greatest at the beginning, its tenor most specifically expressed at the end. Clearly the bard does not intend to indicate a habit of dividing speeches into regular parts.

Of course only a few of the speeches of the Homeric poems approximate the conditions of real oratory; many could better be regarded as conversation. A few decidedly formal speeches can be found among those addressed to single individuals, as the ambassadors to Achilles in book nine or Priam to Achilles in book twenty-four of the *Iliad*, and in the great debates of books one and two—all of which involve formal attempts at persuasion. Most of the speeches are in the general class of deliberative oratory, though the debates over Agamemnon's right to Briseis are essentially concerned with a legal point. The shield of Achilles portrayed litigants trying a case before a board of judges (18.497 ff.), but we have no examples of speeches made in a court of justice in the heroic age. Presumably court speeches were similar to deliberative speeches in being based on nonartistic proof, perhaps on an exculpatory oath which persists into the legal practice of the historical period.[25] In all early invention the most important fact is the absence of what was to be the greatest weapon of Attic oratory, argument from probability. The speakers in Homer are not even conscious that the subject of their talk is limited to probable truth.

Beyond its historical significance as a contrast with later oratory, the most interesting aspects of Homeric rhetoric are its native vigor and its relation to the concept of the orator which was later to develop. The characteristics of rhetoric which eventually monopolized the ancient mind are implicit in the Homeric poems: the power of speech, the resources of the speaker, and the aesthetic and practical significance of his task. There are two ways to achieve the heroic ideal: to be a doer of deeds or to be a speaker of words. Only the very greatest heroes like Achilles and Odysseus can do both; most excel in only one or the other. In either case the object is to win honor, which is a form of immortality, insured only by speech itself, that is, by the activity of the oral bard. Hector dies doing a great deed to be learned of by men to come (22.305), and Helen claims (6.358) that woes were sent upon herself and Paris that they might be subjects of song. Art is thus exalted to the status of an end in itself as was rhetoric in later times. The process of composition is significant and needs no practical goal to accomplish. We are not told that we should imitate the heroes or even perform rites for them, only that the poet will sing of them. The poetry is not didactic, but exists for itself alone.

Hesiod took the step of identifying oratory as a gift of the Muses and thus comparable to poetry (*Theogony* 81 ff.). The oratory he describes has apparently no technical

[25] Cf. J. W. Jones, *The law and legal theory of the Greeks*, Oxford, 1956, 136.

advantages over that found in the Homeric poems—it is a gift and a property of kings[26]—but it is more fundamental to the poet's concept of his own work, for the *Works and days* is itself an attempt at persuasion. The same is true of much of Greek elegiac poetry and of some lyric. Solon describes his exhortation to the Athenians to conquer Salamis as a poem in place of a speech, while Sappho seeks to persuade Aphrodite to come to her.

The earliest scene in Greek literature approximating a court trial is probably the dispute between Apollo and Hermes in the Homeric *Hymn to Hermes*.[27] Hermes tries first to dissuade Apollo from taking any action against him, arguing that he, a day-old babe, is hardly like a cattle thief (261) and offering to take an exculpatory oath (274). The second point reflects the force of the oath in early trials; the first is, it seems, the earliest attempt to employ argument from probability. This is a sign that self-conscious oratory is at hand and is an important indication of intellectual maturity, for it presupposes a philosophical mind, willing to generalize and classify: day-old babies act according to one pattern, cattle thieves according to another. Since Hermes belongs to the first category he cannot belong to the second, and it is improbable that he would commit the characteristic act of such a thief. Apollo is not to be put off, however, and drags the dissembler off to Zeus as to a legal arbitrator or judge. Zeus examines the case before an assembly of the gods (326), but they are only spectators, not a jury. Both Apollo and Hermes deliver speeches; Apollo has evidence in the cows' tracks and a witness in an old farmer, whom Hermes in the best classical style has tried to bribe, but he only narrates his case and does not attempt close argumentation from his evidence. In reply, Hermes tries to

[26] Cf. Solmsen, *op.cit.* supra n. 22, 4 ff.

[27] It is probably a product of the sixth century, cf. Jean Humbot, *Homère, Hymnes*, Paris, 1951, 113. One indication of a fairly late date is the absence of digamma.

awaken the judge's sympathy and again offers to swear an oath. Neither of the speeches are divisible into the parts of later judicial oratory. Zeus decides against Hermes, orders him reconciled with Apollo (391), and sees this order carried out (506).

The next stage in the development of both legal procedure and oratory is the trial scene in Aeschylus' *Eumenides*.[28] There is first a preliminary hearing in which Athena, functioning as a magistrate, hears and examines the charge of the prosecution (397 ff.). She then examines Orestes, who has refused to swear an exculpatory oath (429), and asks specifically about his descent, nationality, alleged crime, and defense. He duly answers these in something close to a set speech. Athena turns the trial over to a jury and departs to return after a choral interlude, which marks some passage of time. Then (566 ff.) comes the actual trial, which consists first of the testimony of Apollo, who is the witness for the defense and virtual advocate, and second of the altercation between the litigants. Athena charges the court (681 ff.), the votes are taken, and the decision given. The important role of the jury is the major change from the trial of Hermes. Neither side seems to deliver a full speech: the nearest approach is that of Orestes in the preliminary examination which contains an attempt to remove prejudice at the beginning and a narration of facts. Bonner and Smith[29] describe the trial of Orestes as "reminiscent of the time when the trial took place before a single magistrate who had final jurisdiction. Each litigant, no doubt, presented his side of the case largely in the form of answers to questions of the magistrates, constantly interrupted and stimulated by pro-

---

[28] Cf. Wolf Aly, "Formprobleme der frühren griechischen Prosa," *Philologus Supplementband* 21.3 (1929) 34 ff. and Van-Groningen, *op.cit.* supra n. 8, 238 ff. The trial of Orestes is a real part of the rhetorical tradition and used as a source of examples, cf. e.g. *Rhetorica ad Herennium* 1.17; Cicero, *De inventione* 1.18; Quintilian 3.11.4.

[29] 128.

tests." It is easy to see that great oratory could not develop under conditions where constant interruption debarred art in the arrangement and development of the case. Athena the magistrate plays an important role in controlling the whole process, and she makes the actual decision, for the jury, though important in the thought of the play, balances itself out. The replacement of magistrates by large juries must have encouraged greatly the development of judicial oratory. A single experienced magistrate can allow interruption and still secure some coherence in the presentation of material; he is free to make inquiries and has only himself to satisfy. A large jury, however, must demand a far more orderly procedure designed to present the case in a way comprehensible to an average amateur listener. The extended, carefully arranged, and reasoned speech which we find as the work of the Attic orators was thus a product of the democratic state, where the large juries necessitated a continuous statement including a narration of the events leading to the crime, a systematic argument based on this narration, together with an attempt to secure attention and good will from ordinary citizens, and a conclusion designed to drive home the crucial points.

Orestes seems to have the choice of two forms of defense. He can claim that he did not kill his mother, or he can admit that he did but claim that he did it justly. He chooses the second as the only possible basis or *stasis* of his argument. The elaboration of the types of *staseis* eventually came to take a great deal of the time of rhetoricians. Orestes claims that his action was just and that this is proved by Apollo's approval. Apollo in turn claims that Zeus had approved and describes the wicked conduct of Clytemnestra. To this the Furies say (640 ff.):

> "Zeus according to your account honors more the
> part of the father.
> But he himself bound his father Cronos.
> How is not the one inconsistent with the other?"

In other words, they introduce an example of the conduct of Zeus. Aeschylus skillfully uses one of the weapons of rhetorical argument—the example. Moreover, the argument is inherently one of probability, though Aeschylus does not use the term. The example is used to induce not what Zeus invariably does, but what he probably would do. It is the recognition and development of the basis of rhetorical, as opposed to scientific, argument in probability that is the greatest characteristic of fifth-century rhetoric. Notice also how short the example is, as contrasted with the Meleager story. A single line suffices to prove the point. In Cronos himself, the Furies, turned rhetoricians, have no interest.

Apollo replies (657 ff.) by denying the applicability of the example: bonds may be loosed, but death may not be undone. He then goes on to explain that the mother is not the parent of the child, "but the nurse of the newly planted embryo." The proof of this, and the technical word *tekmêrion* is used, is that there may be fatherhood and no mother. An example is Athena herself. This is a second proof by example, but this time it is not one of the probability, but of the possibility of the fact. The heart of the argument is in the definition of a "parent," that is, it is a verbal matter. By questioning the assumed and common definition of parenthood, Apollo, at least temporarily, raises doubts whether Clytemnestra had any real right to special respect from Orestes. Here again are new devices at work: a concern with verbal matters sets aside the moral traditions which were generally valued. To put it another way, by agility of argument, the worse, from the point of view of common sense, is made to seem the better cause. Further consideration and opposite examples might easily destroy the argument. But for the moment it stands, and the moment is long enough for Apollo, for he is the last speaker and he wins his case.

Similar indications of the growth of interest in argument and in devices later associated with rhetoric are to be seen in Herodotus.[30] Beginning with him, history is second only to oratory as a genre influenced by rhetoric. Collingwood went so far as to see in Herodotus' method the influence of the practice of the law courts.[31] He says that evidence to Herodotus consists of eyewitness reports, examined and evaluated by the historian in the same way that the orator examines witnesses in litigation. An example might be the account of Argive policy in book seven (148 ff.). The test of truth in both oratory and history is probability, and the immediate object is the same in both cases, the construction of a persuasive (i.e. probable) argument. A further sign of judicial influence may be seen in the motif of retribution recurring in Herodotus: as in the opening stories of the first book, history is conceived as a series of events in a sphere of activity or historical period where judicial process was not available.

The influence of the growing rhetorical consciousness on Herodotus is most evident in the speeches.[32] Some of these show little change from the type found in the Homeric poems. There are two speeches of the long example or Meleager type, that of Sosicles in 5.92 and that of Leotychides in 6.86. The outburst of Xerxes to Pythius the Lydian in 7.39 is not unlike recriminations in the *Iliad,* and the methods of persuasion used by Cambyses in his death-bed speech to the Persians are definitely pre-sophistic (3.65).

As in the Homeric poems, and in contrast with Thucydides, the better part of the direct discourse in Herodotus is conversation rather than oratory. Solon talks with Croesus,

[30] On rhetoric in Herodotus cf. Aly, *op.cit.* supra n. 28, 48 ff. and 76 ff., and his "Herodots Sprache," *Glotta* 15 (1926) 84 ff.; Hermann Diels, "Herodot und Hekataios," *Hermes* 22 (1887) 411 ff., esp. 424 ff.; W. Nestle, *op.cit.* supra n. 19.

[31] R. G. Collingwood, *The idea of history,* Oxford, 1946, 25.

[32] Cf. Norden 38 ff.; Erwin Schulz, *Die Reden im Herodot,* Greifswald, 1933, 11 ff.; Lieselotte Solmsen, "Speeches in Herodotus' account of the Ionic revolt," AJP 64 (1943) 194 ff. and "Speeches in Herodotus' account of the battle of Plataea," CP 39 (1944) 241 ff.; VanGroningen, *op.cit.* supra n. 8, 236 ff.

Xerxes confers with Artabanus, then with Damaratus. Many of these conversations are as carefully planned as scenes from Greek tragedy: for example, the stories of Gyges or Atys or Solon in book one or that of Lycophron in three or of Masistes in nine. Beginning with the account of the Ionian revolt there is a more complicated use of speeches as a way of commenting on the action, much like that seen in Thucydides. The great debates of the later books (e.g., 7.8 ff.; 7.157 ff.; 8.140 ff.) are the most conspicuous rhetorical products, but there is one famous debate in book three (80 ff.) in which the Persian leaders discuss the best form of government. The historical improbability of such a debate in Persia, though Herodotus protests that it did take place, points to its composition as a means of expressing the author's own ideas. It is thus close in spirit to the work of those sophists who, like Gorgias and Protagoras, used oratory to expound philosophy and to the speeches in Thucydides. The contents, which seem to recommend democracy but to be conscious of its dangers and to recognize the need for a helmsman, would probably also be acceptable to Thucydides. The practicality of the arguments is close to later rhetorical practice.

In fact, the four characteristics of rhetorical consciousness are all to be found in Herodotus: the interest in division of speeches is less marked, but it is occasionally present as, for example, in the speech of the Greek envoys to Syracuse in 7.157, which falls into the four parts of introduction, narration, argument, and conclusion taught in the rhetorical handbooks. Schulz pointed out[33] the careful organization of the speeches in the debate on the advisability of the Greek invasion in 7.8-11. Herodotus is, moreover, interested in etymologies and philology. See, for example, the discussion of θεοί in 2.52, where he seems to be disagreeing with

[33] *op.cit.* supra n. 32, 24 ff., but cf. Marcel Delaunois, "Le plan rhétorique dans l'éloquence grecque d'Homère à Démosthène," LEC 23 (1955) 273.

Heraclitus and following the opinion of Anaxagoras.[34] Thirdly, Herodotus is not untouched by the new prose styles: a good example of antithesis is 7.51.[35] Finally, there is considerable subtlety of argument. Herodotus is clearly aware of the possibilities in argument from probability. A passage in which this occurs is his defense of the Alcmaeonids (6.121 ff.). Here he tries to show that it is not probable that the Alcmaeonids would hold up a shield in the light of the sun to signal the Persians at Marathon, for they were haters of tyrants and were held in esteem by the Athenians; therefore, they could not have been offended with the people and have decided to betray their country.[36] An excellent example of argument, including argument from probability aiming at demonstrating the expedient, and also of rhetorical style, including antithesis, rhetorical question, and maxim, is the little speech of Artemesia in reply to the question whether Xerxes should risk a sea battle at Salamis (8.68).

Herodotus' opportunities for direct contact with the intellectual currents of the middle fifth century, with sophistry and the democratic process at Athens, and perhaps with rhetoricians at Thurii, were adequate to justify the claim that the appearance of rhetorical devices in his work is the result of direct and conscious imitation. What he found to be the fashion at Athens would appeal to his instinct. This does not, however, mean that he is as permeated with the spirit of rhetoric as is Thucydides. He has not been trained in rhetorical methods. What techniques he employs he has picked up from observation. He is not altogether convinced

[34] Cf. Nestle, op.cit. supra n. 19.

[35] On Herodotus' style cf. Paul Kleber. *Die Rhetorik bei Herodot* 1, Löwenberg, 1889, and *De genere dicendi Herodoteo quaestiones selectae*, Löwenberg, 1890; John C. Robertson, *The Gorgianic figures in early Greek prose*, Baltimore, 1893, 33 ff.; M. Wundt, *De Herodoti elocutione cum sophistarum comparata*, Leipzig, 1903; Norden 27 f.

[36] Other examples of argument from probability are to be found in 7.103, 104, and 167 and probably elsewhere.

46

of the effectiveness of rhetorical persuasion. Artabanus (7.10) at first failed to persuade Xerxes, and then it seems that this persuasion was wrong and must be countermanded by the gods. But still, opposite opinion, as Artabanus says, is necessary before choice can be exercised. To put it in other terms, Herodotus is only partially convinced that the truth can be achieved by rational process. The world is too complex a place for all things to be that simple. To this extent Collingwood's thesis is overextended. But Herodotus, like any Greek, enjoys debate and will make what use of it he can.

The state of rhetoric in Aeschylus and Herodotus thus contributes to our understanding of the fact that rhetoric in argument, in style, and in arrangement was not introduced into Greece suddenly and dramatically in 427 B.C. by Gorgias, but was already present in most respects. This does not mean that the speeches of Gorgias did not strike the Athenians as extraordinary. The jingles, the obsession with technique, the excesses of Gorgias are what was remarkable, not the principle behind them. One conclusion from this is that the oratory of the fifth century, as Finley has shown,[37] was surely not unlike what Thucydides puts into the mouth of his speakers. Pericles was perhaps a good deal more fluent, less tortuous than the historian, but there is not the slightest reason to doubt that his arguments were what we think of as sophistic, that is, aimed at proving expediency by means of probability, and that his style was antithetical. In the latter respect he was perhaps following the model of Themistocles, who is said by Herodotus (8.83) to have delivered a speech in which throughout he contrasted what was noble and what was base.

Although Thucydides wrote his work subsequent to the arrival of Gorgias in Athens, this survey of early rhetorical

[37] *op.cit.* supra n. 11, 35 ff. The same conclusion might be drawn from Edward B. Stevens, "Some Attic commonplaces of pity," AJP 65 (1944) 1 ff., who discusses especially Cleon's speech on Mytilene.

practice may logically be extended to include his *History* if only because that magnificent work does not properly fit into the topics considered in any subsequent chapter. Thucydides' oratorical technique differs from that of Herodotus chiefly in degree and intensity, and this in turn suggests, what one might assume on chronological grounds, that he was quite aware of the theories of sophists and professional rhetoricians about oratory.[38]

In the absence of documentary evidence Herodotus had apparently constructed many of his speeches on the basis of what he thought ought to have been said.[39] Thucydides has elaborated this into a major principle of historical composition. He claims (1.22) to reconstruct what the speaker ought to have said (τὰ δέοντα). "Ought," that is, in the rhetorical sense, the right topics and techniques for the occasion, not in the sense of politically or morally right. There is thus a right and wrong oratorical technique, a principle much encouraged by the writers of rhetorical handbooks. Thucydides' statement is indicative of self-consciousness in oratorical composition and important in suggesting the rhetorical problem of much of ancient literature. Composition, whether historical, dramatic, or epic, raises problems of writing speeches suitable to the character of the speaker and the occasion, and all of literature was destined to become more and more an exercise in answering a rhetorical challenge.[40]

Even in its over-all composition Thucydides' work shows some similarity to rhetorical methods. It begins with an introduction which secures the readers' attention and sympathy by showing the importance of the war in contrast to previous wars (the so-called archaeology) and the difficulty

[38] Cf. Paul Moraux, "Thucydide et la rhétorique: étude sur la structure de deux discours (III.37-48)," LEC 22 (1954) 3 ff.

[39] Cf. L. Solmsen, CP article *cit.* supra n. 32, 242.

[40] Cf. Peter J. Fliess, "Political disorder and constitutional form: Thucydides' critique of contemporary politics," *Journal of politics* 21 (1959) 614 ff.

of the task, and which makes a virtue of the lack of entertaining narrative much as an orator makes a virtue of his inability at public speaking. After stating the immediate points at issue, the historian proceeds to a narrative in simple style, introduced by the regular particle γάρ; this is the so-called pentecontaetea, which the author describes as a digression and an *apodeixis* (1.97) but which performs the background function of the narration of a speech. Whether an epilogue was planned we do not know; the Sicilian campaign, which follows a similar general pattern, has a very short one with strong emotional impact (7.87.5 f.).

Thucydides appears to have been in sympathy with those sophists who thought that truth was known only through specific instances. Thus historical fact exists and can be determined by a kind of judicial method as described in chapter twenty-two of book one. Knowledge of historical fact may then make possible historical generalization about cause and effect, as in the case of the effects of plague or revolution upon society. But Thucydides does not look for any absolute truth in the sense of a divine plan in history nor does he write to illustrate virtue rewarded and evil punished. His is a rhetorical view of the world: he sees no particular goal in life and views the process of existence as the only thing which can be known. Since life is basically an intellectual process, understanding of life is an essential part of life. Motives and historical processes thus must be explored, stated, and understood as fully as possible. In this supreme intellectual task history and rhetoric join hands.

The Melian dialogue (5.85 ff.) is perhaps the best illustration of Thucydides' mind.[41] Readers have sometimes thought that he intended to discredit the power politics of Athens, but surely that is unlikely: the Melians put their trust in the gods (5.113) and are disappointed; Athenian

[41] On its form and for some arguments against its historicity, cf. H. Ll. Hudson-Williams, "Conventional forms of debate and the Melian dialogue," AJP 71 (1950) 156 ff.

expediency is completely successful. Nor are future events in any way a nemesis upon the Athenians for Melos. The Sicilian campaign failed not because it was too audacious, but because it was not thoroughly pursued (2.66), and the loss of the war is specifically attributed to internal disorders. In all of this Thucydides is a pragmatist, and any dogmatic morality found in him is the product of the moral sensitivity of his readers or a feeling that he must be made to conform to the scruples of Aeschylus and Herodotus. But at the same time, Thucydides is not content simply to state the facts, and he represents the Athenians as unwilling simply to impose their will on the Melians. The dialogue performs no practical, political function, but that does not necessarily prove its lack of historicity, for its function in Thucydides' work, and perhaps in fact, was intellectual. Things must be talked out first, an attempt at persuasion must be made, the events must be understood, there must be no doubt that expediency is in operation. The dialogue, as one reads it, is full of concern with motives expressed, in other words with rhetorical arguments, but its composition by the historian was not for the sake of its composition, not for the art alone, not just to answer a rhetorical challenge. He wrote it to explain the incident of Melos and to express the specific truth for the comprehension of future readers. History may have no goal, but the historian created one for himself.

The principal stylistic method used by the historian to obtain comprehension of contrasting concepts or motives is the sharp focus of antithesis in clauses, sentences, or whole speeches. Within each of the paired speeches a similar focus in thought is obtained by concentrating on a single argument. In some speeches justice or honor or possibility is the subject of interest, but most frequently and especially in successful speeches expediency holds sway. Justice and expediency are regarded as mutually exclusive. For example, in the Mytilenean debate of book three (37 ff.) Cleon admits that justice might be a consideration, but argues for expediency against it. Diodotus in the opposing speech, though supporting the more humanitarian position, rejects justice as a basis of action and similarly concentrates on what is expedient. The tremendous rhetorical impact of his speech is a result of this rejection of justice and acceptance of reality. It seems likely that Greek deliberative oratory of Thucydides' time tended toward a similar focus on one argument,[42] but doubtless the concentration is greater in the historian. It was not destined to remain a permanent feature of Greek oratory.

In Thucydides all the virtues and vices of rhetoric are inherent. The clarity and power which his work achieves and the ruthless vision of the world which it reflects suggest a force which might intoxicate a pupil less devoted to veracity and make composition itself into an end and means regardless of all responsibility, aimed solely at persuasion rather than comprehension. Thucydides' own work is a possession forever, not a prize contest, but there were many anxious to utilize the same means in vying for honor for themselves.

[42] Cf. George A. Kennedy, "Focusing of arguments in Greek deliberative oratory," TAPA 90 (1959) 131 ff. On the Cleon-Diodotus debate, cf. L. Bodin, "Diodote contre Cléon: quelques aperçus sur la dialectique de Thucydide," REA 42 (1940) 36 ff. and Moraux, *op.cit.* supra n. 38.

CHAPTER THREE

Early Rhetorical Theory, Corax to Aristotle

Instruction in rhetoric in the fifth century was given in two rather different ways.[1] One way may be seen from a passage in Aristotle's *Sophistical refutations* (183b36 ff.):

"The educational system of those who taught eristic for money was like the approach of Gorgias. He and his fellows assigned rhetorical discourses to be learned by heart, the teachers of eristic assigned discourse of question and answer. It was presumed for the most part that these discourses included the arguments on both sides of the issue. As a result, the teaching was quick, but unsystematic. The teachers thought they could educate by imparting not art, but the products of art, just as if someone were to claim to furnish knowledge for the prevention of sore feet and then did not teach shoemaking nor how suitable shoes could be procured, but offered many varieties of all sorts of foot gear. Such a teacher has come to the practical aid of a want, but has not taught an art."

Cicero in the *Brutus* (46 ff.), probably quoting from Aristotle's lost collection of early rhetorical handbooks, adds a little more information. He speaks of Protagoras' disputations on important subjects, "which are now called *communes loci*" or commonplaces. Gorgias, Cicero says, did much the same thing in writing his *laudes* and *vituperationes*; he thought that the characteristic act of the orator was to exalt a subject by praise or weaken it by criticism. The common-

---

[1] Cf. George A. Kennedy, "The earliest rhetorical handbooks," AJP 80 (1959) 169 ff. Cf. also A. Gercke, "Die alte τέχνη ῥητορική und ihre Gegner," *Hermes* 32 (1897) 341 ff.; Navarre; Peter Hamberger, *Die rednerische Disposition in der alten τέχνη ῥητορική*, Paderborn, 1914; Barwick 1 ff.; Stanley Wilcox, "The scope of early rhetorical instruction,' HSCP 53 (1942) 137 ff.; H. Ll. Hudson-Williams, "Conventional forms of debate and the Melian dialogue," AJP 71 (1950) 156 ff.

places are thus like arguments and are inserted into a speech to support some position. The orator has memorized them and no doubt uses each one again and again in different speeches. By their use he can lengthen a speech to any desired length. Isocrates' speech *Against the sophists* (12) refers to the same kind of composition. In all references it is clear that these commonplaces or specimens of oratory were like building blocks from which a speech could be constructed. The actual composition was often largely extempore, the orator drawing on the material in his memory in the way described by Plato in the *Menexenus* (236a8 ff.). The orators usually memorized their commonplaces, but, except for that feature, the construction of the speech resembled the composition of oral poetry out of themes and formulae.

There are a few preserved complete speeches which seem to belong to this sophistic tradition and to have been written as examples or fair copies. The *Tetralogies* of Antiphon are three sets of four speeches, two for the prosecution and two for the defense, in imaginary cases of homicide and assault. Gorgias' *Encomium of Helen* and *Defense of Palamedes* are also good examples of the techniques of argument, and also of prose style. Another example might be the speech pleading the cause of the non-lover attributed to Lysias in Plato's *Phaedrus* (230e6 ff.). Phaedrus is intent upon studying, perhaps even memorizing it as an example and raw material of oratory. Of course the sophists also used oratory to express ideas; Protagoras' mythological speech (320c8 ff.) in Plato's dialogue named for him is a good example.

There was no reason why examples of technique should be whole speeches. We know that collections of introductions and conclusions were made by Antiphon and others, and the Demosthenic corpus contains a collection of prooemia for political speeches.[2] The collections were ap-

[2] Cf. A. Rupprecht, "Die demosthenische Prooemiumsammlung," *Philologus* 82 (1927) 365 ff.

parently not limited to judicial speeches, for in this way all forms of public speaking could be taught. One of the sources of appeal of such instruction was its applicability to all types of oratory and to political and philosophical discussions. The wealthy pupils of the sophists regarded themselves as the future governors and philosophers of the state and demanded a set of commonplaces appropriate for their manifold interests. More modest folk had to content themselves with more modest instruction.

In practice sophists like Gorgias probably commented on the techniques illustrated by their creations, and collections of commonplaces which were published, Thrasymachus' *Eleoi* for example, may sometimes have been accompanied by an introduction or commentary of some sort. Theoretical writing about rhetoric was mostly on an entirely different level. It forms the second type of instruction in rhetoric, the rhetorical handbook. Presumably a handbook might contain some illustrations of its rules, but it was basically an exposition of precepts, not a collection of examples. In a passage in the *Sophistical refutations* just preceding that quoted above, Aristotle refers to the theorizing of Tisias, Thrasymachus, and Theodorus, which he contrasts with the system of Gorgias. They did not write specimens or commonplaces, but discussed technique. The same contrast is evident in the context of the passage in the *Brutus* and in Isocrates. Cicero puts Protagoras, Gorgias, and Antiphon in one category, Corax, Tisias, Theodorus, and, until he turned to speech writing, Lysias in the other. Antiphon and perhaps others really overlapped in that they composed specimens and wrote handbooks, but the two activities are not conflated. When the ancient sources speak of τέχνη or *ars* they always mean theoretical instruction and usually a written theoretical exposition or handbook, never collections of commonplaces.

The best general picture of the early rhetorical handbooks is that in Plato's *Phaedrus* (266d5 ff.):

"*Phdr.*: There's quite a lot in the books written on the technique of speaking, Socrates.

Soc.: Oh, yes, you did well to remind me. As I recall it, they begin by explaining that a prooemium should be spoken at the beginning of the speech. That's what you were referring to, wasn't it, the details of the art?

Phdr.: Yes.

Soc.: And second the books say that you should have a narration and witnesses to the facts, third proof from signs, fourth the probabilities of the case. The admirable and versatile speech writer from Byzantium includes in his speeches, I believe, both a proof and a supplementary proof.

Phdr.: You mean the worthy Theodorus.

Soc.: Who else? And he tells how you should effect a refutation and supplementary refutation whether you speak for the prosecution or for the defense. And we're forgetting the distinguished Evenus of Paros who first discovered insinuation and indirect praise, and they say he also spoke indirect censure, learning stock phrases for this purpose in verse so that he could remember them better. He was a shrewd one! And shouldn't we get Tisias and Gorgias in here somewhere? They saw that probabilities are more honored than the truth. They made small things seem important and big things seem inconsequential by the force of their speech; they made new things sound old and old things sound new. On all subjects they could make the account very short or the length unlimited. Prodicus laughed once when he heard about this from me and said that he was the only one who had discovered how long a speech should be—there was need of neither length nor brevity, but of moderation.

Phdr.: Wisely said, Prodicus.

Soc.: And shouldn't we mention Hippias, for I think that visitor from Elis would agree with him?

Phdr.: Certainly.

Soc.: And what shall we say about those museums of words that Polus made, his diplasiology and gnomology and eikonology? And the collection of nouns which Licymnius gave him so that he could find the most elegant word?

Phdr.: Didn't Protagoras do something of the sort?

Soc.: Yes, he collected the exact meanings of words and quite a few other fine points of style. The artistic ability of Thrasymachus seems to me to have gained him victory in the field of pathetic expressions on old age and poverty. Why he has acquired ability to stir a whole crowd of people at one and the same time to frenzy and then to charm them out of it by magic, as he said. He has become very good, too, at attacking or answering allegations on almost any basis. The end of a speech is a subject of general agreement among all the rhetoricians, though some call it a recapitulation and others use some other name.

Phdr.: You mean the technique of reminding the listeners about each of the points discussed in a summary at the end."

Socrates has begun with the contents of the prooemium and passed through the traditional parts of a judicial speech, the narration, the subdivisions of the proof, and the epilogue. Since many later treatises follow this organization in at least a part of their contents it seems clear that the handbooks consisted of a discussion of each part of the speech in turn, though Plato comments also on the oratorical practice of the theoreticians. Plato's summary is confirmed by Aristotle (*Rhetoric* 1354b17 ff.), who says that handbook writers before his time were concerned only with the parts of the speech. Plato's summary would indicate that there might have been some discussion of argument from probability and means of amplification under the heading of proof, but he does not make clear to what extent examples were given. Certainly long examples were not a part of this kind of instruction in rhetoric. The structure given by Plato is that of the judicial speech; probably, as Aristotle (*Rhetoric* 1354b26) and Isocrates (*Against the sophists* 19) indicate, the handbooks were concerned only with court oratory.

The references in Plato, Aristotle, and Isocrates seem to indicate that written handbooks of rhetorical theory were fairly numerous, though this does not necessarily imply that there were many different copies of each. Like the Peripatetic writings,[3] medical works, and some sophistic treatises they were *hypomnêmata*, notes by a teacher or one of his pupils. They filled a specific need and were soon superseded by other handbooks. Their judicial orientation points to their function. Men who could afford a liberal education for public life attached themselves to a sophist,[4] practiced his commonplaces, and learned almost incidentally the techniques of court oratory. But since Greek law required every citizen to speak in his own behalf in prosecution or defense, a knowledge of judicial oratory might be a real need to anyone among the litigious Athenians. One did not after all have to speak in the assembly, and doubtless only those who felt capable of self-expression did so. On the other hand, countless circumstances could catch even the innocent in the toils of the law. Where could an inexperienced person turn? One way was to a *logographos*, a speech writer such as Lysias, whose published orations advertised his wares. But this was probably expensive: Lysias' customers were mostly prosperous businessmen and farmers, and Lysias and other logographers were artists from whom elegance of style as well as effective argument was to be expected. If the pro-

[3] Cf. Jaeger 31 and n. 21.
[4] This was expensive, cf. Plato, *Apology* 20b9 and *Greater Hippias* 282c5; Diodorus Siculus 12.53.2; Quintilian 3.1.10. Cf. also R. Johnson, "A note on the number of Isocrates' pupils," AJP 78 (1957) 297 ff.

spective litigant could not buy a whole speech and could not afford the time to study with a sophist, he could turn to a rhetorician and learn from him in a few hours, or perhaps even by reading a written summary of his system, the necessary parts of a speech and the chief features of each. Such instruction was cheap. When Lysias gave up theoretical instruction for speech writing, as Cicero says he did (*Brutus* 48), he continued to fulfill a similar function in supplying judicial oratory to those in need, but in a different and no doubt more profitable way. Great sophists such as Protagoras or Hippias or Gorgias probably did not bother with this sort of thing; it was the work of the second-raters like Polus and Theodorus. The public for the rhetoricians would also include people not themselves involved in law suits who were guarding against the future or who were interested in the court processes because of their jury duties.

None of the earliest handbooks have survived; they tended to supersede each other as the details of rhetorical theory were developed, and any possible historical interest in their preservation was reduced by the fact that Aristotle undertook a compendium of the teaching of rhetoric up to his own day, the *Synagôgê technôn*. Presumably he was gathering material in preparation for his own works on rhetoric in the way that he gathered information on constitutions as part of his study of politics. Aristotle's study of earlier rhetoric seems to have survived through most of antiquity, and most, though not quite all, of the references in later authors to theories of early rhetoricians are probably filtered through this collection.

Corax and Tisias[5]

The earliest writers of handbooks and the traditional founders of judicial rhetoric are said to have been Corax

[5] For the fragments of Corax and Tisias cf. Radermacher B.ii. For discussion cf. Aulitzky in R-E 11. col. 1379 ff. s.v. "Korax 3"; Stegemann in R-E 5². col. 139 ff. s.v. "Teisias 6"; Kroll 1041 f.; A. W.

and Tisias of Syracuse. There are references to their activity in the works of Plato, Aristotle, Cicero, and Quintilian and much more detailed but inconsistent reports of what they may have done in the collections of introductions to the art of rhetoric known as the *Prolegomena*.[6] These collections were produced from the third to the thirteenth century A.D. and fall into two groups: one, represented by Sopater and numbers 6A and 13 in the collection of Rabe, is a late reconstruction with little reliable materials.[7] The second group, of which Rabe's number four is an example, apparently goes back to the late fourth-century B.C. Sicilian historian Timaeus.[8] Number four says (p. 25 ff. Rabe) that Corax was active in Syracuse at the time that it became a democracy (467 B.C.). He developed a tripartite scheme of oratory to help the citizens speak in the assembly: prooemium, *agôn*, epilogue. The *agôn* included a narrative. Tisias was a pupil of Corax who refused to pay for his instruction. Upon being dragged into court he argued that if he won the dispute he need not pay by that decision, if he lost, however, payment would be unjust since the art would be proved worthless. Corax replied by reversing the argument. The court turned them both out with the epigram "a bad egg from a bad crow (*korax*)."[9]

Verrall, "Korax and Tisias," JP 9 (1880) 187 ff.; Gercke, *op.cit.* supra n. 1; W. Rhys Roberts, "The new rhetorical fragments in relation to the Sicilian rhetoric of Corax and Tisias," CR 18 (1904) 19 ff.; W. Kroll, "Randbemerkungen xviii," RHM 66 (1911) 164 ff.; Hamberger, *op.cit.* supra n. 1; Bromley Smith, "Corax and probability," QJS 7 (1921) 13 ff.; Barwick; D. A. G. Hinks, "Tria genera causarum," CQ 30 (1936) 170 ff. and "Tisias and Corax and the invention of rhetoric," CQ 34 (1940) 61 ff.; Wilcox, *op.cit.* supra n. 1, and "Corax and the prolegomena," AJP 64 (1943) 1 ff.

[6] The best edition is that of H. Rabe, *Prolegomenon sylloge*, Leipzig, 1931.

[7] Cf. Wilcox, "Corax and the prolegomena," *cit.* supra n. 5, 10.

[8] Cf. Ludwig Radermacher, "Timäus und die Ueberlieferung über die Ursprung der Rhetorik," RHM 52 (1897) 112 ff.

[9] The same story is told of Protagoras and Euathlus by Diogenes Laertius 9.8.56.

This account does not agree with that of Cicero in the *Brutus* (46 ff.). He says, alleging the authority of Aristotle, that after the elimination of the Sicilian tyrants, suits were instituted for the recovery of private property and that Corax and Tisias compiled a handbook of precepts on the technique of speaking in such cases.

The questions raised by a comparison of the two accounts are, first, were the beginnings of rhetoric connected with deliberative or judicial oratory; second, was Corax master, opponent, or colleague of Tisias; and third, what was the nature of the teaching of either or both? The better ancient authorities on rhetoric knew almost nothing about Corax. Neither Plato nor Isocrates ever mentions him. Aristotle refers to him once in the *Rhetoric* (1402a18) and attributes to him the same example of argument from probability which Plato (*Phaedrus* 273a6 ff.) had attributed to Tisias. Theophrastus described him vaguely as an inventor of the art of words.[10] Cicero (*De inventione* 2.6) says that the lost *Synagôgê technôn*, the summary of the earlier handbooks, began with Tisias. On the other hand, the Timaeus tradition shows little interest in Tisias and much in Corax. Thus perhaps Corax did play a political role of historical interest. No work of his survived if he ever wrote one. Tisias, on the other hand, taught a theory of which a written summary was known to Plato and Aristotle. Everything we know about this theory points to the fact that its concern was with judicial oratory. In the passage from Plato just referred to, it is clear that he was applying the technique to court trials. There is even one late reference (Pausanias 6.17.8) to indicate that Tisias may have followed the allied occupation of a logographer.

If Corax was a political speaker and Tisias a writer of judicial speeches the connexion between the two of them need not have been very close. Tisias was perhaps influenced by Corax' use of argument from probability. The threefold

[10] Cf. Radermacher A.v.17.

division of speech that Rabe's fourth *Prolegomenon* (p. 26) attributes to Corax is quite suitable for deliberative oratory and probably correct. The major original feature would be the recognition of need for an epilogue. On the other hand, the characteristic of judicial oratory as described by Plato in the passage quoted from the *Phaedrus* is the *diêgêsis* or narration, and a four-part division seems most logical for Tisias. Probably he said something about the function of each of the parts: the prooemium should secure the attention and the good will of the audience, the narration should put the jury in possession of the necessary information, the proof should demonstrate the truth of the charge or refute the allegation, and the conclusion should sum up what had been said. The discussion of proof would seem to have stressed the superiority of the probable over the factual in demonstration.[11] Some later writers quote Tisias' definition of rhetoric as the *demiourgos,* or artificer, of persuasion; that may be genuine.[12] He is also said to have been the teacher of some of the Attic orators: of Lysias at Thurii and of Isocrates. The former seems more probable than the latter, but neither are certain.

Gorgias[13]

The cultural interchange between Sicily and Athens was so extensive that it is not surprising that the ensuing develop-

[11] Cf. Plato, *Phaedrus* 267a6 f. 272d2 ff., and 273a7 ff., in Radermacher B.ii.15, 16, and 18. Cf. also Friedrich Solmsen, rev. of Radermacher, *Gnomon* 26 (1954) 214 f.

[12] Cf. Radermacher B.ii.13.

[13] The fragments of Gorgias' rhetorical works may be found in Radermacher B.vii. For discussion cf. E. Wellmann in R-E 7. col. 1598 ff. s.v. "Gorgias 8" and Kroll 1043 ff.; Gercke, *op.cit.* supra n. 1; Norden 15 ff.; Navarre 79 ff.; Engelbert Drerup, "Die Anfänge der rhetorischen Kunstprosa," JKP *Supplementband* 27.2 (1902) 219 ff.; Karl Reich, *Der Einfluss der griechischen Poesie auf Gorgias* 1. Munich, 1908, 2. Würzburg, 1909; Wilhelm Süss, *Ethos: Studien zur alteren griechischen Rhetorik,* Leipzig, 1910; Hermann Gomperz, *Sophistik und Rhetorik,* Leipzig, 1912; A. Rostagni, "Un nuovo

ment of the rhetorical handbooks took place at Athens. Oratory there had demands upon it elsewhere unmatched, and the constant throng of philosophers and sophists furnished a tradition of conscious theorizing. The democratic process supplied the need for the handbooks; the philosophers hastened their development. Although, as we have seen, much of the technique of rhetoric was known in Athens at an early date, Gorgias' embassy in 427 is a symbol of the progress of oratorical theory from Sicily to Greece, and in the following years Gorgias himself was probably the best known rhetorical personage both as teacher and practitioner.

The quotation from the *Sophistical refutations* at the head of this chapter seems to make it clear that Gorgias' works did not include any systematic discussion of rhetoric. There are a few references to an *ars*,[14] but probably his verbal discussions are meant. Otherwise his rhetorical instruction was through speeches and collections of commonplaces.

For all of his love of pleasing sounds Gorgias did not regard rhetoric as primarily a form of entertainment. The object of his oratory was persuasion. Plato quotes him (*Philebus* 58a8 ff.) as saying that rhetoric differed from other arts in making all its willing slaves and not accomplishing its end by force. In the *Gorgias* (452e9 ff.) Socrates attributes to Gorgias the definition of rhetoric as the artificer of persuasion which we have connected with Tisias. Rhetoric is an art, and it deals with all subjects, though legal and political ones are especially mentioned by Gorgias himself.[15] Its materials are probabilities rather than scientific

---

capitolo della retorica e della sofistica," *Studi italiani di filologia classica* 2 (1922) 148 ff.; Hunt, 12 ff.; Thomas S. Duncan, "Gorgias' theories of art," CJ 33 (1938) 402 ff.; Untersteiner, 92 ff. and esp. 194 ff.; Friedrich Zucher, "Der Stil des Gorgias nach seiner innherem Form," SBB (1956); Charles P. Segal, "Gorgias and the psychology of the logos," HSCP 66 (1962) 99 ff. See further the discussion of Gorgias as an orator in the following chapter.

[14] Cf. Radermacher B.vii.1-6.   [15] *Ibid.* B.vii.10-17.

facts and it can make the small seem great, the great small, the new old, and the old new (Plato, *Phaedrus* 267a6 ff.). Gorgias' technique (*macrologia* is its technical name) enabled him to spin out a speech to any length appropriate for persuasion at the moment, partly by inserting commonplaces, partly by a logical exhaustion of the subject. Thus if he were speaking of Achilles he might elaborate on the virtues of, first, Peleus, then Aeacus, then the divine progenitor (Aristotle, *Rhetoric* 1418a36), and other subjects could similarly be traced out into all their ramifications and implications.

In addition to logical argument Gorgias recognized the persuasive force of emotion. He regarded an orator as a *psychagôgos*, like a poet, a leader of souls through a kind of incantation.[16] The irrational materials of the orator included, according to Gorgias, not only the serious passion which might be evoked by speech, and which Gorgias' rhyming style was no doubt intended to encourage, but also laughter, which is especially important as a means of refutation.[17] Other sophists of the time who were interested in the emotional element of oratory included Prodicus[18] and Thrasymachus, who wrote something called *Eleoi*, or *Plaints* (Aristotle, *Rhetoric* 1404a14 f.), and discussion of the subject was found in some handbooks (Aristotle, *Rhetoric* 1354a11 ff.). Fifth-century oratory as seen especially in Antiphon and Euripides uses ethos and pathos as forms of proof, but then so did Homeric oratory.

A second subject which gradually made its way into the handbooks was style. The stages in this development are not very clear. Perhaps appropriate stylistic devices were sometimes discussed in connexion with different parts of an oration, for Aristotle (*Rhetoric* 1416b30) objects to the requirement in some (fourth-century) handbooks that a

[16] Cf. Untersteiner 119 f. and Segal, *op.cit.* supra n. 13.
[17] Cf. esp. Plato, *Gorgias* 473e2 f. and Aristotle, *Rhetoric* 1419b3 ff., also Radermacher's notes thereon B.vii.22.
[18] Cf. Radermacher B.viii.3-5.

narration be "rapid." In his discussion of metaphor Aristotle says (*Rhetoric* 1412a23) that Theodorus spoke of novel expressions (τὰ καινὰ λέγειν), by which he seems to have meant not a metaphor, but a figure of speech. References to writing on style by other rhetoricians before the age of Aristotle indicate that these generally took the form of separate treatises. Thus Polus,[19] known chiefly from his role in Plato's *Gorgias*, is said in Suidas to have written a work entitled *On style* (περὶ λέξεως). According to the scholiast on Plato[20] Polus learned from Licymnius definitions of proper words, compound words, related words, epithets, and other categories which contribute to elegant diction (εὐέπεια). Antisthenes, too, wrote a work *On style*, subtitled *On characteristics* (περὶ χαρακτήρων), according to Diogenes Laertius (6.15). Both Polus and Antisthenes were pupils of Gorgias, whose stylistic experiments no doubt encouraged discussion of style, as did the philological work of other sophists. One sign of Gorgias' influence is that the account of style in the fourth-century *Rhetorica ad Alexandrum* is concerned with what we think of as Gorgianic figures.

The stylistic peculiarities of Gorgias may be seen in his *Encomium of Helen*, the *Defense of Palamedes*, and in the fragments of speeches like the *Funeral oration*. In essence Gorgias simply borrowed a number of the techniques of poetry[21] and developed to an extreme the natural Greek habit of antithesis. Diodorus Siculus (12.53.4) says:

"He was the first to make use of figures of speech which were far-fetched and distinguished by artificiality: antithesis, isocolon, parison, homoeoteleuton, and others of that sort which then, because of the novelty of the devices, were thought worthy of praise, but now seem labored and ridiculous when used to excess."

[19] The fragments are collected by Radermacher B.xiv.

[20] Cf. Hermias, *Commentary to Plato's Phaedrus* p. 239, 12 (p. 192 Ast), Radermacher B.xvi.2.

[21] Cf. Navarre 22 ff. and Norden 30 ff.

Of these figures, antithesis is certainly the most important. What it meant to early rhetoricians can be seen from the short account in the *Rhetorica ad Alexandrum* (1435b27 ff.):

"An antithesis is that which has both opposite terminology and meaning in contrasting clauses or either one of these. What follows would be opposed in terminology and meaning at the same time: 'It is not just for my opponent to have my property and be wealthy while I, having parted with my substance, am no more than a beggar.' Opposition in words only: 'Let the rich and prosperous give to the poor and needy.' In meaning: 'I nursed him while he was sick, but he has been the cause of the greatest evils to me.' Here the words are not opposed, but the actions are. Antithesis in both respects, meaning and terminology, would be most effective, but the two other types are also antithetical."

Further examples of antithesis may be found in Aristotle's discussion (*Rhetoric* 1409b32 ff.). Gorgias' fondness for antithesis is a direct reflection of his belief that truth is relative and requires the clear expression of contrasts and alternatives as the basis of definition and choice.

Parison is a parallelism of structure. "Either through lack of funds or through the magnitude of war. . . ." Homoeoteleuton is a series of two or more clauses ending with the same or rhyming words. Isocolon is seen in two or more clauses with the same number of syllables.

Throughout antiquity these and other figures of speech involving word play or jingle were usually treated as a group called the Gorgianic figures. Though not invented by Gorgias, since all of them can be found in earlier poetry and some in the prose of the pre-Socratic philosophers, they are properly called Gorgianic because they are the essential characteristics of his style.[22] Most ancient and

[22] Drerup, *op.cit.* supra n. 13, 258 regards all the Gorgianic

modern critics have regarded them with disfavor;[23] if the highest art is to conceal art, as has often been claimed, the devices hardly qualify, for they are extraordinarily conspicuous. Antithesis is the least bizarre, but even it may be only an apparent antithesis of words without logical antithetical significance. Yet in his own age the style of Gorgias did not seem in poor taste. There was then a general desire to create a literary prose; we can see both Thucydides and Antiphon wrestling with the idiom and occasionally snatching at techniques used by Gorgias. There was further a zest for sound among the Greeks, seen equally in the puns of the dramatists. In the Renaissance a new literary prose in the vernacular languages turned with enthusiasm to a style as flamboyant as that of Gorgias.[24]

Gorgias also influenced the theory of style in one quite different way, through the concept of the opportune, *to kairon*. It has been claimed that the ethics, aesthetics, and rhetoric of Gorgias are all based on *kairos*.[25] That is to say, Gorgias carried over to other fields the sophistic theory, seen also in the *Dissoi logoi*,[26] that two antithetical statements can be made on each subject. Any given problem involves choice or compromise between two antitheses so that consideration of *kairos*, that is of time, place, and circumstance (e.g. Gorgias, *Palamedes* 22), alone can solve

---

figures as only variations of antithesis. He stresses (262 ff.) the fact that prose rhythm is not an important element in Gorgias' style.

[23] E.g. Demetrius, *On style* 24, cf. 250, criticizes antithesis. Quintilian 9.3.74 says that Gorgias was *immodicus* in his concern for it. In the third century A.D. the excesses of Gorgias were still remembered; cf. Aquila Romanus 21 (in Halm).

[24] Cf. Norden 786 ff.; T. K. Whipple, "Isocrates and euphuism," *Modern language review* 11 (1916) 15 ff.; Theodor Gomperz (trans. by L. Magnus), *Greek thinkers*, London, 1920, 478 ff.; M. W. Croll, "The baroque style in prose," *Studies in English philology: a miscellany in honor of Frederik Klaeber*, Minneapolis, 1929, 427 ff.; Gilbert Highet, *The classical tradition*, New York, 1949, 322 ff.

[25] Cf. Untersteiner 161 and Radermacher B.vii.23-24.

[26] Cf. Diels 90 and Untersteiner 272 ff.

the dilemma and lead to the choice of relative truth and to action. In rhetoric *kairos* is the principle which governs the choice of the organization, the means of proof, and particularly the style. It has been defined as "the adaptation of the speech to the manifold variety of life, to the psychology of speaker and hearer: variegated, not absolute unity of tone."[27] Allied with the concept of *kairos* is *to prepon*, the fitting, which was also a term used in the fifth century (Plato, *Gorgias* 503e8 and *Phaedrus* 268d5) and which was to become one of the "virtues" of style.[28] The two together constitute what may be called the artistic element in rhetorical theory as opposed to the prescribed rules. *Kairos* as a rhetorical term is largely restricted to the classical period. *To prepon* is more persistent and is the only provision for latitude and taste which found a permanent place in traditional rhetoric. The subject is, of course, one that by nature cannot be reduced to rules, which is one of the reasons it did not receive great attention in the handbooks. Dionysius of Halicarnassus complains (*On composition* 12) that no definitive treatise had been written on *kairos*, "nor did Gorgias of Leontini, who first tried to write on it, write anything worth mentioning."

The significance of this artistic element was especially appreciated by Isocrates, who gives voice to it most clearly in two passages of the speech *Against the sophists* (12-13 and 16-18). The devices of the rhetorical handbooks he compares to the letters of the alphabet, whose use is fixed and immutable. The art of speech, however, is exactly the opposite (13): "it is not possible for speech to be good

[27] Cf. Untersteiner 197. *Kairos* is peculiarly vital in oratory. "Poetry always is free to fulfill its own law, but the writer of rhetorical discourse is, in a sense, perpetually in bondage to the occasion and the audience," Herbert A. Wichelns, "The literary criticism of oratory," *Studies in rhetoric and public speaking in honor of James Albert Winans*, New York, 1925, 212. Epideictic is only partially an exception.

[28] Cf. Max Pohlenz, "Τὸ πρέπον: ein Beitrag zur Geschichte des griechischen Geistes," NGG (1933) 53 ff.

if it does not contain what is opportune and fitting and novel, but in the case of letters there is no need of these qualities" (cf. also *Panegyricus* 9 and *Helen* 11).

Thrasymachus

Developments in prose style in the late fifth century were not solely the work of Gorgias. Another influential rhetorician was Thrasymachus of Chalcedon, who was well enough known to be satirized in Aristophanes' *Daitales* of 427 (fr.16 Meineke), the year Gorgias first came to Athens. It has been suggested[29] that Gorgias and Thrasymachus were the leaders of two opposed schools and that most other writers of the time may be regarded as followers of one or the other; this seems, however, a considerable exaggeration if one considers the surviving prose writing and fragments of the late fifth and early fourth centuries. Thrasymachus is mostly associated with the use of prose rhythm.[30] According to Aristotle (*Rhetoric* 1409a1 ff.) he employed the paean ($- \smile \smile \smile$) as the basis of his prose style without recognizing what he was doing. Later writers are somewhat more definite, though perhaps not on very good grounds. Cicero, for example, speaking of prose rhythm (*Orator* 175), says that Isocrates was the most skilled, "but the original discoverer was Thrasymachus, all of whose works show an excessive rhythmical quality."[31]

We have very little of Thrasymachus' own writing left; the thirty or so lines preserved by Dionysius of Halicarnassus (*Isaeus* 3) do show attention to rhythm, but not predominantly paeans.[32] What Thrasymachus appreciated, and perhaps he was the first to do so, was the effect of a varied

[29] Cf. Drerup, *op.cit.* supra n. 13.

[30] Cf. Norden 41 ff. and G. M. A. Grube, "Thrasymachus, Theophrastus, and Dionysius of Halicarnassus," AJP 73 (1952) 251 ff. Grube shows that the passage in Dionysius (*Lysias* 6) attributes compactness, not periodicity, to Thrasymachus.

[31] Cf. Radermacher B.ix.13-17.

[32] Cf. Drerup, *op.cit.* supra n. 13, 239 ff.

rhythmic pattern, avoiding on the one hand the regularity of verse and on the other the extended series of long or short syllables together sometimes found in non-artistic prose. Furthermore, the fragment shows a degree of sentence structure more developed than in any earlier writer[33] and a tendency to avoid hiatus,[34] or juxtaposition of a word ending with a vowel before a word beginning with a vowel, which is one of the characteristics of the Isocratean school of polished prose. In both of these respects Thrasymachus differs from Gorgias, as he does in avoiding the artificialities of the latter's style. Antithesis, though it occurs, is not the primary structural device and is more closely tied to some logical value than in Gorgias' writing.[35]

The structural principles of Thrasymachus' style are important because of example and imitation, not because Thrasymachus discussed the subject himself at any length. Thrasymachus did write an *ars*,[36] but this seems to have been, as we would expect, in the tradition of Tisias (Aristotle, *Sophistical refutations* 183b32). The scholiast to Aristophanes (*Birds* 880) speaks of a *Megalê technê* which may mean (*megalê* = "great") that it included more than the usual handbook; the most likely addition would be the *Eleoi*,[37] the emotional appeals. From the passage in the *Phaedrus* quoted early in the chapter it would seem that these appeals were basically a collection of epilogues, but with, possibly for the first time, some brief reference to delivery (Aristotle, *Rhetoric* 1404a14 f. and Quintilian

[33] *Ibid.* 238 f.
[34] *Ibid.* 248 ff. and Blass 1.256.
[35] Cf. Drerup, *op.cit.* supra n. 13, 232.
[36] Cf. Radermacher B.ix.1-3 and Eduard Schwartz, "Commentatio de Thrasymacho Chalcedonio," *Index scholarum in academia Rostochiensi*, 1892. He would like (13 ff.) to attribute to Thrasymachus the "attack on the opponent" as the essential part of the proof.
[37] Cf. Friedrich Solmsen, "Aristotle and Cicero on the orator's playing upon the feelings," cp 33 (1938) 390 ff.; Kroll 1046; Edward B. Stevens, "Some Attic commonplaces of pity," ajp 65 (1944) 1 ff.

3.3.4). Rhythm, like delivery, could have been one of the means of emotional appeal catalogued therein, but if any extensive discussion of rhythm or periodicity had existed we would expect to find more technical discussion than we do in fourth-century sources. As it is, Anaximenes, the treasure house of the sophistic *techne*, never even mentions the subject and the discussion in Aristotle is very brief and characteristically Aristotelian.

Other rhetoricians

Other rhetoricians of the late fifth and early fourth centuries were mostly lesser figures. Theodorus of Byzantium[38] has already been mentioned. He wrote a handbook in which he extended the divisions of a speech to include a pre-narration, a supplementary narration, and probably other subdivisions as well (Aristotle, *Rhetoric* 1414b13 ff.).[39] Antiphon, Lysias, Antisthenes, and Alcidamas are more properly discussed among the orators. The latter two were pupils of Gorgias as were Polus and Licymnius, whose interest in style has been mentioned.

Isocrates

Among the rhetorical theories included by Aristotle in the *Synagôgê technôn*[40] is said to have been that of Isocrates. This is a little surprising, for it suggests that Isocrates had written a handbook, and it would certainly indicate

[38] Cf. Radermacher B.xii.

[39] Aristotle, *Rhetoric* 1400b15, describes τὸ ἐκ τῶν ἁμαρθέντων κατηγορεῖν ἢ ἀπολογεῖσθαι as ὅλη ἡ πρότερον Θεοδώρου τέχνη. The phrase has puzzled many. Can it mean that argument from error was, at first, the only distinctive feature of Theodorus' teaching, though subsequently he developed others? To translate "before Theodorus," the normal meaning, seems impossible. An attempt was once made to attribute to Theodorus the first speech in the corpus of Isocrates, cf. K. Emminger, "Ps.-Isokrates πρὸς Δημόνικον," JKP *Supplementband* 27 (1902) 373 ff.

[40] Cf. *Life of Isocrates* p. 5a, 37, Baiter and Sauppe, and Radermacher B.xxiv.11.

an interest on his part in teaching judicial oratory. Isocrates attacks writers of such handbooks (*Against the sophists* 19 f.), but he also attacks judicial oratory in general, and yet we know that he wrote judicial speeches for pay early in his career. As will be seen in the next chapter, Isocrates made a rather complete about-face sometime in the 390's. He may well have taught the techniques of judicial oratory at one time however he felt about the matter later on, or he may have felt it necessary for his pupils to learn privately something about the conventions of court oratory even though he objected to handbooks and an approach to rhetoric which implied that it was simply a matter of learning a few rules.

There are preserved a number of fragments which purport to be from the *Technê* of Isocrates,[41] but they are not in his characteristic style.[42] The best explanation seems to be that insofar as they may be genuine they come from the summary in the *Synagôgê technôn*.[43] Information could have been available to Aristotle orally from students of Isocrates or from a private document compiled by a pupil which may have circulated within Isocrates' school. One of the ancient lives of Isocrates says[44] that the master wrote such a work but that it was destroyed, perhaps by himself. The puzzling story that Demosthenes learned Isocrates' *technê* secretly (Plutarch, *Demosthenes* 5.5) can per-

[41] They may be found in the back of the Teubner text and in Radermacher B.xxiv.

[42] Cf. Blass 2.98.

[43] There have been a variety of opinions about the work, cf. Leonard Spengel, Συναγωγὴ τεχνῶν sive *Artium scriptores*, Stuttgart, 1828, 154 ff. (genuine handbook); Blass 2.105 ff. (work of a pupil of Isocrates); Georg Thiele, "Das Lehrbuch des Isocrates," *Hermes* 27 (1892) 11 ff. (spurious); Michael Sheehan, *De fide artis rhetoricae Isocrati tributae*, Bonn, 1901 (the material in the fragments is Isocratean, though a spurious *ars* was in existence); Navarre 188 f. (the work of a pupil of Isocrates). Cf. also Münscher in R-E 9. col.2224 s.v. "Isokrates"; Kroll 1049 ff.; J. W. H. Atkins, *Literary criticism in antiquity* 1, Cambridge, Eng., 1934, 129 f.

[44] Cf. supra n. 40.

71

haps be explained if knowledge of this handbook was not supposed to exist outside of the school. In Cicero's time the treatise was not extant, though references to it, presumably in Aristotle, were known (*De inventione* 2.7). Quintilian speaks of a handbook by Isocrates, though with some doubt of its authenticity (2.15.4 and 3.1.14).

The fragments of Isocrates' teaching, even when preserved in late authors, are in most cases quite acceptable fourth-century theory, and in a few instances they can be put in some relation to Aristotle's *Rhetoric*, indicating that Aristotle has either specifically accepted or rejected some rule. The principal points are:

1. Isocrates, in company with other sophistic writers of the time, defined rhetoric as "the artificer of persuasion"[45] (Quintilian 2.15.4, but cf. Sextus Empiricus, *Against the professors* 2.62).

2. Isocrates did not distinguish clearly the three kinds of oratory on which Aristotle insists, but spoke of judicial and deliberative speeches and of speeches of praise and blame.[46] Quintilian (3.4.11) says that Isocrates thought praise and blame were present in all kinds of oratory.[47]

3. Isocrates recognized the usual divisions of the judicial speech: prooemium (including perhaps a *prothesis* or statement),[48] narration (which he perhaps called *katastasis*),[49] proof, and epilogue. Apparently he required the narration to be lucid, brief, and probable (Quintilian 4.2.31), a requirement to which Aristotle partly objects (*Rhetoric* 1416b30).[50]

4. Isocrates included a discussion of style. This is quite possible, since style was of increasing interest among the handbook writers after Gorgias. None of the fragments refer

---

[45] Cf. Radermacher B.xxiv.18-19.
[46] *Ibid.* B.xxiv.20-21.   [47] *Ibid.* B.xxiv.37.
[48] *Ibid.* B.xxiv.29.   [49] *Ibid.* B.xxiv.33.
[50] Cf. Radermacher's note on B.xxiv.34.

to the Gorgianic figures, but that may be simply chance. The most interesting fragment on style is that preserved by Syrianus, a rhetorician of the fifth century A.D., and by several other late writers:[51]

"From the *handbook* of Isocrates we learn the nature of what are called purities (καθαραί) of style, for the man cared so much for purity that even in his private (οἰκείᾳ) handbook he gave advice about style. In good style it is necessary for vowels not to fall in adjacent positions, for this would create a halting effect, nor is it right to end one word and begin the next with the same syllable, as for example εἰποῦσα σαφῆ or ἡλίκα καλά or ἔνθα Θαλῆς, nor should you place the same conjunctions close together, but the second part of a correlative conjunction should follow soon after the first. The words may be metaphors or elaborate words or, in rare instances, coined or familiar. Let the flow of words not be entirely prosaic, which would be dry, but mixed with every rhythm, especially [iambic or trochaic?]. Narrate events in order, the first, the second, and the rest following and do not, before completing the first, go to another subject and subsequently resume the first."

The reference to a "private" handbook is interesting and consistent with what we have said about such a body of theory or rules. Radermacher pointed out[52] that Aristotle (*Rhetoric* 1407a30) follows the same order in mentioning conjunctions, then kinds of words, although this is otherwise unusual. The reference to iambic and trochaic is omitted by Syrianus and most versions of the passage except the anonymous scholia of Walz 7 (934) and John of Sicily (Walz 6.166). If it is genuine, it is another point which Aristotle contradicted.

[51] Radermacher B.xxiv.22. The others include Maximus Planudes in Walz 5.469 and John of Sicily in Walz 6.156.
[52] B.xxiv.24.

What we know about Isocrates' handbook is important in two ways: it shows that the contents of rhetorical theory were gradually expanding with the addition of material on style and on kinds of speeches, and it shows something about the state of sophistic rhetoric at the time when Aristotle turned his attention to the subject. Aristotle's contribution to the theory of style is clearer when compared to what Isocrates said.

Plato's *Phaedrus*

The *Phaedrus* may be divided into two parts which correspond strikingly to the two methods of rhetorical instruction current in classical Greece. From the beginning to 257b6 is principally a small collection of specimen speeches. From 257b7 to the end is a theoretical discussion analogous to a rhetorical handbook, which touches, often critically, upon the usual topics, including the definition of rhetoric, its parts, and forms of argument. The dialogue might also be regarded as something of a counterpart to Isocrates' *Helen*, which consists of an introductory theoretical discussion followed by a specimen speech.[53]

There is little agreement about the subject of the *Phaedrus*.[54] Rhetoric is the subject with which it begins

[53] The *Phaedrus* shows the influence of the *Helen* in other respects too, *cf.* R. L. Howland, "The attack on Isocrates in the *Phaedrus*," CQ 31 (1937) 151 ff.

[54] The basic modern discussion of the *Phaedrus* is Léon Robin, *Platon* 4.3 (Budé), Paris, 1933. Cf. also Karl Mras, "Platos *Phaedrus* und die Rhetorik," WS 36 (1914) 295 ff. and 37 (1915) 88 ff.; Werner Jaeger (trans. G. Highet), *Paideia: the ideals of Greek culture* 3, New York, 1944, 182 ff.; Paul Friedländer, *Platon* 2: *die platonischen Schriften*, Berlin and Leipzig, 1930, 485 ff.; W. C. Helmbold and W. B. Holther, "The unity of the *Phaedrus*," *Univ. of California Publications in Classical Philology* 14.9 (1952) 387 ff.; R. Hackforth, *Plato's Phaedrus translated with introduction and commentary*, Cambridge, Eng., 1952; H. Cherniss, "Plato 1950-1957," *Lustrum* 4 (1959) and 5 (1960). Modern scholars are generally in agreement that the *Phaedrus* is one of the later works of Plato, probably written in the 370's.

and ends and to which it repeatedly alludes, but there is some discussion, mostly in the three orations included in the dialogue, of several basic doctrines of Plato, including love, inspiration, and the nature of the soul, and much of the later part of the work deals with dialectic. Actually it is rather silly to insist that the dialogue is about one of these subjects and not about others; most critics agree that the whole is an admirable artistic unity. Plato's view of rhetoric is that it cannot be divorced from its substance: a speech must be about something and it is that something which is important. The thesis to be demonstrated must be philosophically valid and its nature should mold the form of the speech. Plato chooses love as the substance of the particular speeches of the *Phaedrus* for a variety of reasons. For one thing it was a common rhetorical theme (cf. Demosthenes 61, Diogenes Laertius 5.24). Further, love beautifully exemplifies what he has in mind about rhetoric: rather than being a purely objective rational or artistic matter it involves the soul of the disputants. The orator who pleads the cause of the non-lover is harming both himself and the person he addresses more directly and obviously than if he were giving, for example, expedient but unsound political advice. Moreover, the choice allows a kind of contrast between sincere love on the one hand and rhetoric, which is associated with cynical lust and a cold exercise of technique in violence to human feelings, on the other.[55] Finally, Plato perhaps regards the true rhetoric as best exemplified in the dialectic with which the philosopher persuades and ennobles the soul of his beloved.[56]

The introductory part of the dialogue (up to 230e) sets a beautiful natural scene,[57] demonstrates the intense contemporary interest in rhetoric, and alludes to the nature

[55] Cf. R. G. Hoerber, "Love or rhetoric in Plato's *Phaedrus*," *Classical bulletin* 34 (1958) 33.

[56] Cf. Helmbold and Holther, *op.cit.* supra n. 54.

[57] Cf. C. Murley, "Plato's *Phaedrus* and Theocritan pastoral," TAPA 71 (1940) 281 ff.

75

of rhetorical training and techniques of memory (228d1 ff.), which were to become a formal part of rhetoric. The story of Boreas and Oreithyia (229b4 ff.) is evidently intended to contribute to the tone or theme of the dialogue. Probably it has numerous points of contact with what follows,[58] with the philosophical basis of myth, with the need for concern with man and human problems, rather than with the non-human, and perhaps with the question of the sincerity of the storyteller and the good faith of his audience.

Phaedrus then reads a speech, attributed to Lysias, which attempts to persuade a young man to accept as his lover one who claims not to love him. The speech is by Plato, not Lysias,[59] though it is composed in a style like that of Lysias. Plato always enjoyed demonstrating his literary versatility. Principally the speech is designed to furnish an extreme example of sophistic oratory which considered its achievement proportional to the difficulty of its task. The best seriously intentioned examples of such speeches are the surviving works of Gorgias and some of the speeches of Isocrates such as the *Helen*, but there were doubtless many more by other writers. Plato, of course, had to choose a writer of the fifth century for Socrates to discuss, though the reference to Isocrates at the end of the dialogue (278e10 ff.) shows that Plato meant his remarks to be *applied* to his own contemporaries.[60] We do not know whether Lysias ever wrote this kind of oratory; it is possible. In any event, Lysias was a logical choice, for he was a clever and charm-

[58] Cf. Robin, *op.cit.* supra n. 54, xxviii.

[59] Cf. Paul Shorey, "On the *Erotikos* of Lysias in Plato's *Phaedrus*," CP 28 (1933) 131 f.; George E. Dimock, Jr., "Ἀλλά in Lysias and Plato's *Phaedrus*," AJP 73 (1952) 381 ff. It seems unthinkable that a Platonic dialogue would quote an entire speech by any author, and it is unnecessary: if the speech were available to Plato in the 370's it would be available to others too and could be discussed and referred to without complete republication. Yet Lysianic authorship has had defenders; cf. F. Lasserre, "Ἐρωτικοὶ λόγοι," *Museum helveticum* 1 (1944) 169 ff.

[60] Cf. Howland, *op.cit.* supra n. 53, and infra p. 79.

ing orator, lacking the idiosyncrasies of a Gorgias or a Thrasymachus, and his family was on the fringe of the Socratic circle. Socrates claims to be quite overcome by the diction and delivery of Lysias' speech, but thinks it is very inferior in invention. He denies Phaedrus' claim (235b1 ff.) that the arguments have been exhausted and is finally persuaded to try to compose a better speech himself. Here, as in a number of other works, Plato is at pains to demonstrate Socrates' rhetorical ability.

As a piece of Greek oratory the speech which Socrates then delivers is a very creditable composition. It has, for one thing, full rhetorical form, which Lysias' speech lacked: there is a prooemium (237a7 ff.), narration (237b2 ff.), proof (237b7 ff.), and epilogue (241c6 ff.). More important, it has a much more logical development based on a definition of love (237d1 ff.) and then (238e1 ff.) consideration of relative advantages or disadvantages. The proof is largely indirect: the disadvantages of accepting the lover are demonstrated under such headings as intellectual, physical, and economic. Socrates affects to have been carried away into a poetic seizure and starts to leave before saying more.

Phaedrus significantly remarks (242a3) that they must not leave until the heat of the day passes. Immediately the sign comes to Socrates which forbids him to act whenever he is in danger of doing what is wrong. He feels suddenly that the speech he has delivered, though technically very satisfactory, is in substance immoral and irresponsible, for love is, after all, a god. It does not seem to be sufficient justification that he had alleged (237b4) that the non-lover was in fact a lover, for the philosophical basis of the speech is invalid. Socrates uses of the speech the word *deinos*, often applied to a "clever" orator, but here meaning "dreadful." He then delivers a much longer speech in favor of the lover, demonstrating the nature of the soul and of love at very considerable length by use of the myth of the charioteer.

77

This speech is more acceptable philosophically because it is built on truth and aimed at a valid goal. Even if one disagrees with Plato's notions of truth, the speech has a sincerity and nobility lacking in the earlier attempts to reply to a rhetorical challenge. Most rhetoricians, however, would probably regard Socrates' new speech as too poetic and diffuse, and for all its oratorical form more dialectic than rhetoric.

The rest of the *Phaedrus* consists of a discussion of the nature of the true rhetoric, including the examination of the contemporary handbooks quoted earlier in this chapter. The theory Plato expounds is that an art of rhetoric is conceivable for use in advancing the truth, which must, however, be known by the orator first (260d3 ff.). The perfect orator, a phrase which was to echo through the later rhetorical schools, must have natural ability improved by knowledge and practice (269d2 ff.) and must study philosophy, whence he will derive loftiness of mind and effectiveness (269e4 ff.). An example is Pericles, who learned much from Anaxagoras. The rhetoric which this perfect orator will practice will have a strong logical element (264c1 ff.):

"every discourse must cohere like a living thing having itself a body of its own so as not to be lacking head or foot, but so as to have a middle and extremities suitable to each other and composed with the whole in mind."

The arrangement of a perfect speech will be based on two principles (265d1 ff.): definition, which will impart the qualities (a later writer would say the virtues) of clarity and consistency, and division into classes. Both principles are illustrated by Socrates' two earlier speeches. Finally, since the goal of rhetoric is persuasion in the soul of the hearer, the orator must be a master of psychology: he must be able to describe the soul, its action, and what affects it, and he must classify souls and speeches and understand the impact of each kind of speech on each kind of soul (271a4 ff.).

Plato's account of rhetorical psychology is rather unsatisfactory, for it seems basically a matter of using *ad hominem* arguments and is reminiscent of the so-called "noble lie" of the *Republic* (414b7 ff.), where a hearer of inferior intelligence is brainwashed into acceptance of the truth by an omniscient philosopher-orator. The arguments which the orator uses are not necessarily true in themselves, since many persons may be capable of being persuaded only by attractive lies. Further, no consideration is taken of the fact that most speeches, especially political speeches, have to be addressed to a varied audience of largely unknown individuals; Plato seems to think only of the man-to-man relationship of dialectic. We have already noted that Gorgias stated the concept of the opportune as an essential ingredient of successful rhetoric, and most sophists probably thought they had an understanding of circumstances and audience, which is basically what Plato wants and which, in most actual oratory, is more realistic than what he describes. Aristotle was able subsequently to make psychology, in the form of study of ethos and pathos, into two significant parts of rhetorical persuasion.

In the concluding pages of the dialogue Plato expounds his prejudices against writing (274b6 ff.), a position which is influenced by his primary concern with the direct personal relationship of speaker and listener—a view shared by some contemporary rhetoricians.[61] Then he summarizes what he has said (277b2 ff.) and finally contrasts Lysias with Isocrates (278e10 ff.). Socrates' interest in Isocrates is probably historically genuine, but this reference by Plato is ironic in view of Isocrates' failure to achieve anything that Plato could regard as a philosophical rhetoric.[62]

---

[61] Cf. supra. p. 5.

[62] For a different view cf. Robert Flacelière, "L'éloge d' Isocrate à la fin du *Phédre*," REG 46 (1933) 224 ff.

Theodectes

Aristotle was familiar with the systems of rhetoric expounded by a large number of authors from Corax and Tisias to Isocrates and Plato, and in constructing his own *Rhetoric* he made much use of all of them. There is, however, some reason to believe that he knew best that of his friend Theodectes, the dramatist.[63] In addition to the *Synagôgê technôn*, which covered most of the rhetoricians, he made or had made a special *Compendium of the art of Theodectes*,[64] a work to which presumably he refers (*Rhetoric* 1410b2) as the *Theodectea*.[65] In this passage the *Theodectea* is said to contain additional information on the beginnings of periods, which seems a clear indication that it was a step in Aristotle's earlier study of style. He clearly regards the discussion as a detailed one, and it probably was more extensive than anything in earlier writings on rhetoric. According to Cicero (*Orator* 173) Theodectes discussed the need for rhythm in prose and (194) recommended the paean, as Aristotle himself was to do (cf. also Quintilian 9.4.88). Quintilian (4.2.63) attributes to Theodectes a discussion of five virtues of the narration, which seems to be a development of the three attributed to Isocrates. Theodectes added not only *megaloprepeia*, as had others, but also *to hêdu*, sweetness. In addition Theodectes

[63] Cf. Barwick 23 ff. and Friedrich Solmsen, "Drei Rekonstruktionen zur antiken Rhetorik und Poetik," *Hermes* 67 (1932) 133 ff. Cf. also E. M. Cope, *An introduction to Aristotle's Rhetoric*, London, 1867, 55 ff.; Atkins, *op.cit.* supra n. 43, 133 f.; Kroll 1062.

[64] Diogenes Laertius 5.25 and Radermacher B.xxxvii.1.

[65] Aristotle does not refer to works by others in this way; cf. Cope, *op.cit.* supra n. 63, 22. Valerius Maximus (8.14 ext.3) has a story about how Aristotle allowed Theodectes to claim authorship of one of Aristotle's own works, then became jealous of the fame and inserted a remark in his own writings referring to the treatise in such a way as to show that he had written it himself. Presumably Valerius means either *Rhetoric* 1410b2 or *Rhetorica ad Alexandrum* 1421b2. This story is probably a mistaken attempt to explain the title.

took up the various parts of the speech and gave each an objective: good will for the prooemium, trust for the narration, conviction for the proof, and either recapitulation or emotional involvement for the epilogue (Anonymous, *Prolegomena* 32 and 216 Rabe).[66] Neither the five virtues nor the special objects of the various parts of a speech are specifically stated in Aristotle, though the latter might be said to be implied in the discussion. This seems to indicate that the *Theodectea* and its contents did not constitute a major part of book three of the *Rhetoric* as we now have it except for the discussion of periodicity and rhythm, where Aristotle specifically mentions it. The end of the spurious introductory epistle of the *Rhetorica ad Alexandrum* claims that the *Theodectea* was a source for that work, but comparison with the fragments fails to prove the connexion.

The existence of two complete handbooks from the second half of the fourth century makes it possible, suddenly, to see in detail for the first time the contents of rhetorical theory. One of these handbooks, the *Rhetorica ad Alexandrum*, is probably a fairly typical product of early rhetorical theory. The other is the most admired monument of ancient rhetoric, the *Rhetoric* of Aristotle, which in three books deals with invention, style, and arrangement as well as suggesting the need for a study of delivery. It draws heavily on sophistic rhetoric, but equally heavily on Aristotle's system of logic,[67] and to some extent materials are taken from his study of politics and ethics. In studying the *Rhetoric* two considerations need to be in at least the back of a reader's mind: the first is the fact that Aristotle's thought on rhetoric developed gradually as did other parts of his philosophy; the *Rhetoric* was not written all in one inspired seizure. The second is that many portions

[66] Cf. also *Anonymous Seguerianus* 208 in Spengel-Hammer 389.
[67] The *Rhetoric* was sometimes regarded as part of the *Organon*, cf. Paul Moraux, *Les listes anciennes des ouvrages d'Aristote*, Louvain, 1951, 148, 172, and 177 ff.

of the work were suggested by remarks of Plato. Sometimes Aristotle develops Plato's suggestions, sometimes he answers his objections. The influence of Plato can be dealt with as individual points arise, but it is necessary to consider the development of the *Rhetoric* somewhat systematically.

The Development of Aristotle's *Rhetoric*

Aristotle's *Rhetoric* has several apparent inconsistencies. For example, the beginning of the first book attacks the handbooks, which concern themselves with arousing emotions and cataloging the parts of an oration, but in book two Aristotle himself discusses emotional appeal and in book three he, too, catalogues the parts of an oration. Another problem is the discussion of the "common topics" in book two. Even if one accepts the discussion as generally consistent with the rest of the work, why are these means of logical proof divided from the remainder of that subject by the sections on ethos and pathos? Why do some parts of the work depend on and others ignore the enthymeme?

In 1911 Kantelhardt concluded that the *Rhetoric* contains material written at two different times.[68] He thought that the beginning of book one, book two from chapter eighteen on, and the last half of book three were probably early. Signs of this are the rejection of the use of the emotions to persuade, the treatment of the topics, and omission of the example as the alternative to the enthymeme in logical proof. A decade later Werner Jaeger showed clearly the pattern of development of Aristotle's thought throughout his career,[69] and it thus became possible to explain the inconsistencies of the *Rhetoric* much more definitely. This Friedrich Solmsen did in *Die Ent-*

[68] A. Kantelhardt, *De Aristotelis rhetoricis*, Göttingen, 1911.
[69] Werner Jaeger (trans. by R. Robinson), *Aristotle: the fundamentals of the history of his development*, Oxford, 1934.

wicklung der aristotelischen Logik und Rhetorik in 1929.[70] Some of the details have been questioned,[71] but the thesis itself seems certain.

The development of Aristotle's ideas about rhetoric may be summarized thus: Aristotle's earliest known work on rhetoric was the dialogue *Gryllus*, named for Xenophon's son, whose death in 362 called forth a host of encomia (Diogenes Laertius 2.55). What little we know about the dialogue comes from Quintilian, who refers to it in the discussion (2.17.14) of those who have argued that rhetoric is not an art. He seems to imply that the dialogue advanced arguments against the art of rhetoric which he thought Aristotle could not believe because of the different views expressed in the *Rhetoric*. Probably the criticisms were not unlike those voiced by Plato: the technique was not worthy to be called an art and had no proper subject of its own. Maybe the attempt to arouse emotions, at least ignoble emotions, was questioned; maybe the immorality of rhetoric was deduced from the facility of the rhetorician in proving opposites. Since the work was a dialogue there was room for a variety of opinion, and perhaps final judgment was suspended. But the *Gryllus* definitely voiced criticisms and was thought of by Quintilian as inconsistent with the attitude of the *Rhetoric*.

The essential harmony of the views of Plato and the young Aristotle on the subject of rhetoric is indicated by the attack of Cephisodorus on both philosophers (Eusebius, *Praeparatio evangelica* 14.6.9). Cephisodorus was a pupil of Isocrates who saw in works like the *Gryllus* an attack on the work of his master and himself. Although the relationship between Isocrates and the philosophers will be discussed in the next chapter, we may remark here that the success of Isocrates' school was probably a challenge first

[70] In *Neue philologische Untersuchungen* 4, Berlin, 1929.
[71] Cf. Paul Gohlke, "Die Entstehung der aristotelischen Ethik, Politik, Rhetorik," SBW 223.2 (1944).

to Plato and later to Aristotle to take a position on the nature of rhetoric and the importance of rhetorical education.

Aristotle's next work on rhetoric was a draft of a treatise of which portions still exist imbedded in the *Rhetoric*, especially at the beginning of book one and in the discussion of *topoi* in book two. According to Solmsen[72] it drew upon Aristotle's ideas on logic as seen in the *Topica* and clearly acknowledged that rhetoric could be treated as an art. The theory of the enthymeme and example as the two means of logical proof was still undeveloped, and, although Aristotle was departing from Plato in the direction of the sophists, he still had not admitted ethos and pathos into a place in legitimate persuasion nor accepted the value of technical divisions of the rhetorical handbooks.

The *Rhetoric* as we have it seems to have been the result of three further steps, though their order is uncertain.[73]

---

[72] Cf. Solmsen 213 f.

[73] It is probably impossible to be exact about the dates of composition of different parts of Aristotle's rhetorical work. Aristotle arrived in Athens in 367, shortly after Plato had written the *Theatetus* and the *Phaedrus*. Until Plato's death he seems to have written only "Platonic" dialogues, among them the *Gryllus*, which was *perhaps* more antagonistic to rhetoric than the *Phaedrus*. Probably he started to teach rhetoric during the latter part of his first stay in Athens (cf. Solmsen 208). The better part of the groundwork on the *Rhetoric* was presumably done in Macedon (342-335 B.C.), which may be one reason why Isocrates is quoted frequently and Demosthenes virtually ignored; but cf. J. D. Meerwaldt, "De Aristotelis erga Demosthenem anima," MN 54 (1926) 348 ff., who thought that Aristotle and Demosthenes were drawn together by the former's disappointment in Macedon. Aristotle is said to have opposed Philip's proposed expedition against Persia (cf. Philodemus, *Rhetoric* 6.col.56,ii.p.61 Sudhaus). The material on style in the *Rhetoric* was preceded by the *Theodectea*, and it seems possible that this was published shortly after the death of Theodectes in the mid 330's, since other named works of Aristotle like the *Gryllus* and *Eudemus* are more or less memorial. ("Nicomachean" of the *Ethics* was not a term used by Aristotle himself.) The final stage of the *Rhetoric* was achieved during Aristotle's second residency at Athens, perhaps around 330. The latest historical event referred to

Aristotle applied to rhetoric his theory of logic which had been developing coincidently and which is found in the *Prior analytics*. This is the source of the theory of enthymeme and example as the two forms of logical proof. Secondly, he recognized that the logical conclusion of Plato's examination of rhetoric in the *Phaedrus*, in which the possibility of a good rhetoric was admitted, was to add ethos and pathos to logical argument as means of rhetorical persuasion. Thirdly, he added to the system a discussion of style and arrangement which constitutes a third book, the portion of the work closest to traditional rhetorical theory as we have reconstructed it. These changes imply a considerable change in attitude toward rhetoric resulting from an increased interest in the nature of existing practice and much less desire to impose an ideal system upon contemporary life as Plato had tried to do in the *Phaedrus*. Such a development is paralleled in other of Aristotle's interests, for example, in politics.

Aristotle's observation of actual oratory no doubt convinced him of the need to deal with all kinds of oratory. The early handbooks, as we have seen, were concerned only with the oratory of the law courts, though the techniques taught by the sophists were useful in all kinds of speaking. Aristotle distinguishes three and only three kinds of oratory: judicial, deliberative, epideictic. He first states these categories in the third chapter of the first book, and he makes use of them in his discussions of invention, style, and arrangement. They become a standard part of traditional rhetoric; although later authors like Cicero and Quintilian may question the system, they do not succeed in uprooting it. Presumably earlier writers apprehended a dis-

---

is apparently the "common peace" of 336 B.C. (1399b12). It is possible that "editing" of Aristotle's rhetorical thought was continued by his pupils after his death. On the date and composition cf. M. Dufour, ed., *Aristote: Rhétorique*, Paris, 1932, 14 ff.; Moraux, *op.cit.* supra n. 67,317; Felix Grayeff, "The problem of the genesis of Aristotle's text," *Phronesis* 1 (1956) 105 ff.

tinction between speeches delivered in the law courts and in the assembly. Alcidamas speaks (*On the sophists* 9) of the oratory of the public assembly, of the courts, and in private intercourse, a classification similar to one found in Plato's *Phaedrus* (261a7 ff.) and *Sophist* (222c9 ff.). In the *Rhetorica ad Alexandrum* (1421b8 ff.) a sevenfold division into species is the important classification. These species are substantially the same as the six species into which Aristotle subdivides his three kinds, with the addition of investigational oratory. Up until Aristotle's time the species were the more generally recognized distinctions: Plato mentions accusation and apology (*Phaedrus* 267a2) and Isocrates apology, encomium, accusation, and admonition (*Helen* 14 f. and *Panegyricus* 130). The distinction between public and private suits, which is of considerable legal significance and in practice influences style and structure, has no importance at all in rhetorical theory. Unfortunately we have no evidence about what if any discussion existed in sources other than rhetorical handbooks and which may have influenced Aristotle and Anaximenes too.[74] From their accounts and from actual deliberative speeches it appears that the customary topics of deliberative oratory were discussion of the expediency, justice, honor, possibility, or the like, of courses of action involving ways and means, war and peace, national defense, trade, legislation, and such subjects. Deliberative oratory was clearly much influenced by the rules for invention, arrangement, and style that had been developed for judicial oratory. Epideictic was probably not thought of as a unity until Isocrates seized upon it, though a traditional set of topics can be seen in funeral orations. As far as we know the definition and systematic discussion of the three kinds of oratory may be attributed entirely to Aristotle (Quintilian 3.4.1).

[74] Cf. Hinks, "Tria genera," *cit.* supra n. 5 and Wilcox, *op.cit.* supra n. 1. Friedrich Solmsen, "The Aristotelian tradition in ancient rhetoric," AJP 62 (1941) 42 f., sees Platonic influence in Aristotle's method.

Aristotle's three kinds of oratory correspond to the three kinds of hearers; he will not admit the possibility of other kinds existing, for a hearer must be either judge or spectator. If he is judge he will judge what has been done (judicial oratory) or what is going to be done (deliberative oratory). The spectator is most interested in the existing condition (epideictic oratory).[75] Each kind may be divided into two species, depending on whether the intent is positive or negative. Thus, deliberative oratory is either hortatory or dissuasive, judicial is accusatory or defensive, epideictic is concerned with praise or blame. Each kind has, further, its distinctive concern: judicial with the just, deliberative with the expedient, and epideictic with the honorable.

Although in making this classification Aristotle wants to cover the *fields* of existing oratory, he is not classifying existing *speeches*. Even works of his own time do not always show clearly the characteristics of only one of his kinds of speeches. His criteria have been criticized:[76] they shift from hearer to time to end in view. Nor does Aristotle distinguish form from content, a point which enters into classification of speeches like those of Isocrates. There is no particular reason why he should; his classification is convenient for what he has to say about the different kinds of topics of speeches, it is of some value in discussing arrangement, and also style, but the classification should not be regarded as a keen perception of the types of speeches in fourth-century Greece.

Aristotle on Invention

The first two books of the *Rhetoric* are concerned with invention. Aristotle is not very generous to his predecessors in rhetoric and least of all in this branch. He claims

[75] Cf. Franz Joseph Schwaab, *Ueber das Bedeutung des γένος ἐπιδεικτικὸν in der aristotelischen Rhetorik,* Würzburg, 1923.

[76] Cf. Richard Volkmann, *Die Rhetorik der Griechen und Römer in systematischer Uebersicht,* Leipzig, 1885, 19 ff. and Hinks, "Tria genera," *cit.* supra n. 5.

(1354a12) that they have almost completely neglected what was the most important part of their subject and have devoted their attention to either the arousing of emotions or the technical divisions of the speech. His criticisms are of course aimed at the formal judicial handbooks, which were unphilosophical; but the handbooks did discuss, at the very least, argument from probability, and rhetoricians in practice were presumably somewhat more mindful of logic than Aristotle represents them. Similarly, he criticizes rhetorical theory for being concerned only with forensic oratory because that was the subject of the handbooks. Actually, as we have seen, deliberative oratory was not neglected in the schools of the sophists, though there was not so much in the way of rules that could be said about it, as Aristotle's own writings illustrate.

After an initial discussion of the nature of rhetoric, Aristotle defines it as the faculty of discovering the means of persuasion on each subject. He then proceeds (1355b35 ff.) to distinguish two kinds of proofs, artificial and inartificial, or artistic and non-artistic. By the latter category he means direct evidence not the product of the speaker's art: laws, witnesses, testimony exacted from slaves under torture, contracts, and oaths. In the fourth century such evidence was ordinarily secured beforehand, written down, put in sealed urns, and read out in court.[77] Aristotle discusses the different types of direct evidence in the last chapter of book one of the *Rhetoric*. In the fourth century these types were regularly regarded as a group by themselves and are similarly treated in the *Rhetorica ad Alexandrum* (1431b7 ff.), where they are called supplementary (*epithetai*) proofs. The orators often distinguish them from argument.[78] We saw in chapter two that such direct evidence furnished the

[77] On the judicial procedure cf. Bonner and Smith 1.346 ff.
[78] Cf. Antiphon, *On the choreutês* 18; Isocrates, *Against Callimachus* 16 and *Against Euthynus* 4; Demosthenes, *Against Andro-tion* 22 and *Against Callipus* 32.

proof in earlier Greek oratory, a natural state of affairs which continued among orators not trained in the sophistic tradition. It is, for example, noticeable in Andocides, who prefers direct evidence and hesitates to trust the new form of argument.[79]

In the fifth century, however, litigants began to attack direct evidence with argument from probability, and their opponents were forced to bolster testimony by further argumentation. The increasing interest in rational argument is clearly associated with the rational speculation of the Greeks as seen in sophistry and also with the kind of moral decay which overtook the democracy during the course of the Peloponnesian war. The speculation on laws is of the first type: it was recognized that conflict could exist not only between two laws, but also between the words and intention of a single law.[80] Of the second type is the growing realization that witnesses could be bought and documents forged.[81] This was apparently a real problem. According to Isocrates (*Against Callimachus* 53 f.) fifteen people once swore in court to the death of a slave who was subsequently produced from hiding alive and well. Probabilities, however, as Aristotle says (1376a19 ff.), do not deceive for bribes. In the *Laws* (948d6) Plato forbids oaths to be taken by parties to a suit in his state "for it is somehow dreadful,

[79] Cf. George A. Kennedy "The oratory of Andocides," AJP 79 (1958) 32 ff. Another conservative was Aristophanes, who makes little use of argument from probability, though he lets Socrates employ the technique in *Clouds* 393; cf. Charles T. Murphy, "Aristophanes and the art of rhetoric," HSCP 49 (1938) 93 and n. 3.

[80] The classic example of the clash between two laws is, of course, the *Antigone* of Sophocles. For the clash between the letter and spirit of a law, cf. Aristophanes, *Clouds* 1186 ff.; Demosthenes, *Against Androtion* 30; *Rhetorica ad Alexandrum* 1443a31 ff.

[81] Bribery of jurors was difficult in the fourth century because of the elaborate system under which they were chosen. There had been, however, examples earlier. Anytus is said by Plutarch (*Coriolanus* 14.4) to have been the first man to bribe an Athenian jury. He was prosecuted for failing to relieve Pylos in 410.

when there are so many lawsuits in a city, to know well that almost half of the people are perjurers who meet each other readily at meals and other assemblies and private meetings."

The use of argument from probability to attack direct evidence appears already in Antiphon. In reply, commonplaces were built up in support of direct evidence, especially on the reliability of evidence secured under torture.[82] By the time of Isaeus there is little hesitation to dispute the validity of a well attested will. (Isaeus' methods will be discussed in the next chapter.) If he has direct evidence to support him an orator of course makes use of it. If he has not, he must reply on probabilities.[83] Usually the situation is somewhere in between: there is some evidence, but it will not take the orator all the way. Aristotle stresses (1396a4 ff.) the need for an orator to have a firm knowledge of the facts of his case.

Opposed to the inartificial proofs are the artificial, those that can be constructed by the art of the orator. In practice they are basically argument from probability, but this is only a subdivision in Aristotle's system, which divides artificial proof into three types: that found in the character of the speaker, that found in the state of mind produced in the hearer, and that found in the speech itself insofar as it proves or seems to prove (1356a1 ff.).[84]

[82] E.g. Antiphon, On the choreutês 25; Isaeus, Ciron 12; Demosthenes, Against Onetor 1.37 Cf. A. P. Dorjahn, "On slave evidence in Greek law," cj 47 (1952) 188.

[83] Cf. Aeschines, Against Timarchus 91 and Against Ctesiphon 45-46; and Isocrates, Against Euthynus 4. The speech was the thing in a trial, and direct evidence was only a kind of supplement; cf. J. W. Jones, The law and legal theory of the Greeks, Oxford, 1956, 141: "the evidence of witnesses read out during intervals . . . was regarded rather as a means of adding force to the party's speech than as the primary means of proof." Cf. also Bonner and Smith 2, 12 and 117 ff.

[84] Cf. William Grimaldi, "A note on the πίστεις in Aristotle's Rhetoric," AJP 78 (1957) 188 ff.

Proof found in the character of the speaker is called ethos, a term which is, however, applied by rhetoricians, including Aristotle, to several different "characters." The most important to Aristotle is the moral character which the speaker exhibits and which causes the audience to trust him. Some unknown writers had denied (1356a10 ff.) that the worth of a speaker contributed to his persuasiveness. In practice as early as Antiphon a Greek orator concentrates in the prooemium on presenting the character of the speaker in a favorable light.[85] Usually, like Socrates in the *Apology*, the speaker claims to be unskilled in speaking, simple, honest, deserving, but caught up in circumstances; his opponent is sly, cunning, and worthless. The real challenge to the ability of the orator was to sustain the moral impression through the speech. Andocides in *On his return*, for example, fails to do so and resorts to the older concept of nobility which is similar to the authority of the Homeric orators and which is not necessarily moral.

Insofar as it appears in the prooemium, ethos is not a direct element of persuasion, as Aristotle would have it, but a means of conciliating the minds of the judges in order that they can subsequently be persuaded. In fact, however, ethos is used by the orators as an actual topic of persuasion so that Aristotle's category is by no means only theoretical. This ethos is especially marked in Lysias, who is fond of developing the characters of the litigants to show that the jury should favor his client.[86] Indeed, the regular structure of the Lysianic proof is 1.) direct evidence, 2.) proof or refutation by probability, 3.) proof by character.

Under Greek law it was customary for a man to plead his own case, though he might deliver a memorized oration

[85] The persuasive force of character can be seen in Thucydides and Euripides and was apparently recognized by Pericles; cf. Thucydides 2.65.8 and John H. Finley, Jr., "Euripides and Thucydides," HSCP 49 (1938) 42 and 46 f.

[86] Cf. e.g. 1.37 ff.; 7.30 ff.; 13.61 ff.; 19.55 ff.; 22.13 ff.; 24.15 ff.

which another had written and might introduce advocates who would speak for and after himself. In the former case ethos came to have a peculiar importance, for to achieve a successful effect the speech writer had to weave into the speech the actual character of the speaker, or at least he had to keep from saying things in a way that would be completely foreign to him. An old man and a young man must show quite different attitudes; a rich man would not think of things in the same way as a poor man. Such dramatic character is treated by Aristotle under style (1408a25 ff. and 1417a15 ff.) and is called ethopoiia by critics (e.g. Dionysius of Halicarnassus, *Lysias* 8). It is especially important in the narration. The technique itself is in all probability modeled on the portrayal of characters by the poets. Ion in Plato's dialogue (540b2 ff.) says that a rhapsode knows what a man or a woman or a freeman or a slave ought to say, and Nestor in the *Iliad* and the watchman in the *Agamemnon* are excellent examples of the technique. The greatest master of oratorical ethopoiia is, again, Lysias, who assumes with equal fidelity the mask of a man about town or a shrewd farmer.[87] This kind of ethos is not found after the fourth century, which is the only period in which the paid logographers flourished.[88]

A third type of rhetorical ethos of interest to Aristotle is the character of the audience to which the speaker must suit his language and argument (1365b22 ff. and 1388b31 ff.). This is the psychological approach to rhetoric inherent in Gorgias' theory of *kairos*, or the opportune, and developed slightly by Plato in the *Phaedrus* (271a4 ff., cf.

[87] Lysias seems to have published some examples of his technique, cf. Radermacher B.xxxiii.13-15; Navarre 166; Blass 1.381 ff. Cf. also W. Motschmann, *Die Charactere bei Lysias*, Munich, 1906, and O. Buechler, *Die Untersuchung der redenden Personen bei Lysias*, Heidelberg, 1936.

[88] They were replaced by the πραγματικοί, who gave advice on legal technicalities to clients, but did not write speeches, cf. Cicero, *De oratore* 1.198.

also *Gorgias* 513b8 f.). Though most elaborated by Aristotle, it is a persistent element in later rhetorical theory where it, too, is treated under the prooemium.[89]

Aristotle's second kind of proof, that resulting from putting the audience into a certain state of mind, is known as pathos and is, like ethos, another element common to drama and oratory. Probably no Greek orator needed to be taught how to make an emotional appeal, for even Homeric speakers do so with great finesse. One of the most striking examples is Priam's appeal to Achilles in *Iliad* twenty-four (486-506), which might be and no doubt was envied by a Roman declaimer. Priam first equates himself with Achilles' father to secure filial affection in addition to the natural pity for an aged and unhappy man. His present wretched state he portrays vividly and completely, realizing that the completeness of the detail is one of the most effective qualities in such an appeal. Finally, he introduces the gods and addresses himself to Achilles' awe of them and comes full circle to conclude with a final allusion to Achilles' father. These emotions, filial love, pity, reverence of the gods, respect for the aged, are feelings to which orators appealed throughout antiquity.

Emotional appeal in oratory is most clearly developed in the peroration. After the judges' sympathy has been secured by exhibition of the good character of the speaker, the facts are narrated for their instruction and the proof advanced for their conviction. It remains to stir them so

[89] William Süss published (Leipzig, 1910) a book entitled *Ethos: Studien zur älteren griechischen Rhetorik* in which he distinguished three kinds of ethos which do not quite correspond to those distinguished here: 1. objective and psychological—the development of the character of the litigants, 2. subjective—the development of the moral character of the speaker, and 3. what he called subjective-dynamic ethos—the character of the speech itself and its capacity to influence the audience. Subjective and objective aspects of ethos are discussed by W. M. Sattler, "Conceptions of *ethos* in ancient rhetoric," SM 14 (1957) 55 ff.

that they will want to believe and will feel the immediacy of the charge either for themselves or all society and thus the need for action. The prosecution makes most use of indignation or anger, which the speaker tries to arouse against the crime and person of the defendant. The latter needs most of all to arouse the feeling of pity. Such appeals can be found in the perorations of Greek speeches even in the *Tetralogies* of Antiphon, but they are especially characteristic of Aeschines and Demosthenes. A clever orator is not content to leave pathos entirely to the end of a speech; much of his art consists in the subtle way in which he insinuates his cause into the soul of his hearers, evoking their unconscious sympathy, horror, astonishment, and indignation as the case unfolds. A good example is Isocrates' early forensic speech against Callimachus.[90] Pathos and ethos are always closely related, and later rhetoricians (e.g. Quintilian 6.2.8 ff.) were not altogether without logic in treating them as degrees of the same thing. Both are elements which oratory shares with drama. It might be added that except in a few speeches neither pathos nor ethos is ordinarily present in historical writing and, indeed, their presence is one of the principal differences between an oratorical and historical presentation of what might be called historical material. This can be seen well in the narrative-historical sections early in Demosthenes' *On the crown* (e.g. 17 ff.), where the orator uses ethos and pathos to focus the facts in the way he desires.[91]

Aristotle's promotion of pathos from an element of the peroration to an important form of artistic proof may seem extraordinary on the part of a philosopher devoted to scientific proof. It corresponds directly to his definition of ethos as an element of proof rather than a quality of the prooemium and narration and is similarly to be traced to the im-

[90] Cf. esp. 27 ff.; 35 ff.; 42 ff.
[91] Cf. the comments thereon by Francis P. Donnelly, *The oration of Demosthenes on the crown*, New York, 1941.

portance of emotional appeal in actual oratory and to the influence of Plato. After examining the nature of the sophistic handbooks in the *Phaedrus*, Socrates, as we saw above, rejected them all and accepted as the only true rhetoric a system of eloquence based on a knowledge of mind. Oratorical ability is defined (271c10) as *psychagôgia*, the art of enchanting the soul. The orator must know (271d2 ff.) that some people are affected one way, some another by certain things, and he must learn to apply this principle to individuals, that is, learn what arguments to use with what man. When he knows this and understands moreover the right and wrong time for speaking and keeping silent and for brevity and pathetic appeals and emotionalism, then has he truly mastered his art.

It is this knowledge which Aristotle undertakes to impart, and it is Plato's emphasis here on psychology, the need to understand character and the way character is "enchanted" by argument and by emotional elements, which eventually moved him to give such a prominent place in his theory to character and pathos.[92] In the first half of book two Aristotle discusses the disposition of mind which creates emotion, the persons at whom it is directed, and the occasion which produces it; anger and mildness, love and hate, shame, favor, pity, and envy are the principal emotions discussed. It is not Aristotle's intention to recommend a change in practice—he points out the special need for a knowledge of the emotions in the peroration (1419b10 ff.)—but only to provide depth of knowledge and to emphasize those features of oratory which are in fact most important in successful speaking.

The last observations are true to a still greater degree of the third and most important type of proof, rational argu-

[92] Cf. Solmsen, *op.cit.* supra n. 37. Hunt 58 points out that Aristotle's treatment of the emotions in the *Rhetoric* is "a popular and inexact discussion of the external manifestation of character and emotions."

ment. This is discussed in the second chapter of book one and again, in what is perhaps an earlier version, in the twentieth chapter of book two. Aristotle repeatedly says that the logical side of rhetorical theory is undeveloped and yet is the most important (1354a14 ff. and 1354b21 ff.). He wishes to correct this situation and to offer practical help to the orator by an application of logic to rhetoric. Considerable sections of the discussion in book one (1359b19 ff.) are excerpts from his logical, political, or ethical notebooks and seem to wander far from oratory, but Aristotle believed it was a part of his task to itemize the substantive topics with which the three kinds of oratory deal, just as in book two he felt it necessary to catalogue emotions and states of character on which pathos and ethos as forms of proof are dependent. From the point of view of the practicing orator Aristotle may be considered as providing materials for amplification.

Aristotle recognizes three levels of reasoning: scientific demonstration (discussed in the *Prior* and *Posterior analytics*), dialectic or the art of discussion by question and answer (discussed in the *Topics*), and rhetoric, the faculty of discovering the possible means of persuasion in reference to any subject. Dialectic and rhetoric both employ for the most part argument from probabilities rather than from certainties and differ in the subjects they cover, in their literary form, and in the fact that rhetoric may also make use of proof by ethos and pathos.

Now the two processes of logic on all levels of reasoning are deduction and induction (1356a35 ff.). If the premises of an argument are scientifically provable facts and if the argument is expressed in a valid form, the result achieved will be scientific certainty. This is, however, rarely true in dialectic and rhetoric, which usually deal with things which are only true for the most part. Their premises and thus their conclusions are generally probabilities, not universals.

Deductive scientific proof takes the form of the syllogism: "all men are mortal (major premise); Socrates is a man (minor premise); therefore, Socrates is mortal (conclusion)." Deductive rhetorical proof takes the same form, but is called by Aristotle an enthymeme, an argument based on what is true for the most part: "good men do not commit murder; Socrates is a good man; therefore, Socrates did not commit murder." This is probably true, and the premises are probably good reasons why Socrates would have been innocent of a charge of murder; but there are individual circumstances when both premises, though generally true, might not justify the conclusion. The argument would then have formal validity, but would still be false. Brutus and Cassius, for example, were good men too.[93]

In actual speeches, as Aristotle recognized (1357a16 ff.), enthymemes are rarely expressed in the full logical form: "it is inconceivable that Socrates, who is a good man, has committed this murder" is still an enthymeme, although the major premise is suppressed or taken for granted. Thus, any of the very frequent explanatory statements of Greek oratory may be called an enthymeme.[94] Later writers, misunderstanding Aristotle, sometimes regarded such suppression as the factor distinguishing an enthymeme from a syllogism and adopted the term epicheireme to refer to a rhetorical syllogism in full form. In the last hundred years there has been a general return to the Aristotelian definition. If the premises are scientific, demonstrable, known to be absolutely true, the argument is a syllogism. If they

[93] Another way to express the difference is to say that in a syllogism the minor premise explains why the conclusion is true (*ratio essendi*): "Socrates is mortal because he is a man." In an enthymeme the minor premise explains why the fact of the conclusion is believed (*ratio cognoscendi*): "because he is good we do not believe Socrates committed murder." Cf. James H. McBurney, "The place of the enthymeme in rhetorical theory," sm 3 (1936) 56.

[94] Isaeus is distinguished by a fondness for complete expression of premises, cf. Jebb 2.290 ff.

are only true for the most part, or usually true, the argument is an enthymeme.[95]

Similarly, induction can be scientific or only probable. It is scientific if all instances are enumerated. This is not usually the case, or even possible, in oratory, and rhetorical induction is thus distinguished by the name *paradeigma*, example, from which is induced a probable conclusion about the matter in question (1356b5 ff.).[96] Aristotle distinguishes two classes of example (1393a25 ff.): historical and fictitious. As an example of the first he suggests: "it is necessary to make preparations against the Persian king and not let him get control of Egypt. For Darius did not cross over to Greece until he had obtained possession of Egypt, but when he had taken it he crossed over" (1393a33 ff.). Isocrates says (*To Demonicus* 34) "when you are deliberating, regard things which have happened as examples of what will happen. For the unknown may be learned most quickly from the known." The orators often use historical examples, but they are timid about claiming more historical knowledge than their audience and are quite free in editing history to fit their contexts.[97] Fictitious examples are mostly comparisons or fables. An example of comparison given by Aristotle (1393b4 ff.) is: "officials

[95] On the enthymeme cf. Cope, *op.cit.* supra n. 63, 99 ff.; R. C. Seaton, "The Aristotelian enthymeme," CR 28 (1914) 113 ff.; Wilhelm Kroll, "Das Epicheirema," SBW 216.2 (1936); McBurney, *op.cit.* supra n. 93, 49 ff.; Solomon Simonson, "A definitive note on the enthymeme: crossroads of logic, rhetoric, and metaphysics," *Philosophical review* 61 (1952) 368 ff.

[96] In theory the example can also be reduced to syllogistic form, cf. *Prior analytics* 68b38 ff. and *Rhetoric* 1402b12 ff., though the latter may represent an earlier stage in the development of Aristotle's thought, cf. Solmsen 23 f.

[97] Cf. Karl Jost, *Das Beispiel und Vorbild der Vorfahren bei den attischen Redern bis Demosthenes*, Paderborn, 1936; Gisela Schmitz-Kahlmann, "Das Beispiel der Geschichte im politischen Denken des Isokrates," *Philologus Supplementband* 31.4 (1939); Lionel Pearson, "Historical allusions in the Attic orators," CP 39 (1941) 209 ff.

chosen by lot ought not to rule, for that is as though some-one were to choose athletes by lot, not those who might be able to contest, but those to whom the lot fell." Aristotle also gives in this chapter examples of fables. The following chapter (1394a19 ff.) discusses maxims, which are premises or conclusions of possible enthymemes, but usually lack any logical proof. The speaker relies on the general accept-ance of his maxim—sometimes it is a proverb—or on his own character. Aristotle says that the use of maxims is appropriate for older speakers and that they help to make clear the speaker's moral character.

Aristotle was the first to regard the enthymeme and the example as the two logical devices of rhetoric, but he did not invent the techniques nor the names. We have already noted examples in oratory as early as the speeches of the *Iliad.* Enthymeme in fifth-century Greek means an argu-ment or reason (e.g. Sophocles, *Oedipus at Colonus* 292 and 1199). In Isocrates it appears to refer to elaborately developed sentences (*Panathenaicus* 2). In the *Rhetorica ad Alexandrum* (1430a23 ff.) it designates an antithesis. Aristotle, like Isocrates and the author of the *Rhetorica ad Alexandrum,* has taken a word which could mean any kind of statement and applied it to a statement of a particular form. With the development of the syllogism itself we need not be concerned here, though it too developed out of a Platonic beginning.[98]

Aristotle employs some special terms to designate the materials from which enthymemes are made. There are, first of all, the "signs" or "tokens." Thus, bloodstains on a cloak might well be a "sign" that the wearer had committed a murder. Aristotle uses *sêmeion* as a general word for sign

---

[98] Cf. Paul Shorey, "The origin of the syllogism," CP 19 (1924) 1 ff.; Friedrich Solmsen, "The discovery of the syllogism," *Philo-sophical review* 50 (1941) 410 ff., and "Aristotle's syllogism and its Platonic background," *Philosophical review* 60 (1951) 563 ff.; W. D. Ross, *Aristotle's Prior and Posterior analytics,* Oxford, 1949, 25 ff.

in this sense and reserves the term *tekmêrion* for a necessary sign, one from which a certain conclusion can be drawn (1357a32 ff.). The orators generally make use of both to mean a sign pointing to a probable conclusion.[99] There is, however, a further distinction between *eikota*, probabilities, and *tekmêria*, signs, to be found in Plato (*Phaedrus* 266e3) and Aristotle (*Prior analytics* 70a2 ff.) and also in the orators (e.g. Demosthenes, *Against Androtion* 22). In the works of these men *eikota* refer to probabilities of human conduct: what a man might logically be supposed to do. *Tekmêria*, on the other hand, are signs like bloodstains or footprints pointing to some conclusion in the immediate situation and not involving human nature.

A second way of viewing the materials of the enthymeme is offered by Aristotle. He says (1358a10 ff.) that enthymemes are concerned with *topoi*, "topics," of two types. Some (*idioi topoi* or *eidê*) belong to a particular study like physics or politics. Though used by the orator these topics are not by nature rhetorical and may even be the first principles of some science. Beginning in the fourth chapter of the first book Aristotle makes an extensive collection of such topics, catalogued under the kind of oratory to which each is most appropriate. Thus deliberative oratory includes the subject of finance and the orator who would discuss it must be familiar with topics like the extent of the city's resources and its expenses, which are in modern terms the topics of economics. Opposed to these are the common (*koinoi*) topics, the rhetorical and more general topics which may be applied to all subjects alike, for example the topic of the more and the less. The discussion of the particular topics takes up most of book one; pathos

[99] A fragment of Antiphon's τέχνη preserved by Ammonius (Radermacher B.x.8) says that *sêmeia* refer to things past, *tekmêria* to things future, but this cannot be illustrated from anything except Andocides 3.2. On *tekmêria* in the fifth century cf. Finley, *op.cit.* supra n. 85, 30 and Murphy, *op.cit.* supra n. 79, 94.

and ethos, the two other types of artistic proof, intervene
at the beginning of two, presumably because they as well
as the particular topics were worked on by Aristotle at
about the same time, which was late in the development
of the *Rhetoric*.[100] It is not until chapter eighteen of book
two that Aristotle gets back to the common topics, of which
he enumerates (1391b28 ff.) four: the possible and impossible; what has happened and what has not; what will
or will not happen; and greatness and smallness.

Chapter twenty reintroduces enthymeme and example
as forms of proof common to all kinds of oratory. Chapter
twenty-one is concerned with maxims, appropriate here
since they are equally usable whatever the nature of a
speech. Finally (1395b20 ff.), there appears another approach to the enthymeme, which is divided into two types,
demonstrative and refutative. These enthymemes are said
to be built up from topics of which twenty-eight valid and
ten fallacious ones are enumerated. But these topics are the
topoi of the *Topics* and are formal rather than material.
That is, they are lines of argument such as argument from
contraries and argument from definition and argument
from mistake, and they do not supply subject matter at all.
Most, but by no means all,[101] of these are common devices
of the orators. Solmsen has shown that this account is
probably a remnant of Aristotle's earlier rhetorical theory.
Possibly it has even been combined into the *Rhetoric* by
some of Aristotle's pupils.[102]

Topics are, then, to Aristotle the materials of which
proofs are made, whether specific as outlined in book one
or general as outlined in book two, and secondly the form
of arguments as outlined in the last part of book two.

[100] Cf. Solmsen 222 ff.
[101] Cf. Georgiana P. Palmer, *The τόποι of Aristotle's Rhetoric as
exemplified in the orators*, Chicago, 1934.
[102] Cf. Solmsen 223 ff.; McBurney, *op.cit.* supra n. 93; J. L. Stocks,
"The composition of Aristotle's logical works," CQ 27 (1933) 115
ff.; Simonson, *op.cit.* supra n. 95.

Topos means place and may be translated into Latin as *locus*, the place where the orator finds the needed argument. None of Aristotle's topics should be confused with *loci communes*, those commonplaces or expanded formulae which were a leading aspect of the knack of oratory as taught by the sophists. The conclusion of the *Sophistical refutations* shows that Aristotle was well aware of the existence of these, but they are unscientific and, thus, play no part in his theory.[103] Conversely, the topics of Aristotle were not, apparently, recognized as such by any of the orators; although they use many of the arguments he classifies, they do not apply any collective term to them. The *Rhetorica ad Alexandrum* does not utilize the term either, but it does discuss the materials of oratory, both those peculiar to one type (1421b17 ff.) and those common to all types (1427b39 ff.).

All types of Aristotelian topics continue throughout the rhetorical tradition, though altered. The formal topics are best represented in Cicero's *Topica*, which shows the influence of Aristotle's *Topics* and the second book of the *Rhetoric* as well as that of Roman legal practice and Hellenistic logic. The subject is also discussed in *De oratore* 2. The material topics are systematically developed in later rhetoric. Aristotle's classification by the three kinds of oratory is thrown out of perspective by the emphasis given to judicial oratory, but the topics are systematically arranged so that the student can go down the list and draw from each all appropriate material in the order needed. The topics thus become a kind of check list which enables the

[103] On commonplaces cf. Julius Brandenburger, *De Antiphontis Rhamnusii tetralogiis*, Schneidemühl, 1888; U. von Wilamowitz-Moellendorf, "Die sechste Rêde des Antiphon," SBB 1900, 1.398 ff.; Ernest Pflugmacher, *Locorum communium specimen*, Greifswald, 1909; Walter Plöbst, *Die Auxesis*, Munich, 1911, 6 ff.; Karl Hiddeman, *De Antiphontis Andocidis Lysiae Isocratis Isaei oratorum judicialium prooemiis*, Münster, 1913; Kroll 1044; Pearson, *op.cit.* supra n. 97; Stevens, *op.cit.* supra n. 37; Dorjahn, *op.cit.* supra n. 82.

orator to make sure that he has left out nothing. An example might be the list in Cicero's *De inventione* 1.34-43.

The Third Book of Aristotle's *Rhetoric*

The third book of the *Rhetoric* contains a discussion of style followed by a discussion of arrangement not unlike that which made up the greater part of earlier handbooks. The book gives something of the impression of an afterthought and may well have been originally a separate treatise which Aristotle subsequently united to his discussion of invention.[104] Solmsen[105] showed that there exist side by side two introductions to the discussion of style linking it, respectively, to an earlier and to a later version of the first two books. The earlier in composition is that which now stands as the first paragraph of book three. Although it recognizes three forms of proof, logical, ethical, and pathetical, it knows nothing of the example as the sister tool of the enthymeme in logical demonstration and is in general to be referred to the "topical-dialectical" period. The other introduction stands at the end of book two. It fits less well into the context, admits the example and maxim among the proofs, and generally conforms to the last period of the development of Aristotle's theory of logic. Now, if the third book has two introductions, one connecting it with an earlier, one with a later version of the first two books, it is clear that the third book was not tacked on to the end of the completed work, but that it was regarded by Aristotle as a part of the whole treatise during at least two stages of

[104] The list of the works of Aristotle in Diogenes Laertius (5.24) contains a *Rhetoric* in two books and a separate work in two books *On style*, but no *Rhetoric* in *three* books; cf. Moraux, *op.cit.* supra n. 67, 96 ff. Before the development of Aristotle's thought began to be understood it was suggested that the third book might be wholly spurious; cf. Hermann Diels, "Ueber das dritte Buch der aristotelischen *Rhetorik*," *Abhandlung der Akademie der Wissenschaft,* Berlin, 1886, no. 4.

[105] 31 ff.

its development. If this is so, it is possible that the discussion of style itself has seen some development.

Development in other portions of Aristotle's writings can often be recognized by inconsistencies, either in theory or in the use of terms. In the discussion of style in book three a number of inconsistencies or at least apparent inconsistencies appear when the section from chapter five through chapter seven is compared with the rest of the account. These chapters are the basis for the important theory of the virtues of style which was subsequently developed by Theophrastus and is found in virtually all later writing on rhetoric. The later virtues are all mentioned by Aristotle, but not as systematic and exclusive categories. In chapter two, for example (1404a 2), Aristotle states that the virtue of style is clarity. As a kind of corollary he adds that style must not be mean, nor above the dignity of the subject, but appropriate; clarity is to be obtained by using nouns and verbs in their literal meanings; ornamentation appropriate to the subject is the result of the proper use of metaphors. The greater part of the chapter is given over to the discussion of metaphor. Chapter three is devoted to the corresponding vices of style. Chapter four takes up the simile, which Aristotle regards as a form of metaphor. So far, although there are some problems, and perhaps chapters two and three do not altogether fit together, there are no startling inconsistencies.

Chapter five, however, seems to begin all over again. Aristotle says that the basis ($\dot{a}\rho\chi\dot{\eta}$) of style is hellenism ($\tau\dot{o}\ \dot{\epsilon}\lambda\lambda\eta\nu\dot{\iota}\zeta\epsilon\iota\nu$). This is usually interpreted to mean purity, to speak good Greek, a meaning which may seem to gain some support from the discussion of purity which we quoted from the handbook of Isocrates; but Isocrates' rules really aim at euphony and clarity rather than purity. According to Aristotle hellenism depends upon five rules: proper use of connectives (a $\delta\dot{\epsilon}$ to follow a $\mu\dot{\epsilon}\nu$), use of specific rather than general words, avoidance of ambiguities, observance of gender, observance of number. The last two undoubtedly go to make up good Greek and their misuse can lead to ambiguity (*Sophistical refutations* 173b26 ff.), but the list is a strange one if the object really is purity, whether of diction or of composition or both. The *Rhetorica ad Alexandrum* (1435a32 ff.) includes the first and third as two of the principal ways to obtain *clarity*, and this seems to be considerably more meaningful. In later rhetoricians hellenism undoubtedly does mean purity of style, but in the classical period the few occurrences of the verbal form used by Aristotle point rather to speaking Greek, making oneself understood, as opposed to speaking some other language or failing to make oneself understood at all.[106] Its opposite is τὸ βαρβαρίζειν, which does not mean to speak bad Greek, but to speak gibberish (e.g. *Sophistical refutations* 165b21).

However they explain hellenism critics have generally recognized that the chapter as a whole is devoted to clarity in fact if not in name.[107] They have sought to reconcile two discussions of the same subject by the assumption that chapter two is devoted to clarity as a virtue of diction whereas in chapter five Aristotle has turned to the subject of composition. But neither in the *Rhetoric* nor in the *Poetics* does Aristotle distinguish diction from composition, and the *Poetics* never discusses composition at all. The rules for hellenism in the *Rhetoric* clearly involve both diction and composition. Presumably the basis of the traditional interpretation is the first sentence of chapter five: ὁ μὲν οὖν λόγος συντίθεται ἐκ τούτων. This is interpreted to mean "speech is put together from these elements; we will now discuss composition." The second part of this translation is certainly not implied.

[106] E.g. *Rhetoric* 1413b6; Thucydides 2.68.5; Plato, *Meno* 82b4 and *Charmades* 159a6; Aeschines, *Against Ctesiphon* 172.

[107] Cf. e.g. E. M. Cope and J. E. Sandys, *The Rhetoric of Aristotle* 3, Cambridge, Eng., 1877, *ad loc.*

"These elements" should refer to something immediately preceding. That which precedes is, however, the discussion of the simile. Before that is the discussion of the vices of style. If one goes back to chapter two one can find mention of different kinds of words, which is the usually accepted antecedent. These kinds of words are not enumerated, but a cross reference is given to a list in the *Poetics*. The different kinds of nouns referred to in chapters five to seven of the *Rhetoric* do not, however, correspond very well to the list in the *Poetics* (1457a31 ff.), where the kinds are simple and double, then proper, rare (foreign), metaphorical, ornamental, coined, lengthened, curtailed, and altered. In *Rhetoric* 5-7 the kinds mentioned, in addition to specific and general, are metaphor, epithet, and foreign. There is also a reference to double words (1408b10) as though they were a parallel category. From the passages in which it occurs in the *Rhetoric* it appears that an epithet is really any adjective and thus can be excluded from our list. This leaves only three categories—proper, foreign, metaphorical—which correspond approximately to the list given by Isocrates in the *Evagoras* (9): proper, foreign, new, metaphorical.[108] The kinds of words recognized in Isocrates' handbook were familiar (proper), elaborate, coined (new), and metaphorical. We may conclude that in chapters five to seven Aristotle seems to be closer to the conventional categories of contemporary rhetoric than to the careful list of the *Poetics* which is cited in chapter two.

To be fully comprehensible chapter five should have been preceded by a section listing the types of nouns. Perhaps this once existed, but was later replaced by the discussion now found in chapter two. The five rules of clear hellenism, though not removed, have been rendered obsolete by the simple statement that clarity is best achieved by the use of proper words; all the other kinds make the style ornate.

[108] In the *Rhetorica ad Alexandrum* (1434b34) the categories are simple, compound, and metaphorical.

Discussion of ornament and especially of metaphor was then added. The account is a subtle one and seeks to penetrate to an understanding of the psychological effect of a metaphor. With it we should compare chapter six, which is devoted to weight (ὄγκος), a quality later taken to be bombast, but not regarded by Aristotle as a fault. He lists five ways to obtain it: by a description instead of a name or vice versa, by metaphors and epithets, by substituting the plural for the singular, by repeating the article with attributives, and by describing a thing by the qualities which it does not possess. These are clearly matters of both diction and composition. Aristotle advises the use of metaphors "to make clear what you mean," which is at least a verbal departure from chapter two. Finally, the first device is to be used in avoiding mention of anything shameful. In this sense weight corresponds to the avoidance of what is mean in chapter two, and generally it may be said to be a form of ornamentation in which metaphor plays a subsidiary role.

The third characteristic of good style according to chapter two is that it should be appropriate, neither mean nor above the dignity of the subject. This reappears as the subject of chapter seven, which begins by stating the same thought, that important matters should not be treated in an off-hand way nor trifles in a lordly manner. The chapter recognizes two other sources of propriety, expression of emotion and of character. By the latter is meant, apparently, ethopoiia, or the dramatic character of the orator, which the later version in chapter two has almost, but not completely, omitted (1404b12 ff.); the comparison with drama makes the reference clear. The conclusion drawn is that those who practice the technique must conceal it, which observation is also taken over from the earlier version (1408b8).

It might be argued that chapters five to seven are not an earlier version of material found elsewhere, but only a more detailed discussion of the matters outlined in chapter two;

this is disproved, however, by the differences in scope, content, and spirit between the two discussions. If chapters five to seven merely developed chapter two we should expect the discussions to be more detailed. But in fact they are more detailed only in the discussion of points inconsistent with chapter two, like the five rules of hellenism, and much less detailed in matters like the metaphor. The greatest difference between the two sections is the spirit or even the intellectual level. Five to seven is in the sophistic tradition. If a short discussion of the different types of words is prefixed, the whole section will constitute a discussion of style roughly corresponding to that in the *Rhetorica ad Alexandrum* (1434b33 ff.) and in the same relative position in the work. On the other hand, chapters two to four are comparable not to this sophistic tradition, but to the *Poetics*, which is repeatedly referred to. This fact offers the answer to the question of why Aristotle decided to replace chapters five to seven. The greatest difference between the two accounts is the treatment of the metaphor. Chapter two seems to be in essence a later version of chapter five, written after Aristotle had developed a theory of the metaphor, a topic which is conspicuously lacking in the *Rhetorica ad Alexandrum* and, indeed, was surely not to be found in any sophistic handbook. This development came about largely through Aristotle's study in the *Poetics* where four classes of metaphor are distinguished (1457b6 ff.): "metaphor is the substitution of the name of something else, and this may take place from genus to species or from species to genus or from species to species or according to proportion." The resulting discussion of style in the *Rhetoric* is particularly thorough in its treatment of metaphors; not only is the metaphor treated as the principal device of ornament, and when misused a leading cause of frigidity, but in chapters ten and eleven it becomes the basis for *asteia*, similes, proverbs, and hyperboles. Metaphor in this sense is characteristically Aristotelian. Its occurrence in Isocrates found it coupled with lexicographical categories which are no doubt the origin of Aristotle's concept, but Isocrates thought of metaphor as simply one of many types of words, whereas to Aristotle it is the basis of good style: "metaphor more than anything else imparts clarity, pleasure, and novelty, and it is not possible to learn the use of metaphor from anyone else" (1405a8 ff.).

The remaining chapters on style (8-12) are relatively late and resume the level of criticism found in chapters two to four: the theory of the metaphor is to be assumed throughout. Chapter eight on prose rhythm owes a lot to poetic metrics and something to Plato's concept of the limited as seen, for example, in the *Philebus* (25c1 ff.), but the rest is probably Aristotle's.[109] Thrasymachus' preference for the paean is mentioned (1409a2) but is hardly a major source, since Thrasymachus apparently did not understand why the paean should be preferred. The paean is, says Aristotle, rhythmic without being a meter. This is the primary consideration. What he seems to mean is that a passage of good prose will avoid a series of short or long syllables, which might produce a choppy or lumbering effect, but it will also avoid a series of iambs, trochees, dactyls, and anapests, which would have too regular a beat. Patterns which may recur without obviously turning the line into verse are especially _ ⌣ ⌣ ⌣, which Aristotle thought a good way to start a sentence, and ⌣ ⌣ ⌣ _, which is a recommended close. These are the first and fourth paeans respectively. Aristotle does not mention, but probably would accept, the cretic _ ⌣ _, a temporal equivalent of the paean, which is in practice a cornerstone of much ancient prose rhythm.

This, the earliest extant account of prose rhythm, is the ancestor of the very extensive chapters of later writers, including that in Cicero's *Orator* and Quintilian (9.4). The

---

[109] There is a good discussion of this chapter in the article by Drerup, *op.cit.* supra n. 13.

two persistent elements are the statement that prose must not become metrical and the reference to the paean. Later accounts, however, continue the examination of suitable feet to such an extent that the principle of rhythmic variety is eclipsed, and modern critics are thus encouraged to scan prose sentences and divide them, often rather arbitrarily, into metrical feet. In practice, fortunately, ancient writers did not observe their own rules and the rhythmic principle of Aristotle remains the mark of good prose.

A second characteristic of later accounts is the emphasis on the beginning and particularly the end, called the clausula, of a period. Aristotle was pointing in this direction when he distinguished the use of the two different kinds of paeans. The trend is in accord with both Greek and Latin practice in which the rhythmic character of the last few words of a sentence is certainly most marked. It is here, of course, that it is easiest to distinguish feet, and this is no doubt the cause of the emphasis.

Chapter nine on periodicity has been generally misunderstood. By a period Aristotle means not the typical long sentence with subordinate clauses as seen in Isocrates, but the basic structural device of the earlier prose of Antiphon and Gorgias, antithesis or parallelism with a twofold division.[110] This is made clear by his comparison of the period to the strophe-antistrophe structure of the dithyramb and by his continual reference to the *two* parts of the period, the beginning and the end he calls them once (1409a36). Each of these parts he calls a colon, which is not a clause in our sense, since it is not necessarily an independent grammatical unit, but simply a group of words balanced by some other group. The period itself, though it

[110] Cf. George A. Kennedy, "Aristotle on the period," HSCP 63 (1958) 283 ff. The chapter is discussed rather differently by T. B. L. Webster, *Art and literature in fourth century Athens*, London, 1956, 75 ff.

must be complete in sense, need not consist of an entire sentence as we know one. Such a concept of the period is reminiscent of the twofold statement of chapter twenty-four of the *Rhetorica ad Alexandrum*, and indeed, the latter work in all its stylistic examples makes use of a style in which two cola are evident. A few traces of Aristotle's concept of the period survived in later times, especially in the attempts of rhetoricians to restrict the number of clauses in a period, but in general it was replaced by our present conception of a period as an organized paragraph, with some grammatical connexion between the clauses.

The discussion of the period follows that of rhythm, and presumably the two are to be viewed together; but the rhythmical requirements of the period or of the cola are not spelled out. Both the structural elements and the rhythm are forms of limit, and perhaps Aristotle regarded them as complementing each other. The structure imposes a limit through the laws of grammar: a preposition is not complete without its object nor a subject without its predicate, but a prepositional phrase or a simple clause is in a sense complete and thus limited. A series of short syllables at the end of a phrase or clause is without pattern and thus unlimited; the addition of a long syllable creates a pattern in the form of a fourth paean, which is thus a limit. This completion or limit gives the reader or hearer a sense of pleasure.

Chapters ten and eleven are devoted to what would later be called figures of speech, all of which Aristotle treats as metaphors. This is a part of the theory of style which was destined for enormous amplification in the following centuries, but none of the later Greek or Roman accounts seem to share Aristotle's philosophical concern with the psychological bases of figures of speech. All four kinds of metaphor teach us something and as a result produce pleasure. The key passage reads as follows (1410b10 ff.):

"To learn easily is by nature pleasant to all. Words contain meaning. As a result, whatever words impart new knowledge to us are pleasantest. But glosses are not understood and we already know proper words. It is a metaphor which most produces knowledge."

In other words, metaphor is a mean between the extremes of the unintelligible and the commonplace. We already know commonplace words, and we can learn nothing from completely unknown words; but from words with which we already associate some meaning we can get a new insight into the nature of some object or action. Aristotle cites as an example a reference to old age as stubble. We already know what old age is and the words "old age" teach us nothing. Nor would we be edified by some strange or foreign word for the same thing. But we do know what "stubble" is, and if we think of old age as stubble we get a sudden tragic or pathetic vision, for the two do indeed have something in common. This knowledge, in turn, like rhythm and like the sense of grammatical completion, produces a feeling of pleasure or satisfaction and is thus a characteristic of good style. Happiness is as much the object of Aristotle's theory of style as of his ethics.

Aristotle's discussion of style concludes with a very interesting chapter (12) on stylistic variation, a topic which was to play an important part in the later history of rhetoric. According to Aristotle (1413b3 ff.) a different style is appropriate to each kind of oratory. A division is first made between those speeches designed to be read (something like the epideictic oratory of Isocrates) and those composed for delivery; the latter are then divided into demegoric or political and dicanic or judicial. The kind intended to be read is precise, but would appear too thin in actual debate. Speeches written for delivery, on the other hand, seem repetitious when read. The judicial will be more polished

than the deliberative, which is compared to shadow painting—effective only at a distance.[111]

This is not the earliest attempt to differentiate types of
style, but it is perhaps the most important one since Theophrastus began where Aristotle left off.[112] Plato (*Republic*
397c8 ff.) recognized different types of poetic style, and
Isocrates (*Panegyricus* 11) did much the same for prose.
The topic was one necessarily developed, for the standardi-
zation to which rhetorical theory seemed to point was
foreign to the stylistic instinct of all good writers.

Aristotle's discussion of arrangement (1414a30 ff.) shows
the influence of his doctrine of three kinds of oratory and
his impatience with some of the rules of sophistic rhetoricians. It is possible that chapter thirteen, which begins
the account, is earlier than the rest of the treatment, for it
insists that a speech has only two necessary parts: statement
and proof. Four parts are admitted as a maximum, but
they are introduction, statement (*prothesis*), proof, and
epilogue rather than the introduction, narration, proof, and
epilogue of the sophistic handbooks. Yet in the actual discussion which follows, Aristotle describes a narration. In
discussing each part of a speech he makes a few apparently
original observations: the introduction of an epideictic
speech need not have much to do with the speech, but is
just a showy beginning (1414b21 ff.);[113] appeal to the audience is logically outside of the function of an introduction
(1415b4 f.); epideictic (1416b16 f.) and apparently other
(1417b10 f.) narrative should not all be in one place,
but introduced as needed and should demonstrate moral

[111] Aristotle is not interested here in the old dispute over the
written and unwritten word nor in the technique of extempore
speech.

[112] Cf. George A. Kennedy, "Theophrastus and stylistic distinctions," HSCP 62 (1957) 93 ff. and chapter five infra.

[113] Cf. George A. Kennedy, "Isocrates' *Encomium of Helen*: a
panhellenic document," TAPA 89 (1958) 77 ff.

character (1417a15 ff.) and draw upon the emotional (1417a36); the discussion of proof recognizes four kinds of *staseis* or bases of defense (1417b21 ff.): a denial of the fact, or its injuriousness, or its importance, or its injustice. Chapter eighteen unexpectedly appends to the discussion of proof an account of interrogation, ambiguous question, and jests as useful in refutation. The work concludes chastely with an account of the peroration and an echo of the end of Lysias' speech *Against Eratosthenes*.

The *Rhetorica ad Alexandrum*

The other, and more typical, handbook surviving from the fourth century B.C. is the work commonly known as the *Rhetorica ad Alexandrum*. The title comes from the dedicatory epistle at the head of the treatise in which "Aristotle" addresses the work to his most famous pupil, Alexander the Great. This epistle is certainly not by Aristotle and is very inept. The treatise may well have been written during Aristotle's lifetime, though not by himself, for it is quite unlike his manner or thought at any point in his development. A *terminus post quem* for the date of composition is furnished by a reference in chapter eight to the Corinthian expedition to Sicily in 341 B.C., and a candidate for author is suggested by Quintilian (3.4.9), who says that Anaximenes distinguished between judicial and deliberative speeches and seven species: hortatory, dissuasive, laudatory, invective, accusatory, defensive, and investigatory. The text of the *ad Alexandrum*, as we have it, speaks (1421b7) of *three* kinds of oratory, including epideictic, but it immediately (1421b14) abandons the latter and the discussion deals with oratory in terms of the seven species or in some passages deliberative, forensic, laudatory, and invective. It seems very probable that someone has adjusted the text to conform to the categories of Aristotle and that the treatise is basically the work of Anaximenes.[114] About him we know that he came from Lampsacus, that he lived through the middle of the fourth century, and that he was an instructor of Alexander the Great. He is described by Dionysius of Halicarnassus (*Isaeus* 19) as a man who wanted to show ability in all departments of literature, including history, criticism, and oratory, but who excelled in none.

The importance of the *Rhetorica ad Alexandrum* is not so much in its direct influence, which was apparently negligible, but in the fact that it represents better than anything else the tradition of sophistic rhetoric. Attempts have been made to see in it the teachings of one school or another, but such attempts emphasize small details and overlook significant differences. The influence upon it of the Isocratean handbook is, however, perhaps not entirely imaginary.[115] Anaximenes appears to agree with Isocrates in thinking of oratory as judicial, deliberative, and the oratory of praise and blame, in using the term *prothesis* (1440b7) (*katastasis* occurs too, though it seems to mean "arrangement" 1438a2), in accepting the three virtues of the narration (1438a21 f.), in objecting to hiatus (1435a33 f. and 1435b16 ff.), in the concern for the right use of conjunctions (1435a38 ff.), and in the demand for logical

[114] It was first attributed to him by Petrus Victorius. For a while the theory of F. Susemihl, *Geschichte der griechischen Literatur in der Alexandrinerzeit* 2, Leipzig, 1891-1892, 457, that the work was produced in the third century was popular, but the discovery of a papyrus fragment (Hibeh no. 26, London, 1906) of the early third century indicated that the treatise must have been written well before that time. Vinzenz Buchheit, *Untersuchungen zur Theorie des Genos epideiktikon von Gorgias bis Aristoteles*, Munich, 1960, attempts unsuccessfully to refute the attribution to Anaximenes. G. M. A. Grube, *A Greek critic: Demetrius on style*, Toronto, 1961, 156 ff., stresses the inconsistency of the evidence.

[115] Cf. H. Rackham, *Aristotle: Rhetorica ad Alexandrum* (Loeb Library), Cambridge, 1937, 258 ff.

115

order (1438a27 ff.). On the other hand, the emphasis on the species of oratory is much greater in the *Rhetorica ad Alexandrum* than in other works, though not greater than what is implied by the actual oratory, and there is no discussion of prose rhythm, nor are the categories of diction (1434b33 ff.) quite those of Isocrates. Since the treatise shows no influence at all of the concept of philosophical rhetoric developed by Isocrates, it is definitely not the work of a member of his school. It is possible that there is some influence of Zoilus, whose definition of a figure, the earliest known (1437a17): "to pretend one thing and to say another"[116] is reminiscent of Anaximenes' definition of irony as "saying something while pretending not to say it" (1434a17). The end of the dedicatory epistle says that the work is indebted to the handbook of Corax and the *technai* written by Aristotle for Theodectes. Wendland tried to prove this by a comparison of the contents of the *Rhetorica ad Alexandrum* and what is known of the theories of Corax and of Theodectes.[117] He believed that both the *Rhetorica ad Alexandrum* and Aristotle's *Rhetoric* were considerably indebted to a common source, which he identified as Theodectes' handbook.

The reference to Corax, if it means anything, only indicates that the treatise stands in the tradition of the early handbooks. Wendland found some similarity of terminology (the term *katastasis*, for example) and of doctrine (argument from probability), but the first has different meanings and the second was common to all handbooks. There is a little correspondence between Theodectes and Anaximenes, but Theodectes' extensive discussion of periodicity, referred to by Aristotle, is missing as are the five virtues of the

[116] Cf. Phoebammon, *On figures*, in Walz 8.493; Radermacher B.xxv.2-3.

[117] Paul Wendland, *Anaximenes von Lampsacus*, Berlin, 1905, 30ff.

116

narration. Insofar as there are similarities we are dealing with a common tradition.

Wendland did not believe that there was any influence of Aristotle's *Rhetoric* upon the *Rhetorica ad Alexandrum*, as Ipfelkopfer had claimed.[118] There are indeed great differences between the two works. Anaximenes has nothing to say about the three types of proof, the theory of the enthymeme (though the word is once used of a proof, 1438b35), the three and only three kinds of oratory, the theory of the metaphor, or the types of style. On the other hand, there is a parallelism of structure evident between the *Rhetoric* and the *Rhetorica ad Alexandrum* which cannot be proved to have existed in any earlier work and which, if it is not a result of the influence of the *Rhetoric*, is at least a sign of a more extensive concern with the materials of oratory and the rational side of rhetoric. The nature and contents of the *Rhetorica ad Alexandrum* can perhaps be best understood if we pursue this parallelism.

The *Rhetorica ad Alexandrum* falls into three parts which correspond to the three parts of the *Rhetoric*. The first part, chapters one to five, corresponds roughly to the first book of the *Rhetoric*. This is what the author calls a discussion of the *dynameis* (1421b16) of the seven species of oratory. He first takes up exhortation and dissuasion and the topics peculiar thereto: the just, the lawful, the expedient, the honorable, the pleasant, the practicable. The subjects are seven in number: religious ritual, legislation, the form of the constitution, alliances, war, peace, or finance. Lines of argument appropriate to each subject are outlined; legislation is discussed both for democracies and for oligarchies. The arguments are quite specific, and one can see that they could be learned as commonplaces and adapted to almost all possible speeches. For example (1425a10 ff.), "these are

[118] Adalbert Ipfelkopfer, *Die Rhetorik des Anaximenes*, Würzburg, 1889, 54 f.

excuses for making war against someone: that we have been wronged in the past, but now since there is an opportunity we ought to requite the evildoers, or that we ought to defend ourselves against those who are wronging us now, or that we ought to fight for relatives or benefactors, or go to the help of allies who are being wronged, or that it is to the advantage of the city, or for its glory or wealth or power or something of that sort. . . ." What Aristotle says about deliberative oratory (*Rhetoric* 1359a30 ff.) is indeed quite different in detail, but satisfies the same purpose. He says that deliberative oratory is concerned with the expedient and the harmful; its subjects are five in number: finance, war, defense, commerce, legislation. Aristotle then adds a discussion of subjects which the deliberative speaker will need to know, including the nature of happiness, the good, and constitutions. Anaximenes proceeds (1425b36 ff.) to the discussion of eulogy and vituperation, then (1426b22) to accusation and defense, and finally (1427b12) to investigation, which is really adaptable to all species and is simply a demonstration of inconsistencies. Similarly, Aristotle proceeds in the same order to epideictic and then to forensic oratory. Plato's outline of the early rhetorical handbooks gave no hint of any such discussion as this, but the correspondence between Anaximenes and Aristotle indicates that it is a standard fourth-century pattern. It was no doubt a result of the dissatisfaction, expressed by Aristotle, with the limitation of the early handbooks to judicial oratory.

Chapter six of the *Rhetorica ad Alexandrum* begins a new section which the author had earlier (1421b17) labeled the *chrêseis*. These are the topics common to all species of oratory. Modes of proof take up most of the space. The corresponding section of Aristotle's *Rhetoric* is book two, from chapter twenty on, although the inartificial proofs have already been covered at the end of the first book. There is little similarity in what is said about enthymemes, examples, and maxims because this is the subject on which Aristotle most developed his own line, but the same general subjects are discussed, and in the same general relation to the rest of the work.

Beginning in chapter twenty-three, still under the heading of *chrêseis*, Anaximenes discusses style, restricting himself pretty much to the Gorgianic figures.[119] Probably the account was put together from a variety of sources; it is not very well thought out. The much more extensive, but still corresponding passage in Aristotle is the first half of the third book.

All of this material was added to the traditional handbook after the time of Plato. Chapter twenty-nine of the *Rhetorica ad Alexandrum*, corresponding to the second half of the third book of Aristotle, is the fourth-century version of the original rhetorical handbook, the discussion of arrangement. The principal change in both works is the introduction into the discussion of the kinds or species of oratory, but the two works differ in their approach. Aristotle takes the parts one by one and discusses the nature of each in each type of oratory. Anaximenes, on the other hand, takes up the kinds or species and discusses the parts of each.

We have mentioned the parts of an oration several times already. Perhaps it will be worth while to look briefly at the discussion of arrangement as known in the fourth century B.C. The most characteristic part of the prooemium theory is the requirement that it make the hearer well-disposed, attentive, and tractable. According to the *Rhetorica ad Alexandrum* (1436a33 ff.) the introduction must inform the hearers of the topic of the speech and enable them to

[119] On the discussion of style cf. Augustus Mayer, *Theophrasti περὶ λέξεως libri fragmenta*, Leipzig, 1910, xlvii f.; J. Börner, *De Quintiliani institutionis oratoriae dispositione*, Leipzig, 1911, 27 ff.; T. Herrle, *Quaestiones rhetoricae ad elocutionem pertinentes*, Leipzig, 1912, 5 f.

follow the argument and exhort them to attend and make them well-disposed. Theodectes, it will be remembered, had called good will the object of the prooemium. Aristotle (1415a11 ff.) regards everything except a "sample of the subject" as a "remedy." He does, however, discuss the methods of combating prejudice in considerable detail. All the rhetoricians find this necessary and usually create numerous subdivisions: thus in the *Rhetorica ad Alexandrum* (1441b36 ff.) it is said that the audience may be friendly, neutral, or hostile. In the latter case the hostility may be caused by the personality of the speaker, the subject, or the speech itself. The extent to which these topics were studied is evident in the almost formulaic technique of the prooemium of Greek judicial oratory and can be seen clearly in the advice given in the *Rhetorica ad Alexandrum* in the following fairly typical section (1442b2 ff.):

"There are two principles common to all cases. The first is to anticipate whatever arguments you think will impress the judges and make the impression yourself. The second is to blame the deeds on your opponents or, if that is not possible, on some other people, using the excuse that you have not become involved in the suit of your own will, but under compulsion by your antagonists. The following excuses must be alleged against each prejudice: a youngish man must claim a lack of friends to plead the case on his behalf, or the magnitude of the crimes or their number, or the limited period of time or something of this sort. If you are speaking for another person you must say that you are speaking as his advocate because of your friendship or because of your enmity for his opponent or because of your having been present at the deeds or because of interest in common or because the one for whom you speak is desolate and is being wronged. If he is a logical candidate for the charge against him or if the charge which he is bringing is out of his character, make use of anticipation and say that

120

it is neither just nor legal nor expedient to convict someone on the basis of an opinion or a suspicion before hearing the matter out. The prejudices against a man we shall dissipate in this way. . . ."

A characteristic feature of the accounts of the narration in the rhetoricians is the three qualities or virtues required of it: clarity, brevity, and persuasiveness. To these Theodectes added magnificence and sweetness. Proof of early interest in magnificence—*megaloprepeia*—as a quality of style is afforded by a papyrus fragment (*Oxyrhynchus papyrus* 410) in the Doric dialect on that subject.[120] Anaximenes describes succinctly how the three virtues which he regards as important may be obtained (1438a26 ff.). Clarity comes either from facts or language: from the facts if they are told in the order in which they happened and without digression, a rule found also in the Isocratean handbook; from the language if proper and common words and a simple word order are used. Conciseness or brevity will be obtained if superfluous facts are omitted, but enough is told to avoid obscurity. The narration will be persuasive if improbable facts are supported with reasons, or at least if reasons are promised.

Aristotle (1416b16 ff. and 1417b10 ff.) says that often, and particularly in epideictic, the narrative should not be continuous, but interspersed with proof. This is known to the author of the *Rhetorica ad Alexandrum* (1438b14 ff.) and was a feature of some Greek oratory. The speech *On the mysteries* by Andocides, for example, has to deal with several charges which are narrated and proved one by one for the sake of clarity. The technique is also fairly common in Isaeus and may be seen in the third speech of Aeschines.

An idea of the discussion of the proof may be gained from the following description in the *Rhetorica ad Alex-*

---

[120] Cf. W. Rhys Roberts, "The new rhetorical fragment in relation to the Sicilian rhetoric of Corax and Tisias," CR 18 (1904) 19 ff.

andrum of confirmation in a speech of accusation (1442b32 ff.):

"The next part will be confirmation. If the facts are denied by the opposite party, it will be based on proofs, but if they are admitted, on considerations of justice and expediency and the like. It is necessary to put first the witnesses and confessions that we have obtained by torture, if any are available, then to confirm by means of maxims and general considerations, if the evidence is convincing, but if it is not entirely convincing, by argument from probability and then by examples, tokens, signs, and refutations, and finally by enthymemes and maxims. If the facts are admitted, proofs may be omitted and legal arguments employed. . . ."

According to Aristotle (1419b10 ff.) the epilogue is composed of four parts: one part is intended to dispose the hearer favorably toward oneself and unfavorably toward the adversary, another to praise and deprecate, a third to excite the emotions of the hearer, the fourth to recapitulate. The *Rhetorica ad Alexandrum* is not so systematic, but the elements are similar. According to the *Anonymous Seguerianus* (208, p. 389 Spengel-Hammer) Aristotle in the *Theodectea* distinguished three elements in the epilogue: praise and blame, awakening of emotions, and recapitulation. The constant elements in the treatment of the epilogue are some form of emotional appeal and a recapitulation of the proof. These are evident also in surviving Greek speeches.

Additional parts occur in some speeches: a refutation especially may be regarded as a separate part, though it is really a form of proof. The *Rhetorica ad Alexandrum* is much concerned with anticipation, though this may occur in any of the parts as well as standing alone. Partition and digression do not usually constitute formal parts in Greek rhetoric as they do in Roman. In general, the early rhetoricians, and especially Aristotle, regard the structure as fluid. The philosopher insists only on two parts, the statement and the proof. The narration was sometimes not necessary if the subject had already been discussed and was well known. In deliberative speeches even an introduction could be dropped. Judicial oratory tended to keep four parts and the emphasis in the teaching of rhetoric on court oratory thus tended to stereotype them. By the first century B.C. some rhetoricians insisted on the necessity of always including all the parts.[121]

If one looks back over the first hundred and fifty years of rhetorical theory, Aristotle's *Rhetoric* seems to tower above all the remains, for it is infinitely more imaginative and richer than the *Rhetorica ad Alexandrum* and undoubtedly more so than any lost handbook of the age. Its influence has been enormous and still continues. Furthermore, this influence has been largely salutary. Aristotle, unlike most rhetoricians, was not intoxicated with speaking; he does not glorify the art. He simply acknowledges its usefulness while warning against its dangers. The art itself he regards as amoral, but his discussion of it is moral in intent, and the orator must always keep a moral purpose clearly in mind: we must not persuade what is wrong, he warns (1355a31). The practicality of the *Rhetoric* is difficult to assess. Probably no one would learn how to speak in the first instance from reading Aristotle, but any speaker might well profit from much of his advice. In fact, the work is more analytical than instructional, despite an occasional lapse into the imperative mood of the speech manuals. The analysis is not based on actual speeches, but on an abstract conception of speeches of different kinds, just as the *Poetics* is not an analysis of tragedies, but of what Aristotle regarded as characteristic of tragedy.

The *Rhetoric* shares with other handbooks, perhaps grudgingly, the conviction that rhetoric is an art. This is important. It means that oratory can be reduced to rule

[121] Cf. infra p. 335.

and that there exists a right, and thus presumably also a wrong, response to every rhetorical challenge. By the second half of the fourth century B.C. there were probably few educated men in Greece who would deny this. What was true of rhetoric was true of other fields of thought and endeavor too. Poetry, which had once been the product of a god-sent inspiration, was now similarly a creation of the rules of art. Politics was being defined and fixed into a classical pattern. Aristotle repeatedly says that a legal system should be spelled out in as much detail as possible to avoid difficulties of interpretation; broad principles of justice are not adequate, specific rules are needed. The acceptance of rules of art, of right and wrong answers, meant the beginning of that process of ossification which overtook all of ancient creativity. Practice within the art was controlled more and more by strict rules. The artist was more and more a virtuoso, exulting in the game and its rules. The only place for enlargement was in the rules themselves, and thus we may expect to find the detailed working out of most of the subjects outlined in the early handbooks. Aristotle's suggestion of an art of delivery could be taken up and developed. Countless more figures of speech could be added to the Gorgianic few. The uses of direct evidence could be specified. The *stasis* of a speech could be specified beyond the little which Aristotle said. Rhetoric had been created by the needs of Greek society in the fifth century, but once created it perpetuated itself and began in its turn, through its influential role in education, to affect Greek society. The development of rhetoric into a closed system was the prelude to a concept of life and thought as a closed system. This did not take place only in theory, however. The virtuosity of the artist and the decay of serious creativity can be traced in practicing orators in the fourth century coincident with the definition of rhetoric. This process is the subject of the next chapter.

According to tradition the Attic orators are ten in number: Antiphon, Lysias, Andocides, Isocrates, Isaeus, Demosthenes, Aeschines, Lycurgus, Hyperides, and Dinarchus. This "canon" may be Alexandrian or it may have been originated by Caecilius of Calacte, the Augustan critic; his lost work *On the character of the ten orators* is the basis of the *Lives of the ten orators* preserved among the works of Plutarch.[1] The canon was not recognized by Dionysius of Halicarnassus, a contemporary of Caecilius, but was familiar to Quintilian (10.1.76) a hundred years later. Due partly to the canon, orations of these ten writers have survived, and no doubt partly as a result of its existence certain other writers' works are largely lost. We have only a very few orations by other Greek orators of the classical period. Some of the speeches attributed by the manuscripts to Lysias and Demosthenes are the work of others; Plato's *Apology* and *Menexenus* can be regarded as speeches; and there are speeches in other dialogues of Plato. Speeches based on spoken words are found in Thucydides and Xenophon, and Dionysius of Halicarnassus quotes bits from some works which we do not have by authors both in and out of the canon. Finally, there exist in manuscripts short speeches, often dismissed as rhetorical exercises, by Gorgias and Antisthenes.

Studies of Greek oratory have tended to do one or both of two things: to analyze the characteristics and especially the stylistic characteristics of separate orators, largely

[1] Cf. J. Brzoska, *De canone decem oratorum Atticorum quaestiones*, Breslau, 1883; P. Hartman, *De canone decem oratorum*, Göttingen, 1891; O. Kröhnert, *Canonesne poetarum, scriptorum, artificium per antiquitatem fuerunt*, Königsberg, 1897; Ernest Offenloch, *Caecilii Calactini fragmenta*, Leipzig, 1907, xxi ff. and 89 ff.

under the influence of categories set up by Dionysius of Halicarnassus, or to study the legal or political situation which produced the speech.[2] Perhaps there should be added a small group of works, mostly articles, designed to show some of the insight and interest which can be found in the orators, who are often even closer to private realities than was contemporary comedy.[3] These goals have been more or less satisfactorily dealt with and will not be stressed here. The subject of this chapter will be the course of oratory as a literary genre and the relationship between its development and the development of rhetorical theory, a subject which seems to have a universal significance as a study of literary causation.

Judicial Oratory from Antiphon to Isaeus

Chapter two considered the beginnings of Greek oratory in Homer, the Homeric hymns, and the dramatists and historians of the fifth century. This history may now be resumed with the writers of judicial speeches, which was the most characteristic form of Greek oratory. Their activities, as has been said, were made possible by Athenian laws requiring litigants to speak in court on their own behalf.[4]

[2] Of these studies of oratory the two most famous are the works of Blass and Jebb. There is also J. F. Dobson, *The Greek orators*, London, 1919. On the legal side cf. J. H. Lipsius, *Das attische Recht und Rechtverfahren*, 3 vols., Leipzig, 1905-1915; Robert J. Bonner, *Lawyers and litigants in ancient Athens*, Chicago, 1927; Bonner and Smith 1 and 2.

[3] Cf. e.g. Robert J. Bonner, "Wit and humor in Athenian courts," CP 17 (1922) 97 ff.; E. S. Forster, "Guilty or not guilty?" *Greece and Rome* 12 (1943) 21 ff.; Kathleen Freeman, *The murder of Herodes and other trials from the Athenian law courts*, London, 1946.

[4] Male citizens or citizens of allied states under treaty of reciprocity with Athens could bring suit. Others, including women and slaves, had to be represented in litigation by a citizen, though women and children could give evidence and evidence could be taken from slaves under torture. A litigant could ask the aid of an advocate who would speak after himself or in place of himself if he was incapaci-

There was no requirement that litigants write their own speeches, however, and a number of gifted artists developed a brisk trade in custom-made speeches. We get a fleeting glimpse of the transaction in Aristophanes' *Clouds* (459-475):

Chorus: If you learn these things (rhetoric) from me you will have enormous fame among men.

Strepsiades: What shall I get?

Chorus: For all time with me you will lead the life men envy most.

Strepsiades: Shall I really see this?

Chorus: Yes, many men will always be sitting at your gates wishing to meet and have an interview with you and bringing counteraccusations involving many talents and consulting about business with you worthy of your genius.

Presumably a litigant or prospective litigant would call upon a speechwriter, a logographer, and furnish him with information about the case. The latter worked this up into a speech, perhaps consulting the litigant along the way, and perhaps, but not necessarily, interviewing witnesses. The prices were probably relatively high, but no doubt the zeal of the speechwriter was proportional to the price promised. It would be interesting to know to what extent the speechwriter acted as a lawyer, searching for evidence, examining the law, advising on the conduct of the case, and to what extent his function was simply literary. Isaeus surely furnished not only a literate speech but legal advice on the complexities of the law of heredity. On the other hand, Lysias in the eighteenth and twenty-first speeches seems to have composed only the peroration. Could a

---

tated. Nominally the court had to give its consent for the introduction of an advocate. It was illegal to pay advocates, but they doubtless often received valuable "gifts." Cf. Bonner and Smith 1.310 ff. and 2.7 ff.

litigant ask several writers to submit speeches and then choose between them? Did writers offer unsolicited speeches to litigants? Both seem unlikely, though Lysias is said to have offered Socrates a completed *Apology* (Cicero, *De oratore* 1.231). Did the speechwriter help the litigant to rehearse, listening to his delivery and advising him about gestures? We do not know. Did the general public know who had written a speech at the time of delivery? Sometimes, but there are very few references by litigants to the speechwriter of the opponent (e.g. Isaeus 1.7 and Aeschines 1.94). Usually the skill of the opponent himself is attacked and the whole convention of ghostwriting carefully masked. Subsequently the speechwriter published speeches or collections of speeches which he had written for various clients, no doubt choosing successful ones for the most part.[5] Some polishing was often done between the oral and written presentation; Lysias 12.25, for example, could not have been written ahead of time, and there was always a temptation, to which Cicero was to yield in the case of Milo, to publish what a writer wished he had said and to insert anticipations of the arguments of an opponent. The ordinary motives of literary publication were reinforced among the logographers by a desire to advertise the writer's ability. Sometimes the litigant's manuscript may have been the basis of publication; for example, it is not altogether clear whether Isocrates personally published the speeches which he wrote for hire.

We have speeches written to be delivered by others from the pens of Antiphon, Lysias, Isaeus, Isocrates, Demosthenes, Hyperides, and Dinarchus. Many others, including

---

[5] In most cases we do not know the outcome of the trial. The following certainly or probably failed: Andocides 2 and 3, Lysias 26, Isaeus 6, Aeschines 3, Demosthenes 19, Dinarchus 2 and 3, and Lycurgus 1, also the published, but now lost speech of Antiphon in his own defense. Lysias' published speeches are said (*Lives of the ten orators* 836a) to have lost only twice.

writers represented by spurious speeches in the corpus of Lysias and Demosthenes, engaged in the same activity. Antiphon, Lysias, and Isaeus are primarily known as logographers, and the development of the form may be seen by a study of their works.

Antiphon

Antiphon was born about 480 B.C. and was tried and executed for treason in 411 as a consequence of his influential role in the oligarchical revolution of that year.[6] His extant works include the three *Tetralogies*,[7] written sometime between the 440's and 420's, *On the choreutês* (419/8), *Against the stepmother* (about 416) and *On the murder of Herodes* (about 414).[8] In antiquity there were at least thirty-five genuine speeches in existence, including the famous defense of himself on trial for his life.[9] We have fragments of this and other speeches. All the extant speeches are concerned with homicide, but none of the fragmentary speeches are. Stylistically Antiphon was regarded as "austere," and his works have been compared to those of Aeschylus and Thucydides. Both in ancient and

[6] The principal sources of Antiphon's biography are Thucydides 8.68 and 90 and the first of the *Lives of the ten orators* in the corpus of Plutarch, cf. the edition with translation by Harold N. Fowler in the tenth volume of the Loeb Library's *Plutarch's Moralia*, Cambridge, 1936. The speeches and fragments of Antiphon are adequately translated in the Loeb Library *Minor Attic orators* by K. J. Maidment, Cambridge, 1941.

[7] Speeches will be cited either by their English titles or occasionally by their number as given in standard texts (Oxford, Teubner, Budé, Loeb). Tradition calls for Latinization of titles, but the results are often cumbersome or contrived. The principal subtlety in the Greek titles is the use of κατά (Latin *in*) for prosecution "against" someone; πρός (Latin *adversus*) for replies "to" someone's attack; ὑπέρ (Latin *pro*) for speeches "in behalf of." Sometimes (e.g. *On the crown*) a speech bears a traditional title with the preposition περί (Latin *de*).

[8] Cf. K. J. Dover, "The chronology of Antiphon's speeches," CQ 44 (1950) 44 ff.

[9] According to Caecilius as reported in *Lives of the ten orators* 833c.

modern times he has frequently been confused with Antiphon the sophist and other writers of the same name.

According to Thucydides (8.68.1) Antiphon was the man most able to help anyone who consulted him about a case in the courts or the assembly; he was a complete legal advisor, not just a speech writer. From the tone of Thucydides' account it seems that Antiphon's works represent the best technique of the time. Three of the extant works, the so-called *Tetralogies*, are not real cases, but model speeches, two for and two against a defendant in three different murder cases. They are apparently genuine, but earlier than the other three speeches, which seem to deal with real cases.[10] In general the *Tetralogies* are in accord with the teachings of the rhetorical handbooks: they rely on argument from probability, and they follow the prescribed divisions of judicial speeches except that the narrative is omitted. Is this because these are not real cases and there are no facts to narrate? The cases are specific enough to have made it possible to include a narration if Antiphon had wished. A better explanation might be that the *Tetralogies* were written before knowledge of the techniques of Tisias in Sicily had reached Athens and that it was not yet the custom to set aside a separate narrative.[11] This seems possible if they were written in the late forties or early thirties—a date supported by the fact that Pericles and Protagoras are said (Plutarch, *Pericles* 36.3) to have discussed the question of how responsibility should be fixed

[10] Cf. H. Richards, "On Greek orators," CR 20 (1906) 148 ff. and G. Zuntz, "Once again the Antiphontean *Tetralogies*," *Museum Helveticum* 6 (1949) 100 ff.

[11] The *hypothesis* to the first *Tetralogy* comments on the absence of a *katastasis* and blames it on the fact that the art was not yet "perfected." *Katastasis* is sometimes used to mean narration (e.g. Radermacher A.v.16), sometimes prooemium (e.g. Radermacher A.v.22). Reliable accounts of early rhetoric indicate that *diêgêsis* was the usual term for narration from the beginning.

for the death of a boy accidentally killed by a javelin in a gymnasium, which is the subject of the *Second tetralogy*.[12] Antiphon is never very good at narrative; his first speech omits it entirely, and it is short and slightly confused in the fifth and sixth speeches. Perhaps he recognized the logic of having a narrative section but never quite learned how to make use of its peculiar advantages to present the character of the speaker and color the audience's picture of what had happened.

The three speeches delivered in actual court cases, with the exception of the omission of the narrative in number one, are also in general accord with the teaching of fifth century rhetoric,[13] although Antiphon shows greater freedom in his arrangement of material than do later speechwriters. He tends to pick out one argument and present it early in the speech, and he does not systematically exhaust all possible arguments. Argument from probability plays an important role, but it is less conspicuous than in the *Tetralogies* or in his speech in his own defense, where he argues (col. 3) that it is improbable he would have worked for establishment of an oligarchy. The major problem in the three speeches written for delivery seems to be how to correlate direct evidence and argument from probability.[14] In comparison with Lysias or Isaeus, Antiphon often seems almost at a loss; there is little sureness of touch in proof, little of the self-confident manipulation of argument which

[12] Protagoras seems to have visited Athens twice during Pericles' lifetime, once about 444 and once about 432; cf. Kathleen Freeman, *Companion to the pre-Socratic philosophers*, Oxford, 1949, 343 and Untersteiner 3.
[13] Cf. Eduard Schwartz, "Commentatio de Thrasymacho Chalcedonio," *Index scholarum in academia Rostochiensi* (1892) 9-10. Schwartz pointed out what he regarded as a characteristic fifth-century feature of the proof, namely, the attack on the opponent, τὰ πρὸς τὸν ἀντίδικον, to be found also in Gorgias and Euripides.
[14] Cf. Friedrich Solmsen, *Antiphonstudien* (*Neue philologische Untersuchungen* 8), Berlin, 1931, 4 ff. and 17 ff.

the writers of the fourth century attain.[15] The contentions of Antiphon are rarely *proved*, either logically or apparently, and in most of the speeches more could have been done in preparation or could have been said in the speech. In *Against the stepmother* no direct evidence or witnesses of any kind are produced; in a kind of fatalistic way the speaker makes what he can of the refusal of the defense to hand over slaves for examination.[16] Granted that the slaves would have been the best witnesses, an impression of veracity could have been produced by direct substantiation of some minor points in the narration. *On the choreutês* would have been much improved by a detailed discussion of the way the medicine which caused the choir boy's death was administered and why.[17] A fourth-century orator would perhaps have done considerably more to discredit the opponents. The fifth speech, *On the murder of Herodes*, is apparently the latest of the three and is somewhat better in all these respects than the other two, though still without complete self-assurance and polish.

The speeches of Antiphon as examples of rhetorical art, then, have weaknesses. Argument is not satisfactorily handled, opponents are attacked, but the ethos of the speaker is not used as a means of proof, and pathos is not very much developed.[18] Failure to exhaust the possibilities of argument can be compared to the fifth-century habit of concentrating on a single argument in deliberative oratory, but there the technique is much more effective than it is in judicial speeches. Yet the orations of Antiphon

[15] Cf. Dover, *op.cit.* supra n. 8, 45. For a more complimentary view of Antiphon's abilities cf. Umberto Albini, "Antifonte logografo," *Maia* 10 (1958) 38 ff. and 132 ff.

[16] The speech is sympathetically discussed by U. von Wilamowitz-Moellendorf, "Die erste Rede des Antiphon," *Hermes* 22 (1887) 194 ff.

[17] Cf. Kathleen Freeman, "The mystery of the choreutes," *Studies in honor of Gilbert Norwood*, Toronto, 1952, 85 ff.

[18] On ethos in Antiphon cf. Ivo Bruns, *Das literarische Porträt der Griechen*, Berlin, 1896, 430 ff.

have certain virtues, which were sometimes to be lost later. He is generally fair to his opponents; he attacks them (e.g. *Against the stepmother* 21 f.) without introducing irrelevant scandals.[19] He sticks very close to the subject and avoids any diversionary temptations. He feels free to arrange the material in what seems the best way rather than feeling bound by rhetorical rules. Stylistically, too, the speeches are quite free.[20]

Lysias

Born, perhaps, in 444 B.C. in Athens, Lysias was the son of Cephalus of Syracuse, a metic, or resident alien, who was a friend of Pericles and whose home is the scene of Plato's *Republic*.[21] About 429 Lysias transferred his residence to the colony of Thurii in southern Italy, perhaps for political, perhaps for business reasons, and lived there as a citizen until Athenian connexions led to the expulsion of himself and about three hundred others after the failure of the Athenian expedition to Sicily (415-413). Returning to Athens he prospered as a manufacturer of shields during the latter part of the Peloponnesian war. In 404 much of his property was confiscated by the Thirty Tyrants, his

[19] Cf. Schwartz, *op.cit.* supra n. 13 and Dobson, *op.cit.* supra n. 2, 34 f.

[20] Cf. Jebb 1.18 ff.; Richards, *op.cit.* supra n. 10; Dover, *op.cit.* supra n. 8.

[21] The traditional date of 459 for the birth of Lysias seems too early; it probably resulted from a belief that he must have gone to Thurii in the year of its foundation (444 B.C.). Since he was allegedly fifteen when he emigrated, he must have been born, it was reasoned, in 459. Cf. Friedrich Ferckel, *Lysias und Athen*, Würzburg, 1937, 12 f. The principal sources of the life of Lysias are the references in the twelfth speech (*Against Eratosthenes*), the fragments in *Oxyrhynchus papyri* 1606 (vol. 14, London, 1919), the essay by Dionysius of Halicarnassus (there is no English translation, but for a French version cf. A. M. Desrousseaux and Max Egger, *Denys d'Halicarnasse: Jugement sur Lysias*, Paris, 1890), and the *Lives of the ten orators*, cf. supra n. 6. A complete translation of Lysias by W. R. M. Lamb, London, 1930, is available in the Loeb Library.

brother Polemarchus was put to death, and Lysias himself barely escaped with his life to Megara, where he aided the cause of the Athenian democrats. On their return to Athens he was briefly a full-citizen, but lost the right because the grant had not had the recommendation of the council before its adoption by the assembly. His interest in rhetoric and oratory may have begun under the influence of sophists at his father's house in Athens or he may have met Tisias in Thurii as the ancient biographer says. According to Cicero (*Brutus* 48) Lysias conducted a school briefly, perhaps in the period 403-401. After 401 he supported himself largely if not entirely from the sale of speeches to litigants.[22] Caecilius accepted two hundred and thirty-three speeches as genuine, a very large number in comparison with the other orators. We have, in addition to some fragments, thirty-four speeches attributed to Lysias, including three large portions of speeches preserved by Dionysius of Halicarnassus. Of the speeches one is a funeral oration, one is part of an epideictic speech written for someone to deliver in the assembly. The rest are judicial. The speech attributed to Lysias in Plato's *Phaedrus* is a parody.[23] The sixth speech (*Against Andocides*), the eighth speech (a strange accusation of calumny not made before a court of law), and the twentieth speech (*For Polystratus*) are probably not by Lysias.[24] The authenticity of the *Funeral*

[22] An unsatisfactory attempt to disprove this was made by Angela C. Darkow, *The spurious speeches in the Lysianic corpus*, Bryn Mawr, 1917, 7 ff. She seems to have thought that Lysias wrote and published two hundred and thirty-three or more speeches as literary exercises.

[23] Cf. Alfred Croiset, *Histoire de la littérature grecque* 4, Paris, 1900, 435 ff.; Paul Shorey, "On the *Erotikos* of Lysias in Plato's *Phaedrus*," CP 28 (1933) 131 f.; George E. Dimock, Jr., "Ἀλλά in Lysias and Plato's *Phaedrus*," AJP 73 (1952) 381 ff. and esp. 392 ff.; supra p. 76.

[24] In the case of the sixth speech the diction, composition, arrangement, tone, and lack of tact all seem unlike Lysias; cf. Jebb 1.280 ff. Blass 1.259 notes that a speech *Against Andocides* was attributed to Theodorus of Byzantium. The eighth speech, besides being a very unlikely case for Lysias to undertake, is not in his style; for example, it seems to avoid hiatus, cf. Blass 1.640 ff. The twentieth speech was

oration (2) cannot be proved, but has always had sup-porters.[25] The greatest of the speeches, that *Against Eratosthenes* (12), was written to be delivered by Lysias himself in 403. The *Olympic oration* (33) of 388 was also probably spoken by Lysias: it attacks Dionysius of Syracuse and urges the Greeks to cooperate among themselves. Lysias seems to have been active until about 380 and may have lived well into the 370's (Demosthenes 59.21).

Lysias made two great contributions to Greek oratory. The first was a prose style which, though influential and appreciated in his own day, was to become the standard of Attic purity and grace three hundred and fifty years later. It is the simple style in all its elegance, unadorned, yet never bald, unenlivened, yet never dull. The basis of it was first a vocabulary which consciously distinguished the proper word for each object, action, and quality and which was the practical and artistic objective at which the philological and lexicographical researches of the late fifth century aimed. In addition, Lysias profited from the experience in composition of Herodotus, Thucydides, Gorgias, Antiphon, Thrasymachus, and his other predecessors; without their mannerisms, he makes use of period, antithesis, claus-ulae, and asyndeta woven together as he sees fit. Since there had been a Gorgias and was to be an Isocrates it was well that there was a Lysias.[26]

Lysias' second great gift to oratory was ethopoiia, his technique of conveying something of the character of the speaker into the orations he wrote for a customer to de-

---

written for a trial soon after 411 and is probably too early to be by Lysias.

[25] The most extensive recent defense seems to be J. Walz, "Der lysianische *Epitaphios*," *Philologus Supplementband* 29.4 (1936). Cf. also Marcel Bizos' defense in Louis Gernet and Marcel Bizos, *Lysias: Discours* 1, Paris, 1955, 41 ff.

[26] On the style of Lysias cf. the essay of Dionysius (cf. supra n. 21); Blass 1.383 ff.; Jebb 1.155 ff.

liver. This is one part of a practical recognition, to be made later on the theoretical level, that character is an important means of proof or refutation. The speech was expected to appear more genuine and less rehearsed if it seemed to be the work of the speaker himself. All speakers must aim at securing the good will of the judges, but Lysias tried to counteract the bad effect of the sameness of such attempts by presenting a variety of personalities. By showing some trivial human weaknesses of character he establishes a rapport with the audience and convinces them of the general human virtue of his client. In the first speech, for example, the defendant is old-fashioned and blunt in his ways; one might not choose him for a friend or even much respect him, but because of Lysias' portrayal it is difficult to believe that he has laid a subtle trap for his wife's lover and very easy to believe that he killed the lover when taken in the act of adultery. The young man in speech sixteen bluffs his way through a tight spot by a candid self-confidence. Most famous of all, perhaps, is the so-called cripple of speech twenty-four, who is in danger of losing his pension from the state; Lysias wins considerable confidence for a rather suspicious customer by a kind of sarcastic humor. In general this character portrayal is effected by the thought rather than the style. What the speaker says, his demonstrations of pride or folly, show what he is like. Lysias does not attempt to vary the diction to suit the speaker, and farmers, merchants, and aristocrats all speak the same simple, flawless Attic.[27]

It is possible to use character as a form of proof in a more direct way. A speaker can openly defend his own character, especially if he is being attacked by someone else, or he can attack the character of his opponent, whether he is

[27] Cf. W. Motschmann, *Die Charactere bei Lysias*, Munich, 1906, and O. Buechler, *Die Unterscheidung der redenden Personen bei Lysias: eine stylische Untersuchung der Diêgêsis*, Heidelberg, 1936, 31 ff.

prosecutor or defendant. We have noted that Antiphon does only a little of this; Lysias, as might be expected, does much more. In many speeches a section on character follows directly after the specific proof or refutation of the charge. In *Against Eratosthenes*, for example, after the initial proof of the part of Eratosthenes in the arrest of Polemarchus (25-36), Lysias remarks (37 f.) that what he has said is probably sufficient indictment, for Eratosthenes cannot follow the common custom of ignoring the specific charges and pointing out his services to the state. Apparently diversionary tactics were already becoming common. Lysias, however, takes the opportunity to attack his opponent with a list of the latter's disservices to the state, supported by witnesses. This runs for ten sections; it is not relevant to the specific charge made, but it helps to discredit Eratosthenes further by acquainting the audience with his habitual conduct. Later on in the same speech (70 ff.) Lysias further extends the scope of his attack to include the emotionally weighted name of Theramenes. All of this is logically irrelevant, but it is rhetorically effective in producing an impression of character and in directing the judges' emotions. It seems at least possible that the strong party feelings arising out of the troubles at the close of the Peloponnesian war and during the period of the Thirty Tyrants were in part responsible for the appearance of invective and for the introduction of emotional, semi-irrelevant proof. Another example is the speech *Against Agoratus*. Agoratus was prosecuted for causing the death of a relative of the speaker under the Thirty. In section thirty-three and more specifically in forty-three Lysias begins a systematic extension of the charge so that virtually all the misfortunes of Athens are blamed on the villainous, but insignificant, person of Agoratus. Later (62 ff.), as in other speeches, Lysias specifically deals with the character of those involved, and the patriotic citizens who were murdered are contrasted with the slave-born Agoratus who survives. A further step has actually been taken here toward the irresponsible character assassination of mid-fourth-century oratory in that Agoratus' slave birth is harped upon and his private vices of slander, immorality, and adultery are brought in (67 f.).[28]

The violence of Lysias' feelings against the oligarchs as expressed in the speeches *Against Eratosthenes* and *Against Agoratus* is understandable. Most of the other speeches also show a preference for the democrats, but in a couple of cases Lysias seems to have agreed to write on behalf of those who were at least compromised. The *Defense of Mantitheus* (16) is perhaps a case of this: Mantitheus was accused of having served in the cavalry in 404-403 under the Thirty. He denies the charge, however, and asserts that he is a supporter of the democracy. The twenty-fifth speech is a defense on an unspecified charge, probably as a part of a scrutiny, by a man who had remained in Athens under the Thirty and probably sympathized with them, although he held no office. Another speech which has been partially recovered on papyrus, the *Defense of Eryximachus* on a charge of having remained in Athens in 404, is a very similar case.[29]

On the basis of these speeches Lysias has been sternly attacked as a political opportunist who avoided all personal danger in the Peloponnesian war and the revolution, yet constantly aspired to citizenship, who talked about democracy, but whose concern was primarily with money and whose views on most subjects varied with what appeared to be his own advantage.[30] Such a stricture seems excessive;

[28] On the general subject of slander and invective cf. Walter Voegelin, *Die Diabolê bei Lysias*, Basel, 1943, and Bruns, *op. cit.* supra n. 18, 438 ff.

[29] Cf. H. J. M. Milne, "A new speech of Lysias," *Journal of Egyptian archaeology* 15 (1929) 75 ff.

[30] Cf. Ferckel, *op.cit.* supra n. 21. The concluding pages show that Ferckel is in part influenced by a Nazi attitude toward the

real participation in and identification with the cause of the democracy was naturally difficult for metics, and if this is to be blamed, the exclusiveness of the Athenian democracy is equally at fault. Lysias was not an Athenian citizen with the secure ties of family and clan, but a foreigner forced to live by his own wits. None of those defended by Lysias were active oligarchs; none of them had apparently committed personally any acts of violence. It seems possible that Lysias was liberal enough to undertake the defense of these men in the same way a modern lawyer might. The right to defend oneself was part of the democratic tradition. Lysias' technical agility in expressing that defense was not a political act on his part, for to refuse a client under these circumstances would be analogous to a refusal on the part of a magistrate to hear a defense. This view of oratory had not been shared by Antiphon, who seems to have restricted himself largely to oligarchic clients and to have felt much more of a sense of positive political purpose. Lysias' comfort to oligarchs is limited to their legal defense. He did not write prosecutions in their interests.

A second way of viewing Lysias' attitude toward clients and the presentation of their cases is to regard each speech as an intellectual challenge. Rhetoric tends to dissociate itself from philosophy or creed. While still pretending to be a tool to the attainment of truth, each individual speech becomes a thing in itself to be admired and enjoyed. The necessity of fairness in presenting both sides of the case is forgotten and immediate persuasion becomes the sole object, divorced from all considerations of the subject which might detract from persuasion. Writing a speech is therefore a technical, artistic challenge. This view of the work seems to be strong in some later orators and present at least occasionally in Lysias, especially in the speeches *For*

Jews, to whom he compares the metics. Despite this blemish the thesis contains some shrewd insights into Lysias' activities.

Mantitheus and *For the invalid*. In both cases by deft combination of argument and skilful portrayal of character,
Lysias manages to make what really must be called the
worse seem the better cause. Only by careful critical reading, which of course the judges in court could not give,
does the art become evident. Lysias was not necessarily
willing to write for anyone who would pay him, but he was
willing to write in any case which interested him. He is not
primarily a political philosopher, but an artist.

Chronologically the next logographer is Isocrates, who was
born in 436 and engaged in the writing of judicial speeches
in the period between 403 and 393 B.C. Isocrates' later
epideictic works were to overshadow his early productions
of which six have, however, survived. These are relatively
simple in style, but there is enough of the characteristic
manner of Isocrates to show that the law courts of the first
decade of the fourth century heard something other than
the style of Lysias from time to time. The *Aegineticus* is
probably the best of the six, persuasive in argument, fitted
out with an ethopoiia worthy of Lysias, and achieving a
natural and effective pathos as the speaker narrates his
faithful care of the friend whose estate he claims. This is,
incidentally, the only extant speech written for delivery
in a non-Athenian court (Aegina). Despite the ability
demonstrated it does not appear that Isocrates made any
special contribution to this form of oratory. The use of
political prejudice as a form of proof is striking in four of
the speeches (16, 18, 20, and 21), but had been used by
Lysias. These works are important for the historical, economic, and legal information they contain.

Isaeus

Very little is known of the life of Isaeus, probably
because his activities were limited to writing speeches
for litigants. Dionysius of Halicarnassus says only that
he came from Athens or Chalcis, lived in the fourth

century, was a pupil of Isocrates, and taught Demosthenes. With this the biography in the *Lives of the ten orators* is in general agreement. The fifth speech is apparently the earliest and may be dated 390/389 B.C.; the latest of the speeches (12) belongs to 344/343. This suggests that the orator was quite young in 390. Perhaps he was born around 415. The connexion with Demosthenes is probable, since the latter's four early speeches against his guardians show similarities to passages in Isaeus.[31] Out of sixty-four speeches attributed to Isaeus in antiquity, of which Caecilius accepted fifty, we have twelve—eleven on testamentary cases, which was probably his specialty, and one preserved by Dionysius of Halicarnassus, (*Isaeus* 17) on a case of civil rights. There are also a number of fragments.

The oratory of Isaeus is the triumph of technique. No testamentary case, for his art was specialized, seems to have been too great a challenge for him to undertake. Isaeus himself and his opinions are never evident, of course. Furthermore, the morality of the case is no concern of his. His sole object is to solve a rhetorical and legal problem, to effect persuasion out of given materials. Like the other orators he was aided by the fact that the speech would be orally delivered only once before a large jury which would have little opportunity to examine it carefully, and the particular field of testamentary law especially lent itself to his tactics since many of the cases were of limited interest and great complexity. It is easy to see why the litigants needed the services of a logographer, and in Isaeus they undoubtedly found an authority on the delicate points of the law of inheritance. The jurors could not be expected to be deeply and personally interested nor to carry very many of the facts long in their minds. An impression of righteousness, logic, and clarity for a few minutes was all

[31] Cf. William Wyse, *The speeches of Isaeus*, Cambridge, Eng., 1904, 591 f., 597 f., 606, 624. For a translation of Isaeus cf. E. S. Forster in the Loeb Library, London 1927.

that was needed, and this Isaeus could secure. Despite a deserved reputation for slyness (Dionysius of Halicarnassus, *Isaeus* 4) he seems to have been very successful.

Something of his boldness and technique can be illustrated from the very first speech. A certain Cleonymus has died without issue and left a will bequeathing his property to relatives who are not the closest by blood. Some nearer relatives claim the property, relying no doubt on the prejudice in favor of blood over testamentary wish. Isaeus' problem in writing for these relatives is to invalidate the will, which is unfortunately quite legal, well attested, and even deposited with a magistrate for safe-keeping. His general approach is to show that the friendship between Cleonymus and the two sets of relatives reversed itself in the period after the will was written, so that the testator came to favor the nearer relations. Even if such a reversal had taken place, legally the will would still be valid, but Isaeus maintains that to have failed to change the will under the altered circumstances would be irrational. Thus, either Cleonymus was *trying* to change his will and being prevented by its beneficiaries, in which case justice demands the rejection of the will, or else, since he should have wanted to change it, he must have been insane, in which case (21 and 50) the will is invalid. In preparation for this dilemma Isaeus appears to confirm each step of his narration and argument, though actually the witnesses do not establish the crucial fact of any intent to alter the will. In the development of the argument each admission of the opponents is seized upon and interpreted: they admitted that the dying Cleonymus asked to see his will, but claimed he did not intend to change it. Isaeus (22) describes the situation as follows:

". . . alleging Cleonymus to be calling the magistrate to confirm their bequest, though ordered, they did not dare to bring him in, but they even sent away the one of the archons who came to the door. Of two alternatives, either to possess the inheritance more securely or to annoy Cleonymus by not doing what he asked, they preferred his enmity to the bequest! How could anything be less believable than this?"

On reflection it is perfectly clear that many other interpretations of the action, if it took place at all, are possible and the alternatives suggested by Isaeus, which seem so clearcut, are entirely imaginary. Perhaps Cleonymus was too sick to see anyone; perhaps the archon who came to call was a friend who had nothing to do with the will or the "magistrate" who kept it. But the jury was not intended to have time for such doubts; all was too positive not to be accepted.

Or consider this argument (36 f.):

"I think that you might learn what is just in our case most clearly from the men themselves. If someone should ask them why they think it right for them to become the heirs of Cleonymus, they might reply that they are related to him in such-and-such a way and that he was on friendly terms with them for some time. But would not these reasons be more appropriate for us than for them? For if one becomes an heir on the basis of affinity of blood, we are more closely related. If it is through the existence of friendship, all know that he was more familiarly associated with us."

Up to this point the genuineness of the will has not been questioned, but with assumed candor, relying on the respect for blood ties, Isaeus is even ready to suggest that it is a forgery (41 f.):

"You all know what a tie of blood is, and it is not possible for this to be misrepresented to you. But many in the past have produced false wills, some complete forgeries, or wills not accomplishing the intent of the deceased. In our case you know our relationship and the fact of our familiarity with the deceased on which we base our claim. Not one of you really knows the authenticity of the will, trusting in which they make their slanderous allegations."

And so on to a repetition of the dilemma of insanity or undue interference. This speech is not unusually tricky, but represents the standard technique of Isaeus. Somewhat similar attacks on the validity of wills are also to be found in the fourth, ninth, and tenth speeches.

Isaeus did not or could not imitate Lysias' techniques of ethopoiia: the speakers in the twelve speeches all reveal the same intense earnestness.[32] This is the most effective way to carry off sophistic arguments. On the other hand, most of the speeches make direct use of character as means of proof; both the worthiness of Isaeus' client and the worthlessness of the opposition are demonstrated (e.g. 4.27 ff. and 8.40 ff.), and the motives of characters are carefully revealed. Occasionally an attempt is made to evoke some particular emotion in the judges. In the second speech, for example, there is repeated and effective insistence on the horrors of childlessness and the fact that the opponent wishes to deprive Menecles of a son (e.g. 2.1, 7, 10, 11, 12, 13, 14, 20, 22, 23, 24, 25, 27, 33, 35, 37, 43, 46). It is in logical argument, however, that Isaeus is most successful. Better than any of his predecessors, he can make what direct evidence there is seem to go a long way by careful extensions of it with argument from probability. Jebb describes Isaeus' "art of grappling," in which the speaker seems to engage in a kind of rapid-fire debate with his opponent, though in monologue.[33] Dionysius of Halicarnassus had quoted what we now call the twelfth speech as an example of this; it is undoubtedly the best one available, but many other speeches (e.g. 8.28-34) contain similar passages. One of the secrets of the technique is a logical fullness of expression

[32] Cf. Bruns, *op.cit.* supra n. 18, 531 ff.   [33] Jebb 2.304 ff.

by which each of the steps in the argument is expressed. Dionysius (*Isaeus* 16) said that Isaeus differed from Lysias in speaking by epicheireme rather than by enthymeme, by which he means that Isaeus expresses full logical syllogisms whereas Lysias tends to suppress one part.

The technical supremacy of Isaeus is aided by an artistic sense which shows him the master rather than the slave of his own rhetoric. Although in general he conforms to the pattern of prooemium, narration, proof, peroration—the latter a short recapitulation only—he is alive to the great effectiveness of departing from this scheme in specific cases. In the seventh and eleventh speeches the conventional type of prooemium is discarded for direct confrontation of the points at issue. The third speech begins directly with a short narration; the sixth speech consists almost entirely of narration (3-50). This freedom is solely a result of devotion to persuasion as the object of oratory. Probably it, as well as the logical force and earnestness of Isaeus, contributed to the eloquence of Demosthenes. The two differ chiefly in that Isaeus' art was much more specialized and circumscribed. Whether this was because of difference in political status or of personality we cannot judge.

Not all litigants hired the services of a logographer, but unless a litigant was thoroughly familiar with the conventions of the courts and had studied the handbooks of the rhetoricians he was at a decided disadvantage. This can be seen in the case of Andocides, who came of an old and distinguished family and may have felt some scorn for upstart speechwriters, many of whom were metics.

Andocides

Born about 440 B.C., Andocides early became active in a political club which opposed the radical demagogues and especially Alcibiades.[34] He was implicated

[34] Sources for his life are first of all his own speeches *On his return* and *On the mysteries*, to a lesser extent the biography in the

in the mutilation of the herms in 415, by which his political friends tried to prevent the sailing of the Sicilian expedition, and was exiled. Three times he attempted to return: in 411 under the oligarchy unsuccessfully; about 408 under the restored democracy, also unsuccessfully; and successfully in 403 under the general amnesty. The speech *On his return* was delivered as part of the second attempt. In 399 the old charges were revived by his opponents, who argued that the amnesty could not apply to him. In his defense he delivered his greatest speech, *On the mysteries,* and won his case. In 392 he was sent as an ambassador to Sparta and after his return delivered the speech *On the peace.* The speech was a failure, and he was again exiled. There exists under Andocides' name also a fourth speech, *Against Alcibiades,* relating to the political situation of 415. It has usually been regarded as spurious. Nothing is known of the orator after 392.

Andocides did not write speeches for hire nor was he one of the leading political orators of his time. *On his return* and *On the mysteries* are both defenses of himself, the former a failure, the latter successful. He published them presumably to secure a wider audience for his defense, not to advertise himself as a writer of speeches. *On the peace* is a deliberative speech resulting from his own embassy. Furthermore, the speeches are clearly not the work of one trained in all the conventions and techniques of contemporary rhetoric. It appears that as time passed Andocides became more adept at speaking, and the speech *On the mysteries* is a creditable product, but he is never a typical orator.[35]

The earliest speech, *On his return,* is the least satisfactory. It has a prooemium, narration, and proof, but no satis-

---

Lives of the ten orators (cf. supra n. 6). A translation of the speeches by K. J. Maidment is available in the Loeb Library vol. *Minor Attic orators* 1, Cambridge, 1941.

[35] Cf. George A. Kennedy, "The oratory of Andocides," AJP 79 (1958) 32 ff. *On the peace* is discussed further infra p. 204.

factory conclusion. The proof is weak and based largely on a list of services to Athens; there is little development of the usual topics of argument. Ethos and pathos are lacking; the tone of the speech at times verges on the insolent. In a word, the whole work is what an indignant aristocrat with little knowledge of or patience with the new rhetoric might compose. It is not at all surprising that it was completely ineffective.

In 399 when he delivered *On the mysteries*, Andocides was somewhat more familiar with rhetorical convention and considerably more in control of his tone. He had picked up some of the commonplaces of the courts and had learned to project his character. On the other hand, effective though his defense is, the organization is not what Andocides would have learned from a handbook or a rhetorician. There is still no recapitulation, though one would have been serviceable because of the number of issues involved. The narration and argument are interspersed, a technique later to be recommended by rhetoricians, but probably not noted in the fifth-century handbooks. Most conspicuous is the virtual reliance on direct evidence, even in sections such as the account of the mutilation of the herms, where argument from probability could have been put to good use. As has been said, reliance on direct evidence is characteristic of the older methods of litigation before the development of rhetoric.

After ten years of residence in Athens Andocides became much more familiar with rhetorical convention. *On the peace* has a relatively loose organization, but it does end with a proper peroration carefully drawing the lines of peace and war and appealing to the good will of the audience. The speaker is careful to avoid offense throughout, and most important of all, he deals with all the usual topics of deliberative oratory: necessity (13), practicability (15), honor (17), expediency (17 ff.), and justice (23). The failure of the speech was political rather than rhetorical.

Thus Andocides' career may be taken to show a gradual awareness of rhetorical convention. He has usually been regarded as the poorest of the orators,[36] rightly from a rhetorical view. His importance is derived from the detailed information he preserves, especially on the great scandal of 415, and also from the fact that he shows the conflict between an older and a newer oratory, the one relying on direct evidence and aristocratic self-assurance, the other on argument from probability and winning persuasion.

The fourth speech, *Against Alcibiades*, is something of a puzzle. It is a speech for Phaeax at a meeting of the assembly in 415 considering the ostracism of Alcibiades, Nicias, or the speaker. The situation is unprecedented and improbable historically. From what we have concluded about the art of Andocides the speech cannot have been written by him for delivery on that occasion. It is a competent rhetorical product of the period around 400 and much beyond the abilities, and probably the inclinations, of Andocides in 415. Raubitschek has been able to defend much of the contents of the speech as the possible work of Andocides and suggests that if it were not written on the occasion in 415 it may have been published ten years or so later as a pamphlet in the persistent Alcibiades dispute; in such a case the author has been very careful to avoid anachronism.[37] If the work is by Andocides it must have been written in the period between 403 and 392 when he was gaining familiarity with rhetorical conventions. From what one sees of him in the genuine speeches the prospect of his carefully composing such a pamphlet either for political reasons or as a rhetorical exercise seems improbable, but it cannot

[36] Cf. e.g. Hermogenes, *On characteristics* 2.11 *ad fin*; Quintilian 12.10.21; Philostratus, *Lives of the sophists* 2.1.14. Cf. also Jebb 1.87 ff.

[37] A. E. Raubitschek, "The case against Alcibiades (Andocides iv)," TAPA 79 (1948) 191 ff. In reply cf. C. Hignett, *A history of the Athenian constitution*, Oxford, 1952, 395 f.

entirely be ruled out. On the other hand, the work might well have been attributed to him falsely since he had opposed the Sicilian expedition and the plans of Alcibiades as shown by his involvement in the mutilation of the herms.

Trial of Socrates

No account of Greek oratory would be complete without reference to the single most famous courtroom scene, the trial of Socrates. Plato's *Apology* is obviously not exactly what Socrates said, but critics have varied greatly in the degree of invention they allow to Plato.[38] There is considerable evidence to support the view that Socrates did not deliver a formal defense in the usual way: Plato speaks frequently of the helplessness of a philosopher in the law, though there was no good example other than Socrates;[39] Xenophon (*Apology* 4) reports that Socrates had twice considered the nature of the defense he should give and twice felt himself constrained by his *daimôn* so that in the end he went into court without making any preparations at all, and there is the explicit, but unreliable evidence of Maximus of Tyre (3) that Socrates offered no defense. The large number of defenses published for Socrates after his death[40] and the attempts of Plato in the *Menexenus* and the *Phaedrus* to show that Socrates could construct good oratory, if he wished, contribute to the same impression.

It seems likely that Xenophon wrote his *Apology* for Socrates after the publication of Plato's and endeavored to correct some of the misapprehensions which he felt derived

---

[38] Cf. esp. the attacks on the historicity of the *Apology* by Bruns, *op.cit.* supra n. 18, 203 ff.; Heinrich Gomperz, "Sokrates' Haltung vor seinen Richtern," ws 54 (1936) 32 ff.; W. A. Oldfather, "Socrates in court," cw 31 (1938) 203 ff.

[39] Cf. esp. *Gorgias* 484d-e, 486a-c, 521b ff., 526e, 527a; *Theatetus* 172c ff.; Oldfather, *op.cit.* supra n. 38, 203 and 205.

[40] Oldfather, *op.cit.* supra n. 38, 204 cites works by Plato, Xenophon, Lysias, Theodectes, Demetrius of Phaleron, Zeno of Sidon, Plutarch, Theo of Antioch, and Libanius. Cf. also the discussion of Isocrates' *Busiris* infra pp. 180 ff.

from that work.[41] He deals much more specifically with the charges than does Plato, who composed a more general defense addressed to a wider audience than just the court.[42] Xenophon also felt that Socrates could have defended himself in such a way as to persuade the judges, but would not do so on moral grounds. He blames especially the arrogance (μεγαληγορία) of the address. This arrogance is more clearly marked in the passages which Xenophon puts into Socrates' mouth than in the *Apology* of Plato, though it is present in the latter work. Plato as a skillful rhetorician has attempted, rather successfully, to preserve the character and principles of Socrates and to present him in a way which, though it still probably would not have won a victory in court, has at least won the good will of posterity. From the point of view of the history of rhetoric the trial seems to show much what the speech *On his return* by Andocides showed, that success in court demanded observance of certain rhetorical conventions, of which the most important was the establishment of a sympathetic rapport between speaker and audience. Lysias is said to have offered Socrates a written defense, and Cicero (*De oratore* 1.231) seems to have believed that it would have secured Socrates' acquittal, but Socrates refused to use it. (Cf. also Diogenes Laertius 2.40).

Though he cannot stoop to flattery or indulge in emotional appeal, and though the argument of the speech is not developed in the usual way—the cross-examination of

[41] Cf. Anton Hermann Chroust, *Socrates, man and myth*, London, 1957, 17 ff. Chroust dates the *Apology* of Xenophon sometime after 385/384 since it mentions Anytus as dead and Lysias 22.7 speaks of an Anytus as alive in that year. But they are not necessarily the same person, and the *Apology* may not be quite that late. The view that Xenophon's account is prior to Plato's is defended by R. Hackforth, *The Composition of Plato's Apology*, Cambridge, Eng., 1933, 8 ff.

[42] Cf. Chroust, *op.cit.* supra n. 41,43. The two apologies are compared by L. R. Shero, "Plato's *Apology* and Xenophon's *Apology*," cw 20 (1927) 107 ff.

Meletus is particularly striking—Plato's Socrates does employ many of the commonplaces of contemporary judicial oratory and in general observes the rules for oratorical partition.[43] There is first a prooemium which points out the speaker's lack of court experience and apologizes for his language. That Socrates is truthful in these claims while ordinary litigants often were not is beside the point; Socrates is made to say the conventional things in the conventional place. There follows (18a35 ff.) a statement of the case which fulfills the functions of a narration, then the refutation of the charges,[44] a section (28a1 ff.) like those found in speeches of Lysias demonstrating Socrates' character, and finally a peroration (34b6 ff.) which tries to achieve its objective of demonstrating moral integrity by specifically rejecting the usual pathetic conventions.

There is no hint of this organization in Xenophon, who implies that Socrates dealt immediately and directly with the charges made. We must remember, of course, that Xenophon was not present at the trial and that by his own admission (22) he is not trying to present the entire speech. Both Plato and Xenophon incorporate dialogues with Meletus which, if historical, would indicate that Socrates tried to undertake direct examination like that seen in the trial in the *Eumenides*.

Even if Socrates in delivering his defense tried to abandon the framework of organization taught by the rhetoricians, and this is not certain, Plato in writing the *Apology* did not. He portrays a Socrates thoroughly familiar with the

[43] Cf. A. Rabe, *Platos Apologie und Kriton logisch-rhetorisch analysiert*, 2 parts, Berlin, 1897-1898, and Robert J. Bonner, "The legal setting of Plato's *Apology*," CP 3 (1908) 169 ff.

[44] As in Demosthenes' *On the crown* it is difficult to draw a line between what is properly narration and what is properly refutation: the discussion of the old accusations, which Socrates "refutes" first, forms a valuable narration of background material for the actual present charges. Probably the refutation really begins with the treatment of those present charges in 24b2 ff. Refutation of the earlier charges begins in 19a7.

commonplaces of judicial oratory. Traditional rhetoric was already so deeply implanted in the Greek consciousness that there was no question of any successful deviation from it. In the history of rhetoric that is the great significance of the *Apology*.

Epideictic Oratory[45]

The majority of Greek speeches were written to be delivered in courts of law. There are a few extant works written either before or after their delivery in a political assembly and a couple of dozen other speeches, mostly but not solely the work of Isocrates, which really belong in neither of these categories. Although some of them take the outward form of judicial or deliberative speeches, they were not intended for actual delivery, and though certain conventions exist, the speaker is free to depart from the practical limitations of these genres whenever and however he wishes. In some cases, whatever the real purpose of the speech, the result is a degree of stylistic ornamentation and an indulgence of whim which has caused the works to be regarded as *paignia* or playful exercises by an oratorical virtuoso. More generally these speeches are classed as *epideixeis*, or demonstrations, and the genre is called epideictic. According to Aristotle (*Rhetoric* 1358b2 ff.) they are addressed to spectators, who are concerned with the ability of the speaker, not to judges; they deal mostly with the present, though they may recall the past or anticipate the future; their end is usually the demonstration of the honorable or

---

[45] For ancient theories cf. the little *Art of rhetoric* attributed to Dionysius of Halicarnassus and two treatises on epideictic under the name of the third-century A.D. rhetorician Menander, Spengel 3.331 ff. There is also some discussion in *Rhetorica ad Herennium* 3.10 ff. and Cicero, *De inventione* 2.176 f. and *Partitiones oratoriae* 70 ff. The principal modern studies are Theodore C. Burgess, "Epideictic literature," *Studies in classical philology* 3 (Chicago, 1902) 89-261, usually found bound separately, and Vinzenz Buchheit, *Untersuchungen zur Theorie des Genos epideiktikon von Gorgias bis Aristoteles*, Munich, 1960.

disgraceful, and they are adapted to being read as well as being heard by the exactness and detail of the style (1414a18). Aristotle clearly thinks of epideictic as a speech or pamphlet written to praise or vilify someone or something. The *Rhetorica ad Alexandrum* speaks of the species of praise and blame rather than the genus of epideictic, though such speeches are delivered "not for the sake of contest, but of demonstration" (1440b13). The subdivisions of epideictic recognized in later antiquity, for example, panegyric, encomium, invective, and funeral oration, are all concerned with praising or blaming, and from the rhetorical point of view the more apparently unworthy the subject the greater the achievement: anyone can praise Penelope, but it is more difficult to praise Helen, especially when the rules of the game emphasize the fact that such praise must be largely moral rather than physical (*Rhetorica ad Alexandrum* 1440b20 ff.). This is a form of literature which has relatively few admirers today, but if we are to understand the Greeks thoroughly it seems necessary to understand, if not to share, their love for it. Epideictic is the form of oratory closest in style and function to poetry; both epic and drama are also delivered before spectators rather than before judges of fact or policy. There is no intrinsic reason why the content of epideictic could not be as profound as the content of tragedy. In later antiquity, when the victory of rhetoric in literature was complete, virtually all poetry was regarded as a subdivision of epideictic.[46] The extant remains of epideictic literature can best be dealt with if we discuss first two classes of speeches designed for special occasions and then look one by one at the other principal examples. Such an examination will furnish an introduction to the greatest of the epideictic orators, Isocrates, who experimented with virtually all species and types,

[46] Cf. Hermogenes, *On characteristics* 2.10, p. 389 and 393 Rabe, and Burgess, *op.cit.* supra n. 45, 91 ff.

separately or in combination, and developed to its highest point the peculiar epideictic style.

Funeral Orations

Six documents exist which can, without question, be classified as funeral orations (*epitaphioi*), though perhaps only one or two of them were actually delivered in anything like their present form at one of the memorial services for those who perished in war. Poetic laments were an ancient custom and private funeral orations were probably delivered in many places, but public funeral addresses in honor of all those killed in one year were a peculiar institution of Athens (Demosthenes, *Against Leptines* 141). The custom surely does not antedate the Persian war and it may have been instituted by Cimon in 475,[47] though Plato (*Menexenus* 242c1 f.) says that there were no public funerals between the Persian wars and the battle of Oenophyta in 457. Pericles (Thucydides 2.35) speaks as though the custom were long established. According to Thucydides (2.34) public funeral orations were delivered regularly throughout the Peloponnesian war. The most interesting rhetorical feature of such speeches is the highly formulaic quality which they achieved almost immediately. Not only general organization but the topics to be mentioned became traditional in the way that gradually happened in other forms of oratory and poetry. The religious nature of the occasion no doubt helped to effect this; it was a kind of rite. But it also was consistent with the nature of rhetoric for an oratorical problem to be supplied with a fixed answer, tolerating of course some individual variation to give an illusion of novelty. The traditional funeral oration led the way toward a traditionalism in all of literature.

[47] Cf. A. Hauvette, "La Eleusiniens d'Eschyle et l'introduction des discours funèbre à Athenès," *Melanges Henri Weil*, Paris, 1889, 159 ff. But cf. also H. Caffiaux, *De l'oraison funèbre dans la Grèce païenne*, Valenciennes, 1861; F. J. Snell, *Lysias' Epitaphios*, Oxford, 1887, 9; Burgess, *op.cit.* supra n. 45, 146 ff.

Pericles delivered a funeral oration in 440 (Plutarch, *Pericles* 8.6) and again in 431. The latter was the occasion for the great speech attributed to him by Thucydides (2.35 ff.) in which opportunity is seized for a magnificent presentation of Athenian ideals. Since the speech was famous in antiquity (e.g. Plato, *Menexenus* 236b5) the extension of the subject is probably not an addition of Thucydides. As we shall see, Gorgias also used the occasion of a funeral speech for a political end. Pericles' opening words clearly indicate that a traditional pattern was expected, beginning with a commendation of the custom of such speeches and continuing on to the deeds of ancestors and then of the present generation. From the accounts in later rhetoricians it appears that the usual structure was threefold: praise, lament (sometimes a denial of the propriety of lamentation), consolation.[48] The praise, after a brief introduction, dealt first with the ancestors of the dead and in a general way with the greatness of the country, proceeding chronologically. This is true already of Pericles' speech, though he quickly dismisses the deeds of the past as too well known. A second part of the praise was devoted to those who had died, to which Pericles turns in chapter forty-two. He skips quickly over the lament with just a mention at the beginning of forty-four and turns then to the consolation. The last sentence of the speech sounds like a formulaic dismissal.

Rhetorically Pericles' funeral oration is very effective. It may be slightly too compressed and intense to be understood at first hearing, but the choruses of drama make at least as great demands. The tone is most striking: austere, realistic, stern, not at all typical of the usual attempts to secure the attention of the audience, but Pericles had the advantage of a well-advertised Olympian character and consciously uses the contrast between his tone and that expected so that he startles the audience's attention. Most

[48] Cf. Burgess, *op.cit.* supra n. 45, 148 ff.

stern is the absence of pity at the end and most realistic is the admission of the faults of the dead in chapter forty-two, only to wipe out these faults in the glory of death. That chapter concludes with one of the most emotional, and perhaps the finest, sentence in Greek prose. But then, the speech has had the benefit of the combined abilities of Thucydides, Pericles, and, according to Plato, Aspasia. They kept the standard form, aimed at a goal beyond that of the common speech, and achieved by the force of the thought alone a magnificent product.

A second example of funeral oratory is the fragment of twenty-two lines from a speech by Gorgias quoted by Diony-sius of Halicarnassus, probably in a lost part of the intro-duction to the essay on Demosthenes, but preserved at second hand by Syrianus.[49] Since the fragment deals with the praise of the dead it must have come from the second section of the first major division of the speech. It is in Gorgias' characteristic balanced, rhyming style which seems frigid today but was particularly influential on epideictic; all surviving funeral orations are considerably more Gor-gianic than are other kinds of oratory. It is strange that a foreigner should participate in such a purely Athenian occasion; if Gorgias was asked to deliver the speech it was an extraordinary tribute to his popularity. Perhaps he wrote the speech and someone else delivered it or more likely it was not intended for actual delivery at all. The most inter-esting aspect is the political intent, if we can believe the story of Philostratus (*Lives of the sophists* 1.9), who says that Gorgias dwelt on Athens' victories over the Persians and said nothing about wars against the Greeks, showing to the Athenians that victories over barbarians call for hymns, victories over Greeks for laments. Gorgias was not merely playing with words, and modern attempts to see

[49] Cf. the edition by H. Usener and L. Radermacher of *Dionysius Halicarnasseus: Opuscula* 1, Leipzig, 1899, 127 f.; Radermacher B.vii.42; W. Vollgraff, *L'oraison funèbre de Gorgias*, Leiden, 1952.

serious intent in epideictic speeches are somewhat bolstered.

The *epitaphios* among the works of Lysias is a much more ordinary product and perhaps more typical of the average funeral oration. The author's concern with the contemporary situation was very slight; he devotes only two (67-68) out of eighty-one sections to the Corinthian war. What he is interested in is the rhetorical opportunity for display offered in the earlier part of the speech, which of course follows the standard pattern. There is first the praise of ancestors. It runs to fifty-three sections and is concerned with legendary times and with the period of the Persian wars. The fantastic and the poetic take the place which the objectives of contemporary Athens held in Pericles' speech. The second part of the praise, that of the men themselves (54-68), is only slightly concerned with them and deals largely with fifth-century history. The lament (69-76) and the consolation (77-81), both short in comparison with the discussion of the mythological achievements of Athens, contain the usual commonplaces on death and valor. It is tempting, but rash, to say that the speech shows the decay in intellectual intensity from the fifth to the fourth century. Intellectual activities of the early fourth century were of a different sort. What the speech does show is a love of rhetoric for its own sake, which had existed in the fifth century and which continues throughout antiquity with mounting volume. There is a general tendency in the fourth century for the speech to rule the speaker and for him to be lured or intoxicated by rhetorical opportunities into words which are either devoid of relevance or, in political speeches, irresponsible and often untrue. We will see more of this oratorical inebriation later. Gorgias loved words, but he was exceedingly cold-blooded in his use of them. He was in complete control. Fourth-century orators, especially the second-rate ones, do not have this control. Their awareness of the nature of their impact is scant. They call into their speech whatever comes to mind. The Lysianic *epitaphios* is by no means the worst example of this kind of thing, it is simply the first one we have met. Epideictic was naturally much more prone to artistic disunity and contextual irrelevance than deliberative or forensic oratory, but such men as Pericles and Abraham Lincoln proved that great epideictic oratory is possible.

One of the most interesting studies of funeral oratory is the dialogue of Plato called the *Menexenus*. In an introductory discussion Menexenus reports to Socrates that the council is about to choose someone to deliver a public funeral oration. There is nothing difficult about composing such a speech, Socrates replies, the speaker just strings together commonplaces. This takes hardly any time and the result is spellbinding. Nor does the speaker even have to stick to the truth. Socrates then proceeds to deliver a funeral oration which he claims to have learned from Aspasia, the mistress of Pericles. It is an excellent speech which conforms in general to the usual structure. When he has finished there is another short discussion in which Menexenus expresses his approval of the speech.

The *Menexenus* is difficult to interpret. Socrates betrays a knowledge of Greek history down to the Peace of Antalcidas, which occurred a dozen years after his death (245e5 ff.)—a rather extreme anachronism—and it is not immediately evident just what the references to Aspasia signify. But more puzzling than that, why should Plato, the most illustrious opponent of rhetoric, take the trouble to compose a *good* funeral oration? It would perhaps be convenient if the little dialogue could be regarded as spurious, and in the past a few scholars so labeled it, but it is quoted by Aristotle (*Rhetoric* 1367b6 and 1415b31), and its style is so Platonic that the most numerous, most qualified, and most recent Platonists all accept the work.

A common interpretation has been that the dialogue and the speech which it contains are intended as satire of contemporary rhetoric and its indifference to truth.[50] But there are objections to this view. First of all, it has no ancient authority. Cicero (*Orator* 151) says that the speech was so admired it had to be read in public every year in Athens. Secondly, the mood of the work as a whole is against such an interpretation. The introductory dialogue does make fun of oratory and orators—when Socrates says that he feels more handsome as he hears his country praised we can hardly take it as anything but humor—but when he begins the speech his tone becomes quite serious, and as he rises to the climax in the series of messages to be reported from the dead to the living there is no memory of the playful beginning. This difference of tone between the introduction and the rest of the work was noted by Plutarch (*Pericles* 24.3), and it is difficult to imagine Plato being satiric on the subject of death and immortality. Elsewhere Socrates sometimes affects a serious tone when he does not mean to be taken seriously in the final analysis, but in such cases, for example in his first speech in the *Phaedrus*, the real situation is made clear before the dialogue is over. It is important to note that the concluding dialogue of the *Menexenus*, though humorous and charming, reveals none of the bitterness of satire. No moral is drawn. Menexenus is apparently genuinely impressed. He sees through the ruse of Socrates: this is not Aspasia speaking, this is a creation of the master himself. Socrates has no regrets for delivering the speech, as he does for his immoral product in the

[50] Cf. P. Wendland, "Die Tendenz des Platonischen *Menexenus*," *Hermes* 25 (1890) 171 ff.; Max Pohlenz, *Aus Platos Werdezeit*, Berlin, 1913, 244 ff.; A. E. Taylor, *Plato: the man and his work*, London, 1920, 41 ff.; R. G. Bury, *Plato* 7 (Loeb Library), London, 1929, 330 f.; Louis Méridier, *Platon* 5.1 (Budé), Paris, 1931, 74 ff.; G. M. Lattanzi, "Il *Menesseno* e l'epitafio attribuito a Lisia," *Il mondo classico* 5 (1935) 355 ff.; Hermann Gauss, *Philosophischer Handkommentar zu den Dialogen Platon* 2.1, Berlin, 1956, 223 f.; E. R. Dodds, *Plato: Gorgias*, Oxford, 1959, 23 f.; Buchheit, *op.cit.* supra n. 45, 94 ff.

Phaedrus, and promises to write more. The very excellence of the speech argues against a satiric intent.

For all the joking, practically everything said by Socrates in the introduction to the *Menexenus* has some serious basis in Plato's thought. The force of inspiration, which Socrates seems to ridicule (235a1), is made quite clear in the *Ion* (535e7 ff.), nor can we doubt that the effect of such a speech as that of Pericles might linger for days. At first it seems wrong that orators should, as Socrates says, ascribe to the dead not only the virtues which they actually had but those which they had not, and Pericles had refused to do so. But in the sequel the orator is presenting the world as it ought to be rather than as it is, and making the ignoble seem noble is not quite the same as making the worse seem the better cause, for public morality may thus be improved.

A second explanation of the dialogue quite different from the satire theory is to say that Plato is merely trying to out-do the rhetoricians at their own game, that the dialogue has a literary objective rather than an educational or philosophical purpose.[51] Plato regards rhetorical composition as a knack rather than a difficult achievement, but he is pleased to be able to represent a philosopher as a successful speaker. Socrates' condemnation may have been regarded by some as due to ignorance of rhetoric rather than refusal to use it, and perhaps Plato, as in the *Apology,* would like to refute such a charge. This explanation is more satisfactory than the satire theory; probably it has some truth in it. But it seems a little unusual that the dialogue should have no positive educational contribution to make, especially since it must have been written soon after Plato opened his school and in the midst of the educational rivalry with Isocrates. Alfred Croiset suggested many years ago

[51] This seems substantially the view of U. von Wilamowitz-Moellendorf, *Platon* 2, Berlin, 1920, 126 ff., though he regards the introductory dialogue as satire. Cf. also Bruns, *op.cit.* supra n. 18, 356 ff.

that in fact the speech in the *Menexenus* might be regarded as a model of a proper oration, something like the second speech of Socrates in the *Phaedrus*.[52] This point of view has much to recommend it, though doubtless all scholars will not find it convincing.

First, if the speech in the *Menexenus* is a model of a good speech the work ceases to be an unparalleled literary production. Not only does it resemble the speech of the *Phaedrus* and to a lesser extent the Diotima speech of the *Symposium*[53] but it corresponds to the common type of the sophistic specimen speech as composed by Gorgias and others for imitation by their pupils. Further, we have seen Pericles and Gorgias both using funeral oratory for positive educational purposes. Since Plato regards oratory as a knack rather than an art he, unlike Aristotle, has no need to protest against such unscientific methods of teaching as the memorization of commonplaces.

Secondly, as Croiset pointed out, the speech does accord with the requirements for a philosophical rhetoric laid down in the *Phaedrus* (277b5 ff.). Clarity of definition and logical divisions are well illustrated by the beginning of Socrates' speech, and knowledge of the psychology of the audience, a second requirement, is equally well illustrated by the close of the speech. Of course the most important requirement of the philosophic rhetoric is that the contents of the speech be true, and this has been, probably, the big stumbling block to regarding the *Menexenus* as a serious work consistent with Plato's other teaching, for it is exceedingly clear that some statements of Socrates' speech are not true to historical fact. But what Plato means by "true" can be seen by a comparison of the speech with the standards for literature in the *Republic*.

[52] Alfred Croiset, "Sur le *Ménexène* de Platon," *Mélanges Perrot*, Paris, 1903, 59 ff.

[53] Cf. Werner Jaeger (trans. by G. Highet), *Paideia: the ideals of Greek culture* 2, New York, 1943, 178 f.

Such a comparison constitutes a third, and perhaps crucial, argument for regarding the speech of Socrates as a serious model for funeral oratory. The *Republic* (607a4) will admit two forms of poetry into the ideal state: hymns to the gods and praises of good men. A funeral oration is a form of the latter in prose. The proper form of oratory itself is touched upon in 392a13 ff.: it is that which shows the just are happy and the unjust unhappy. The speech of the *Menexenus* presents the contentment of those who have done their duty and died for their country. In keeping with the injunctions of the *Republic* (387d1) the conventional lament is omitted and the emphasis is instead upon the immortality of those who have died.[54] The *Republic* appears to have two principal criteria for literature (377e6 ff. and 379a1 ff.): is it true, and does it produce a right effect upon the audience? These, however, are essentially the same thing, for that which produces a right effect is, for that reason, true. In this same sense the Platonic myths are true, for they expound a view of morality or reality which is true and universal; in this sense the historical material of the *Menexenus*, however much it departs from Thucydides, is acceptable to Plato. Democrats and oligarchs alike in classical Greece regarded history as a means to an end, and such a view seems entirely consistent with Platonism. Plato can call the Athenian constitution an aristocracy (238c5 ff.) because it ought to be a rule by the best. In his treatment of wars his object, like that of Gorgias in his funeral oration, is to play down expediency and imperialism and to exalt courage, forgiveness, and virtue. Thus the Sicilian campaign is represented as a war of liberation rather than what it actually was, a war of aggrandizement. The concern of Socrates' speech is not really with the past at all, but with the right effect upon the audience, to return to the criteria of the *Republic*. To secure this end, Plato specifically says

[54] Cf. G. M. Lattanzi, "Il significato e l'autenticità del *Menesseno*," *La parola del passato* 31 (1953) 303 ff.

(*Republic* 389b7 ff.) that *the rulers of the city may tell lies.*

Just as it has been thought that the *Menexenus* was inconsistent with Plato's view of rhetoric, so it has been thought that he would not or should not enter into Athenian traditions to the extent of composing an oration for her dead.[55] In part this topic is well treated by Friedländer:[56] he claims that Plato's feelings for Athens are complex and ambivalent, much as are his feelings for rhetoric and poetry. On the one hand, Plato is an aristocrat with a sense of public service and a love of country; on the other hand, he is revolted by the goals and methods of the democracy and above all by the injustice of Socrates' execution. Friedländer sees in the *Menexenus* an equilibrium between these sentiments and regards the dialogue as an attempt by Plato to relate himself to historical reality. Could Plato be expected to subscribe to the fundamental principle of funeral oratory, *dulce et decorumst pro patria mori?* The guardians in the *Republic* (468a1 ff. and esp. 468e4-6) are clearly expected to die for the state, but that is an ideal state. If one can judge from the experience of Socrates, who served as a soldier and who died to obey the law though he had refused to commit injustice to others to fulfill the law, the morality of giving one's life for one's country depends on the morality of that country and its war. This brings us back again to the misrepresentation of history in the *Menexenus.* For a great funeral oratory, in Plato's view, not only the conduct of the individual but of the state must be noble. As an educator who may influence the conduct

[55] Cf. Pohlenz, *op.cit.* supra n. 50. Pamela Hubbe, "The *Menexenus* reconsidered," *Phronesis* 2 (1957) 104 ff., regards the speech as a serious effort by Plato to prevent the suspension of customary payments to Athenian war orphans about 386 (thus the deliberate anachronism). The prospect of Plato composing such a specific bit of propaganda is startling and the approach does not explain the use of rhetoric by Plato.

[56] Paul Friedländer, *Platon* 2: *die platonischen Schriften,* Berlin and Leipzig, 1930, 217 ff.

of future generations the orator must present the state as good, as engaged in good causes, whether in fact it is or not. In blotting out the errors of the past the orator educates his citizen audience to a new future virtue. This serious view of the function of the orator need not in any way contradict the fact that the actual composition is, in Plato's view, an easy task: Socrates shows how easy it is to do it properly.

The anachronism of Socrates' speech is more difficult to explain. The only apparent reason for an anachronism or any specific temporal reference would seem to be to link Socrates' speech with an actual occasion and thus suggest a contrast between it and some other speech. The funeral oration attributed to Lysias relates also to the Corinthian war, but, beyond that, direct connexion between the two works cannot be established. It has always been uncertain whether or not Lysias, a metic, could have delivered a funeral oration. If in fact he wrote it for someone else to deliver, as he did judicial speeches, the introduction of a logographer for Socrates is more meaningful and the choice of Aspasia humorous, since she had been regarded as the real source of many of the ideas of leading statesmen (Plutarch, *Pericles* 24). It is also possible that some reference is intended to the *Aspasia* of Aeschines the Socratic.[57]

The funeral oration preserved as the sixtieth speech of Demosthenes is a very inferior product which one hopes he did not write. Perhaps the speech that he delivered over those who fell at Chaeronea (*On the crown* 320) was lost and someone, not much later, composed this work as an exercise. It is of course possible that some of it draws on what Demosthenes actually said. Dionysius of Halicarnassus knew the speech and regarded it as spurious (*Demosthenes* 44), which shows that it has considerable antiquity. It has

[57] Cf. Bruns, *op.cit.* supra n. 18, 359. He compares the references to Aspasia to mention of Connos in the *Euthydemus* 272c1 and 295d3.

many of the characteristics which mark the decaying oratory of the late fourth century: there is a traditionalism at the beginning and a lack of verisimilitude in the introduction of topics which seems to show that the author is primarily interested in the rhetorical problem of discovering everything which might be said rather than of fitting what is said to the occasion. No clear moral picture emerges and if the speech was ever delivered the effect on the audience must have been one of watching an orator perform a perfunctory task. The greatest rhetorical problem of the speaker is the fact that the dead whom he would honor lost their battle and the war. This he tries to get around with feeble arguments (19 ff.) and by the typical diversionary treatment of introducing some other subject which can be better discussed, in this case the legendary stories of each of the tribes to which the dead belonged (27 ff.). These commonplaces would be of some local interest and helped greatly to fill out the speech.

The final funeral oration is that by Hyperides, preserved in papyrus and somewhat fragmentary.[58] It was delivered in 322 over those who died in the Lamian war. Hyperides is an able orator and this is perhaps his best speech. Although it fulfills the usual functions of funeral orations and contains praise of the city and consolation to the living, the speaker showed a remarkable independence in leaving out the mythological commonplaces and concentrating on the actual historical occasion. Furthermore, he gave specific attention to Leosthenes, the able commander killed in the war. Both of these facts give the speech a much greater immediacy and sincerity than has any other funeral oration except that of Pericles. The reason is that Hyperides, like Pericles, was deeply and emotionally involved in his subject. He was using an occasion to say something close to his heart, a tribute to the general and his soldiers, and he was

[58] Cf. Hans Hess, *Textkritische und erklärende Beiträge zum Epitaphios des Hypereides*, Leipzig, 1938.

not simply reacting to a rhetorical challenge or fulfilling a formal task. There are, of course, great differences between the speeches of Pericles and Hyperides and to some extent they are the differences between the two ages. The concern of the former is civic, philosophical, austere. The latter is personal, historical, and emotional.

Festival Orations

Both the festivals of a single city like Athens and the great games which brought together all of Greece furnished occasions for oratory. Since these were among the very few manifestations of panhellenic unity it is not surprising that that theme often appeared in such speeches. We hear (Diogenes Laertius 6.2) of a speech which Antisthenes intended to give at an Isthmian festival criticizing the Athenians, Thebans, and Lacedaimonians. Perhaps it would have suggested that their energies would be better used against the barbarians than against each other, but Antisthenes never gave the speech. According to Philostratus (*Lives of the sophists* 1.9) Gorgias delivered at least one striking speech at both a Pythian and an Olympian festival. In the latter, given at a time when Greece was torn by faction, he advised the Hellenes to turn against the Persians and contend for their land rather than each other's cities.[59] Philostratus' use of the word ἆθλα as though quoted from the speech suggests that an athletic symbolism ran through it as it does through Isocrates' *Panegyricus*, and there may well have been considerable development of an antithesis between the horror of war and the blessings of peace.[60] Hippias also is known to have spoken at the Olympic games, though the specific subject is not recorded (Plato, *Lesser Hippias* 363c7 ff.). Dionysius of Halicarnassus preserves (*Lysias* 29 f.) the first nine sections of the *Olympicus* of Lysias. It too

[59] Probably at the 97th Olympiad, 392 B.C.; cf. Blass 1.59.
[60] Cf. Wilhelm Nestle, "Neues zu Sophistik: 1. zu Gorgias," BPW 52 (1932) 1357 ff.

was concerned with panhellenic unity against the barbarian and attacked particularly Dionysius of Syracuse (Diodorus Siculus 14.109, who gives the date 388 B.C.) with such vehemence that violent action against the person and gold pavilion of Dionysius was averted with difficulty. Perhaps we may see here some of the irresponsibility of oratorical inebriation. Not enough of the speech survives to reconstruct its structure. In the *Art of rhetoric* attributed to Dionysius it is said (1.2 ff.) that a panegyric, the technical name for a festival speech, consists normally of praise of the god associated with the festival, praise of the city in which the festival is held, praise of the contest itself and of the crown awarded, and finally, praise of the king or officials in charge. Lysias' speech begins with Heracles, but otherwise the formula does not seem entirely suitable. Probably it belongs to a later time when panegyric had adopted a fixed structure like that of the funeral oration.

Sophistic Oratory

Epideictic speeches of the kinds discussed so far performed a public function and offered legitimate opportunities for an orator to develop a significant line of thought. It is a sign of decadence if an orator feels no involvement in the occasion and delivers a speech which is only a rhetorical display. There are, however, a number of speeches which have often been regarded simply as rhetorical displays of stylistic ornamentation, mostly because of their subject matter, which is mythological and apparently irrelevant to the period in which they were written. Attempts have been made to prove that most of them are late forgeries, but we know that a number of the authors to whom they are attributed were interested in problems suggested by Homeric mythology or other early poetry. Furthermore, they are rather similar in substance to two undoubtedly genuine works of Isocrates, and in most cases their style is very much what one would expect from the authors. As a result it is generally believed today that the *Helen* and *Palamedes* actually are original works of Gorgias, the *Ajax* and *Odysseus* works of Antisthenes, and the *Odysseus*, though not a work of Alcidamas as it claims, probably a genuine product of the fourth century.

In Plato's dialogues we get some feeling for the manner in which sophists performed in public. They show a wide variety of individual idiosyncrasies, and the dialectic resulting from Socrates' questioning is not represented as quite what they are used to. In general, however, they show a willingness to join a discussion into which they may attempt to introduce a somewhat formal speech or myth, as Socrates himself does occasionally, or if they have given a speech they show willingness to interpret it and discuss the presentation or substance.[61] Protagoras, Hippias, Prodicus, Gorgias, and Thrasymachus are all presented as concerned, rightly or wrongly, with education rather than with entertainment. With that background it seems fair to expect that the sophist, after delivering a speech about or in the person of Ajax or some other legendary figure, might informally discuss what he had said and derive from it some principles or precepts which he regarded as important. The surviving speeches all lend themselves to such a treatment.

Gorgias' speech for Helen shows all the wildness of his jingling style, but it is also a masterful illustration of the apagogic method by which the orator enumerates a series of possibilities and deals with each in turn.[62] After a brief

---

[61] Cf. H. Ll. Hudson-Williams, "Conventional forms of debate and the Melian dialogue," AJP 71 (1950) 156 ff.

[62] For the text cf. Otto Immisch, *Gorgiae Helena*, Berlin and Leipzig, 1927; Diels 82.B.11; Radermacher B.vii.39. For discussion cf. Blass 1.72 ff.; E. Maass, "Untersuchungen zur Geschichte der griechischen Prosa: über die erhaltenen Reden des Gorgias," *Hermes* 22 (1887) 572 ff.; M. L. Orsini, "La cronologica dell' *Encomio di Elena* di Gorgia e la *Troiane* di Euripide," *Dioniso* 19 (1956) 82 ff.; Friedrich Zucker, "Der Stil des Gorgias nach seiner innerem

introduction in which Gorgias seeks to justify the choice of subject—it is right to praise the praiseworthy and defend the maligned—he states (6) that Helen must have yielded to Paris either through fate or the wishes of the gods, or else she was ravaged by force or persuaded by words or maddened by love. No other possibilities are presumed to exist. Each of those enumerated is examined in turn and it is demonstrated by what Aristotle would call enthymeme or example within the limits of probability that in each case Helen cannot be blamed for her action. The most interesting discussion is that of persuasion by words (8 ff.), where Gorgias develops an analysis of psychological effects.[63] The speech ends with a brief conclusion echoing the statements of the introduction. In four and a half pages Gorgias has given a vivid, even unforgettable, example of the same logical method which he employed in his famous discussion of being.[64] He refers to the little work as a λογισμός or "reasoning" in section two, and this seems entirely appropriate; but it is not out of place nor inconsistent with his purpose for him to call the production a παίγνιον, a "trifle," at the very end. It is playful in mood, but it also has a serious purpose in demonstrating a method of logical proof.

The *Palamedes* is similar except that it takes the form of a courtroom defense on a formal charge of treason.[65] The conventions of courtroom oratory are adhered to, though there is no narration; rhetoricians allowed it to be dispensed with if the facts were well known. Palamedes

---

Form," SBB 1956.1. Blass' date of 393 B.C. seems too late; Orsini suggests before 415. For an English translation of most of the speech cf. LaRue Van Hook, "The *Encomium on Helen*, by Gorgias," CW 6 (1913) 122 ff., reprinted in vol. 3 of the Loeb Library *Isocrates*, 55 ff.

[63] Cf. Thomas S. Duncan, "Gorgias' theories of art," CJ 33 (1938) 402 ff.

[64] Cf. Untersteiner 140 ff.

[65] Cf. Diels 82.B.11a; Radermacher B.vii.4; for a brief description Schwartz, *op.cit.* supra n. 13, 7 f.

proves first that he was unable to betray the Greeks and second that even if he had been able he could have had no desire to do so. In the first part various ways are considered and shown to be impossible in turn; thus the apagogic method is again followed. Similarly in the second part various reasons why he might have wished to betray the Greeks are suggested and rejected. In section twenty-two the speaker turns to a defense based on his character and services to the Greeks and at the end of the speech arouses considerable pity for his lot. There is, thus, logical proof, ethos, and pathos in the speech.

In examining methods of instruction in rhetoric we found that Gorgias required his students to learn complete or partial speeches. The *Palamedes* seems to be one of these speeches. The mythological situation furnishes a background of material without the difficulty of invention, and it makes the work somewhat more entertaining than are the *Tetralogies* of Antiphon. Like them it is not an epideictic speech, but an example of arrangement, argument, and style. The mythological situation does not in any great way mitigate against the usefulness of the work as a lesson in method, and many of the arguments could be taken out for use in treason cases and sometimes perhaps in other cases too.

The two speeches of Antisthenes, *Ajax* and *Odysseus*,[66] are also imaginary courtroom speeches, this time on the claim of each to the arms of Achilles, but they do not appear

---

[66] Antisthenes was a follower of Socrates and often wrongly regarded as the first Cynic, cf. Donald R. Dudley, *A history of cynicism*, London, 1937, 1 ff. For the text cf. Radermacher B.xix. 11-12. For discussion cf. Blass 2.310 ff., L. Radermacher, "Der *Aias* und *Odysseus* des Antisthenes," RhM 47 (1892) 569 ff.; Wilhelm Altwegg, "Zum *Aias* and *Odysseus* des Antisthenes," *Juvenes dum sumus: Aufsätze zur klassischen Altertumswissenschaft der 19. Versammlung deutscher Philologen und Schulmänner zu Basel*, 1907, 52 ff.; A. Bachmann, *Aiax et Ulixes declamationes utrum iure tribuantur Antistheni*, Münster, 1911.

to be models of structure and argument. Neither of them has the divisions of a judicial speech: not only narrative but also prooemium and peroration are lacking. The argument is reminiscent of what we have regarded as pre-rhetorical. Ajax, with some indignation, objects to the competence of the jury, which has no direct knowledge of the case. Antisthenes was interested in knowledge as the basis of virtuous activity, but if that is the point we would expect Odysseus' reply to bear on the topic in some way. It does not, but argues that the arms should go to Odysseus because of his many services to the Greeks, in much the way that Andocides in his first speech argues for his restoration. The only hint of Antisthenes' objective comes from Diogenes Laertius' list of his works (6.15). They were ten in number, each divided into several books. The first collection contained *On style or on characteristics*, *Ajax or the speech of Ajax*, *Odysseus or concerning Odysseus*, *Orestes' apology*, *Concerning judicial copying or Desias and Isographes* (apparently a pun on Lysias and Isocrates, but the text is in doubt), and *In reply to the unwitnessed speech of Isocrates*.[67] The two extant speeches are probably identifiable with the second and third works mentioned in the list,[68] since our *Ajax* is a speech of Ajax and our *Odysseus* is concerned with Odysseus' services. The fourth and the last of the works mentioned were apparently also speeches. If so, there was an introductory essay, three speeches, another essay, and another speech. The last two works constitute a unit, connected by the interest in Isocrates. The others could constitute a unit also illustrating something discussed in the introductory essay. But what was *On style or on characteristics* about? The word translated

[67] On the text of the list cf. J. Humblé, "Antisthenica," *Antiquité classique* 3 (1934) 163 ff.
[68] There is no doubt about the *Ajax*, a little about the *Odysseus*. The discussion of *polytropos* is also "concerning Odysseus"; Porphyry (*Commentary on the Odyssey* 1.1) says that the latter comes from the *Homeric questions*, a work not contained in Diogenes' list.

"style" is λέξις, which is the ordinary word for literary style, but the speeches seem not at all striking in this respect and do not differ among themselves stylistically. The word translated "characteristics" is used by later rhetoricians to refer to the three kinds of style, grand, middle, and plain; but such a meaning around 400 B.C. would be unexpected and does not fit the examples. The word could, however, mean any kind of characteristics or idiosyncrasies. Since the two speeches which we have are quite different, primarily because of the different way of thought, manner, and moral character of the speakers, it seems possible that this is what Antisthenes was trying to illustrate. Ajax is aristocratic, indignant, and resentful. He scorns the jury and will not stoop to techniques of persuasion. Odysseus is more clever, inventive, ready to claim military ability, even self-confident. We know from Porphyry's scholia to the first line of the *Odyssey*[69] that Antisthenes was interested in Odysseus' ability to speak and in his moral character and that he discussed the meaning of πολύτροπος, the adjective used of Odysseus in that line, in both senses. Thus, it is possible that Antisthenes is trying to illustrate something like ethopoiia, the manifestation of personality in speech, a subject which was clearly of contemporary interest.[70]

The fifth surviving mythological speech is an *Odysseus* bearing the name of the fourth-century sophist Alcidamas.[71] Almost certainly he did not write it, for we have his pamphlet *On those writing written speeches or on the sophists*, which appears to be genuine and which inveighs heatedly against literary composition of oratory as opposed to ex-

[69] Cf. A. Rostagni, "Un nuovo capitolo della retorica e della sophistica," *Studi italiani di filologia classica* 2 (1922) 148 ff.

[70] Cf. H. J. Lulofs, *De Antisthenis studiis rhetoricis*, Amsterdam, 1900, 86 ff., and George A. Kennedy, "The ancient dispute over rhetoric in Homer," AJP 78 (1957) 23 ff.

[71] Cf. Radermacher B.xxii.16.

temporaneous composition.[72] Toward the end of the work (29 ff.) Alcidamas mentions his use of writing in it and claims that this was a justifiable exception. As far as we know he never changed his mind and never published speeches, for his whole career lies in opposition to that of Isocrates, whose vehicle was the carefully polished written speech and who, though unnamed, is the object of attack in the pamphlet.[73] It is difficult to suggest a name for the real author of the *Odysseus*, but it seems to be a product of the school of Gorgias. The style shows his influence and the speech is, like his *Palamedes*, apparently intended as an example of judicial technique. There is a prooemium (1-4), which aims at the good will of the audience; a narration (5-7); introduction of direct evidence in a message from Paris to Palamedes, as well as witnesses to attest it; then a proof based on probability (10-12); an over-long section (13-21) which seems designed to show that Palamedes' father couldn't be trusted, but which digresses into an account of the abduction of Helen; a refutation (22-28) of Palamedes' claims of services to the Greeks; and a short peroration (29). The section on the character of the father as evidence for the character of the son points to a date well into the fourth century; the earliest orators, like Antiphon and Lysias, use no such techniques, but they are marked in the public speeches of Demosthenes and Aeschines. The other striking feature of the *Odysseus* is its use of antiphilosophical sentiment to discredit Palamedes (4, 12, and 22 ff.). Probably this is simply a rhetorical technique without any contemporary significance.

[72] Cf. Radermacher B.xxii.15 and Marjorie J. Milne, A *study in Alcidamas and his relation to contemporary sophistic*, Bryn Mawr, 1924. Herber Auer, *De Alcidamantis declamatione quae inscribitur* Ὀδυσσεὺς κατὰ Παλαμήδους προδοσίας, Monasterii Guestalorum, 1913, regards the *Odysseus* as genuine despite the inconsistency.

[73] Cf. Milne, *op.cit.* supra n. 72 and Georg Walberer, *Isokrates und Alkidamas*, Hamburg, 1938.

Isocrates

Isocrates was born in 436 B.C., the son of Theodorus of Erchia, a manufacturer of flutes.[74] His teachers are said to have included Prodicus, Gorgias, Tisias, and Theramenes, and he was acquainted with Socrates. When his father's estate was lost in the Peloponnesian war Isocrates turned to writing judicial speeches. About 393 he opened a school which trained, a few at a time, some of the most distinguished men of their generation, among them the general Timotheus, the historians Theopompus and Ephorus, and Nicocles the king of Cyprus. Dionysius accepted twenty-five orations as genuine; we have twenty-one, including six judicial speeches, in addition to nine letters. Due to poor delivery Isocrates did not speak in public or take part in politics. Most of his speeches were published as pamphlets after long and careful revision. His style is one of the most distinctive in Greek:[75] the diction is pure, the expression full in the extreme, rhythmical, highly antithetical, but the jingling excesses of Gorgias are avoided. Isocrates particularly disliked hiatus, the clash resulting from ending a word with a vowel and beginning the next word with a vowel. He died in 338 at the age of ninety-eight.

It is with Isocrates the orator, rather than the political theorist, that we are here principally concerned, though political theory is often the subject of his oratory and cannot be entirely ignored. Nor are we concerned with the educator, though it was Isocrates' school which helped solidify the tradition that made rhetoric the accepted basis of education. As an orator Isocrates illustrates many of the

[74] The principal sources are Isocrates' own works, the essay *Isocrates* by Dionysius of Halicarnassus, and the *Lives of the ten orators*, cf. supra n. 6. Useful translations of all the works are available in the Loeb Library *Isocrates*, vols. 1 and 2, London, 1928-1929, by George Norlin, vol. 3, Cambridge, 1945, by LaRue VanHook.

[75] On Isocrates' style cf. Blass 2.121 ff.; Jebb 2.51 ff.; Norden 113 ff. On types of speeches cf. K. Wenig, "Essai de classification des discours d'Isocrate," *Listy filologicke* (1920) 259 ff.

influences which were developing in Greek oratory. He has great technical ability; he shares with earlier sophists a belief that truth is elusive and that the appropriate is the most suitable standard of judgment;[76] he loves the sound and fury of words and the feeling of power that they give.[77] But most contemporary orators were restricted by practical necessities. They had to win cases or persuade assemblies. Isocrates' income was derived from his school, not from his speeches. Objective results did not determine his success; his speeches are literary products worked out in detail at leisure, and their success was measured principally by his own sense of the extent to which they answered the particular rhetorical challenge from which he began. Technical mastery of rhetoric was a tool which Demosthenes polished and wielded with creative force. Isocrates was an intellectual of no very certain convictions whom rhetorical ability reduced to straw-snatching opportunism.[78]

Isocrates says (*Antidosis* 161) that he was financially ruined by the Peloponnesian war. It is probable that he attempted to continue his father's business of flute manufacture. He may possibly have been involved in the ruin of Theramenes and may even have withdrawn from Athens briefly. Perhaps it was at that time that he went to Thessaly and studied with Gorgias (Cicero, *Orator* 176).[79] For ten years (about 403-393) he became a logographer, a pro-

[76] Cf. e.g. *Against the sophists* 8 and 12 f.; *Helen* 5; *Panathenaicus* 9 and 30.

[77] Cf. e.g. *Panegyricus* 48 ff.; *Nicocles* 5 ff.; *Antidosis* 311.

[78] In addition to Blass and Jebb cf. Jaeger, *op.cit.* supra n. 53, 3 1944, 46 ff., and in reply Norman H. Baynes, "Isocrates," *Byzantine studies and other essays*, London, 1955, 144 ff.

[79] On the involvement with Theramenes cf. *Lives of the ten orators* 836 f. and Paul Cloché, "Isocrate et la politique théraménienne," LEC 5 (1936) 394 ff. *Lives* 837b indicates that some time was spent in Chios. Cicero (*loc.cit.*) describes Isocrates as an *adulescens* when he studied with Gorgias, in which case it was perhaps earlier than this date, but Cicero may have assumed that a student would be an *adulescens*.

fessional writer of judicial speeches, but sometime late in the 390's he abandoned his speech writing and opened a school.[80] Later on in his life Isocrates always speaks of judicial speech writing in terms which imply that he never had anything to do with it.[81] Dionysius of Halicarnassus reports (*Isocrates* 18) that Isocrates' adopted son absolutely denied that his father had ever written court speeches, but that according to Aristotle the bookstores were full of them. As we have seen, six such speeches survive; neither Dionysius nor anyone else has seriously doubted their authenticity. Artistically there is no reason why Isocrates should want to disown them. Another author might have suppressed them because of the political temporalizing, but Isocrates is always a political opportunist. At most he might have regretted the flagrant inconsistency between certain specific statements and positions he adopted later. All he actually does in these early speeches is to utilize with some cleverness the democratic sentiment which was strong in Athens after the overthrow of the Thirty. The speech *Against Lochites*, for example, was written for a person of humble circumstances against a young aristocrat and tries to present the latter as an oligarch, the kind of person who had twice overthrown the democracy (10 f.). Another example is the speech entitled *On the team of horses*,

[80] The date cannot be absolutely established. According to Jebb (2.216), it must be after the last of the judicial speeches, the *Aegineticus*, which he puts in 394/393, and before *Against the sophists*, the exact date of which is equally uncertain, though most often put around 390. Jebb (2.124) would place the latter speech before the *Gorgias*. H. D. Verdam, "Quo ordine Isocratis *Busiris, Adversus sophistas, Helena* orationes inter se succedant et quid Plato ad eas responderit," MN 44 (1916) 373 ff. regards *Against the sophists* as written about 384 in reply to the *Gorgias*, but the educational situation criticized seems more suitable for the late 390's before Plato opened the Academy, which he probably did shortly after his return from Sicily in 387.

[81] The most explicit passages are *Antidosis* 36 ff. and 49. References like *Panegyricus* 11 and 188, though disparaging judicial speech writing, are not necessarily inconsistencies.

written for Alcibiades' son and strongly pro-democratic. Alcibiades is glorified as the people's hero, although later, in the *Philip* (58), he is represented as the one man most responsible for Greece's misfortunes. The position adopted in these speeches is purely rhetorical; the writer needed to win his case in return for his fee.

The real reason that Isocrates probably wanted to overlook the early speeches is that they were written for hire and are essentially mundane. A logographer was of questionable respectability, unacceptable in intellectual and political circles. This life he completely casts aside, and from the dull cocoon emerges the resplendent educational butterfly. The opening of the school can be compared to a kind of conversion. All of Isocrates' past was blotted out from his mind. He never says anything about his first forty years except that he had a good education and lost his property. Apparently he stopped what he was doing and tried to forget it and started something quite different.

At the end of the fragmentary work *Against the sophists*, one of the first he wrote after opening his school, he indicates that he was persuaded of the importance of the disciplines which he taught by certain arguments. The part of the speech which contained the arguments is lost, though perhaps they were no more than an early statement of his "philosophy." He has the convert's zeal: he vigorously attacks both in this speech and in the *Helen* all other educators of his day, for only his own school is on the right track.[82] It aimed at what he calls "philosophy" (*Antidosis*

[82] Cf. A. Gercke, "Isokrates 13 und Alkidamas," RhM 54 (1899) 404 ff., and "Die Replik des Isokrates gegen Alkidamas," RhM 62 (1907) 170 ff.; F. Susemihl, "Ueber Isokrates xiii.9-13, und x.8-13," RhM 55 (1900) 574 ff.; K. Hubik, "Alkidamas oder Isokrates? Ein Beitrag zur Geschichte der griechischen Rhetorik," WS 23 (1901) 234 ff.; H. Raeder, "Alkidamas und Platon als Gegner des Isokrates," RhM 63 (1908) 495 ff.; W. Nestle, "Spuren der Sophistik bei Isokrates," *Philologus* 70 (1911) 1 ff.; G. Walberer, *op.cit.* supra n. 73; Stanley Wilcox, "Isocrates' fellow-rhetoricians," AJP 66 (1945) 171 ff.

270 ff.),[83] a wisdom in practical affairs resulting in high moral consciousness and equated with a mastery of rhetorical technique (293). Rhetoric and philosophy are the practical and theoretical sides of the same culture. Isocrates would avoid too much stress on argumentation as leading to purely verbal answers to problems and also too abstract an approach directed toward virtue or the good as divorced from individual facts (*Helen* 4 ff.). We know little about the techniques Isocrates used in teaching,[84] but rhetorical composition was the central exercise; students were expected to have a natural ability to start with which was developed by practice and theory (*Against the sophists* 14 ff.). In this approach Isocrates was no doubt influenced by his sophistic teachers like Gorgias. The "philosophy" is in large part that of the fifth century sophists: intellectual development is equated with rhetorical technique and abstract truth is dismissed as impossible or useless. Peculiar to Isocrates, perhaps, is the insistence upon moral consciousness as actually growing out of the process of rhetorical composition. A passage from the *Antidosis* (274 ff.) ex-

[83] Cf. Blass 2.24 ff.; Jebb 2.34 ff.; Harry M. Hubbell, *The influence of Isocrates on Cicero, Dionysius, and Aristides*, New Haven, 1913; August Burk, *Die Pädagogik des Isocrates* (*Studien zur Geschichte und Kultur des Altertums* 12.3-4), Würzburg, 1923; P. G. Neserius, "Isocrates' political and social ideas," *International journal of ethics* 43 (1932-1933) 307 ff.; F. Taeger, "Isokrates und die Anfänge des hellenistischen Herrscherkultes," *Hermes* 72 (1937) 355 ff.; H. Wersdoerfer, *Die philosophia des Isokrates im Spiegel ihrer Terminologie: Untersuchungen zur frühattischen Rhetorik und Stillehre* (*Klassisch-philologische Studien* 13), Bonn, 1940; H. Ll. Hudson-Williams, "A Greek humanist," *Greece and Rome* 9 (1940) 166 ff.; Stanley Wilcox, "Criticisms of Isocrates and his φιλοσοφία," TAPA 74 (1943) 113 ff.; Jaeger, *op.cit.* supra n. 53, 3.46 ff.; W. Steidle, "Redekunst und Bildung bei Isokrates," *Hermes* 80 (1952) 257 ff.; S. E. Smethurst, "Cicero and Isocrates," TAPA 84 (1953) 262 ff.; E. Mikkola, "Isokrates: seine Anschauungen im Lichte seiner Schriften," *Annales academiae scientiae fennicae* 89 (1954).

[84] Cf., however, R. Johnson, "Isocrates' methods of teaching," AJP 80 (1959) 25 ff.

presses this clearly (cf. also Dionysius of Halicarnassus, *Isocrates* 4):

"I think that there has never been any art which could create virtue and justice in those bad by nature, neither in the past nor now, and that those making promises about this will grow weary and stop speaking before such an education is found, but *I do believe that men may become better and worthier if they are anxious about speaking well and if they desire to be able to persuade their listeners* and moreover if they set their hearts on their advantage, not that which the ignorant think is advantage, but what is advantage in the true sense.

"For first of all, one who chooses to speak or write speeches which are worthy of praise and honor cannot possibly support unjust and insignificant causes or those of private quarrels, but great and honorable and philanthropic causes concerned with the common good. For if he does not find such subjects he will do nothing worth doing. Secondly, from those deeds which illustrate his hypothesis he will select the most distinguished and the most edifying. And he who accustoms himself to look at and evaluate such examples will feel their influence not only on the discourse at hand, but in all his other deeds. So that the ability to speak and think well will reward those who train themselves in a love of wisdom and honor with regard to words."

Isocrates' emphasis on rhetoric has obscured what was probably a great influence in his life. Modern scholars tend to think of him as an opponent of Plato, which is true, and presumably, therefore, an opponent of the Socratic tradition. But Isocrates regarded himself as a follower of Socrates; the anonymous life (line 8, Budé Isocrates 1) even labels him a pupil of the philosopher. It may be that Socrates would have disowned him or that he did not understand Socrates, but that is irrelevant to his feeling.

In addition to the reference to Isocrates in the *Phaedrus*, there are a number of indications of Isocrates' attitude toward Socrates. One is the story in the *Lives of the ten orators* (838f) that Isocrates was greatly grieved by the death of Socrates and appeared in mourning the day after his death. Secondly, Isocrates' criticisms of educators are certainly not directed against Socrates. In *Against the sophists* and in the beginning of the *Helen* he objects both to teachers of disputation like those ridiculed in Plato's *Euthydemus* and to the traditional sophists who taught political discourse by a system of commonplaces. A student learned their topics in the way he learned the letters of the alphabet. These teachers are probably the successors of Gorgias, people like Polus and maybe Alcidamas. Isocrates has been frequently thought of as a follower of Gorgias, but what he says against sophists here was true of Gorgias, and in the *Helen* (14) he specifically criticizes a work of Gorgias on the acceptable Socratic ground that it did not fulfill its function.

Far from criticizing Socrates in any way, Isocrates even defends him. One of the early speeches is the *Busiris*, named for a mythical king of Egypt. This speech is primarily an example of how to develop the topics of an encomium. It takes the form of a letter addressed to Polycrates, who, under the press of poverty, had decided to become a philosopher. Isocrates' sarcastic reference (1) to the mercenary instinct is consistent with Socratic practice, though Isocrates did himself subsequently teach for pay.[85] Polycrates had written a so-called defense of Busiris and a more famous work, an accusation of Socrates. Isocrates says (4) that he will make it clear that Polycrates failed in both discourses. Subsequently he says very little about Socrates, but a number of elements in the speech seem to be Socratic: the feel-

[85] Cf. *Antidosis* 2 f. and 155 ff.; *Lives of the ten orators* 837 b-c; R. Johnson, "A note on the number of Isocrates' pupils," AJP 78 (1957) 297 ff., which discusses his wealth.

ing of responsibility to correct error (3), the criticism of the pretense of knowledge (24), the view of the gods as being by definition virtuous (41-3), the implied comparison be-between Busiris and Socrates as having both been unjustly accused (4-6), and the attribution to Busiris of political theories (15-20) somewhat similar to those which Plato makes Socrates outline in the *Republic*. Busiris is moreover presented as responsible for the development of philosophy in Egypt (22). Isocrates has apparently derived knowledge of Egyptian institutions from the second book of Herodotus and simply attributed these institutions to Busiris by a sophistic argument from probability. The speech indicates at least an enthusiasm for Socrates and a willingness to be counted on his side. It furthermore does so through the use of myth, a device characteristic of many of Socrates' followers including Plato, Antisthenes, and Xenophon. Critics have not usually regarded the *Busiris* as a serious speech any more than they have the *Helen*, but it seems likely that a serious idea underlies both works for all their bizarre subjects.

Later in his career Isocrates poses as a kind of Socrates on a number of occasions. In the *Panathenaicus* (200 ff.), for example, he breaks off his discussion and argues with himself in somewhat the manner of Socrates in the *Phae-drus*. The best example, however, is the *Antidosis*, Isocrates longest speech, which takes the form of a defense of himself on the same charge (30) of having corrupted the youths which had been made against Socrates. The speech repeatedly recalls remarks in Plato's *Apology*.[86]

There is, in addition, much in Isocrates' general cast of thought which reminds one superficially of Socrates. Norlin cited his aloofness from public life, his critical attitude

[86] Cf. George Norlin, *Isocrates* 1 (Loeb Library), London, 1928, xvii, who refers esp. to sections 21, 27, 33, 89, 93, 95, 100, 145, 154, 179, 240, 321, and Georg Misch, A *history of autobiography in antiquity* 1, Cambridge, 1951, 154 ff.

toward the Athenian democracy and hatred of demagoguery, his criticism of much of sophistry, his insistence on definition of objectives and terms (though definition is only a rhetorical technique to Isocrates), his prejudice against philosophical speculation on the origin of things, his feeling that education should aim at right conduct, and a rationalism combined with acquiescence in forms of worship.[87]

The fact that Isocrates regarded himself as a follower of Socrates helps to explain the initial features of his teaching career. The end of the Peloponnesian war brought to him financial ruin and perhaps even intellectual chaos. To support himself he turned to the writing of judicial speeches for others. The death of Socrates was a shock to him. It seemed to show how insecure was the position of any intellectual. For a number of years he temporized, continuing to write and sell speeches and to flatter the democracy. Late in the 390's things began to be clearer. Athens was stronger, the long walls were rebuilt, fear of intellectualism abated. Responding to the example of Socrates, Isocrates took the plunge, abandoned what he was doing, and turned his efforts to education in what he hoped, perhaps, was the spirit of Socrates, though he was also influenced by the examples of Gorgias and other teachers. The success of Isocrates' school probably prompted Plato to open the Academy when he returned from Sicily a few years later. The very existence of the Academy shows that there was nothing essentially un-Socratic in the organization of a school.

Isocrates' teaching was distinguished by a concern with morality which was not particularly evident in sophists such as Gorgias. The most likely source of such feelings was the

[87] Cf. Norlin, *op.cit.* supra n. 86, xvi ff. The biggest apparent difference between the two is in their attitudes toward rhetoric. What we know of Socrates' trial points to a real opposition to rhetorical methods, but he may not have made the clear-cut division between philosophy and rhetoric found in Plato, cf. Arnim 20.

Socratic circle. Surely one safe statement about the historical Socrates is that he rejected apparent expediency as a
basis of conduct. This is evident in the *Apology*, where he
will not use rhetoric for his own advantage; in the *Crito*,
where he will not violate the laws to save himself; and in
the story (*Apology* 32c4 ff.) of how he refused to execute
an order of the Thirty which he believed wrong. We are
accustomed to think of expediency as the basis of political
action, and that attitude is represented in sharp focus in the
pages of Thucydides, where expediency is often contrasted
with justice. Sharp focus on a single argument and especially
argument from expediency is apparently characteristic of
fifth-century deliberative oratory.[88] Toward the end of the
century it began to be abandoned in favor of a synthesis of
arguments: a course of conduct was recommended not as
expedient only but also as just and honorable. The experience of the Peloponnesian war may have influenced this
change, but the movement was hastened by moralists like
Socrates continually insisting on the same theme. In no
Greek orator is moral synthesis of arguments so much developed as in Isocrates, and if he is in fact the only one of
the Greek orators under direct Socratic influence one does
not have to look very far for the reason. He discusses the
need for moral synthesis most explicitly in the speech *On
the peace* (28 ff.), but it can be traced already in the *Panegyricus*, where it is said that the invasion of Persia (179 ff.)
will be just, expedient, honorable, and possible, and still
more in the *Plataicus*, where from the very beginning aid
for the Plataeans is called for mostly as just and honorable.
It is perhaps the most important element in the *Archidamus*: the allies of Sparta are presumed to have argued
for peace and recognition of Messenia on the basis of expediency. Isocrates makes Archidamus reject this and advance instead arguments for justice and honor in accord

---

[88] Cf. George A. Kennedy, "Focusing of arguments in Greek
deliberative oratory," TAPA 90 (1959) 131 ff.

with Spartan traditions (37), which constitute true expediency. All of the succeeding speeches have this element in them, especially *On the peace*, where (28 ff.) the argument that justice and honor are the true forms of expediency is made the basis for action. As Athens refuses to act by force, as she finds her true future and self-realization in a life of peace, a new aura of understanding will settle down upon the Greek world to bind up its wounds. Moral synthesis to some extent weakens oratorical effectiveness. A single striking point driven home with insistence and acceptance of all its implications is probably better rhetorically because more vivid than the self-righteous, but diluted arguments of moral synthesis. The speeches in Thucydides are considerably more forceful than those of Isocrates, and Demosthenes, when intent upon oratorical force, reverts to focus on a single argument.

Isocrates' political ideas, too, are partly Socratic. Socrates showed a loyalty to, but decided lack of enthusiasm for Athenian democracy as it existed in the fifth century, and Plato represents (*Gorgias* 515d1 ff.) him as saying that Pericles and the other great statesmen had made the people worse rather than better. In general, the position of Isocrates is similar. There is much love of Athens expressed,[89] but Isocrates' desire for a return to a much more restricted democracy is made clear in the *Areopagiticus* (21 ff.). At the same time he looks more and more toward individuals as the hope of separate cities and of the Greek world. This is a general trend of the fourth century, and part of the transition from the real city state, in which every man was a part of the whole, to the Hellenistic state where an individual ruled and where other individuals found compensatory individuality in an increasingly personal philosophy and religion. In Athens Isocrates most admired his own pupil Timotheus (*Antidosis* 101 ff.). Else-

[89] Cf. esp. *Panegyricus* 21 ff.; *Areopagiticus* 73 ff.; *Antidosis* 299 f.; most of the *Panathenaicus*.

where he looked at one time to the monarchy of Cyprus, later to Syracuse. Isocrates' appeal to Dionysius in his first epistle, where he calls upon him to undertake the leadership of all Greeks, is exactly parallel to Plato's hopes in Dionysius II: both writers were trying to produce in actuality a political dream. The nature of Plato's dream is no doubt ultimately derived from Socrates. In Isocrates' case it is the fact of the dream, the right to dream, the possibility of utopia, which comes from Socrates.

The early publications of Isocrates' school cannot be dated precisely. The speech *Against the sophists* constituted a kind of program (*Antidosis* 193 ff.) and is perhaps, therefore, the earliest, written sometime in the late 390's. Because of its connexion with Socrates the *Busiris* also seems to be early. In the early 380's Plato returned to Athens, found Isocrates' school flourishing, and opened the Academy. There is no tradition of *personal* animosity between Plato and Isocrates,[90] but certainly they did occupy vastly different intellectual positions and viewed each other's schools with disapproval. Some passages by each author clearly have the other in mind. Plato's attitude toward rhetoric at the time of the founding of the Academy can be seen in the *Gorgias*. There is nothing in that dialogue to point directly and specifically at Isocrates; rather it is a criticism of all rhetoric and all rhetoricians. Isocrates had been a pupil of Gorgias and felt the force of the criticism, particularly the implication (454b1 ff.) that rhetoric was not an art because it lacked a subject matter of its own. The criticism was unfair, as Aristotle later realized. Isocrates' answer was not to refute the contention by argument, but to attempt to disprove it by practice. For the next few years he experimented with a variety of subjects and forms until he discovered what he felt was a satisfactory subject for his own conception of oratory.

[90] Cf. Diogenes Laertius 3.8 and Wilamowitz, *op.cit.* supra n. 51, 106 ff.

The first example of this experimentation would be the *Encomium of Helen*. It begins with an extensive introduction, out of proportion to the length of the speech, attacking various groups of philosophers and rhetoricians and finally discussing the proper subject of oratory. Among the philosophers criticized (1) are those who maintain that courage, wisdom, and justice are identical and that there is one knowledge concerned with all three. This presumably means Plato and his followers, but Antisthenes, Protagoras, Gorgias, Zeno, and Melissus are all criticized in the first three sections, so that it is difficult to regard the work as directed primarily against Plato.[91] The criticism of Gorgias is important and resumed again in section fourteen. Gorgias claimed to write an encomium of Helen, but, Isocrates says, actually he wrote a defense of Helen. This is a mild criticism, but it succeeds in putting Isocrates in an independent and middle position between the writers he criticizes. He would not be identified with any of them and avoids all their pitfalls. The subjects for discussion which they choose are mostly a waste of time and quite unlike Isocrates' subjects (11):

"Topics of general applicability and reliability and all similar ones are devised and delivered by means of a variety of forms and occasions which are hard to learn, and their composition is more difficult in the same degree as it is more difficult to be dignified than to scoff and to be serious than to joke."

This statement is reminiscent of the accounts of his own oratory in later speeches.[92] It and the criticism of other writers surely suggest that the speech as a whole is regarded by Isocrates as a serious product and not merely a rhetorical

[91] Though R. L. Howland did so, "The attack on Isocrates in the *Phaedrus*," CQ 31 (1937) 151 ff. He regarded the *Helen* as a reply to the *Protagoras*.
[92] Cf. *Against the sophists* 16 f.; *Panegyricus* 7 ff.; *Antidosis* 46 ff.

exercise. He goes on in section twelve to attack encomia of bumblebees or salt as trivial, but to speak of Helen (14) is to call to memory a remarkable woman.

The ensuing praise of Helen may be viewed as a discussion of panhellenism in which Theseus, the symbol of Athens, and Heracles, the symbol of Sparta, contend for the prize of excellence in a campaign against the barbarian.[93] Panhellenism was a traditional topic of the festival orations and thus ready at hand. It is made explicit in the closing words of the speech:

"We might justly believe that Helen is the cause of our not being slaves to the barbarians. For we shall find that it was because of her that the Greeks agreed together and made a joint expedition against the barbarians and then for the first time made Europe victor over Asia. As a result, we experienced such a great change that, although in the past any among the barbarians who fell upon evil times thought it right to rule the Greek cities . . . after that war our race progressed so much that it took both great cities and much territory from the barbarians. If, therefore, any speakers wish to develop this material and amplify it, they will not be at a loss for a starting point from which, without repeating what I have said, they will be able to praise Helen, but will meet with many new topics concerning her."

Isocrates has a number of objectives in the *Helen*. Criticism of other educators is one; experimentation with a serious theme is another; clearly the composition of a model encomium for imitation by the pupils in his school is a third. Only in the latter sense is the speech to be regarded as rhetorical exercise. To a greater or lesser degree all of Isocrates' speeches interweave educational controversy,

[93] Cf. George A. Kennedy, "Isocrates' *Encomium of Helen*: a panhellenic document," TAPA 89 (1958) 77 ff. Isocrates' immediate inspiration of Helen as a cause of Greek advantage may be Euripides' *Trojan women* 931 ff.

political or philosophical thought, and pedagogic method.

Plato seems to have regarded the *Helen* as requiring an answer, which he incorporated into the *Phaedrus*. That dialogue, which is structurally a reverse image of the *Helen* in that it consists of specimen speeches followed by a theoretical discussion, contains not only reminiscences of Isocrates but "direct and comprehensive attack on the educational system of Isocrates in which Isocrates' own words and methods . . . are turned against him."[94] At the end of the dialogue is a famous passage in which Socrates sends his greetings to Isocrates, expresses his hopes in him, and remarks that there is a "certain philosophy" in his mind. This is probably an allusion to Isocrates' early association with and respect for Socrates compared to what Plato must have regarded as an un-Socratic and even un-philosophic philosophy subsequently pursued.

A second attempt to provide a material for rhetoric was the *Panegyricus* of 380. The material is again panhellenism, but, instead of the form of a mythological exercise, Isoc-

[94] Cf. Howland, *op.cit.* supra n. 91, 152. Note that Socrates criticizes a written speech, that his remarks, like those of Isocrates, are provoked by an unsatisfactory work by another author, that Stesichorus' palinode was concerned with Helen. Howland believed that "Lysias" really meant "Isocrates" and was a way of deflating the would-be educator to the level of the logographer. Cf. also Raeder, *op.cit.* supra n. 82, and Léon Robin, *Platon* 4.3 (Budé), Paris, 1933, xxii ff. Robin (p. ix) appears to date the *Phaedrus* in the 370's, which is satisfactory since the *Helen* is probably an approximate contemporary of the *Panegyricus* of 380. Howland (p. 159) dates the *Phaedrus* about 370 since he sees in it (260a1) a reference to *To Nicocles* 23 f., a speech written after Nicocles became king in 374. Other discussions of Plato and Isocrates include K. Lueddecke, "Ueber Beziehungen zwischen Isokrates *Lobrede auf Helena* und Platons *Symposium*," RHM 52 (1897) 628 ff.; A. Croiset, *op.cit.* supra n. 52; B. von Hagen, *Num simultas intercesserit Isocrati cum Platone*, Jena, 1906; G. Mathieu, "Les premiers conflit entre Platon et Isocrate et la date de l'*Euthydème*," *Mélanges Glotz*, Paris, 1932, 555 ff.; Jaeger, *op.cit.* supra n. 53, 3. 46 ff.; G. J. de Vries, "Isocrates' reaction to the *Phaedrus*," MN 6 (1953) 39 ff.; Dodds, *op.cit.* supra n. 50, 27 f.

rates adopted a combination of a festival oration and a funeral oration. In thought and style this is his greatest speech. The choice of the imaginary situation and the title are expressions of the nature of the subject, which finds Greece in a contest of excellence with the barbarian. There is thus a real union of subject and form which Isocrates never again achieves. The beginning of the speech develops the motif most, with its contrast of athlete and orator (1), Isocrates and sophists (4 and 9), and the audience as judge (11), but throughout the speech words of striving, winning, contesting, and wrestling seem common. One of the claims of Athenian greatness is, significantly, that of her festivals (43 ff.). The end (187) invites a continuation of the contest and challenges other orators to come forth. Athletic motifs are common in all Greek oratory, but only here and in Demosthenes' *On the crown* are they so systematically introduced. Some of the Greek love of speech and argumentation is probably derived from a feeling that oratory is a contest in which man exhibits something of his manliness. Phoenix taught Achilles to be a doer of deeds and a speaker of words. Circumstances of a less heroic age robbed many Greeks of the opportunity to be the former and these made up for it by exercise as the latter. The involvement of personal honor suggested in the *Panegyricus* is part of the reason that the speech stands so far above anything else that Isocrates did, that and the appropriateness of the form and the nature of the audience which was not a court of law or a company of sophists, but the whole Greek world. Yet, although the *Panegyricus* is addressed to all the Greeks, and although at times (e.g. 185) it appears to call for a joint hegemony of Athens and Sparta, it is predominantly an Athenian document. Buchner in a recent study[95] sees in the speech a union of epideictic ad-

[95] Edmund Buchner, *Der Panegyricus des Isokrates: eine historisch-philologische Untersuchung*, Wiesbaden, 1958.

dressed solely to Athenians, as a funeral oration would be, and a deliberative speech addressed to all Greeks. In the latter it was necessary to recognize the claims of other states, but surely what Isocrates most wanted was an Athenian revival. The most important goal of Greek co-operation and of expedition against Persia was to be its effect on Athens, which was still weak from the Peloponnesian war and from Spartan rule of Greece. In the center of the work (100 ff.) Isocrates inserted a defense of Athens' recent past, and the total effect of the portrayal of Athenian greatness is not only to claim for Athens the right to lead but also to show to the Athenians their national character and their potential greatness. Athens' claim is an historical and traditional one, not one of present might. Isocrates already lived in the past; the sense of progress evident through much of the fifth century had vanished.

Of all the speeches of Isocrates the *Panegyricus* is the one which is most likely to have had some real political influence. The second Athenian confederacy, which was formed in 377, contained a number of features reminiscent of its exhortations. Isocrates may claim at least to have helped prepare the public for that event.[96]

In the works of the next dozen years Isocrates abandoned panhellenism as a basis for oratory and experimented with a kind of gnomic oratory, reminiscent of the elegiac poets. This is seen in the so-called Cyprian speeches, *To Demonicus*, *To Nicocles*, and *Nicocles*. The rise of Thebes may have made panhellenism seem a remote possibility so that Isocrates was forced to create a new kind of serious oratory. The results clearly were not satisfactory, and he returned to panhellenism when opportunities were presented. There

[96] Cf. U. von Wilamowitz-Moellendorf, *Aristoteles und Athen* 2, Berlin, 1893, 380 ff.; Charles D. Adams, "Recent views of the political influence of Isocrates," cp 7 (1912) 343 ff.; M. L. W. Laistner, *Isocrates: De pace and Philippus* (*Cornell studies in classical philology* 22), New York, 1927, 16. The connexion was rejected by Baynes, *op.cit.* supra n. 78, 144 ff.

were none for a while. The Cyprian speeches were followed by the *Plataicus*, which deals very specifically with the capture and destruction of Plataea by the Thebans in 373. It was probably also natural to turn to specific and immediate subjects when the one great subject was unavailable. From this time on the desire to discover a subject for oratory seems to fade into the background. Isocrates probably felt that the success of his works and his school was an adequate answer to Plato. He had indeed created a unique treatment of political material.

Although panhellenism is not alluded to in any of the speeches of this period, Isocrates had not forgotten it. A fragmentary letter (number 1) to Dionysius of Syracuse survives in which Isocrates urges him to take the leadership of the Greek world.[97] This letter must be dated about 368, that is, after the defeat of Sparta at Leuctra, during a successful campaign against Carthage, and before Dionysius' own death. In addition to illustrating the general trend of looking toward individuals as the salvation of Greece, the letter shows something about Isocrates. It is the first of several sudden graspings at an opportunity to effect his panhellenic scheme. The original concept of panhellenism was a means of restoring the ancient prestige of Athens. That an Athenian revival continued to be one of Isocrates' main interests is borne out by the *Areopagiticus*, *On the peace*, and the *Panathenaicus*; but panhellenism under Athenian leadership became less and less possible. Athens could hardly have played now the major role in a campaign against barbarians, and in a world ruled by Dionysius she could not have expected any more consideration than the

[97] Attempts to prove the letters spurious have been unsatisfactory; cf. L. F. Smith, *The genuineness of the ninth and third letters of Isocrates*, Lancaster, Pennsylvania, 1940. Cf. also U. von Wilamowitz-Moellendorf, *op.cit.* supra n. 96, 391 ff. and "Unechte Briefe," *Hermes* 33 (1898) 492 ff.; C. Woyte, *De Isocratis quae feruntur epistulis quaestiones selectae*, Leipzig, 1907; G. Weiss, *Zur Echtheit der Briefe des Isokrates: syntaktische Beiträge*, Schwabach 1914.

occasional tokens she received from Alexander. It is the program itself, rather than its objectives, which Isocrates is anxious to effect, or to put it another way, the rhetorical success of the *Panegyricus* made its political program into the policy of the school, valued for itself alone.

Dionysius did nothing to fulfill Isocrates' hopes and soon died. Isocrates fell back into his old pattern and produced the *Archidamus* and *Areopagiticus*, which have no hint of panhellenism but are concerned with the maintenance of the domestic traditions of Sparta and Athens. In 356 he addressed a letter to Archidamus (number 9), a fragment of which also survives. In it he calls upon the Spartan king to lead an expedition to take from the barbarian land on which Greeks could be settled and at the same time to free the Greeks of Asia. Why he chose this moment to appeal to Archidamus is unclear. Athens was embroiled in the Social war; no state was in a position of clear leadership; Philip's future was not yet certain. From the *Archidamus* it is clear that Isocrates admired the king as an individual, and perhaps he had done something we do not know about to demonstrate his great potentialities in Isocrates' eyes. But the same objections which may be made against Isocrates' appeal to Dionysius are relevant. The revival of panhellenism is sudden and, on the basis of other works, unexpected; it is in fundamental inconsistency with Isocrates' original conception of panhellenism as the cure for Athens' decline and his continuing interest in Athenian revival.

Then the pattern repeats itself on an even bolder scale. Isocrates for ten years says nothing about panhellenism. He occupied himself first with the composition of the speech *On the peace*, which is his most pacifistic work and in which a new policy of friendship and nonaggression is outlined. Then comes the *Antidosis*, his defense of his educational system. It refers (57 ff.) to the *Panegyricus* in terms indicating that panhellenism was definitely a thing of the past. Subsequently Isocrates began work on a tract designed to show that the quarrel between Athens and Philip of Macedon over Amphipolis could peacefully, justly, and honorably be resolved, but before he completed it peace was actually achieved. We know a little about Isocrates' projected speech on Amphipolis from the description given at the beginning of the *Philip*, and it seems to have been in somewhat the spirit of the *Areopagiticus* and *On the peace* in its avoidance of the question of a panhellenic expedition. But the Peace of Philocrates, the apparent respect of Philip for Athens, and a situation in which it was no longer traitorous to speak well of the Macedonian presented to Isocrates an opportunity even more tempting than those which had produced the letters to Dionysius and Archidamus. He composed a formal oration to Philip on the scale of his greatest speeches urging him to assume the leadership of Greece, reconcile the Greek states, and undertake an expedition against Persia. The speech captures some of Isocrates' earlier vigor and may be regarded as realistic; yet surely it is, like the earlier letters, an aberration of the moral position which Isocrates had earlier assumed. Isocrates had been striving for the greatness of Athens, the need to effect a moral revival worthy of Athenian traditions, the essential unity of Hellenic civilization, and the fact, seen repeatedly in the moral synthesis of arguments, that the means to accomplish an end are in themselves important. Virtually every one of these principles he is willing to throw aside. He discovers (32) that Philip is a descendant of Heracles, and thus a legitimate Greek, though previously he had restricted that ancestry to the Spartan kings (*Letter to Archidamus* 3). He claims (128 ff.) that Athens has sunk so low that she is incapable of any effort; but the original point of the expedition was to strengthen what Athens stood for. Without central participation by the historic Greek states the campaign was merely an example of individual aggression. There is no reason to believe that the *Philip* had any effect upon Philip or in any way influenced his subsequent actions or his creation of the League of Corinth,[98] nor does Isocrates claim to have influenced Philip, only to have expressed what Philip was considering himself (*Second letter to Philip* 3).

The last of the speeches of Isocrates is the *Panathenaicus*. Readers have often felt that it was a strange and unsatis- factory document.[99] They have sometimes blamed this on the author's advanced age: he was 98 when he completed it. Probably it does show a falling off of powers, but it is quite typical of Isocrates' political theory over the previous decades. Isocrates' pro-Philip sentiment lasted until about 342 and produced the first letter to Philip. Sometime around 342, perhaps still in admiration of Philip, he began the *Panathenaicus*. It is a defense of Athens and an attack on Sparta that is out of touch with political realities. Isoc- rates himself admits (58) that Spartan influence in the political realm hardly deserved this vehement attack, an attack which readers of the *Archidamus* and the letter to Archidamus would hardly have predicted. On the other hand, the names of Macedon and Philip, which were surely the objects of all interest at the time, are never mentioned.

The explanation for the *Panathenaicus* can be found in its defense of Athens. Isocrates' later life is overshadowed by a feeling of being misunderstood (*Panathenaicus* 5): it is hardly surprising. How could his feeling for Philip be justified in terms of patriotism or of his own adherence to a Socratic tradition? Especially must his position have been difficult after the war between Athens and Macedon re- sumed in 340. It was the peace of 346 which made his appeal to Philip possible. His last official words had been the *Philip*, and his sentiments were doubtless regarded as pro-

[98] Cf. Laistner, *op.cit.* supra n. 96, 21, and Baynes, *op.cit.* supra n. 78, 145.

[99] Cf. Blass 2.292 ff.; Jebb 2.122 ff.; Norlin 2, *op.cit.* supra n. 86, 369 f. For attempts to explain the speech cf. P. Wendland, "König Philippos und Isokrates," NGG (1910) 137 ff.

Macedonian. The *Panathenaicus* is designed to show his love of Athens (35 ff.). He looks back over his life's work and tries to draw it together, revising things he had said (172), suppressing panhellenism, trying to achieve again the moral synthesis of his earlier triumphs. Sometimes (e.g. 86 f.) it is justice that is to be the basis of action, but then a kind of cynicism breaks out (e.g. 114 ff.). If this interpretation is correct, the emphasis on Sparta is diversionary. Isocrates wants to show that the real opponent of Athens has not been Macedon, but Sparta. The speech was written over a long period of time. When half of it was finished Isocrates became too ill to work, he says (267); then three years later he took it up and completed it. We do not know what parts he wrote when, but it seems likely that the parts most like the *Philip* were composed earlier. This would include much of the first section of the speech, including the praise of Agamemnon, which some critics have regarded as a covert eulogy of Philip,[100] while the latter part of the speech, in which the criticism of Sparta is mitigated, represents perhaps less of a desire to direct opposition against Sparta and thus less interest in diverting it from Macedon.

This is the last of Isocrates' major works, but it is not the end of the story. There is still another reversal. The war between Athens and Macedon ended in the battle of Chaeronea in 338 and the defeat of Athens. Shortly after, Isocrates addressed his second letter to Philip. He reminds Philip of his earlier advice. He exults in Philip's victory over Greece. And he makes the startling assertion that after the expected victory over the Persians nothing will remain but for Philip to become a god. The letter in recent times has been accepted as genuine; it is not unexpected. If it is genuine, the romantic biographical tradition that Isocrates committed suicide on learning of the victory of

[100] Beginning with Arnold Schaefer, *Demosthenes und seine Zeit* 3, Leipzig, 1887, 6.

Philip has to be rejected and with it the historicity of Milton's Sonnet:

> Daughter to that good Earl, once President
> Of England's Council and her Treasury,
> Who lived in both unstained with gold or fee,
> And left them both, more in himself content,
> Till the sad breaking of that Parliament
> Broke him, as that dishonest victory
> At Chaeronea, fatal to liberty,
> Killed with report that old man eloquent.

Isocrates' political thought is characterized by startling reversals brought on by opportunities to see his scheme for a panhellenic expedition realized. The ordinary course of his development, and most of his speeches, is concerned with Athens, with her moral responsibilities, her national character, and her domestic policy. But whenever someone appeared who might effect his other plan he was willing for the moment to forget Athens and dash off a letter or speech in quite a different mood. This happened roughly every ten years and recipients included Dionysius of Syracuse, Archidamus of Sparta, and Philip of Macedon. Isocrates admits to opportunism (*Philip* 118 and *Panathenaicus* 172).

These vacillations no doubt helped to produce some of the feeling of dissatisfaction evident in Isocrates' educational activities. He does not seem to have retired, but speaks of pupils as though still with him in advanced age. The most extensive exposition of his educational ideals is the *Antidosis* of 353. It grew out of an actual occasion when Isocrates, who was suspected of considerable wealth, was challenged under a valid Athenian law either to perform a liturgy, which would mean to fit out a warship at his own expense, or to exchange property with another citizen originally assigned the same liturgy. *Antidosis* means exchange of property. Isocrates lost the suit and it opened his eyes to his unpopularity. Subsequently he composed this apology, modeling it on the speech of Socrates. For all the speech's literary echoes nothing could show more clearly the extent to which he had developed into a figure quite unlike his master. The artificiality of the occasion—this is not the defense in the antidosis suit, but an imaginary defense on a capital charge—the enormous length of the speech in which every conceit is developed to the fullest possible extent, the annoyance of Isocrates that he should be misunderstood, his pride as seen in his extensive quotations from himself and his listing of his pupils, all are un-Socratic. It is doubtful that the *Antidosis* reversed the trend in Isocrates' popularity. In the later speeches, the *Philip* and the *Panathenaicus,* there is even some evidence of increasing rifts between Isocrates and his own pupils. For example, in the *Philip* (18 ff.) he says that when he described the work he was writing his followers were dismayed and tried to dissuade him. The objections which he cites involve mostly the impossibility of advising Philip, but the master could hardly be told that he was vitiating his life's work for the sake of apparent expediency, a policy against which he had always protested. Similarly, in the *Panathenaicus* (200 ff.) there is a kind of dialogue between Isocrates and his pupils on the subject of his treatment of Sparta in that speech.

Isocrates' strange inconsistencies and vacillations can be explained, and a unified concept of his career can be achieved. As usual the reactions of antiquity are a valid starting point. Isocrates was generally viewed as an orator and stylist, occasionally as an educator, hardly ever as a political thinker. His political influence, if it existed, was slight.[101]

[101] Isocrates sways so much with the times that it sometimes appears he is influencing the course of events and it is probable that at least a few people took him seriously. As stated above, the *Panegyricus* may have helped pave the way for the Second Athenian Confederacy, but real influence on later events or on the policies of Philip seems unlikely. For a good statement of a variety of early

Philip of Macedon compared Isocrates' speeches to athletes since they furnished pleasure for spectators (*Lives of the ten orators* 845d). Isocrates is never concerned with the bases of political judgment, with sources of political information, with the theory of politics. He is neither a political theorist like Aristotle nor a practical politician like Demosthenes. What he is concerned with are the means of expression of political thought: not what Athens, or even Philip ought to do, but how to demonstrate what ought to be done, how to marshal arguments, how to say something new on the same theme. He states (*Panegyricus* 10):

"I think that both the other arts and the philosophy of words would make the greatest progress if admiration and honor were paid not to the originators of deeds, but to those who best perfected each, and not to those seeking to speak on subjects which no one has previously discussed, but those knowing how to speak as no one else could."

Not just *Busiris* and *Helen* but all of Isocrates' works composed after he opened his school are in some degree sophistic specimen speeches (*Panathenaicus* 134) addressed to the Greeks in general and to the school in particular.

---

views cf. Adams, *op.cit.* supra n. 96. Ernest Barker, "Greek political thought and theory," *Cambridge ancient history* 6, Cambridge, Eng., 1927, 518, took the position that Isocrates' pamphlets were without effect. G. Mathieu, *Les idées politiques d'Isocrate*, Paris, 1925, supported an opposite view, but is rightly criticized by Jaeger 199 ff. The latter believed that Isocrates sometimes wrote works at the suggestion of political leaders and gives the *Plataicus*, commissioned by Timotheus, as an example. This seems possible. M. L. W. Laistner, "The influence of Isocrates' political doctrines on some fourth century men of affairs," cw 23 (1930) 129 ff. stated the view that Isocrates had practical influence, but the article is lacking in any satisfactory proof. Probably Isocrates' pupils learned more rhetoric than political theory from him; the achievements of Timotheus and others cannot be credited to Isocrates without specific evidence.

They contain serious thoughts, of which the theory of panhellenism is the most obvious, but they were composed in response to rhetorical rather than political challenges. In the *Panegyricus* Isocrates rather transfigured himself and achieved something close to political thought. His pride therein is enormous (14). The rest of his career he lived in the shadow of that work; he was always predisposed in favor of its theme because of its rhetorical success. He can rise with equal enthusiasm to the rhetorical challenge of a speech for a Spartan king or a Plataean exile. He can find arguments to address any foreign tyrant. He can argue against the Peace of Antalcidas as a disaster or for it as the basis of all security and happiness.

What this means can be shown more specifically from an analysis of the *Philip*, perhaps the most vigorous of his later speeches and one which might be thought to be the product of a realistic political concern. Some of the political thought may be sincere enough, but it was not the motivation of composition. The *Philip* may be divided into three main parts: an introduction (1-29), the body of the speech (30-122) urging Philip to reconcile the Greeks and undertake the leadership of an expedition against Persia, and an epilogue (123-155) elaborating the glory of the task. Though the introduction contains considerable praise of Philip and performs the normal function of preparing the audience to listen with favor to the rest of the speech, it also contains a great amount of discussion of the speech itself, of the rhetorical problem involved, of an earlier speech, and of Isocrates. It is doubtful that this would have much effect on Philip, whereas it was of consuming interest to Isocrates and to his pupils, who were intended to regard the speech as a model of how to address a king. Isocrates is much concerned throughout with novelty. He begins (1) by telling Philip not to be surprised at the unusual beginning of the speech, which is the more or less irrelevant matter of what Isocrates would have said if he had been

199

able to complete a speech on the subject of Amphipolis. It is clear that he regarded that occasion as a rhetorical rather than political challenge (2-3):

"When I saw that the war between you and Athens was the cause of many evils *I endeavored to say* on the subject of the city and its territory *nothing similar to what was said* by your companions or by our statesmen, *but what was as remote as possible from their policy.* . . . I expressed no opinion about the subjects under debate. . . ."

What he did was enunciate a clever paradox (3):

"It was to your advantage for us to have this territory and it was to our city's advantage by no means to acquire it."

He describes with some satisfaction in what follows the reaction of his pupils to the brilliant, but unrealistic sophistry with which he supported this dictum.

It was also the rhetorical challenge which inspired him to write on the present occasion (10):

"Having thought about these matters and believing that I would never find a nobler subject than this nor one of more general interest nor one more advantageous to us all, I was moved to write on the subject again. . . ."

"Us" no doubt can be taken to include Philip and the Athenians, but Isocrates is really thinking of himself and his school. He is again thinking of the latter when he says (12):

"I wished by means of these words addressed to you also to show and make clear to my pupils that to bore the national festivals and to address all the people coming together at them is in reality to address no one. . . ."

The orator must instead win over a champion like Philip. Isocrates momentarily at least admits the ineffectiveness of oratory! Some of his pupils objected to the appeal to

200

Philip (17 ff.), and we have already suggested that their objections may have been well-founded. Isocrates inserts the objections at length (18-21) for two reasons: they glorify Philip and they glorify his own achievement in rising to the enormous task of addressing Philip in a worthy speech. In this he was of course successful, and he reports the shame and repentance which his pupils expressed when they read the magnificent work he had produced (23). The speech is now submitted to be judged by Philip (29) and it is with this request for literary judgment rather than a request for political action that the introduction ends.

The body of the speech is a good example of rhetorical amplification of a rather meaningless sort. The first general topic (32-80) is the reconciliation which Isocrates would have Philip effect. This is subdivided into discussions of the benefits which the Greeks have bestowed on the Macedonians (32-38), the *possibility* of reconciliation (39-56), the *ease* of accomplishment (57-67), and the *worthiness* of the task (68-80). Possibility is "proved" by arguments from probability: the probable reaction of the Spartans, Argives, Thebans, and Athenians in turn. Ease is "proved" by historical examples, all irrelevant, of men who did great things: Alcibiades, Conon, Dionysius, and Cyrus. The section thus constitutes a good example of method for maintaining practically any kind of argument.

This first general topic is separated from what follows by a brief (81-82) explanation of Isocrates' right to give advice, his wisdom, and his education—considerations which must never slip from the reader's mind. The second general topic of the speech is the expedition which Isocrates recommends against the barbarian (83-123). It begins with discussion of the rhetorical difficulty of saying something new since Isocrates had already treated the topic in the *Panegyricus*. But he can at least furnish an outline of argument for others (*i.e.* his pupils) to elaborate (85). There are two main subdivisions: one argues that success is assured on the basis of the expedition of the Ten Thousand (89-105); the other avers that Philip's predecessors would also argue in favor of the expedition (105-115). In the first of these Isocrates is particularly proud of the rhetorical paradox that he is arguing from the example of a failure in order to prove the possibility of success (89-90), though apologetic that he had already used the example in the *Panegyricus* (93-4). He shows remarkable restraint in not introducing one possible avenue of amplification (98). The second subdivision of the general topic of the expedition, the argument that Philip's predecessors would approve, is an example of Gorgianic amplification as described by Aristotle (*Rhetoric* 1418a33 ff.):

"In epideictic there is need of episodic praise, like that found in Isocrates. For he is always dragging in somebody. This is what Gorgias meant when he said he was never at a loss for words. If he speaks about Achilles he praises Peleus, then Aeacus, then the god. . . ."

Isocrates is happy to have a novel thought in portraying Heracles: he elaborates his moral rather than physical virtues, though he does not feel up to a complete treatment of the subject (109-110). The pupils are no doubt to carry on the work.

The peroration, too, betrays the primarily rhetorical concern of the speech. Philip is to think up new arguments himself (138), although in general Isocrates' field is speech, Philip's action (151). The final section of the work (155) is still concerned with itself as a work of art.

Similar analyses could be made of other works of Isocrates and would bring the reader close to his central interests. From some passages, the last section of the *Philip* for example, it might be possible to argue that Isocrates regards his speeches in the way that fifth-century sophists looked at rhetoric—as a way of arriving at a relative truth by the development of crucial issues and arguments. But this is to pay him too high a compliment. He never argues both sides of a question. He wants his side to win, and he wants his pupils and the world to be impressed with his wisdom, but his concern with the subject matter is largely incidental. It is grist for his technique. This technique, Isocrates himself, his school, and virtually everything connected with him need occasion no great wonder. The Greeks were not taken in by him, though the Romans sometimes were. He was tiresome, long-winded, and above all superficial. His style is typical of him. It says as little as could be imagined in as many words as possible (*Panathenaicus* 84 f.). Just as he develops each possible argument, so he develops each possible grammatical antithesis. It is not communication, but decoration, not persuasion, but obfuscation.

Deliberative Oratory[102]

The statesmen of the fifth century did not publish their orations and perhaps made little or no use of writing in composing them. Historians like Herodotus and Thucydides sometimes reconstructed what was said on the basis of men's memory and probability, but deliberative oratory was not regarded as a literary form. According to Plato (*Phaedrus* 257d5 ff.) politicians were afraid of being regarded as sophists if they published speeches. The earliest rhetorical handbooks concerned themselves solely with judicial oratory, and the only training for political speaking came in the schools of the sophists, some of whom composed and taught specimen speeches and commonplaces adaptable to a variety of political occasions. The *Demegoric prooemia* of Critias (Hermogenes, *On characteristics* 2.11) would be an example. According to Thucydides (8.68.1) Antiphon helped speakers in the assembly: perhaps he wrote portions of speeches as a logographer. As far as we know the theory

[102] Cf. in general, H. Ll. Hudson-Williams, "Political speeches in Athens," CQ 1 (1951) 68 ff.

of deliberative oratory did not receive formal expression until the time of Aristotle and Anaximenes, but in the late fifth and early fourth centuries, judging from speeches in the historians and a few other examples, deliberative orators were much influenced by the rules for judicial speeches. Prooemia and perorations like those in court speeches appear, there is occasional need for narration, argument from probability and historical examples are employed, and there are developed commonplaces and topics, the expedient in particular, but also the just, the honorable, and the possible, which served as a framework for the central part of many speeches. We have already noted in Isocrates a tendency to combine all of these topics together as arguments recommending one particular course of action.

Publication—by which is meant circulation in written form—of political speeches may well have been begun by aliens who were desirous of influencing Athenian political opinions, but who were barred from speaking in the assembly. We hear (Clement, *Miscellanies* 6.16) of a work by Thrasymachus, who was a citizen of Chalcedon, *On behalf of the Larissans*, and Dionysius of Halicarnassus (*Demosthenes* 3) quotes a considerable fragment from the beginning of "one of the demegoric speeches" of Thrasymachus. It is concerned with the "ancestral constitution" and presumably, therefore, to be dated in the period 411-403, when that was an important political slogan. The fragment is interesting as foreshadowing the way Isocrates and Demosthenes try to arouse Athenian patriotic emotions. The thirty-fourth speech of the metic Lysias, *Against the subversion of the ancestral constitution of Athens* belongs in a similar category, though it was delivered by someone according to Dionysius (*Lysias* 32) so that Lysias was really a political logographer.

The earliest extant deliberative speech both delivered and published by its author seems to be the third oration of Andocides, *On the peace with Sparta*. The circumstances leading to publication are relatively clear. Andocides, who was of course an Athenian citizen, and his fellow delegates failed to persuade the Athenians to accept the terms of the treaty which they had arranged with Sparta; they were consequently exiled in 391. During his previous exile Andocides had published what is now known as his second speech, *On his return*, and, bad as it is, he perhaps believed that it had helped his cause. He therefore committed this speech to writing as a more permanent justification of his embassy. We have no way of knowing whether it was publicly circulated before or after his death, although it was probably before. In any event, Andocides is in somewhat the position of an alien, anxious to plead a cause, but unable to speak in person in Athens. The speech has a narration, rare in deliberative oratory but appropriate here, and the body of the work as was stated above consists of treatment of the topics of necessity (13), practicability (15), expediency (17-23), and justice (23), in a fashion not unlike the synthesis of arguments later used by Isocrates.[103] There is also a peroration which recapitulates the argument and appeals to the audience.

Some of the speeches of Isocrates belong formally to the deliberative category and were published during his lifetime—the *Plataicus, On the peace*, and *Areopagiticus*, for example. Although these are primarily educational and rhetorical products and only secondarily attempts at political persuasion, they may yet be thought of in the same tradition we have been discussing. Isocrates did not feel capable of delivering speeches and personally participating in public life; instead he published the speeches which he might otherwise have delivered.

Other orators in the first half of the fourth century may have published speeches which they had previously delivered, but there are no extant examples. From what we know it appears that Demosthenes initiated the custom,

[103] Cf. supra p. 183.

and though Hyperides and others followed him, none of their deliberative speeches survive. It has sometimes been thought that even the extant deliberative speeches of Demosthenes were not actually delivered, but were pamphlets generally based on one or more actual speeches, but concerned with general policy rather than specific questions.[104] The theory cannot be flatly denied: most of the speeches are concerned with a definite occasion,[105] but opportunities for editing between delivery and publication existed. The relation between a delivered speech and its published version has been demonstrated only in the case of *On the Chersonese* and the *Fourth Philippic*.[106] It seems clear from Plutarch (*Demosthenes* 11) that Demosthenes published a collection of deliberative speeches during his lifetime, presumably to prolong their political influence.

Demosthenes

Demosthenes was born in Athens in 384 B.C.[107] When he was seven his father died and the guardians appointed for him embezzled most of a large inherit-

[104] Cf. Eduard Schwartz, *Demosthenes erste Philippika*, Marburg, 1894.
[105] Cf. Charles D. Adams, "Are the political 'speeches' of Demosthenes to be regarded as political pamphlets?" TAPA 43 (1912) 5 ff.
[106] Cf. Stephen G. Daitz, "The relationship of the *De Chersoneso* and the *Philippica quarta* of Demosthenes," CP 52 (1957) 145 ff.
[107] The primary sources for Demosthenes' biography are the *Lives of the ten orators*, the life by Plutarch, references in Demosthenes' own speeches, especially the three speeches *Against Aphobus* and *On the crown*, and the attacks in all three speeches of Aeschines. Other ancient discussions of Demosthenes as an orator include the *First letter to Ammaeus* and the essay *On the style of Demosthenes* by Dionysius of Halicarnassus, the comparison of Demosthenes and Cicero in *On the sublime* (12), Lucian's *Encomium*, and numerous references elsewhere, esp. in the rhetorical works of Cicero. Translations include those by Charles R. Kennedy (Bohn Library) 5 vols., London 1913; by J. H. Vince, A. T. Murray, et al. (Loeb Library) 7 vols., London and Cambridge, 1930 ff.; A. W. Pickard-Cambridge, *The public orations of Demosthenes*, 2 vols., Oxford, 1912.

ance. On coming of age he prosecuted them in a series of suits; though he recovered only a portion of the money, he thus earned a reputation as a skillful writer of judicial oratory which led to a career as a logographer. Subsequently he was asked to write speeches in cases of political significance: *Against Androtion*, written for Diodorus in 355 was the first. The following year Demosthenes may have undertaken personally the politically motivated prosecution of Leptines. He also delivered in that year his earliest extant deliberative speech, *On the symmories*. At this time he appears to have been in general agreement with the conservative statesman Eubulus. In the following years, however, as seen in the *Philippics* and *Olynthiacs*, he became increasingly alarmed at the growing strength of Philip of Macedon and tried to arouse his fellow citizens to the threat to their liberty, urging that they strengthen their forces and seek alliances. Only temporarily did he acquiesce in the Peace of Philocrates (346). After the defeat of Athens by Macedon at Chaeronea (338) he persisted in anti-Macedonian activities when they seemed possible and in 330 defended his entire career in the greatly admired speech *On the crown*. The end of his life is clouded by charges that he received bribes from Alexander's fugitive treasurer, Harpalus. He was convicted and assessed a heavy fine, which he could not pay, but instead escaped into exile. Recalled at the death of Alexander (322), he enjoyed a brief period of favor, but with the defeat of the Greeks by Antipater in the Lamian war (322) he was condemned to death, fled to the island of Calauria, and drank the poison concealed in his pen.

The corpus of works bearing Demosthenes' name consists of sixty speeches, an erotic essay, a collection of prooemia, and a collection of letters. Of the speeches seven are perhaps by Apollodorus (46, 47, 49, 50, 52, 53, 59). Number fifty-eight has sometimes been attributed to Dinarchus. Numbers 26, 40, 42, 43, 44, 48, and 56 are generally regarded as not by Demosthenes. The *Funeral oration* (60) and the *Erotic essay* may be spurious as are at least the fourth and fifth letters. The deliberative speech *On the Halonessus* is generally attributed to Hegesippus and the speeches *On organization* and *On the treaty with Alexander* to unknown authors. This leaves forty-one speeches, the prooemia, and perhaps some of the letters as probably genuine. In antiquity sixty-five speeches were regarded as genuine by the author of the *Lives of the ten orators* (847e). Some nine speeches once published, but now lost are known to us by title; the greatest loss is probably Demosthenes' defense in the Harpalus incident. Many speeches were published by Demosthenes himself, no doubt after some editing. Others, including the fourth *Philippic* and *Against Midias*, were preserved by Demosthenes in his files but probably not published until a collection was made in Athens by an unknown editor shortly after the orator's death.[108] Some spurious speeches became part of this or subsequent collections because of connexions between Demosthenes and the subjects or persons involved in them.

The antithesis of Isocrates as an educator is Plato, as an orator Demosthenes. This is true not only in the specific historical sense that Demosthenes' energies were directed against Macedon but in the attitude of the two orators toward speech and policy. To Isocrates oratory is a thing in itself; artistic creativity is his goal; he looks for what is literarily expedient. Demosthenes, though he begins as a rhetorician and logographer, subdues his art and constrains it to be his tool in the defense of his country. Once his political instincts are fully awakened they establish absolute standards: he can be inconsistent about all things except patriotism, and to that end his oratory is the single greatest means.

There is a very weak tradition (*Lives of the ten orators* 844b) that makes Demosthenes a pupil of Isocrates, and attempts have been made to point out specific influences

[108] Cf. Erich Bethe, *Demosthenis scriptorum corpus ubi et qua aetate collectum editumque sit*, Rostock, 1897, and Engelbert Drerup, "Antike Demosthenesausgaben," *Philologus Supplementband* 7 (1899) 533 ff.

of one on the other.[109] But Demosthenes' whole concept of the function of the orator, of art, of style, and of politics is so essentially different that occasional verbal similarities need only mean that Demosthenes had read and occasionally picked up a phrase from Isocrates. We have said before that he may have studied some kind of judicial handbook circulated in Isocrates' school, for he was to a great extent self-taught.[110] When he was still a boy the oratory of Callistratus first roused in him a desire to be a great speaker (Plutarch, *Demosthenes* 5). He definitely learned something from Isaeus when preparing his prosecution of his guardians,[111] and the story (Plutarch, *Demosthenes* 7) that his delivery was criticized and improved by the actor Satyrus may well be true. Although they have not always admired him, all critics, ancient and modern, have felt the uniqueness of Demosthenes: it is seen in his Periclean isolation, his disinterest in the gymnasium, his water-drinking among the wine bibbers, his autodidacticism, his ability to draw something from everyone.

In the oratorical career of Demosthenes certain speeches illustrate critical steps in his development. The following discussion will deal with them in an attempt to outline the most satisfactory critical approach to his rhetoric. Any greater discussion covering all the speeches would be out of proportion to this work.

Demosthenes' earliest speech, his prosecution of his guardian Aphobus, is a remarkable product, as much a piece

[109] Avoidance of hiatus, a favorite stylistic feature of Isocrates, can be seen in Demosthenes, and some of the verbalization of patriotism in Demosthenes may come from Isocrates; cf. Josef Mesk, "Demosthenes und Isokrates," ws 23 (1901) 209 ff.; Paul Wendland, "Isokrates und Demosthenes," ngg (1910) 289 ff.; Jaeger 31 ff.

[110] Cf. Jaeger 31 f.

[111] Cf. Blass 3.1.14 ff. and 199 ff. and Octave Navarre, introduction to the Budé *Démosthène: plaidoyers politiques* 1, Paris, 1954, xxx f.

of accounting as of rhetoric.[112] Despite the attested influence of Isaeus, the character of the speech is much more open than is usual in Isaeus. The direct evidence is relevant and extensive: statement and substantiation, statement and substantiation, again and again. Argument from probability finds only a limited use (e.g. 55). There is no indulgence of love of speech, no unnecessary word. The shamelessness of Aphobus is shown repeatedly (e.g. 38), but there is no scurrility. Though the speech falls into the standard formal parts: prooemium 1-3 (with the usual attack on the intractability of the opponent, expression of inexperience—justified for once—and request for a fair hearing), narrative 4-6, proof 7-48 (with 47-8 as a recapitulation), refutation 49-59, and peroration 60-69 (with indirect recapitulation and effective pathos), the impression of the speech is entirely narrative, as though the orator were telling his story and proving every word. Except for the increase in pathos at the end the parts do not show the stylistic differences found in parts of other such speeches. Nothing is probably more reassuring and convincing to a jury than this candid technique. An orator can only use it if he has a very good case with many documents and witnesses and is himself the complete master of the material.

The second speech against Aphobus is a reply in the same trial to Aphobus' charge that Demosthenes' father was a public debtor. It is less successful, less thought out. Direct evidence was not procurable, for the attack had come unexpectedly, and Demosthenes apparently delivered the first part of the speech extempore.[113] There is no formal narra-

---

[112] Cf. Blass 3.1.199 ff.; Jaeger 244; Walther Schwahn, *Demosthenes gegen Aphobos: ein Beitrag zur Geschichte der griechischen Wirtschaft*, Leipzig, 1929, tried to work out the financial details but was not entirely successful; cf. the review by George M. Calhoun, CP 25 (1930) 86 ff. Cf. also J. Korver, "Demosthenes gegen Aphobos," MN 10 (1941) 8 ff.

[113] Cf. Alfred P. Dorjahn, "A third study of Demosthenes' ability to speak extemporaneously," TAPA 83 (1952) 164 ff. Dorjahn has

tion, which is not unusual in "second" speeches; however, one is really needed here to explain the basis of the charge, and the orator fills up the void with a representation of facts from the first speech and a proportionally larger peroration, perhaps to be expected since this is the conclusion of his case. The speech is not a poor one. Demosthenes did what he could at the time, he does not allow himself to be led into any wild statements, and the impression of the case which the jury had from the first speech was doubtless confirmed.

The third speech against Aphobus was delivered some time later, after Aphobus had brought a suit of false witness against Phanus, who had testified for Demosthenes.[114] It was necessary to discuss the earlier trial, and the nature of the attack meant that little direct evidence was available; thus, the use of argument from probability (e.g. 22 ff.) makes the speech seem more regular than the two earlier works, though at the end of the narration (10) the speaker makes a distinction between probabilities and argument from what seems just to all. The speech has great versatility not only in argument but also in style, for example in the liveliness of the imaginary debate between Demosthenes and Aphobus in 40-41. The speech ends abruptly, but perhaps the peroration was not published or has been lost.

Although Demosthenes continued to have difficulties with his guardians and soon afterward delivered the first and second speeches *Against Onetor*, it must have been the prosecution of Aphobus which gave him a limited fame as a writer of courtroom speeches. For the rest of his life he was a logographer; we cannot say with what frequency since many of the works he wrote probably were not preserved

---

shown in this and other studies that there is no good evidence for the tradition that Demosthenes was unable to speak extemporaneously.

[114] Cf. George M. Calhoun, "A problem of authenticity (Demosthenes 29)," TAPA 65 (1934) 80 ff.

or published. His clients seem to have been carefully chosen from among friends and equals: he was not the defender of the downtrodden, but of the affluent, of the creditor against the debtor. Birth was not important to him, as his defense of Phormio shows, but money was. Even when his clients claim poverty one finds it difficult to believe them. In the speech *Against Callicles* the client says that he has small means, but he does not care about the money (35) and has recently paid something over a thousand drachmae in fines (2). Of all the clients the most modest in circumstances was perhaps Euxitheus, who prosecutes Eubulides in the fifty-seventh oration. His opponents claimed that he was rich, but he denies this (52) and there are indications of poverty in the speech (25 and 31). If Euxitheus was indeed poor, it is tempting to see a political significance in Demosthenes' acceptance of the case, for the speech was delivered in the mid 340's during the great campaign against Philip, when Demosthenes wanted to arouse popular sentiment.

The surviving private orations of Demosthenes show him to be a business-like logographer. He can portray the character of a client with conviction, he can narrate with clarity and vigor, and he can construct a logical proof without an impression of slyness. He usually follows standard rhetorical structure and employs many of the commonplaces of prooemium, proof, and peroration. But for all Demosthenes' technical skill there is virtually no evidence in the private speeches of that point of view, seen in Lysias, Isaeus, and Isocrates, which regarded rhetoric as a joy in itself. Demosthenes accepted cases, it would seem, not to find occasions to prove his cleverness, but to gratify his friends and make money. He did not seek sensationalism, did not deal with adulterers and courtesans, did not introduce spectacular pathetic effects.

There is perhaps only one instance in which a charge of questionable practice could be brought against Demosthenes.

In the thirty-sixth speech he ably defended the banker
Phormio in a suit brought by Apollodorus for recovery
of twenty talents. Phormio had been an employee of Apollodorus' father, and after the latter's death became the trustee
of his estate. Releases were given for all claims, but after
many years had passed Apollodorus again insisted that
money was owed to him. Phormio, with Demosthenes'
speech, won more than four-fifths of the jurors' votes and
Apollodorus had to pay a fine. Soon afterward Apollodorus
brought suit for false witness against a minor witness in
Phormio's defense, one Stephanus. We have a speech (45)
apparently written by Demosthenes on behalf of Apollodorus which contains a virulent attack on Phormio (71 ff.).
The orator's change of clients has been much discussed.
Was he simply available to the higher bidder without himself feeling any involvement in the cases? This would seem
more probable in the case of other orators than Demosthenes, who apparently picked his clients with care. Aeschines (*On the embassy* 328) criticizes Demosthenes for
showing the speech for Phormio to Apollodorus before the
trial, not for writing a speech for him. Several hundred
years later Plutarch criticized the action and regarded it as
clearly morally wrong, but Plutarch may not have understood the conventional standards of logography. Blass suggested and others have agreed that Demosthenes' change
of sides was influenced by political consideration, since
Apollodorus took the personal risk about this time of proposing transference of the theoric fund to the war chest
(*Against Neaera* 4), a motion consistent with Demosthenes'
recommendations in the *Olynthiacs*.[115] A political trade of
this kind is probably no more admirable than a lack of

[115] Blass 3.1.32 ff. and Jaeger 40. J. E. Sandys and F. A. Paley,
Select private orations of Demosthenes 2, Cambridge, Eng., 1896,
xxxix ff. discuss the matter thoroughly, but do not accept Blass' view.
On the portrait of the disputants cf. Bruns, *op.cit.* supra n. 18,
534 ff.

involvement and purely literary attitude toward a client's case, but it does show that Demosthenes' actions were based on what he thought to be patriotic principles. The personal attack on Phormio is, however, an acceptance of rhetorical convention, maybe insisted upon by Apollodorus, but regrettable.

Among the private orations is one (51) which does not belong to that category, a claim for a trierarchic crown, delivered some time after 361 by a speaker who was supported by Cephisodotus. We know that Demosthenes as a trierarch carried Cephisodotus as general on board his ship to the Chersonese in 360/359 (Aeschines, *Against Ctesiphon* 51 f.), an occasion vividly described by Demosthenes later (*Against Aristocrates* 163 ff.). The facts fit well enough to make it probable that Demosthenes is speaking in his own person and the speech is, therefore, evidence that he was wealthy enough to be required to furnish a warship at this time, not indeed the only occasion on which he did so (*Against Midias* 78 and 161). It is also evidence of a difference of opinion between Demosthenes and certain supporters of Aristophon (16), then the first man in the city. The speech is not impressive rhetorically; it is querulous in tone and has none of the breadth of vision which Demosthenes later develops: no mention is made, for example, of what the ships did or were intended to do.

As a result of his success in private cases (*dikai*) Demosthenes gained an opportunity to write speeches in suits involving an offense against the state (*graphai*), where there was usually an underlying political rivalry. Greater public interest was aroused by these, and the speeches are often two or three times as long as speeches in private cases. Since Athens had no public prosecutor, individuals had to bring charges in the public suits, and the actual speeches delivered might be written for the prosecutors by logographers, just as in private suits. Demosthenes' function has not changed, therefore, in his speeches *Against Androtion*

(355), *Against Timocrates* (353), and *Against Aristocrates* (352), but opportunity for imaginative treatment and fame are much greater. The speech *Against Leptines* (355) is not essentially different from the private speeches, though Plutarch (*Demosthenes* 15) reports that Demosthenes spoke it in public himself, which would be a further step toward an active public career. Nor has Demosthenes' economic view altered. *Against Androtion, Against Timocrates,* and *Against Leptines* are all directed against a taxation policy that had been especially hard on Demosthenes' prosperous friends and clients.[116] All these works may be regarded as support for the conservative, peace-minded Eubulus. This does not, of course, mean that Demosthenes' views are in any way oligarchic.[117] Eubulus was not an oligarch nor was his supporter Aeschines, nor, in fact, was oligarchy an important ideology in fourth-century Athenian politics. The democratic sentiments of Demosthenes' early speeches can be quite sincere and yet his sympathies can be with the wealthy. The Athenian system of relying on the rich for large capital expenses meant that the state's finances were only as sound as the finances of wealthy individuals. Demosthenes' bias for wealth was to him a bias in favor of financial order.

[116] Cf. L. Vorndran, *Die Aristocratea des Demosthenes als Advokatensrede und ihre politische Tendenz,* Paderborn, 1922 and Jaeger 56 ff. The difficulties of associating terms descriptive of policy to the basically personal groupings of Athenian politics are well brought out by Raphael Sealey, "Athens after the social war," *JHS* 75 (1955) 74 ff. Sealey discusses the political circumstances of the three speeches in question and prefers to regard Aristophon and Androtion as members of two groups personally opposed, but promoting the same policy.

[117] Pierre Orsini, in the introduction to the Budé *Démosthène: plaidoyers politiques* 1, Paris, 1954, ix ff., desiring to make Demosthenes a democrat, has wrongly tried to deny that he was a defender of wealth and position. Orsini's hero worship of Demosthenes' wisdom is counterbalanced in the second part of the introduction where Octave Navarre, the co-editor, writing a number of years earlier, discusses Demosthenes' technique in these speeches.

Since the speeches are consistent in function and social viewpoint with what Demosthenes had been doing, it seems appropriate to ask whether there is any rhetorical difference between these speeches and the private orations, taking *Against Androtion* and *Against Leptines* as examples.

In the public orations of Demosthenes it is often necessary to distinguish the object of a speech from its subject, or, to put it another way, the real from the ostensible and legal issue. The real objective of the speech against Androtion is to discredit a political faction which had been hard upon the wealthier class of society. Androtion as a tax gatherer had especially won the ill will of many. We do not know whether his motives were patriotic or demagogic. An excuse for prosecuting him was found in his proposal to crown the members of the outgoing council, a traditional mark of honor, although in this year (356/355) they had not fulfilled the technical requirement of building new ships because the treasurer had absconded with the money. The charge of illegality was, in other words, a legal technicality. The two prosecutors, coming from the same humble class as the jury, were personal enemies of Androtion, which was satisfactory since personal enmity was a tolerable ground for litigation in Athens and could effectively mask more complicated motives. We do not know who wrote the first speech for the prosecution, perhaps Euctemon, who delivered it. Demosthenes composed the second speech, delivered by Diodorus.

The rhetorical problem involved was to make the action of Androtion seem sufficiently grave to justify condemnation. Demosthenes had to convert a legal technicality into a threat to Athens. He no doubt believed in his cause, and he was aided by Androtion's arbitrary methods and the fact that, as a former pupil of Isocrates (Anonymous life of Isocrates, line 104, Budé), he could be presented as a tricky sophist. Demosthenes' chief technique, and the striking feature of the speech, is the interweaving of three

216

themes: Androtion is vicious, Androtion's crimes are a public concern, Androtion is a sophist. There is a systematic generalization of the charge, or elevation of it from the immediate and legalistic to the symbolic and patriotic. These techniques, first used here, become permanent features of Demosthenes' art.

The three themes are stated in the prooemium (1-4). Androtion has done dreadful things to Euctimon, but worse things to Diodorus. Worse than that, he has attacked Diodorus' uncle. Worse than that, he now has harmed the entire state. But the judges must be careful and not misled, for Androtion is a clever sophist. The themes are rhetorical commonplaces, but usually they are restricted to the prooemium. The distinctive feature of Demosthenes' treatment is that throughout the systematic discussion that follows these threads are never dropped; perhaps the first is the most prominent, but the others continually appear.

The generalization of the charge begins with the first words of the speech, where Euctemon is said to have come to the aid of the city as well as of himself. Androtion's assertion that the council was not responsible for the loss of the funds and its consequent inability to build ships presents an opportunity for amplification of the importance of the navy (12 ff.) with examples from Persian, Peloponnesian, and fourth-century wars, all leaving the clear impression that Androtion is undermining national defense. Androtion must be convicted as a warning to future councils that they must build ships to be honored (19-20). The charge that Androtion was technically incompetent to take part in the assembly is likewise made the occasion for amplification of the wisdom of Solon in guarding Athens against immoral leaders (31-32). Gradually Demosthenes builds up a picture of Androtion as a would-be oligarch: his conviction will make the council more democratic and Athens a better place (37). Are the constitution, the laws, the oaths of the jurymen to be bartered away for the small

217

amount of overdue taxes collected by the plaintiff (45)? The methods of Androtion are oligarchic and exceed the violence of the Thirty Tyrants (47 ff.). The citizens are in fact being treated as slaves (55). Thus Androtion becomes a symbol: whatever kind of man is honored in the state will be imitated (64); the golden crowns which he destroyed are a symbol of merit and honor, qualities held highest by Athenians (75); the bowls dedicated by Androtion are only symbols of wealth. What impiety for Androtion to be conducting the sacred rites of Athens (78)!

By the time Demosthenes has finished speaking Androtion seems a monster and the charge a crucial one in the preservation of the state. The problem of social prejudice is cleverly avoided by granting that rich men were wrong to fail to pay their taxes (42) and subsequently speaking as though Androtion were mainly exacting taxes from the poor (65). Demosthenes has likewise avoided attacking the council members of the past year and asserts that no disgrace will be brought upon them by condemning the actions of these few culprits (36). The speech was heard but once, and in once hearing or once reading today the logical fallacies and exaggerations are not easily perceived. It is possible that some of the facts were more adequately dealt with in the speech given by Euctemon. Demosthenes does not *prove* that the methods of Androtion were oligarchic, nor that he had been a prostitute, nor that his father had been a state debtor—a charge which had been used against Demosthenes himself by Aphobus—certainly not that he had defrauded the treasury as is implied toward the end of the speech (76). It is highly unlikely that Androtion's methods were worse than those of the Thirty Tyrants: Demosthenes produces nothing to equal the experience of Lysias and his family. Demosthenes objects to the use of alternative defenses by Androtion (18) but introduces alternatives himself later on (e.g. 37 and 44). He is also unfair in denying the right of a defendant to dispute the method by which he is brought to trial (28). In other words, there are sophisms and tricks to be found and Demosthenes is clearly a rhetorician. But his motives, unlike those of Lysias, Isocrates, and Isaeus, are not rhetorical, they are political or economic. The end, the discrediting of Androtion, is what is really important and personally important to Demosthenes, though he does not personally deliver the speech. If unfair and tricky, he is yet personally consistent and sincere.

The speech *Against Androtion* has regularity of form and clear structural members. There is a prooemium (1-4) dealing with plaintiff, defendant, motive, and significance as usual. A narration is strictly unnecessary, since this is a second speech for the prosecution; but sections five through seven function as a narration in making a statement of the case, and the usual word introducing the narration ($\gamma \acute{\alpha} \rho$) is found. The proof extends from section eight to sixty-eight. It is divided into a demonstration, with enthymemes and examples, of the illegality of Androtion's action (8-20), of his immorality (21-24), of the legality of the prosecution (25-34), then a refutation of the points made by Androtion (35-46) and an attack on Androtion's character (47-68). The peroration is introduced as though it was a further discussion of the faults and errors of the defendant. There is no recapitulation, but the pathos increases in the presentation of the crowns and bowls as symbols and in the introduction of the religious motif at the very end.[118]

[118] Navarre, *op.cit.* supra n. 111, xxx ff., has a very different notion of the structure of the speech, as does William Wayte, *Demosthenes' Against Androtion and Against Timocrates*, Cambridge, Eng., 1893, xxvi ff., but they do not recognize that introductory words betray the vestiges of a "normal" structure and that ethos, invective, and pathos can be regarded as forms of proof—are so regarded by Aristotle. There is no necessity to restrict the contents of the *pistis* to rational argument. The term epilogue, applied by Navarre (xxvi ff.) to the better part of the speech, is exceedingly inappropriate for such use.

Against Leptines is part of the same political program and is an attempt to repeal a law invalidating grants of immunities to the ordinary recurring liturgies or financial burdens imposed upon the rich. Some wealthy citizens, Chabrias for example, had at one time been exempted because of unusual services to the state. Leptines had abolished the exemptions ostensibly to equalize the financial burden on other citizens. Demosthenes is no doubt sincere in believing that these honorable grants served an important function in encouraging public responsibility, but it is nevertheless true that the class with which he has been identified benefited most from the immunities. The speech contains (24-25) a spirited defense of the existence of private wealth in the state in which Demosthenes' viewpoint is clearly seen. Furthermore, the law of Leptines abolishing the immunities was clearly a part of the same political program as Androtion's tax gathering activities. Aristophon, the statesman in power at the time, was one of the commissioners defending the changes made by Leptines (148), and Eubulus, the leader of the opposite group and soon to become the leading Athenian statesman, was one of those who had been granted an immunity (137). According to Plutarch (*Demosthenes* 15) Demosthenes spoke in person, perhaps in hopes of marrying the widow of Chabrias, whose son, deprived of his father's immunity, nominally was bringing the charge against the new law. The speech is unique in being a prosecution of a law rather than an individual. Since the statue of limitations prevented prosecution of Leptines himself, Demosthenes attacked his law instead and proposed a substitute for it. Commissioners were appointed to defend Leptines' law.

If Demosthenes did speak in person we can see his image in the ethos of the speech. Jaeger drew a picture of a restrained, dignified, somewhat aristocratic advisor—in a word a humanist.[119] Critics have admired the polished tone and

[119] Jaeger 65 ff.

assured elegance of the speech, but its conservatism is equally striking. The laws and constitution are viewed as a political framework evolved with care throughout the past, unexcelled in wisdom. Change is most to be distrusted. What has made Athens great once will do so again (e.g. 88 ff.).

The rhetorical problem of *Against Leptines* is a simpler one than in the case of *Against Androtion*. Obviously the matter is not just a technicality; the speaker must show that the benefits of granting immunities more than balance the immediate financial advantages of abolishing immunities. His theme invites a wide discussion of national self-interest and public service. This is the earliest speech in which Demosthenes begins to formulate his vision of a national character, and he uses that actual phrase a couple of times (11 and 64). He also (61) views Philip of Macedon with some alarm.

Rhetorically the most interesting feature of the speech is its structure. This at first appears loose in the extreme, merely a series of points strung together and introduced by an almost unvarying τοίνυν, "well then." Such a technique contributed to the ethos of the speaker, who seems no slick and ranting professional, but a respectable citizen saying what he has to say. On closer inspection, however, the structure turns out to be somewhat more complex. Demosthenes' proposal for a substitute law is set in the very center of the speech (88-104) and framed by two attacks upon the law of Leptines, each divided into two parts. Thus, after a very brief prooemium (1) there comes first (2-28) the general objections against Leptines' law based on the topics of justice, expediency, honor, profit—the typical topics of fourth-century deliberative oratory—rather artlessly woven together. Then follows (29-35) a section devoted to historical examples of those who deserved and received immunities, what Blass called the "positive" side of

221

the case.[120] Such examples are relevant to the issue, unlike those introduced by Isocrates in the *Philip*. After the discussion of the substitute law comes the negative side of the case, the refutation of claims made in support of Leptines' law (105-133), and finally a section which returns to the general considerations of the beginning: justice, honor, and expediency (134-156). The speech ends with a not unemotional peroration of recapitulation. A modern Belgian school of critics has stressed Demosthenes' use in many speeches of a "psychological" structure rather than the traditional rhetorical arrangement;[121] certainly it can be agreed that he shows no signs of being the docile follower of rhetorical rules. He carries along simultaneously a number of different themes, all of which are repeatedly illustrated and each of which is repeatedly brought to the surface. The symmetry which the speech contains may seem rather artificial, but Demosthenes' artistic independence and ability to synthesize standard topics into a whole which will effect a practical end, and not simply stand as a monument of words, are already evident.

In 354 Demosthenes delivered his earliest surviving deliberative speech, *On the symmories*. It is much more compressed than any of the works we have been discussing, too compressed, perhaps, for oral presentation; therefore, we may well have a revision of what was actually said. The topics are more systematically treated than in *Against Leptines*, but the structure is again symmetrical: after a brief prooemium attacking impractical orators Demosthenes deals first with the proposed Persian war, which he opposes

---

[120] Blass 3.1.235.

[121] Cf. Marcel Delaunois, "Du plan logique au plan psychologique chez Démosthène," LEC 19 (1951) 177 ff., "Le plan rhétorique dans l'éloquence grecque d'Homère à Démosthène," LEC 23 (1955) 267 ff., and an amplification of the subject under the latter title, Brussels, 1959. Cf. also H. de Raedt, "Plan psychologique de la première *Philippique* de Démosthène," LEC 19 (1952) 227 ff. These studies show on graphs the interweaving of motifs in Demosthenes.

(3-13); expediency (3), honor (6), justice (7), and possibility (9) are the topics touched upon. This takes us about a third of the way through the speech. At the center is the discussion of ways and means for war: Demosthenes does not oppose preparations, but money must be allowed to remain in the hands of its owners (24 ff.), a course which is possible, honorable, and expedient. Roughly the last third of the speech is devoted to a refutation of the need to fight Persia, a peroration emphasizing justice, and the concluding, matter-of-fact recapitulation. This topical approach can also be seen in the early speech *On the liberty of the Rhodians* (351): practicality, expediency, and honor all point in one direction (2, 8 and 28).

About this time two changes take place in Demosthenes' work. One is political. After supporting the program of Eubulus, which was based on financial security at home and peace abroad, Demosthenes rather suddenly turns against Eubulus in alarm at the continued growth of the power of Philip. The change can be attributed largely to Philip's unexpected successes in Thessaly and Thrace.[122] The first fruit of the new point of view is the first *Philippic*.[123] Since such a change must have alienated many of Demosthenes' friends he could only have had a sincere and patriotic belief that a determined opposition to Philip was best for Athens. The personal concerns of Demosthenes' wealthy associates are swept aside as trivial.

Corresponding to this political change is a rhetorical change. New vigor appears in the first *Philippic*, unlike anything in Greek oratory since the sharply focused speeches

[122] Cf. Jaeger 114.
[123] The dates of the speech *On the liberty of the Rhodians* and the first *Philippic* are in doubt. Jaeger seems right, 230, n. 41, in regarding the Rhodian speech as similar to that *On the symmories* and *For the Megalopolitans*, but "still far removed from the impassioned national feeling of the Philippics" (94). A good discussion of Demosthenic chronology is Raphael Sealey, "Dionysius of Halicarnassus and some Demosthenic dates," REG 68 (1955) 77 ff.

in Thucydides. There is no question of weighing the relative expediency of courses of action and of attributing to them justice and honor. It is assumed that Philip acts in his own interest, and Athens must act in hers. Territory in the north is the prize of war. The property of the careless belongs to those willing to run a risk (5). Demosthenes so focuses Athenian interests that the question seems not one of advantage, but of necessity, not the choice of a course of action, but the pursuit of the only possibility. His major point is that success is possible (2-12). All other rhetorical arguments are only accessory: Athens' failure to act will bring on her the deepest disgrace and will allow Philip to go unpunished (42-43), but no honor is promised Athens for action, and disinterested justice is not involved. It seems that Demosthenes' patience has been suddenly exhausted; the futility of expecting right to triumph in the course of nature has overwhelmed him.[124]

Succeeding speeches show a similar intensity. The first *Olynthiac*, for example, makes no mention of the honor or justice to be observed in helping Olynthus, only of the fact that it is to Athens' interest to seize the opportunity presented to fight Philip near his own home (11). Finally, in the second and third *Philippics* Demosthenes takes a further step. His idea of expediency had never been that of the speakers in Thucydides. Perhaps expedient policy was not so evident in the bewildering fourth century as it had been a hundred years before. The ugly principle that might makes right was no longer acceptable: the fourth century demanded at least an appearance of justice, morality, and rectitude, which is no doubt at the bottom of the common synthesis of topics. Beginning with the second *Philippic* Demosthenes finds a basis for his argumentation in a higher principle than self-interest, and one which combines ethical nobility with rhetorical force. This is the concept of the national character. Philip looks only

[124] Cf. Kennedy, *op.cit.* supra n. 88.

to the immediately expedient, and most other Greek states are as bad, Demosthenes says, but Athens has the tradition of her past to demand her loyalty (7-10). Self-interest and expediency for her are thus primarily the maintenance of this tradition. The third *Philippic*, Demosthenes' most forceful speech, carries on this same spirit. Justice in the old sense is not discussed and expediency is coupled with the possibility of preserving Athens (4). There are none of the self-conscious topics of the professional rhetoricians, yet the whole speech is concerned with the necessity of action in Athens' interest. Failure to act will inevitably bring disgrace for all that Athens has been, and the orator's vision of the national character is the point on which the whole speech focuses and under which all arguments are subsumed. It is also the physical center of the speech (36 ff.) framed symmetrically by considerations of practical concerns of the moment. A battle for Athens, decadent and fond of flattery, forgetful of her past, is fought out between Demosthenes the unpopular patriot (2) and Philip, the violent foreign king, compared successively to a fever (29) and a hailstorm (33).

Surely this viewpoint, like Demosthenes' political position, is one of stubborn, unselfcentered patriotism. The normal goals of the rhetorician and politician are equally rejected for the faith of the prophet. There appears to have been an austerity and loftiness in Demosthenes even in his early career; perhaps this finds expression in his deliberate self-devotion to a cause which, it must have been increasingly clear, was impossible. A splendid passage of *On the crown* (190 ff.) betrays the instinct of the martyr. It must be read with recognition of Demosthenes' assumption that no fundamental change could be admitted into the Athenian constitution and traditional way of life, an assumption which others did not accept and which could not permanently be maintained. In his lonely radicalism, Demosthenes was a pure conservative.

225

Patriotism, to one who does not share an enthusiasm for a particular cause, can be very distressing, for the patriot is capable of ignoring details of specific and inconvenient facts, social conventions, or even ordinary responsibility. The more he believes in his goal, the more it seems to justify all means of attainment. His cloak is his sincerity and his shield the fact that he defends others who cannot or will not defend themselves; but his position can become absurd. In responding to a purely rhetorical challenge the rhetorician, perhaps with tongue in cheek, colors and molds his case within the limits of probability; the patriot, in pursuit of what seems essential, is occasionally blinded to probability. The unattractive aspect of Demosthenes' oratory is mostly the result of the purity of his patriotism; it can best be seen in the prosecutions which arose from the Peace of Philocrates.

After the fall of Olynthus Demosthenes apparently became convinced that at least a temporary truce with Macedon was necessary, because Athens was not making any progress in the war. Negotiations were conducted in 346 and Demosthenes took part, together with Philocrates, Aeschines, and others. Aeschines describes (*On the embassy* 21 ff.) Demosthenes' conduct during the trip to see Philip: he had promised fountains of words and boasted that he would sew up Philip's mouth with an unsoaked rush. His speech was to be the climax of the interview, but, when the moment came, Demosthenes collapsed completely. He fumbled his prooemium and finally stopped, helpless. Philip, Aeschines relates, was rather condescending and encouraged Demosthenes, but that just aggravated the orator. Finally the herald imperiously commanded the withdrawal of the ambassadors. Various inferences can be drawn from the story: one is that Demosthenes did not have the instinct for replying to a sudden rhetorical challenge, which Aeschines shows; another is that his collapse represents his painful horror at speaking, more or less as an inferior, before a barbarian; in other words, it was a result of the greatness of his love of Athens. It may well also be true that this incident is the source of his great hatred of Aeschines, who claims to have distinguished himself oratorically, perhaps for the very reason that he was less emotionally involved in the situation. It was to Aeschines that Philip addressed his reply.

The peace was achieved, though Philip dallied and secured more territory before swearing to it. Contrary to Athenian expectations, which had been encouraged by Aeschines, Philip then advanced into central Greece and reduced the cities of Phocis, which he had prevented from being expressly included in the treaty. Inevitably those responsible for the peace found themselves attacked. Demosthenes, no doubt anxious to show that he had played no active role in making the peace (*On the false embassy* 223), turned his guns on Aeschines. But he showed the irresponsibility of the frenzied patriot in so doing, for the hatchet man he chose to oppose the hated Aeschines was one Timarchus, a man long active against Philip (*On the false embassy* 286), but whose private life was notorious. Aeschines immediately charged that Timarchus' crimes made it illegal for him to participate in public deliberations and to bring actions. Aeschines prevailed, but Demosthenes remembered.

Three years later, encouraged by Hyperides' successful prosecution of Philocrates, Demosthenes personally pressed the prosecution of Aeschines. The speech, known as *On the false embassy*, attempts to achieve on a very large scale (three hundred and three sections) the passion of the *Philippics*, the clarity of Demosthenes' earlier prosecutions, and the subtlety of interwoven themes, especially the vision of Athenian national character, which underlies all of Demosthenes' work. All in all the speech is a failure. Despite some fine bursts of rhetoric, it is unpersuasive and misleading. Demosthenes is most interested in an opportunity to discredit Aeschines generally. As in the prosecution of Androtion he wishes to amplify a charge into a sweeping denunciation, though here the specific indictment is no legal technicality, but the grave accusation of receiving bribes from Philip. This Demosthenes does not come near to proving: there was in fact no evidence for what Demosthenes had talked himself into believing. His secondary charges are also in some cases equally unsubstantial and flatly denied by Aeschines. The allegation, for example, that Aeschines had mistreated a freeborn woman of Olynthus (196) is sheer spite; Aeschines says in reply (4) that the audience shouted down the charge as it was made. Among the more serious indictments are, first, that Aeschines and the other ambassadors, this time not including Demosthenes, deliberately tarried on the trip to exact the oath to the treaty from Philip, although it was desirable to ratify the treaty as soon as possible; second, that Aeschines promised the Athenians that Philip would respect Phocis and move against Thebes, when in fact he did just the opposite. The first charge is easier to answer: it had no doubt been perfectly clear to the ambassadors and many other Athenians that Philip simply was not going to swear until he had accomplished certain preliminaries. This is shown by the slowness with which he took the oaths when the ambassadors did meet him. The ambassadors need not have been bribed to realize that following Philip around when he was not minded to see them would not increase their influence. Aeschines says (97 f.) that a journey straight to Philip in Thrace was not part of the instructions and that the ambassadors could not have reached Philip before he left Thrace. To the second charge, that he made the assembly promises on behalf of Philip, Aeschines replies with a flat denial. It seems unlikely that a seasoned diplomat would have promised anything on behalf of a foreign king, but Aeschines on other occasions was carried away with himself and he may have said more than he intended or have been deceived by Philip. It is as possible that Demosthenes regarded Aeschines' unofficial explanation of Philip's probable intentions as a "promise" and felt that the assembly had been hoodwinked.

Another unattractive feature of the speech, and of several speeches of Demosthenes, is the personal attack on the background, private life, or appearance of an opponent. Aeschines' mother and father and his career as an actor are frequently mentioned to discredit him. Aeschines, of course, makes similar attacks on Demosthenes. These techniques reflect the fourth-century interest in personality and are a kind of perverted ethos.[125] To Demosthenes some explanation of the wickedness of Aeschines must be found, and it seems probable to associate it with his background and upbringing.

Aeschines made a very creditable reply to Demosthenes' attack and was acquitted, quite rightly. The bad blood between the two continued, however, and produced years later (330) the most celebrated oratorical duel of antiquity, Aeschines' *Against Ctesiphon* answered by Demosthenes' *On the crown*. The latter of the two has traditionally been venerated as the masterpiece not only of its author but of ancient eloquence and perhaps of the spoken word. Such a judgment, of course, cannot be proved, though it may possibly be true. Twentieth-century students on first reading the speech often are not greatly moved, but then they are rarely conditioned to respond to any oratory. The critic who reads and rereads frequently ends by embracing the verdict of the centuries. In any event, *On the crown* is a splendid compendium of all those features which in other speeches seem most characteristic of Demosthenes.

In 337, a little over a year after the battle of Chaeronea at which Philip had decisively defeated the Athenians and

[125] Cf. Bruns, *op.cit.* supra n. 18, 557 ff., and T. B. L. Webster, *Art and literature in fourth century Athens*, London, 1956, 85 ff. and esp. 98 ff.

their allies, Ctesiphon proposed in the assembly that Demosthenes should be honored with a crown at the Great
Dionysia of the following spring because "he continues
to speak and do what is best for the people." We have seen
that the Athenians voted crowns to the council regularly
and crowns were often used to honor individuals (*Lives of
the ten orators* 843c). There was not, therefore, anything
necessarily remarkable about the award of a crown, but
the circumstances made this particular motion a question
of confidence in the policies of Demosthenes and a tribute
to him in the period of Athens' discouragement and
defeat. Aeschines, continuing his personal feud with Demosthenes and opposing any expression of confidence in his
leadership, immediately introduced a charge of illegal
motion against Ctesiphon. This made the award of the
crown impossible until the trial had been held, an event
which did not take place until 330, perhaps because Philip's
assassination in the summer of 336 strengthened Demosthenes' position. Strictly speaking, Ctesiphon, not Demosthenes, was on trial, but Demosthenes appeared as an advocate with him and delivered the major speech for the
defense. Ctesiphon probably did little more than introduce
Demosthenes.

Aeschines' able speech for the prosecution has survived.
It is most successful in the clarity with which it presents
the technical argument against the legality of Ctesiphon's
motion. Broader issues are raised, but they are rather a
second string to the orator's bow. Aeschines calls upon
Demosthenes to reply in the same order. The first rhetorical problem of the defense is, therefore, to avoid this,
for it would mean putting weak arguments in a conspicuous
place early in the speech. Ctesiphon's motion probably had
not been made at the legal time and place. Yet this avoidance must not be evident either. The cleverness with which
Demosthenes solves this problem has long been recog-

nized:[126] he denounces Aeschines for making charges foreign to the indictment and insists upon his right to answer
these first. What he means are the charges relating to his
part in the Peace of Philocrates, foreign to the indictment
only in the sense that the events were more remote in time
from the date of Ctesiphon's motion. Since the basis of
awarding the crown was Demosthenes' statesmanship in
general, there was no reason why Aeschines should not discuss any period of the orator's activity. Presumably he
omitted the very earliest events either because Demosthenes
had then been cooperating with Eubulus or because they
antedated his own public career.[127] Actually Demosthenes
is well satisfied to be able to discuss his services to Athens
over a long period. This preliminary issue extends as far as
section fifty-two, after which comes the main refutation of
Aeschines' charges; but even here the substantive issue
of Demosthenes' statesmanship is dealt with first and at
great length. Only when he feels that the audience has
begun to appreciate his viewpoint does the orator venture
to deal, and then but briefly, with the technical charges
(110-125). An invective against Aeschines is next introduced, and the great torrent of abuse which pours forth
effectively removes any attention the audience might have
paid to weakness in Demosthenes' replies to the technical
charges. In other words, what Aeschines wished to be the
main issue of the trial becomes a kind of overlooked valley
of detail, lost between the enormous cliffs of Demosthenes'
statesmanship and Aeschines' crimes.

A second rhetorical problem which Demosthenes faced
was occasioned by the fact that his policies had been unsuccessful. Aeschines made much of Demosthenes' ill for-

[126] Cf. esp. William Watson Goodwin, *Demosthenes on the
crown*, Cambridge, Eng., 1901, 310 f.
[127] Cf. Paul Cloché, *Démosthènes et la fin de la démocratie
athénienne*, Paris, 1937, 225 ff.

tune and tried to identify Athens' troubles with the person of his enemy. Even without Aeschines' vilification Demosthenes had to plead in the dark shadow of the Battle of Chaeronea. This challenge he meets head on, and from it achieves great pathos. The most striking passage is that beginning at section 199 which contains the great oath by those who fell at Marathon, much admired by the author of *On the sublime* (16.2). As in the *Philippics*, Demosthenes insists upon loyalty to Athenian traditions; that is the only true expediency. Success or failure are of secondary interest. Athens has won a moral victory:

"If what was going to be had been clear to all, and if all had known ahead of time, and you, Aeschines, had foretold and prophesied with cries and shouts, though in fact you said not a word, not even in that case should the city have abandoned her traditions. . . ." (199)

Again and again he hammers at the theme "what else could I have done?" (e.g. 28, 62, 66, 69, 101, 188, 190 ff., 301) meaning by "could," within the framework of Athenian traditions. The possibility of shutting eyes at what seemed inevitable he expressly rejects as impossible (63). This loyalty to national traditions is the foundation on which Demosthenes builds his defense. Neither blunt expediency nor justice to individuals nor honor in the narrow sense play any separate role, but all are synthesized into the single obsession.

Three ways, then, in which *On the crown* resembles earlier speeches of Demosthenes are its attempt to concentrate attention on wider issues rather than on legal technicalities, its presentation of the need for loyalty to Athenian traditions as the central issue logically and the central topic rhetorically of the trial, and its effective use of recurring themes. A fourth way is in the structure of the speech, which shows the tendency to symmetry already noticed in other speeches and an ability to adapt rhetorical conventions to specific occasions.[128] Formally speaking, *On the crown* has all the traditional parts of a courtroom speech: there is a prooemium that performs the usual functions (1-17) including (9-17) a preliminary consideration of the procedure which Aeschines has demanded and which Demosthenes knows he cannot successfully follow. Then comes a narration, introduced by the narrative word γάρ (18-52), though it does not deal with the entire circumstances, only with what Demosthenes labels as outside the present case. Because these are earlier events it is possible for Demosthenes to give here an excellent background for the subsequent body of the speech. When the background is set (52) he can break off the narrative abruptly and return to it whenever he wishes later. Thus he gains several advantages at the same time: he disposes of some of Aeschines' arguments, he gives the impression of logical order and clear narration, he does not tire his audience with an excessively long narrative account, and finally he does not run any danger of repeating himself when he takes up later events further on in the speech. The proof also shows the two usual parts, a logical one, which here is a refutation of Aeschines' charges (53-125), and an ethical one (126-296), largely a contrast between the character of Demosthenes and that of Aeschines. The central point of the speech in terms of bulk comes around section 160, and significantly there appears here a turning point in the thought too, for Demosthenes, having made his shattering charges that Aeschines brought on the war and lost Greek freedom (142-159), turns to his own measures to counteract these deeds and to his noble expression of Athenian traditions. A symmetry is noticeable in the passage as a whole:

[128] For different structural analyses cf. Wilhelm Fox, *Die Kranzrede des Demosthenes*, Leipzig, 1880, 17 ff., and Goodwin, *op.cit.* supra n. 126, 308 ff. Many critics have found the speech confused and have suggested (unnecessarily) that it contains conflations or interpolations, cf. Albert Rabe, *Die Redaktion der demosthenischen Kranzrede*, Göttingen, 1892.

126-140 attack on Aeschines
  141 invocation to the gods, echoing that
     at the beginning of the speech
142-159 deeds of Aeschines

160-198 deeds of Demosthenes
199-210 Athenian traditions, beginning
     with oath by the gods
210-250 deeds of Demosthenes

The contrast between the fortunes of the two orators is then made specific in the following sections. The speech ends with a peroration (297 ff.) which is decidedly recapitulatory. Demosthenes asks again the question "what ought the loyal citizen to have done?" (301) and again (315) demands a comparison between himself and Aeschines.

Just as the structure of the speech follows the traditional pattern, but is free from any constraint which this might have imposed, so the style of Demosthenes is his own delicate instrument. Neither clarity and austerity nor rhetorical fullness occupies his entire attention. The context determines the style, and the orator is the master of all styles: he can narrate vividly, argue with precision, and especially he can mount to moving pathos. One of the greatest passages of *On the crown* shows well his versatility. It comes at that crucial moment, the hinge of the speech, when, after Aeschines has ruined everything, Demosthenes comes forward to save what can be saved. The tension of the scene in Athens is conveyed by the narration, in short sentences, of each step as the assembly is summoned (169): evening, the messenger, his disastrous news, the meal of the prytanes interrupted. The market place is closed, the generals are summoned, and the assembly meets. The herald cries "who wishes to address the assembly?" "But no one came forward." All of this is in a sense irrelevant, but the details of the scene are burned into the mind. The tragic pause comes. Demosthenes looks around at the assembly: there are the generals, there the orators, there Aeschines. None speak. The next touch is typically Demosthenic: the voice of the herald who called for speakers becomes the voice of the fatherland pleading for deliverance. All the qualities of patriotism and tragic suffering are imposed upon the dramatic narrative scene. Thunderous parallel contrary-to-fact conditions roll in to demonstrate the gap between desire to act and ability to advise, then like a red flag the name of Philip, and, finally, Demosthenes stands forward in a sentence remarkable for its emphatic word order: "I showed myself, then, this one, on that day, I." In what follows the tone rapidly changes to one of competent comprehension and logical argument.

The greatness of *On the crown* consists in part of this command of style, in part of the success with which the contrast of Aeschines and Demosthenes is everywhere developed into black and white portraits of evil and of good, and in part of the magnificent moral tone, intense, noble, sincere, transcendent. Demosthenes' defense is by no means all true—some of the unproven arguments of the embassy speech recur, Aeschines' character is slandered, and some questions are unsatisfactorily dealt with[129]—but the orator is, in his own view, dealing with matters of principle which transcend facts. His sophisms are not uttered for the sake of making a good speech, but for the sake of his country. The attitude is very much like that of Plato in the *Menexenus*, where truth is not equated with historical fact, but with a moral absolute like that of myth. In contrast Aeschines' speech seems tricky, gaudy, and superficial. Demosthenes himself was not unaware of the contrast and accused Aeschines (280) of producing a show-piece, of answering a rhetorical challenge and caring nothing about the punishment of wrong-doing. The theme is taken up again in the peroration (308). Against Demosthenes that charge cannot

[129] Cf. Cloché, *op.cit.* supra n. 127, 249 ff.

be made. He knew all the tricks and rules of rhetoric, but they were to him only means to a far more important end. As his career developed he made that end the preservation of Athenian democracy and institutions as he knew them and the recovery of the spirit that had made them. He alone of Greek orators shared, perhaps without much realizing it, Plato's belief in absolute goals and rejection of rhetorical relativism.

The fourth century B.C. in Greece is a period of very great interest and significance, whose like recurs from time to time. Old and valued institutions are confronted with some new and powerful force. When it becomes clear that the new force cannot be crushed, what should be the attitude of those convinced that the old traditions are right? Fourth-century thinkers range from those who embrace the new with enthusiasm to those who demand to die with the old. There are those who prefer not to think about the problem. And there are those who seek the best possible working adjustment. One of the latter is Aeschines.

Aeschines

Aeschines was born in 390 B.C. or earlier at Athens.[130] He was first an assistant in his father's school, then an ephebe and citizen soldier, taking part in the battle of Mantinea, later a tragic actor, a clerk in the assembly, and a protégé of Eubulus, the finance minister. His first known public speech was an invective against Philip on the fall of Olynthus, 348. In the same year he was

[130] D. M. Lewis, "When was Aeschines born?" CR 8 (1958) 103, suggests a date shortly after 403 B.C. Sources for Aeschines' life are his own speeches, the attacks of Demosthenes, the biography in the *Lives of the ten orators* and some later lives printed in Blass' Teubner edition of the text. Modern discussions usually begin as books or papers on Demosthenes; but cf. Blass 3.2.129 ff.; Jebb 2.393 ff.; Dobson, *op.cit.* supra n. 2, 163 ff. Cloché, *op.cit.* supra n. 127, is useful for historical information. There is a translation in the Loeb Library by Charles D. Adams, London, 1919.

an ambassador to Arcadia, in 346 one of the ambassadors to arrange and ratify the Peace of Philocrates, in 339 a delegate to the Amphictyonic council, and in 330 an ambassador to Philip. Three speeches survive: *Against Timarchus*, delivered in 346; *On the embassy*, delivered in 343; and *Against Ctesiphon*, delivered in 330. Since Aeschines did not receive one-fifth of the votes in the latter trial he was subject to a heavy fine; to avoid it, or in general weariness, he retired into permanent exile, probably in Asia and on Rhodes, where he may have taught rhetoric (Plutarch, *Demosthenes* 24) or at least have given readings from his speeches. The date of his death is unknown. A collection of letters dealing with his later years is of doubtful authenticity.

Aeschines was not a professional rhetorician. So far as we know he never wrote speeches for others, and unless he did so during his exile he never undertook to teach others how to speak. Furthermore there is no satisfactory evidence that he had studied rhetoric with any of the orators or sophists.[131] His amateur status might be compared with that of Andocides, but there is considerable difference between the two, for Aeschines, though an amateur, is not amateurish. He is as familiar with commonplaces, argument, partition, and the devices of style as any Greek orator, and because of his experience as an actor he probably knew more about delivery than most. In the half-century between the school days of Andocides and Aeschines great changes had taken place in the Athenian intellectual environment. By Aeschines' time rhetoric was the fabric of any literary education, the conventions of rhetoric were deeply entrenched in all public utterances, and intellectual activity was unthinkable without the color of rhetoric. Aristotle's

[131] The biography of Aeschines in the *Lives of the ten orators* is a double one. The first and less reliable part (840b) makes Aeschines a pupil of Isocrates and Plato or Leodamas, the second, much shorter, but more reliable part says (840 f.) that he did not study under any teachers.

acceptance of and serious concern with rhetoric are evidence of the same development.

The earliest of Aeschines' three extant speeches is *Against Timarchus*. We have already criticized Demosthenes for his choice of Timarchus to prosecute Aeschines after the Peace of Philocrates; Aeschines quickly brought a charge of illegal action on the ground that Timarchus' notorious private life disqualified him under Athenian law from the right to prosecute. The speech has, basically, a regular organization: prooemium (1-8) is followed by a statement of the legal basis of action (9-36), narration, and demonstration of the deeds of Timarchus with some discussion (40-115), anticipation of the defense (117-169), attack on Demosthenes (170-176), and peroration (177-196). Aeschines takes a very moral attitude toward the charges,[132] but he also fairly revels in the details of description. He feigns delicacy, but the shameful word slips out (e.g. 52). The fact that *Against Timarchus* has never had an English commentary is probably due to distaste for the subject matter, but the speech is not a first-rate one. Even the purple passages are rather grimy. Probably Aeschines expected the detail to produce a disgust in the audience which would go far toward winning the case. Such an assumption is typical of his rather superficial concept of this and other cases in which he speaks.

The outstanding characteristics of Aeschines are use of diversionary tactics, legalism, and a preference for vivid description over close logical argument. These are constantly interwoven and contrast sharply with Demosthenes' constant attempts to generalize, broaden, and deepen the content of a trial. In *Against Timarchus* one cannot help but notice the way Aeschines completely ignores the deeper issue of his own defense against the charges inspired by

[132] Apparently a characteristic of the political moderates, cf. Jacqueline de Romilly, "Les modérés athéniens vers le milieu du ive siècle: échos et concordances," REG 67 (1954) 327 ff.

238

Demosthenes. There is no discussion of politics and policy, though Greek ideas of the relevant could easily have been extended to include such topics. Attention is entirely focused on the illegal actions of Timarchus, luridly described, but hardly proved, and on the majesty of the law, which is cleverly developed in the earlier part of the speech. This legalism is in itself not unfair, but Aeschines' solution of the rhetorical problem which it raises is decidedly questionable. How could Timarchus' associates be induced to testify to the moral aberrations of Timarchus without involving themselves in the same charges? Aeschines' solution is to close one legal eye and attempt to get agreement to carefully worded statements which catalogue Timarchus' acts without mentioning the activities of his partners. If they still refuse he really does not care too much since the statement has already been impressed upon the jury, and he can indulge effectively his rectitude against a recalcitrant witness (e.g. 69). A second solution is the extensive and unfair appeal to popular knowledge of Timarchus' crimes (e.g. 44). Aeschines claims (89) that if the trial were being held in a foreign city all Athenians would be competent witnesses against Timarchus. Why should not they be in Athens?

Aeschines was successful in the suit. Legally he deserved to be, but in a sense it was unfortunate, for his self-assurance at his techniques was probably strengthened. He has about him some of the self-satisfaction of Cicero or other self-made men. They are inordinately fond of quoting themselves and proud of their education.[133]

Although Timarchus was disposed of, Aeschines could not avoid his own trial. In his defense he delivered his ablest speech, *On the embassy*. It is clear, vigorous, and largely persuasive. The organization is simple and chronological. Many passages, for example that describing the journey to Macedon and the interview with Philip (20 ff.),

[133] Cf. Dobson, *op.cit.* supra n. 2, 172 f.

are masterpieces of narrative. The introduction of aged parent and relatives (179) did not offend contemporaries. In answer to Demosthenes' charges Aeschines does not expound his intentions and policies. He only says this is what I did on the fifteenth, this is what I did on the sixteenth, and it was all open and aboveboard. Nobody was bribed. Why something was done, what was the desired object, he does not or cannot say. Since Demosthenes' prosecution was not a very responsible one Aeschines' reasonable tone and candid style were successful by a slight margin.

We do not have the speech Aeschines delivered at Delphi in 339, but he describes the situation and the speech in some detail in *Against Ctesiphon* (107 ff.). It is indicative of his methods and their dangers. Under Theban pressures the Amphissians suggested a fine of fifty talents against Athens because she had insulted Thebes by rededicating, in the temple at Delphi, the shields taken from the Medes and Thebans during the Persian war. Aeschines as an Athenian delegate was called upon without warning to go into the council and oppose the motion. He chose an extreme diversionary approach. Instead of answering the charge, he pointed out with utmost vividness the land down below Delphi, visible from the site, which the Amphissians occupied illegally, and he called emotionally for a sacred war to expel them. The spark kindled, the war was declared. When Philip, a member of the Amphictyonic council, intervened, his war with Athens resulted, and Chaeronea was its fruit. As he describes the event years later Aeschines still does not perceive the irresponsibility of his conduct, but he is proud of the success of his speech. He blames Demosthenes for preventing Athens from following up its advantage adequately (125).

Aeschines' quarrel with Demosthenes approached its climax when, in 336, he brought the charge of proposing an illegal motion against Ctesiphon. This is the first time he had attacked. Perhaps he had been lying in wait for an opportunity, but he had won the first round, and it would have been better for the past to remain unexhumed. But Aeschines' feelings of frustration and injustice were too great to allow a vote of confidence to Demosthenes to pass unchallenged. It was he, Aeschines, who had believed that the Macedonian kings, however they felt about the rest of Greece, would respect Athens, as they were doing. It was he who had foreseen the eventual victory of Macedon and worked for an honorable understanding. It was Demosthenes who had worked against all of this and who ought now to have been discredited and rejected. Yet after Chaeronea Demosthenes was more a hero than ever. Aeschines in this third speech is intent on showing the Athenians that Demosthenes was personally the cause of all their misfortunes. It is out of this envenomed feeling that he produces such passages as this (130 ff.):

"But did not the gods foretell, did not the gods forewarn us to take care, all but assuming human voices? No city have I ever seen so protected by the gods and so ruined by a few orators. . . . What unexpected and unforeseen things have not happened in our time? We have lived not the life of men, but we have been born to be a tale of wonder to posterity. Is not the king of the Persians who dug through Athos, who yoked the Hellespont, who demanded earth and water of the Hellenes, who dared to write in his letters that he was master of all men from the rising of the sun to its setting, now not contending for rule over others, but now for the safety of his own skin? . . . And Thebes, Thebes, city of our neighbors, in one day has been snatched from the midst of Greece, justly perhaps, for in the long run her plans were bad, but meeting a god-sent infatuation, a folly not of human, but divine proportions. And the Lacedaimonians . . . who once thought themselves to be the leaders of the Greeks, are now about to set out, making an exhibition of their misfortunes as they are sent to Alexander. . . .

And our city, the common refuge of the Greeks, to which came in the past embassies from Greece . . . now no longer contests for the hegemony of the Greeks, but for the soil of its own land. And these misfortunes have come upon us since Demosthenes came into political leadership. . . . For navy, army, city have utterly been snatched away from the time his influence began. . . ."

The speech contains a number of unsatisfactory features. For example, Aeschines discusses Demosthenes' part in the embassy which arranged the Peace of Philocrates but nowhere indicates that he himself had any part in it at all. Presumably he expects his audience to have a poor memory. There are many unsubstantiated statements and gross misinterpretations.[134] As before, Aeschines relies upon the legal details which are put in a prominent position early in the speech, and as before here he was on good ground. The legalisms are not sufficient, however, to divert all attention, and when he does turn, as clearly he must, to the general subject of Demosthenes' statesmanship it is still not policy, but the details of execution, which he discusses. This is the primary reason why the speech cannot match the reply of Demosthenes, who is in a much stronger position than in *On the false embassy* to express the role of the patriot with rhetorical success, for he has his entire career to draw upon rather than his conduct during one difficult period.

The speech, then, has the legalism and the diversionary attempt characteristic of Aeschines. It has too the vivid narrative (*diatyposis*) such as when the disasters suffered by the Thebans are conjured up before the jury's eyes (157). One must imagine the speech delivered in Aeschines' splendid voice and with the stance of a tragic actor.[135]

Aeschines lost the suit and even failed to receive the neces-

[134] Cf. Cloché, *op.cit.* supra n. 127, 227 ff.
[135] Cf. Alfred P. Dorjahn, "Some remarks on Aeschines' career as an actor," CJ 25 (1929) 223 ff., esp. 229.

sary one-fifth of the votes, thus incurring a large fine which he avoided by going into exile. Stories were sometimes told of his later years, one to the effect that the Rhodians asked him to teach rhetoric and he replied that he didn't know it himself (Anonymous life 6, p. 4 Blass), another that he gave declamations from his speeches and when the islanders marveled at *Against Ctesiphon* and wondered why it did not win he replied dourly, "You wouldn't wonder if you had heard Demosthenes' reply" (*Lives of the ten orators* 840e).[136] Both stories suggest that in his mind his failure was a rhetorical one, not a political judgment.

It seems possible to suggest why Aeschines' works show the characteristics they do. Did he avoid discussion of policy because he had none? Does the superficiality of his political treatment reflect a superficial mind which did not see beyond the immediate facts? Not necessarily, though Aeschines was certainly not a profound philosopher. The general tenor of his activities was to try to find an understanding between Athens and Macedon which would leave Athens independent and avoid war. This was the policy of Eubulus which Demosthenes had also pursued until he became convinced that Macedon was a complete threat to Athenian traditions. Aeschines, confronted with the choice either of resistance to the end and destruction or of compromise and adjustment of Athenian traditions chose the latter as the most expedient for the city as he knew it. He believed that there was for Athens no clear answer within her own traditions, but a difficult course of tightrope walking and of immediate expediency in the light of historical experience. His policy was thus a deliberate resistance of long-range policy, which in turn demanded some confidence in Macedon as less of a threat than Demosthenes believed. One

[136] In Cicero's variant (*De oratore* 3.213) Aeschines also read Demosthenes' speech, but could not reproduce the orator's delivery. Many later rhetoricians tell some version of the story, cf. C. Kunst, "De Aeschine Rhodi exsulante," ws 39 (1917) 167 ff.

passage in particular (*On the embassy* 79-80) may be quoted as indicative of this viewpoint:

"During the war I united the Arcadians and other Greeks as much as possible against Philip, but when no man came to the aid of the city, but some waited to see what was going to happen, others campaigned against us and the orators in the city were making the war an excuse for their daily extravagant expenditures, I confess that I advised the people to treat with Philip and make the peace which you, Demosthenes, think now was a disgrace, you who never lifted a sword. . . . It is right, Athenians, to review ambassadors on the basis of the circumstances under which they served and generals on the basis of the forces which they led."

In a number of passages (e.g. *On the embassy* 131 and 183 and *Against Ctesiphon* 134 ff.) Aeschines expresses a belief in a Fate which seems to make extensive human action or planning useless.

Rhetorical expression of Aeschines' view of Athenian affairs was difficult, for it easily could be made to seem cowardly and opportunistic. The Athenians were willing to make a peace with Philip, to tolerate him, sometimes to cooperate with him, but they probably were not willing to admit that they were following a policy of doing so. Although Demosthenes faced the great problem of arousing the Athenians from their sloth, Aeschines faced an equally great problem in supporting a course of action which was an acceptance of the inferiority of Athens on the world stage. Thus he hesitates to deal openly with the problem and takes refuge in a passionate concern with fact and detail.

Aeschines' political views imply that there are no political absolutes, and this attitude is reminiscent of the rhetorical view, found in Isocrates, that expression in speech was to be determined solely by the rhetorical need of the occasion and that in the solution of a rhetorical problem the orator had performed his entire task. Demosthenes (*On the crown* 280) accuses Aeschines of this kind of rhetoricism, probably justly. Aeschines clearly loves to speak and speaks for the moment only, without much historical responsibility, and he is easily intoxicated by the exuberance of his own verbosity. The Delphic speech is the best example. An inclination in this direction may well have been encouraged by his early experience as an actor and a resulting view of a speech as primarily an artistic performance, also by his self-attained success, and finally by the bitterness which his rivalry with Demosthenes produced and which fostered in him the attitude that anything was permitted in attaining a rhetorical victory. Such a view led him into the trap of his final speech.

Posterity has not been over-generous to Aeschines. He is famous because of Demosthenes, and in the eyes of some he is infamous because of Demosthenes. There is no reason to believe that he was bribed, as Demosthenes alleges, or that he did not speak and act what he thought best for Athens; all of his actions are perfectly explicable on the assumption of patriotic sincerity. Even gullibility is not clearly proved against him, unless it is gullibility to rhetoric. One does not have to like him. Jebb didn't and remarked snobbishly (2.396), "It is not the occasional coarseness of his style, but it is the vulgarity of his soul that counteracts his splendid gift for eloquence." The respectable Blass also detested him. Historians such as Bury and Beloch have liked him better, for they have better understood his problems. He was a self-made man, exceedingly proud of the culture he had acquired, not thoroughly conscious of how to use it. Demosthenes thought he ruined his country by his rhetoric. We may be content with agreeing that he ruined himself.

245

The Lesser Orators of the Later Fourth Century

The workings of rhetoric in Athenian society can be seen in the careers and speeches of a number of approximate contemporaries of Demosthenes and Aeschines.

Apollodorus

Born in Athens 394 B.C., Apollodorus was the son of the freedman banker and manufacturer Pasion, known also from Isocrates' *Trapeziticus*.[137] On Pasion's death his businesses were continued by his freedman Phormio until Apollodorus' younger brother became of age, at which time (362) the shield factory became the property of Apollodorus, the bank going to the brother Pasicles. Apollodorus served repeatedly as trierarch and once as choregus. Early in the 340's[138] he cooperated with Demosthenes in an attempt to convert the theoric fund to military purposes, and as a result Demosthenes wrote for him the first speech *Against Stephanus*. There are six other speeches in the corpus of Demosthenes which were spoken by Apollodorus, but which are clearly not in the style of Demosthenes. They are in a consistent style themselves,[139] and are thus apparently the work of a single author who might as well be regarded as Apollodorus himself for lack of a better candidate.[140] These are *Against Stephanus 2* (Demosthenes 46), *Against Timotheus* (49), *Against Polycles* (50), *Against Callipus* (52), *Against Nicostratus* (53),

[137] Knowledge of Apollodorus' career is dependent on the references in the speeches of himself and Demosthenes. Translations of the speeches are available among translations of Demosthenes.

[138] On the date cf. Jaeger 243 f., n. 38.

[139] On the style of Apollodorus cf. Arnold Schaefer, *Demosthenes und seine Zeit,* 3.2: *Beilagen:* "die Reden in Sachen Apollodors," 130-199, Leipzig, 1858, not reprinted in subsequent editions; F. Lortzing, *De orationibus quas Demosthenes pro Apollodoro scripsisse fertur,* Berlin, 1863; J. Sigg, "Der Verfasser neun angeblich von Demosthenes für Apollodor geschriebener Reden," JKP *Supplementband* 7 (1873) 396 ff.; G. Huettner, *Demosthenis oratio in Stephanum prior num vera sit inquiritur,* Ansbach, 1895; Sandys and Paley, *op.cit.* supra n. 115, xliii f.

[140] Cf. Sandys and Paley, *op.cit.* supra n. 115, xliv f.

and *Against Neaera* (59). *Against Evergus* (47) is sometimes attributed to Apollodorus and *On the trierarchic crown* has been also, though probably wrongly.[141] Apparently it was known that Demosthenes had written for Apollodorus and the latter's papers were examined at the time Demosthenes' works were collected. Apollodorus disappears from history after the speech *Against Neaera*, which was written before 340, but he may have lived some time longer.

Apollodorus is a third-rate orator. He is not a member of the Attic canon and is indeed unmentioned by the rhetoricians. His style is undistinguished, his arrangement not striking, his argumentation feeble. His speeches preserve some information, especially about Athenian banking, which is interesting, but to the historian of rhetoric he is chiefly an example of the kind of litigious rancor which the technique of rhetoric encouraged. Since the law courts were open to him and the formal requirements of oratory known, Apollodorus made use of both for his own ends.

Anyone involved in the banking business or a member of a banking family was probably brought to appeal to the law more than other citizens, and some of Apollodorus' earlier suits were no doubt justified—his defense *Against Callipus* is apparently unexceptionable.[142] Demosthenes (*For Phormio* 53), however, accuses him of ceaseless prosecution on trumped up charges against both great and small, and the number of prosecutions specifically mentioned by Demosthenes and Apollodorus himself, at least fifteen, confirms the allegation. The claims of Phormio were settled by arbitration and raised again by Apollodorus eighteen years later (Demosthenes, *For Phormio* 19) on the basis of no evidence but argument from probability.[143]

[141] Cf. the works cited in note 139.

[142] This Callipus of Lamptrae is not the same as Callipus, son of Philo, against whom Apollodorus brought an accusation (Demosthenes, *For Phormio* 53).

[143] Cf. Sandys and Paley, *op.cit.* supra n. 115, xxiv f.

When the attack failed Apollodorus continued his harrowing of this man—who was now his step-father—by suing for false testimony a witness named Stephanus, who had testified to an inconsequential point. The speech *Against Nicostratus* shows him suing an old friend in return for prosecutions the latter had brought upon him. In *Against Neaera* he is also engaged in a suit of revenge on a subject by modern standards none of his business. Stephanus, not Phormio's witness, but another, had brought a suit for illegal motion which prevented Apollodorus's attempt to transfer the theoric fund to military purposes (6). Subsequently Stephanus brought a charge of murder (9). Apollodorus and his brother retaliated by prosecuting Stephanus' wife Neaera for living with him in wedlock when she was in fact an alien. They do not spare the details of her career as a prostitute. The speech is long, and despite or because of its sordid quality the best work of Apollodorus in vigor and interest. There is one striking passage in which the orator inquires of the jury what they will say when they return home that night (110-113). "Where were you?" their wives will ask. "Judging a case." "Whose?" "Neaera's." "What did you decide?" And there will be the devil to pay if they say "We acquitted her."[144]

Both *Against Nicostratus* and *Against Neaera* show clearly that Apollodorus was not a solitary example of an Athenian with a passion for litigation. Aristophanes alleges that the evil was widespread even in his time and perhaps it was. By the latter half of the fourth century it must have been a general problem. Some of the prosecutions, *Against Neaera*, for example, began with political differences;[145] such speeches are different only in scale and art from the prosecutions of Aeschines and Demosthenes. That kind of

[144] The topic is more briefly used by Lycurgus, *Against Leocrates* 141; cf. also Demosthenes, *Against Aristogiton* 1.98 ff.
[145] Cf. Grace H. Macurdy, "Apollodorus and the speech *Against Neaera*," AJP 63 (1942) 257 ff.

sensational prosecution we do not find in the fifth or early fourth century. The increasing use in the fourth century of the *graphê paranomôn,* or suit for illegal motion, and the *paragraphê* or plea in bar of action, multiplied the amount of litigation. Any such movement put a premium on rhetorical technique and diverted attention from the real issues of a difference of opinion. Apollodorus' prosecutions can be compared to Aeschines' attacks on Demosthenes in that they were legalistic, diversionary, and spiteful.

Lycurgus

Lycurgus was born about 390 B.C. into the distinguished Athenian family of the Eteobutadae.[146] He held the title "Treasurer" (the exact position is unknown) in 338-326, was responsible for many important public works and the author of numerous laws. He appears to have been in general agreement with the policies of Demosthenes. He died in 324. Of the fifteen speeches known in antiquity only one survives.

There has never been any question about the patriotism, sincerity, and integrity of Lycurgus. He was clearly an Athenian Cato, even to the extent of sharing a harshness which regarded all crimes as equal (*Against Leocrates* 65 f.). Lycurgus' public services, especially as finance minister in the difficult years after Chaeronea, are amply documented. The series of prosecutions which he conducted as a private individual seem to have issued from no personal malice, but to have been intended to unite his countrymen against moral weakness or corruption and to inflame their love of

[146] The principal source is the biography in the *Lives of the ten orators.* It does not indicate the date of Lycurgus' birth which must be estimated from Libanius' statement (*hypothesis* to Demosthenes *Against Aristogiton*) that he was older than Demosthenes, cf. in general Blass 3.2.72 ff. There is a translation of Lycurgus by J. O. Burtt in the Loeb Library *Minor Attic orators* 2, Cambridge, 1954, 15 ff.

country. All of this, all of the testimonies to Lycurgus' severe and noble character, leaves the reader completely unprepared for the rhetorical irresponsibility of the single surviving speech, *Against Leocrates*. Only the orator's refusal to employ character assassination (149) prevents it from being a perfect example of the indulgence of rhetorical technique. That the austere Lycurgus should have produced it is another proof of the extent to which rhetorical standards had permeated Athenian thinking in the fourth century.

Leocrates was a prosperous Athenian blacksmith (58) of good family (136) who gave way to panic on hearing of the defeat at Chaeronea and fled, complete with mistress, to Rhodes, where he created consternation by his exaggerated report of the Athenian defeat. Subsequently he went to Megara, where he engaged in the grain trade for five years or so (21). Then, for reasons not specified, he returned to Athens. According to the author of the Greek *hypothesis* to the speech Leocrates was quite candid about his flight and return, and Lycurgus may have felt that public interests would suffer if he went unchecked. In 330, therefore, he indicted Leocrates for treason, but the vote of the jury was a tie and, like Orestes, the defendant was accordingly acquitted.

Leocrates had apparently broken no law by living in self-imposed exile. He had illegally transported grain to foreign ports (27), but Lycurgus uses that as a sign of his disloyalty rather than making it the legal charge. Lycurgus' only basis for prosecution was his own exaggerated indignation, and his only weapon his rhetorical ability. He must make an extended commercial absence abroad by a private citizen appear to be an overt act of treason against the state. To do so, he first pretends that the central issue will be whether or not Leocrates actually settled abroad, and he introduces evidence thereof; it is unlikely, however, that Leocrates would have disputed the fact. Since this is the only real evidence of anything, Lycurgus no doubt wanted to make it go as far as possible. Once (52) he implies that a law of the Areopagus covered the case, but it must not have applied literally since it is not quoted nor substantiated in any way and the orator quickly passes on to other topics. Parallels are drawn between Leocrates and other "traitors," Phrynichus for example (112); but they are hardly applicable. There is much digression of a moralizing, patriotic nature (e.g. 86 ff., 95 ff., 98 ff.), one hundred and three lines of poetry (one should not complain since much of it is not otherwise preserved), and a great deal of emotionalism. For example, Leocrates is said to have no pity for the harbor from which he sailed nor shame for the walls he left undefended (17), and the orator is quite tasteless in making use of the disgrace of Athens to bolster his points (42). Nor does he hesitate, lacking an applicable Athenian law, to quote one of Sparta (129), nor to imply, without evidence, that Leocrates was expelled from both Rhodes and Megara (133).

In a word, the speech, which is completely regular in form, is a fine example of unreasonable prosecution encouraged by confidence in rhetorical technique. Since the Athenian juries were judges both of fact and of law, Lycurgus' method, bolstered by his virtuous reputation, had considerable chance of success. According to the *Lives of the ten orators* (841b) Lycurgus was the pupil of both Plato and Isocrates. Whether or not this is true, he combines the ruthlessness of the philosopher who twisted facts to attain an end he was confident was right with the virtuosity of the orator who could write an accompaniment for any theme. Of course Lycurgus, like Demosthenes, did not choose just any theme: the basis of his choice was patriotism, but he goes beyond Demosthenes in the standards he demands, and the rhetorical techniques he uses seem, therefore, more extreme than they do in the hands of Demosthenes, who is a much greater speaker, more subtle in total effect, and more conscious of the mood he is conveying.

Hyperides

Hyperides was born in 390 B.C. in Athens.[147] Like Lycurgus he is said to have studied with Plato and Isocrates. He was a professional speech writer and politician who for most of his career cooperated with Demosthenes against Macedon. In 343 he successfully prosecuted Philocrates, but in 324 he was one of the ten prosecutors of Demosthenes for receiving a bribe from Harpalus. He spoke the funeral oration for those who died in the Lamian war in 322. Before the year was out his surrender was demanded by Antipater. He fled, was captured, and was executed. Seventy-seven speeches were attributed to him in antiquity. None survived in manuscript, but in the nineteenth century one complete speech (*For Euxenippus*) and portions of five others were found on papyrus in Egypt. The *Funeral oration* has been discussed above.

In the early fourth century it apparently was not possible to combine commercial speech writing and respectable civic activities. Antiphon had done so in the fifth century, but sophistry and with it logography were discredited in many quarters immediately after the Peloponnesian war. The development is parallel to the rejection of pure expediency as a logical argument. Isocrates in the 390's had felt that if he wanted to be a serious educator he must make a break with judicial speech writing. Lysias was not successful in

---

[147] The principal source is the *Lives of the ten orators*. The date of birth is dependent upon *Inscriptiones graecae* ii.941. The best modern study of Hyperides is the introduction to the Budé edition by Gaston Colin, *Hypéride: discours*, Paris, 1946. Cf. also Blass 3.2.1 ff. and P. Orsini, "Démosthène et l'ideal oratoire du ive siècle," *Mélanges de la société toulousaine d'études classiques* 1 (1946) 71 ff. On the characteristic language of Hyperides cf. Ulrich Pohle, *Die Sprache des Redners Hypereides in ihrer Beziehung zur Koine*, Leipzig, 1928. There is an English translation of the speeches and fragments in Burtt, *op.cit.* supra n. 146, 363 ff.

surmounting his metic origin. Isaeus apparently never tried to enter politics. Demosthenes subsequently succeeded in writing speeches for others without jeopardizing his political career, but he had the initial advantage of a personal litigation and was careful in his choice of clients. His example, as in the case of his publication of deliberative speeches, no doubt encouraged others to follow. Time and persistence were gradually bringing more and more acceptance of rhetoric. The young Aristotle scorned judicial oratory, the old Aristotle analyzed it. Hyperides exploited the new conditions: he was a professional speech writer who also dabbled in politics.

The most striking feature of Hyperides' work is the lack of discrimination he showed in accepting cases and in undertaking litigation himself. Lysias defended individuals with whom he may not have had much sympathy, but his action could be justified in that such persons were entitled to defense. Hyperides personally prosecuted or wrote for the prosecution of anyone, including his oldest friends, on virtually all kinds of charges. The speech *Against Demosthenes*, delivered personally, is an example, though it may well have been politically shrewd for Hyperides to take advantage of the absence of charges against himself. Another example is the prosecution of Aristagora for failing to obtain a patron. She had been the orator's mistress—he was famous for maintaining three mistresses at once, including one of the most expensive in Greece—but he wrote two speeches against her and may have delivered them himself. Furthermore, he was quite willing to take on sensational cases which Demosthenes for one would never have touched. His defense of the courtesan Phryne on a charge of impiety was his most famous work. As a finale, according to tradition, he appealed to extra-rational proof and unveiled to the jury the bosom of his client.[148] Of the extant speeches the

---

[148] Cf. Colin, *op.cit.* supra n. 147, 10 ff., and A. Raubitschek, R-E 20 col. 903 ff. s.v. "Phryne." The principal ancient references are

most unsavory is *Against Athenogenes*, which the author of *On the sublime* (34) admired. In an attempt to free a slave boy with whom he was in love, Hyperides' client had, without making an investigation but entirely carried away by passion, bought a whole perfume business from the wily Athenogenes, only to find that the business was loaded with heavy debts for which he was now responsible. Hyperides' success is largely due to the candid ethopoiia of the speaker who appears to put all of his cards on the table and may even succeed in winning some sympathy from a reader. The law was entirely on the side of Athenogenes, and it would be interesting to know whether Hyperides' rhetoric was able to aid his client. The fact of publication and the fame of the speech is slight evidence that he won. Among other speeches known to us are two more involving courtesans, Demetria and Mica; a prosecution of Mantitheus, which looks unsavory; and a prosecution of Patrocles for procuring.[149] The extant speech *For Lycophron* is concerned with adultery.

Hyperides cannot be excused, as Lysias could, on the ground that he defended those in trouble, for he undertook prosecutions on grounds that seem legally weak. In this situation a responsible modern lawyer would advise his client to drop the case, but Hyperides' function was not legal, it was rhetorical. He no doubt expected to publish his speeches, and he looked for opportunities to deal strikingly with rhetorical problems. The developed state of rhetoric and public acceptance of it had made this possible.

Hyperides was greatly admired in antiquity as an orator who could do almost everything well (*On the sublime* 34).

Athenaeus 13.590e ff.; Quintilian 2.15.9; *Lives of the ten orators* 849e. The inspiration of the incident may have been the tradition that Menelaus spared Helen's life at the end of the Trojan war when he glimpsed her bosom, cf. Euripides, *Andromache* 628 and Aristophanes, *Lysistrata* 155.

[149] Cf. Burtt, *op.cit.* supra n. 146, 565 ff.

Judging him is made difficult by the fragmentary nature of the speeches, but he has a wonderful naturalness which seizes upon the occasion to create an extemporaneous effect. The speeches *For Euxenippus* and *Against Demosthenes* begin disarmingly "as I was just saying to those seated beside me . . ." and the former continues with a spirited prooemium dealing with the justification of the use of impeachment against Hyperides' client. The prosecution of Demosthenes, though superior to the attack by Dinarchus, is not distinguished. Hyperides probably spoke third and limits himself largely to the immediate occasion, though referring vaguely (col. 17) to earlier bribery. Since the indictment by the Areopagus was regarded as equivalent to proof Hyperides introduces no evidence. The question, like that at the end of Plato's *Apology*, is one of the punishment. The most effective passage comes when the orator alludes to his old friendship with Demosthenes (col. 21-22): "Will you dare to speak to me of friendship . . . this friendship you yourself dissolved. . . ."[150] Hyperides' prosecution does not represent any political change on his own part, but a capitalization on the difficulties of Demosthenes.

Dinarchus

Dinarchus was born at Corinth about 361 B.C.[151] He is said to have studied under Theophrastus and Demetrius of Phaleron and was a professional logographer in Athens. The three extant speeches were all delivered by clients during the prosecution of those alleged to have been bribed by Harpalus in 324. In the following years Dinarchus was successful in his profession, but in 307 he retired to Euboea to avoid political prosecution. He returned to Athens in 292

[150] On the trial cf. Charles D. Adams, "The Harpalus case," TAPA 32 (1901) 121 ff. and E. Badian, "Harpalus," JHS 81 (1961) 16 ff.

[151] The principal sources are the *Lives of the ten orators* and the essay *On Dinarchus* by Dionysius of Halicarnassus. Cf. Blass 3.2.258 ff. There is a translation in Burtt, *op.cit.* supra n. 146, 161 ff.

and probably died soon thereafter. As many as a hundred and sixty speeches were credited to him in antiquity (Dionysius of Halicarnassus, *Dinarchus ad fin.*)—among them *Against Theocrines*, now number fifty-eight in the corpus of Demosthenes.

Dinarchus has never been very highly regarded. He has no ideas of his own, no style of his own, no integrity of his own; he is a technician who happened to be useful to politicians and litigants for a couple of decades, and this has secured him a dubious immortality. The most important of the three surviving speeches is *Against Demosthenes*, written for an unknown accuser who prosecuted along with Hyperides and eight others. Dinarchus makes the maximum use of Demosthenes' ill-advised proposal of the death penalty for himself if the Areopagus should report that he had accepted a bribe, as unfortunately that body did report. Although the question before the court was apparently the determination of the penalty, a good deal of space is nevertheless spent establishing the moral likelihood of Demosthenes' accepting a bribe, and some of the charges of Aeschines are resumed, as is Aeschines' identification of Athenian bad fortune with that of Demosthenes (29 ff., 41, 72). There is much rhetorical spite (35 f.), and the speech creates an impression of disorganized excitement. The fact that Dinarchus composed the whole thing for pay rather than as an expression of outraged patriotism—which could be said for Hyperides or Aeschines—lurks in the reader's mind. It is impossible to decide what Dinarchus or the speaker thought about contemporary problems, and the orator would have thought it to be irrelevant. He was solving a rhetorical problem, how to convict Demosthenes, and in this he was successful. Relative ability can perhaps be deduced from the fact that the Athenians thought nine orators were necessary to prosecute Demosthenes.

The other two speeches are considerably shorter but show

the same emphasis on ethical rather than logical proof. The infamous career of Aristogiton, the defendant in the second speech, naturally lent itself to this approach, but in both cases Dinarchus was in the position of having almost nothing to say, for the material had been handled in the earlier cases[152] and was perfectly familiar to everybody. The absence of a narration in all three speeches results from the same fact.

There were in fourth-century Athens many more public speakers than those discussed here: the great Callistratus left no examples of his art, nor do we know anything about the oratory of Eubulus. Among Demosthenes' supporters was Hegesippus, who was according to Libanius' *hypothesis* the author of the *On the Halonnesus* (Demosthenes 7). The speaker of that work had been an ambassador to Philip (2), and Philip had subsequently sent a letter to Athens offering to give the small island of Halonnesus to her. The Athenians wanted the island given *back* to them. Hegesippus delivers a strong reply to the letter, attacking the intentions of Philip. Although Demosthenes would have applauded the speech, which is lively and technically competent, it lacks rhetorical distinction.[153] Probably it is a typical deliberative speech of the time. *On organization* (Demosthenes 13) and *On the treaty with Alexander* (Demosthenes 17), both by unknown authors, also found their way into the corpus of Demosthenes because of their consistency with his ideas. Another speaker who supported De-

---

[152] Demosthenes was tried first and was prosecuted by Stratocles, then by Dinarchus' client, who was perhaps Menesaechmus or Himeraeus, cf. Burtt, *op.cit.* supra n. 146, 168. The order of the other trials and also their result is uncertain. The third epistle of Demosthenes is an important but questionable source: it indicates (42) that Aristogiton was acquitted and (31) Philocles condemned, but this may not be right, cf. Burtt 287 f.

[153] Cf. Blass 3.2.111 ff., and L. Heinlein, *Hegesipps Rede περὶ Ἀλοννήσου verglichen mit den Demosthenischen Reden*, Würzburg, 1900.

mosthenes, but of whom no works survive, was Polyeuctus of Sphettus.[154]

One of the greatest of Greek orators in the eyes of antiquity was Demades. None of his works were published (Quintilian 2.17.13), but some of his forceful remarks were long remembered[155] (Demetrius, *On style* 282 ff.). He generally sympathized with Macedon, but was predominantly an orator rather than a statesman. He could apparently be bought and the impression of his contemporaries may be summed up in the remarks with which, for the sake of contrast, Plutarch begins his life of the virtuous Phocion:

"Demades the orator, being in power at Athens because of his political favors to Macedonians and Antipater and being forced to write and speak much which was contrary to the reputation and character of the city, said that he ought to be excused because he was guiding the shipwreck of a state. . . . Demades was himself the wreckage of the city; he lived and governed so outrageously that Antipater said of him, when he became an old man, that as in the case of a victim after a sacrifice, only the tongue and belly remained."

This statement may be taken to represent the fate of Attic oratory, and the historian of rhetoric must inquire why. A popular explanation is that the loss of independence in Athens and the disappearance of a real democracy made

[154] On Pseudo-Demosthenes 13 cf. Blass 3.1.352 ff. and F. W. Levy, *De Demosthenis περὶ συντάξεως oratione*, Berlin, 1919, who regards it as genuine. On no. 17 cf. Blass 3.2.121 ff., and Stanislaus Schüller, "Ueber den Verfasser der Rede περὶ τῶν πρὸς Ἀλέξανδρον συνθηκῶν," ws 19 (1897) 211 ff. On Polyeuctus cf. Blass 3.2.126 ff.

[155] Cf. Blass 3.2.236 ff.; P. Treves, "Dèmade," *Athenaeum* 11 (1933) 105 ff.; Vittorio de Falco, *Demade oratore: testimonianze e frammenti*, Naples, 1954. The fragmentary speech *On the twelve years*, ascribed to Demades, is not genuine, though it may be based on historical information. A translation is available by Burtt, *op.cit.* supra n. 146, 336 ff.

great oratory impossible.[156] This may be true, but it is so easily and so often said that it is well to be sure there are not factors pointing to a more complex answer. The decline is most evident in that point of view which isolated oratory from real political or moral concern and saw in it only an art of winning persuasion for the moment. The reason why none of the myriads of speeches delivered in the Hellenistic period have been preserved is that they were not of significance or interest to anybody. They were compositions for the moment, the work of creatures with tongue but no brain. The trend in this direction antedates the victory of Macedon; it is already implicit in Isocrates' *Panegyricus*, in Isaeus' view of his art, and in all oratory which subordinates content to form. It is what Plato felt to be implied in sophistic notions of rhetoric. That Demosthenes delivered his greatest speeches at the end of Athenian democracy tends to blind critics to the fact that in effectiveness, in ideas, in independence, in content, the greatest period of Greek *political* oratory was in the fifth century. We have some inkling of its nature in Thucydides. Demosthenes should be regarded as an afterglow, and the very ineffectiveness of his violent efforts is probably an indication that the substance of oratory could no longer impart an extended influence. The orators, in the interests of petty causes, had too often cried "wolf."

What then was the cause of this process? Does oratory necessarily degenerate in this fashion? Any such natural tendency was accelerated by the restricted bases of Greek civilization. Greek oratory had marked out its fields, established its classifications, and explored its challenges. It had done what it could with its commonplaces and arguments.

[156] Cf., e.g., Harry Caplan, "The decay of eloquence at Rome in the first century," *Studies in speech and drama in honor of Alexander M. Drummond*, Ithaca, 1944, 319 ff. The experiences of Greece and Rome are not exactly analogous since considerable independence existed from time to time in Hellenistic Greece.

There is a sameness about the subject matter, but there seemed no new things to say, no new arguments to advance, no new examples to cite. Later writers felt that they could not surpass Demosthenes. Epic, drama, and other literary forms in antiquity arrived at the same dead end, for the same reason—the restricted traditional basis on which they were built and especially the absence of any foreign literatures or cultures to reinspire them. Translation of the forms into the Latin language was to produce a momentary renaissance. The brain of oratory decayed. What did survive was the tongue, the concern with style, seeking to make up for lack of content by stylistic adornment, and the belly, the appetite of the orator for pay and applause.

The decline of Athens and Athenian democracy is as much a process coincident with the decline of oratory as it is a cause of waning eloquence. The weariness and futility that the Peloponnesian war bequeathed to all men is at the heart of the fatalism and inertia which Demosthenes could not break. That war itself was fundamentally a product of the formal bases of Greek politics and of the inability of the Greek city states to change. Inability to resist autocracy was, thus, a political counterpart of inability to produce great oratory. In *theory* there need have been no tie between the date of decline of oratory and democracy. Democracy was one of the major causes of the systemization of Greek rhetoric, but only one of several factors in the flowering of Greek oratory, which had existed long before the Athenian democracy. Other factors included the tradition of achieving excellence as a speaker of words; the influence of sophistry, which was not an Athenian product; the general literary milieu of fifth-century Athens, especially the influence of history and drama; and the patriotic fervor resulting from the Persian wars. Oratory might have outlived the democracy. Judicial oratory was the basic form and need for that continued. Epideictic easily lent itself to new conditions and was, in fact, to attain great triumphs under the rule of Roman emperors. Even deliberative oratory might have been offered some scope during subsequent years in the internal councils of Athens and in the workings of the Achaean and Aetolian leagues. It was the nature of Greek oratory and the attitude of the Greeks toward oratory which made it impossible to respond to these challenges with new thoughts and new materials for speech. The analogy of tragedy is valid. Tragedy can exist without democracy and has, in Spain, France, and England. What it needs is an enthusiastic and intellectual age—which sometimes also produces democracy—and tragic subjects capable both of development and new treatments. When opportunities for novelty are gone and excitement wanes tragedy dies. Our present age, though democratic beyond precedent, is not one of great tragedy.

Much of what has been said in this chapter should contribute to an understanding of the relationship between rhetorical theory and oratorical practice in the classical period.[157] There is a general unity of theory and practice. Speeches *do* make use of the kinds of arguments and topics mentioned in Aristotle and Anaximenes. Argument from probability *is* the commonest form of proof. Deliberative speeches *do* discuss the expedient, judicial speeches the just, and epideictic speeches the honorable, though they combine these topics too. Portions of speeches, especially the prooemia, *are* built up of commonplaces. Historical examples *are* commonly introduced. Ethical proof *is* used often, and appeals to emotions *are* regularly found, especially in the peroration. The four parts of an oration discussed in Aristotle and Anaximenes *are* adequate as the structural basis of real speeches. Judicial speeches almost always have the four parts, unless the work is a "second" speech, in which case the narration is sometimes omitted.

[157] Cf. Kroll 1065 ff., "Praxis des 5/4 Jhdts."

The parts regularly perform the functions attributed to them by the theorists: the prooemium secures the unprejudiced, sympathetic attention of the audience; the narration clearly sets forth the facts; the proof, logical and ethical, follows; then the peroration, which usually recapitulates and stirs the passions. Sometimes there is more than one narration, and the proof is divided into subsections. Deliberative speeches show the influence of the judicial form, though there is normally no narration. In style—a subject not discussed in detail here since it has been handled by Blass and Jebb and requires attention to the Greek text— the Gorgianic figures, the periodic style, and the prose rhythms discussed in the handbooks *do* appear. We know further that delivery *was* given attention by such orators as Demosthenes and Aeschines.

On the other hand, there is no evidence that the Attic orators learned how to speak directly from handbooks.[158] These were probably mostly for the untrained not the professionals, who learned from each other and experience, all the while conforming in general to the traditions in the way natural to a Greek literary artist. The handbooks and actual speeches were both products of the tradition, which was the great governing force and which produced the typical rhetorical state of mind. That tradition was not the work of any one man nor written down in any one place. It is only in later writers like Quintilian that a reasonably full statement can be found. The tradition could be and was modified, but not in its essentials, which were matters of form and which were unchanged from the time of their statement in the fifth century.

Within the limits imposed by the forms, the practice goes beyond anything in the theory. This is to be expected. No criticism explains genius, and ancient criticism is espe-

---

[158] Dionysius of Halicarnassus' *First letter to Ammaeus* is concerned with successfully disproving the contention that Demosthenes made use of Aristotle's *Rhetoric*.

cially inadequate in describing the greatness of the literature it accompanies. The theorist does not provide for the cleverness of Demosthenes in solving rhetorical problems, and especially is stylistic criticism inadequate to the actual achievements. Probably the orators worked mostly by ear. This is true in the subtleties of prose rhythms;[159] in the use of the metaphor, where, as in poetry, the orator sometimes achieves a constructive and symbolic force apparently undreamed of by the critics; and in the variety of figures which can be found in oratory but which were not named and classified until the Hellenistic period. Finally, the actualities of oratory do not clearly settle into the three categories of deliberative, judicial, and epideictic, though examples of these three can be found.

The most satisfactory image would be to think of the rhetorical tradition as a great interwoven vine leading from two main trunks. One of these trunks, the practical side, was nurtured by a rich culture and put forth an exceedingly green foliage for a brief time, supported in part by its fellow trunk. Thereafter the other, theoretical trunk alone continued to grow, drawing strength and sap from its dying mate and producing a dry, yellowish leaf which was ground up as an educational fodder for the other arts. From a distance it is sometimes hard to distinguish which branch belongs to which trunk.

[159] E.g. Demosthenes' avoidance of a series of short syllables, cf. Blass's second edition (1893) 3.1.105 ff. and Charles D. Adams, "Demosthenes' avoidance of breves," CP 12 (1917) 271 ff.

CHAPTER FIVE

Hellenistic Rhetoric to the Arrival in Rome of Dionysius of Halicarnassus[1]

During the period from the death of Aristotle to the foundation of the Roman empire, the theory of rhetoric which had been reasonably fully developed in the fourth century was greatly augmented into a detailed system. This system, together with practical exercises, gained a central place first in secondary and then in advanced education. Of the many Greek writings on rhetoric in these three hundred years we have practically none; what we know about Hellenistic developments comes largely from works written by Roman authors or by later Greek authors who refer to Hellenistic rhetoricians and their writings. Sometimes specific theories are attributed to specific rhetoricians or schools—especially to Theophrastus and to Hermagoras. More often there are vague references to discussions which a later author builds upon or disagrees with. The *Rhetorica ad Herennium*, for example, never refers by name to any previous rhetorician; nevertheless, it is exceedingly helpful in gaining a general notion of developments in the two hundred and fifty years after Aristotle's *Rhetoric*. It is a handbook in Latin by a contemporary of Cicero[2] and ap-

[1] In general cf. Friedrich Blass, *Die griechische Beredsamkeit in der Zeitraum von Alexander bis auf Augustus*, Berlin, 1865; Franz Susemihl, *Geschichte der griechischen Literatur in der Alexandrinerzeit* 2, Leipzig, 1892, 448-516; Arnim 73 ff.; Claus Peters, *De rationibus inter artem rhetoricam quarti et primi saeculi intercedentibus*, Kiel, 1907; J. W. H. Atkins, *Literary criticism in antiquity* 2 vols., Cambridge, Eng., 1934; Kroll 1071 ff.

[2] A. E. Douglas, "Clausulae in the *Rhetorica ad Herennium* as evidence of date," CQ 10 (1960) 65 ff., argues in favor of a first-century date considerably after the latest reference in the work, which appears to be the mention of Marius' seventh consulship, 86 B.C. (4.68). The actual date of composition is of less importance than the fact that the work reflects the teaching of the late second and early first century B.C.

parently is based on the teaching of some Roman rhetorician who in turn had learned the traditional system from a Greek source.[3] A second work written about the same time and of almost equal help is Cicero's *De inventione*.

The earliest Greek handbooks, as we saw in chapter three, were built around the parts of the judicial oration. Aristotle regarded this subject as of little significance and composed an account of logical, ethical, and emotional proofs in three different kinds of oratory. Subsequently he added a discussion of style and of arrangement not unlike that in the early handbooks. In the first century B.C. the handbooks begin with a discussion of invention. Three kinds of oratory are dealt with, but the major concern is with the parts of the oration; some vestiges of Aristotle's concepts are discussed under the "proof." There is thus, as Cicero points out (*De inventione* 2.8), a kind of conflation of two systems, Aristotle's and that of the original sophistic handbooks, sometimes referred to as Isocratean.[4] The problem of reconciling the two approaches was complicated by the question of what to do with the extensive discussion of issues or *staseis* which Hermagoras introduced. The *Rhetorica ad Herennium* makes these a part of the discussion of the proof; Cicero relegates them to a second book. In the *Ad*

[3] Cf. Friedrich Marx, "Prolegomena," *Incerti auctoris de ratione dicendi ad C. Herennium libri iv*, Leipzig, 1894; Harry Caplan, *Ad C. Herennium de ratione dicendi* (Loeb Library), Cambridge, 1954, xv ff.; Dieter Matthes, "Hermagoras von Temnos 1904-1955," *Lustrum* 3 (1958) 58 ff., esp. 81 ff. with extensive bibliography.

[4] Cf. Barwick 1 ff. Barwick regarded the basic conflation as having taken place in the fourth century and associates it with Theodectes and Heraclides Ponticus, cf. esp. 40 ff. This is too early, for the rhetorical system of the Stoics (Diogenes Laertius 7.41-43) resembles that of Aristotle with Theophrastus' addition of delivery, and even Hermagoras seems not to have treated the parts of the oration under invention (cf. infra). A better date would be shortly after Hermagoras. The conflation is less thorough in Cicero's *De inventione* than in the *Rhetorica ad Herennium*. Cf. Kroll 1096 ff.; Friedrich Solmsen, "The Aristotelian tradition in ancient rhetoric," AJP 62 (1941) 46 ff.; Caplan, *op.cit.* supra n. 3, xviii ff.

Herennium the new organization is moderately satisfactory from a practical point of view since there is no need to treat topics twice, once under invention and once under subjects to be handled in the separate parts of the speech, but little is left to discuss under arrangement. This is the second big heading of the handbook and consists of a very short discussion of the order in which strong and weak arguments may be placed and of departures from the ordinary order of the parts of the speech (3.16-17). In most subsequent treatises style is handled third, followed by the new parts (called *officia*, "functions," in *Ad Herennium* 2.1) of delivery and memory, but the author of the *Ad Herennium* postpones style to the last because he wants to give it special treatment (3.1).

This description indicates another fact about the changes in rhetorical theory, namely the great increase in categories. The parts of rhetoric have grown from three to five by the addition of delivery and memory, the parts of the oration from four to six by the addition of partition and refutation. The system of three or four different categories of issues has been devised, and each of these has its subdivisions. Memory and delivery have their own subtopics, and, most conspicuous of all, hundreds of different figures of speech are named and described. No doubt the primary reason for this elaboration is the fact that any discipline, once it begins self-analysis, carries on the process relentlessly. In modern times the same trend with the same creation of terminology and definitions can be seen in some of the social sciences. The Hellenistic period was one of general scholarly activity when philologists were much concerned with specific features of literary technique, including that seen in the orators of the fourth century. The subtlety and finesse of Isocrates, Demosthenes, and others certainly encouraged attempts to perceive and classify what had been done.

A third feature is the academic nature of the theory. The early handbooks were composed for practical use by litigants, but Herennius is not expected to go to court immediately, despite the emphasis on judicial oratory. He is to study rhetoric as a discipline of the mind (1.1). Many references are made to declamations on mythological or remote historical subjects, and the wider audience addressed by the author was no doubt intended to consist of students in the rhetorical schools. Nor does the author of the *Ad Herennium* have Aristotle's concern with the place of rhetoric in society. Furthermore, the techniques are entirely amoral. The reader is told how to argue for or against a given case, how to use evidence to prove or disprove a point. No mention is made of any responsibilities, social or intellectual, of the orator. The system is self-consciously complete (4.69) with no need of the disciplines of law or psychology or philosophy for its operations. The point of view throughout is that all the answers are known: if a case is properly presented it will be persuasive. None of the mitigating circumstances of actual life are imagined. This aspect of the system is not, of course, new. We have seen that it was growing in the fourth century and clearly it continued without check. Before the first century B.C. was out it reached the extreme position of imposing absolute rules on the writers of speeches. Even the author of the *Ad Herennium* confines oratorical style (*semper omnis oratoria elocutio*) to three specific kinds (4.10).

Related to the academic quality of rhetoric is the doctrine of imitation which enshrined certain earlier writers as classics and restricted literary creativity to a necessarily imperfect imitation of them. Some Latin writers resisted this trend as less applicable to them than to the Greeks. We see signs of the dispute in the extensive introduction to the last book of the *Ad Herennium*, where the author protests against those Greek rhetoricians who quote all their examples and are unwilling or unable to coin suitable ones themselves.

These are not the only features of Hellenistic rhetoric.

A comparison of fourth-century writings and the rhetorical works of Dionysius of Halicarnassus would bring out certain other characteristics: there was, for example, some tendency toward monographic studies like Theophrastus' influential *On style* and the extant treatises attributed to Demetrius and to Dionysius himself. Another feature is the increasing concern of rhetoric with all literature, not just with oratory. Demetrius and Dionysius have as much to say about poetry or history or the writing of letters as about speeches. This fact no doubt reflects the central position that rhetoric had acquired in education.

Since rhetoric in education is clearly a crucial matter in this period it will be best to look first at that topic and then take up the specific contents of rhetorical theory and its development.

A child spent the first six years of his life at home, treated more or less as a baby.[5] At the age of seven he began to go to primary school, where he was taught by a *grammatistês* to read and write and count. The process was one of rote memorization of the shapes and names of letters, then the sound of syllables, and finally the pronunciation of words and sentences. Passages of poetry were memorized and recited, and sentences of the schoolmaster were laboriously copied out. A third century papyrus containing such exercises has been found.[6]

This process continued rather painfully until a child could read and write, at which time he went on to the school of the *grammatikos*, the grammarian, whose primary task was to teach a basic knowledge of the Greek language and literature. Coincidently a boy had athletic training and often music lessons, but neither was a concern of the school itself,

[5] Cf. Marrou 142 ff.
[6] Cf. O. Guéraud and P. Jouguet, "Un livre d'écolier du iiie siècle avant Jésus-Christ," *Publications de la société royale égyptienne de papyrologie, textes et documents* 2, Cairo, 1938.

which was devoted exclusively to literary studies. Primary education had existed in earlier times, and advanced education had previously been furnished by sophists, but this intermediate phase was largely a development of the Hellenistic period, accompanied on the scholarly level by the development of a science of grammar. Schools were private institutions charging fees to support the teacher, although in a few cities educational foundations were set up by benefactors. Cities did supply the gymnasia and operate the ephebate, the military training program of the late teens.[7]

Our best primary source of information about Hellenistic grammar is the little handbook written about 100 B.C. by Dionysius Thrax, a pupil of Aristarchus.[8] Dionysius defines grammar as an acquaintence (ἐμπειρία) with what is said in the poets and prose writers. The subject has six parts: reading (involving practice in prosody), exegesis of poetic tropes, explanation of rare words (glosses) and historical references, construction of etymologies, practice in inflexion, and judgment of the poets. A common way of grouping these was to say that grammar had three parts, one literary, one practical, and one historical (Sextus Empiricus, *Against the professors* 1.248-252). We may imagine the student reading a text out loud after his master, and proceeding word by word to identify forms, figures, and references in the old-fashioned way still practiced in some Classics courses today.

A line was usually drawn between the teachings of the grammarian and the more advanced instruction of the rhetorician. The former dealt mostly with the poets and with analysis, the latter concentrated on the orators and on increasingly difficult composition. But in practice the two schools tended to overlap. Some teachers taught both

[7] Cf. Marrou 103 ff. and Sterling Dow, "The Athenian *Ephêboi;* other staffs, and the staff of the Diogeneion," TAPA 91 (1960) 381 ff.

[8] Cf. Gustavus Uhlig, *Dionysii Thracis ars grammatica*, Leipzig, 1883.

grammar and rhetoric to different classes;[9] some of the work of grammatical analysis, the study of diction and of figures, for example, was related to rhetoric, and recitation was of course under the general heading of delivery.

Furthermore, grammarians often introduced their students to the first stages of rhetorical composition, the *progymnasmata*.[10] We know about these exercises mostly from extant accounts written in the first and second centuries A.D. by Theon and by Hermogenes, but ancient education was so conservative that we may assume the exercises go back at least to Hellenistic times. For that matter the term *progymnasmata* is used of exercises in the *Rhetorica ad Alexandrum* (1436a25). Hermogenes' list of exercises, in order of increasing difficulty, is fable, narrative, chria (amplification of a statement or action), maxim (also to be amplified), refutation and confirmation, commonplace (generalized moral statement), encomium, comparison, character portrayal, description, philosophical thesis, and discussion of a law. Marrou points out that each of these exercises was to be performed according to set rules and with prescribed subdivisions.[11] Originality, far from being encouraged, would have been regarded as unscholarly and a breach of discipline. Such an attitude toward writing, inculcated in early youth and reemphasized by subsequent study of canonized examples of argument or style, had great effect upon the nature of Hellenistic and Roman literature.

By his middle teens a boy was ready for the rhetorician. Under his direction the student completed the course in the *progymnasmata* and undertook a study of rhetorical

[9] Cf. Strabo 14.650 and Friedrich Marx, rev. of Thiele, BPW 10 (1890) 1007.

[10] Cf. Georgius Reichel, *Quaestiones progymnasticae*, Leipzig, 1909; Ray Nadeau, "The *Progymnasmata* of Aphthonius in translation," SM 19 (1952) 264 ff.; Marrou 172 ff.; Donald L. Clark, *Rhetoric in Greco-Roman education*, New York, 1957, 177 ff.

[11] 175.

theory based on the lectures of the master and perhaps also on some handbook. He also composed advanced exercises. This had been essentially the system of Isocrates (*Antidosis* 183 f.), which was still in full force in the time of Quintilian. Quintilian states (2.4.41 f.) that declamations in imitation of cases in the law courts or speeches in the assembly, the *controversiae* and *suasoriae* of the Romans, were introduced in Greece about the time of Demetrius of Phaleron, that is, at the end of the fourth century. He also says (2.4.3) that in his time, and presumably long before, Greek rhetoricians with help from their assistants continued the analysis of texts in the manner of the grammarians, but concentrated on historians and orators. Quintilian attempted unsuccessfully to follow the same custom with Roman students. Thus the Hellenistic rhetorical schools seem to have exposed their pupils to a threefold system of theory, practice, and study of texts as an object of imitation.

To one who has followed the history of rhetoric to this point, such a one-sided educational system should not be surprising. We have seen that the ability to be a speaker of words was one of the two arts taught to Achilles by Phoenix; we have seen how rhetoric played a central role in the schools of the sophists because of their practical concerns. Isocrates' permanent and formal school, concerned almost solely with rhetoric, was probably the crucial development: it had influenced the founding of Plato's Academy and had been responsible for Aristotle's decision to teach rhetoric. In the fourth century familiarity with rhetoric was the surest path to fame and success. Despite the restrictions on his activities, the orator was for centuries a powerful ideal. Finally, rhetoric was the only one of the learned disciplines which was sufficiently developed and agreed upon to furnish a standard basis for education and to be taught by someone who was not himself an original theorist. The core curriculum must not be beyond the ability of the teachers. Because of its degree of early development and its clarity rhetoric became a model for the codification of other arts, among them grammar and music.[12]

At the pinnacle of the educational system (ἐγκυκλία παιδεία) of the early Hellenistic period was philosophy; if a young man pursued higher education in his late teens and twenties it was probably in the school of a philosopher that he did so. But since rhetoric played such an important part in secondary education and study of it colored all intellectual concerns, most of the philosophical schools included rhetorical exercises in their curriculums and some exercised leadership in rhetorical scholarship (Quintilian 3.1.15 and 12.2.23 ff.). Philosophical interest in rhetoric and the art of persuasion may also have been motivated by the needs of a popular philosophical literature intended to make converts.

Among the philosophers the Peripatetics were the leaders in the study of rhetoric. They had Aristotle's example to begin with, and subsequent important advances were made by Theophrastus. Then came a falling off: according to Strabo (13.609, cf. also Plutarch, *Sulla* 26) the loss of Aristotle's library and many of his works from the time of Theophrastus until the first century b.c. made purely philosophical speculation difficult. The Peripatetics therefore turned to the declamation of commonplaces to fill the void.[13] The story describes the decay of the school rather than explains its cause, whatever the truth about the library. Lycon of Troy, head of the school around the middle of the third century, was known for his elaborate style (Cicero, *De finibus* 5.13), and we have a Latin translation of a bit of one of his speeches (Rutilius Lupus 2.7).

Real advances in rhetorical theory were made by the im-

[12] Cf. Manfred Fuhrmann, *Das systematische Lehrbuch*, Göttingen, 1960.

[13] Cf. Arnim 83 and Felix Grayeff, "The problem of the genesis of Aristotle's text," *Phronesis* 1 (1956) 105 ff.

mediate successors of Aristotle—Theophrastus and to a
lesser extent Demetrius. In no case do their methods involve any basic departure from the master. They clarified
or systemized what he had begun, or they pursued subjects
which he had suggested as worth attention. This was almost
certainly in keeping with Aristotle's concept of how the
school should function, continually engaged in research and
revising its conclusions.

Theophrastus (c.370-c.285 B.C.)

The extant works of Theophrastus are the *Characters*,
two works on botany, a number of short scientific treatises,
and some notes on metaphysics. These represent, however,
only a small fraction of his total output. Diogenes Laertius
(5.42 ff., esp. 47-49) gives a list of writings including some
which may have dealt with rhetoric and a number which
certainly did. The titles show an interest in invention—*On
enthymemes*, for example, and two books of *Epicheiremes*,[14]
which term replaced enthymeme as the name for the basic
rhetorical argument. There was also work in the field of
arrangement, style, and delivery; an *Art of rhetoric* in one
book; works on commonplaces and topics; collections of
theses, which may have been used as rhetorical exercises;
and a treatise *On the ludicrous*, which may have influenced
later rhetorical discussions of humor (e.g. Cicero, *De oratore*
2.217 ff.). Theophrastus lectured to as many as two thousand at once and gave practical attention to the technique
of speaking (Diogenes Laertius 5.37), anointing and dress-
ing himself with care and indulging in gestures (Athenaeus
1.21 a-b).

Theophrastus' influence on rhetoric was greatest in the
areas of style and delivery; in both cases he developed
theories at which Aristotle had pointed. Of his lost rhetorical works we know best the treatise *On style* because
Cicero made repeated use of it. In *Orator* (79) he says:

[14] Cf. W. Kroll, "Das Epicheirema," SBW 216.2 (1936) 16 f.

"The language will be pure and good Latin, it will be clearly and distinctly stated, attention will be given to what is fitting; one thing will be lacking which Theophrastus numbers fourth among the virtues of a speech, ornamentation which is pleasant and abundant."[15]

Theophrastus' four virtues had been taken up also in *De oratore* (3.37 ff.) and made the basis of the discussion of style in that work; that is, each of the virtues was discussed in order and other topics subordinated to it. The long discussion in Quintilian (8.1-11.1) is basically similar. Since accounts of style generally do concentrate on the four virtues and since Cicero attributes them to Theophrastus, it seems highly likely that Theophrastus' *On style* (Περὶ λέξεως) followed the same pattern.[16] It is not surprising that it should, since the virtue of style is a key phrase in the third book of Aristotle's *Rhetoric* (1404b1). Only one virtue is there recognized, namely clarity, though propriety is appended as also necessary. Aristotle subsequently discusses other qualities including ornamentation or weight (ὄγκος) (1407b26 ff.) and propriety (τὸ πρέπον) (1408a10 ff.), and he includes also a discussion of hellenism (1407a19 ff.) which, as we have seen,[17] was really an earlier discussion

[15] "Sermo purus erit et Latinus, dilucide planeque dicetur, quid deceat circumspicietur. Unum aberit quod quartum numerat Theophrastus in orationis laudibus: ornatum illud suave et affluens." Probably some of what immediately follows is also from Theophrastus, but it is difficult to sort it out clearly.

[16] Cf. Johannes Stroux, *De Theophrasti virtutibus dicendi*, Leipzig, 1912. The fragments (and also a great deal that does not come from Theophrastus) are available in August Mayer, *Theophrasti περὶ λέξεως libri fragmenta*, Leipzig, 1910, cf. esp. the *conspectus fragmentorum*, 226 f. G. M. A. Grube's attempt to refute some of Stroux' conclusions seems to me unsuccessful, for it does not recognize the general acceptance of the virtues nor Cicero's clear turn to an earlier rhetoric, cf. "Theophrastus as a literary critic," TAPA 83 (1952) 180 ff. Cf. also Alain Michel, *Rhétorique et philosophie chez Cicéron*, Paris, 1960, 327 ff.

[17] Cf. supra pp. 104 ff.

of clarity, but might be taken to refer to good Greek. Thus the four virtues of Theophrastus may be found, more or less, in Aristotle. Qualities of style had also been discussed by Plato, Isocrates, Theodectes, and others and can be seen in the *Rhetorica ad Alexandrum* (1438a22). What Theophrastus did was to organize the material into a set of clear and teachable categories. In so doing he departed from the logic and unity of treatment which Aristotle's demand for clarity had made, but it must be confessed that the third book of the *Rhetoric* as it stands does not carry through that doctrine with any clarity itself, and a rigorous application could only result in a kind of extreme Atticism. Was a teacher to discuss figures solely in terms of the clarity they imparted to the context? This could hardly be done in an age which tended more and more toward an elaborate literary style almost divorced from the context. Theophrastus gave Hellenistic rhetoricians a usable system which preserved the essential requirements of good style and did not overemphasize adornment.

Purity (ἑλληνισμός, *purus et Latinus*), the first of Theophrastus' virtues, refers mostly to the correct form of a word. Cicero says (*De oratore* 3.40), "we shall preserve case and tense and gender and number. . . ." The brevity of the discussion in Cicero results partly from his opposition to extreme Atticism, which, under Stoic influence, stressed this virtue above others.[18]

Clarity (τὸ σαφές, *dilucide planeque*) is basically the clarity described by Aristotle. Cicero says (*De oratore* 3.49), "by speaking good Latin, with common words which clearly indicate what we wish to signify and declare, without ambiguous work or language, without an excessive number of words, nor with too elaborated metaphors, nor with the

---

[18] Cf. G. L. Hendrickson, "The *De analogia* of Julius Caesar: its occasion, nature, and date, with additional fragments," CP 1 (1906) 97 ff., esp. 105 ff. There was of course some feeling that grammar was "elementary," cf. Stroux, *op.cit.* supra n. 16, 13.

sentence structure broken up, without the tenses altered nor the persons confused nor the order disturbed. . . ."

The third virtue, propriety (τὸ πρέπον, decorum) discusses the adaptation of the style to the circumstances of the speech, the character of the speaker, the sympathies of the audience, and the kind of speech. Frigidity was defined as an overshooting of the proper expression (Demetrius, On style 114). Some of the material included in the discussion can be seen in Aristotle (1408a10 ff. and 1413b3 ff.) and Cicero (De oratore 3.210-212). Cicero and Quintilian both discuss ornamentation *before* propriety, but it is likely that Cicero reversed Theophrastus' order since he calls *ornatus* Theophrastus' *fourth* virtue (Orator 79) and since it comes after propriety in the list of virtues adopted by the Stoics (Diogenes Laertius 7.59).[19]

The fourth and final virtue was ornamentation (*ornatus*). Theophrastus may have used the term κατασκευή, which the Stoics adopted (Diogenes Laertius 7.59); Cicero's *suave* and *adfluens* indicates a subdivision into the two qualities of τὸ ἡδύ or "sweetness" and τὸ μεγαλοπρεπές or "distinction."[20] According to Dionysius of Halicarnassus (*Isocrates* 3) Theophrastus said that style becomes great, lofty, and unusual (μέγα, σεμνόν, περιττόν) through choice of words, harmony, and the use of figures. Dionysius and Quintilian make the distinction between choice of diction and composition a basic one for their whole theory of style, but this should not be attributed to Theophrastus since it is neither in Aristotle nor in Cicero. An indication of the content of Theophrastus' separate parts of ornamentation can be seen in Aristotle's discussion of the several types of words—proper, rare, coined, compound, and metaphorical—of periodicity and prose rhythm, and of the Gorgianic

[19] Cf. Stroux 60 ff.

[20] Cf. Stroux 25 ff. and 37 n. 2; Friedrich Solmsen, "Demetrios περὶ ἑρμηνείας und sein peripatetisches Quellenmaterial," *Hermes* 66 (1931) 241 ff.; Kroll 1073. For evidence that Theophrastus used the term μεγαλοπρεπές cf. Demetrius, On style 41.

figures. It may have been in this section that Theophrastus remarked (Quintilian 10.1.27) that the reading of the poets confers the most advantage to the orator. He also divided words into those beautiful by nature and those paltry and mean (Dionysius of Halicarnassus, *On composition* 16) and defined the beauty of a word as inherent in its sound or in its appearance or in its value in our minds (Demetrius, *On style* 173); he agreed with Aristotle (1408b2) in disliking overly bold metaphors (*On the sublime* 32.3, cf. Cicero, *Ad familiares* 16.17) and discussed in some detail (Cicero, *Orator* 173) prose rhythm, recommending the paean (*Orator* 194 and 218), rejecting the dactyl, iamb, and trochee (Quintilian 9.4.88), and preferring a general and varied rhythmical quality (Demetrius, *On style* 41 and Cicero, *De oratore* 3.184 ff. and *Orator* 228). We have his definition of an antithesis (Dionysius of Halicarnassus, *Lysias* 14) as threefold: when opposites are predicated of the same thing or the same thing of opposites or opposites of opposites (cf. Aristotle, *Rhetoric* 1409b36). The granting of a separate section to the σχήματα or figures is important.[21] Heretofore they had been treated almost incidentally, but from now on they play an increasingly important role in the theory of style. Theophrastus is probably responsible for elevating the subject to a level equal to diction and thus encouraging the process of identification of figures which led to the almost interminable lists in later rhetorical handbooks. Devices of stylistic amplification were also discussed; we have a fragment preserved in the *Laurentian epitome*[22] which attributes to Theophrastus six kinds of amplification, some of them suggestive of categories in Quintilian (8.4.3 ff.).[23] In Aristotle (*Rhetoric* 1368a10 ff.)

[21] The early history of figures is more fully discussed below in connexion with Demetrius.

[22] This is available at the end of the Oxford Classical Text of "Longinus," p. "F." Cf. Grube, *op.cit.* supra n. 16, 177.

[23] Cf. Mayer, *op.cit.* supra n. 16, 142; J. Cousin, *Etudes sur Quintilien* 1, Paris, 1935, 427; Grube, *op.cit.* supra n. 16, 174.

they had been treated as part of the subject matter of epideictic oratory. Quintilian's discussion of maxims (γνῶμαι, *sententiae*) as a device of style (8.5) probably also goes back to Theophrastus since Cicero, immediately after listing the four Theophrastan virtues, demands that the orator provide *acutae crebraeque sententiae* (*Orator* 79, cf. Gregory of Corinth in Walz 7.1154).[24] The maxim was a form of proof to Aristotle (*Rhetoric* 1394a1 ff.), but in the *Rhetorica ad Herennium* (4.24 f.) it has become simply a figure of speech.

Cicero's *De oratore* and to a lesser extent *Orator* are anachronisms in rhetorical theory because they leap back over nearly three centuries to the broader and more philosophical concept of rhetoric found in Aristotle and his pupil. Cicero's action greatly enriched the tradition. He was in turn followed by Quintilian and others. In the Hellenistic period the Stoics followed the approach of Theophrastus to style, but there occurred at some point an adaptation of the system which is found in the *Ad Herennium* (4.17 ff.). There three qualities (*res*) of style are required: *elegantia, compositio, dignitas. Elegantia* is divided into *latinitas* and *explanatio* (clarity), which gives us the first two of the Theophrastan virtues. *Compositio* is part of Theophrastus' ornamentation and so, it turns out, is *dignitas*, which consists of figures of diction and of thought (4.18). Propriety, so necessary a feature to the Peripatetics, is completely omitted.

A second subject of later stylistic theory, the characters or kinds of style, was probably given some impetus by Theophrastus' discussion of styles as applied to diction and genre.[25] Concepts of different kinds of style, all good in

[24] Cf. Mayer, *op.cit.* supra n. 16, 143, and Cousin, *op.cit.* supra n. 23, 435.
[25] Cf. George A. Kennedy, "Theophrastus and stylistic distinctions," HSCP 62 (1957) 93 ff. Objections to attributing the characters to Theophrastus have come primarily from G. L. Hendrickson, "The peripatetic mean of style and the three stylistic characters,"

their own way but appropriate for different subjects, objects, or speakers, are really basic to any literary sensitivity. There was thus from the earliest time in Greece a notion of a grand style,[26] and Plato (*Republic* 397b4 ff.) distinguished two kinds of poetic style which corresponded roughly to dramatic and narrative with the addition of a "mixed" style. This way of viewing style as a concomitant of genre was readily applicable to kinds of oratory and is employed by Isocrates (e.g. *Panegyricus* 11). In the twelfth chapter of the third book of the *Rhetoric* Aristotle developed this concept into a brief outline of a demegoric, dicanic, and epideictic style. He also perceived (*Poetics* 1459a8 ff. and 1460b8 ff.) styles in poetry varying with the diction. The two categories are not specifically mingled, though the discussion of kinds of oratory does make some mention of diction (1414a22 ff.). If Theophrastus developed the topic he did nothing more unusual than he did in developing the topic of the virtues of styles or of delivery.

Since the third book of Cicero's *De oratore* is heavily indebted to Theophrastus' *On style*, the presence of the theory of the three styles in Cicero's work is some indication that they may have been found in Theophrastus. In

AJP 25 (1904) 125 ff. and "The origin and meaning of the ancient characters of style," AJP 26 (1905) 249 ff.; Stroux, *op.cit.* supra n.16, 88 ff.; Theodor Herrle, *Quaestiones rhetoricae ad elocutionem pertinentes*, Leipzig, 1912, 18 ff.; Solmsen, *op.cit.* supra n. 4, 183; G. M. A. Grube, "Thrasymachus, Theophrastus, and Dionysius of Halicarnassus," AJP 73 (1952) 251 ff. and *op.cit.* supra n. 16, 179. Grube admits that Theophrastus discussed kinds of diction, but not three styles in a wider sense. For other discussions cf. W. Schmid, "Zur antiken Stillehre," RHM 49 (1894) 133 ff.; L. Radermacher, "Theophrast περὶ λέξεως," RHM 54 (1899) 374 ff.; W. Kroll, "Randbemerkungen," RHM 62 (1907) 86 ff. (a reply to Hendrickson); Christian Jensen, *Philodemus über die Gedichte, fünftes Buch*, Berlin, 1923, 170 ff. and "Herakleides von Pontos bei Philodem und Horaz," SBB (1936) 303 ff.; Kroll 1074; Franz Quadlbauer, "Die *genera dicendi* bis Plinius d.J.," WS 71 (1958) 63 ff.

[26] Cf. Quadlbauer, *op.cit.* supra n. 25, 55 ff.

3.210 ff. Cicero takes up the virtue of propriety and discusses it in terms of what style to use on what occasion: various judicial speeches, deliberative speeches, or laudations require various kinds of style. The full, the plain, or the middle kind should be chosen on the basis of what is appropriate. The three styles are thus associated with kinds of oratory, as Aristotle had done, in the context of a discussion of one of Theophrastus' four virtues. We have more explicit testimony from Quintilian (3.8.61 f.), who says that Theophrastus wished the diction in deliberative oratory to be free of all affectation. In other words, Theophrastus described certain styles as appropriate to certain kinds of oratory (cf. also Quintilian 3.7.1). In so doing he applied the styles of diction as outlined in the *Poetics* to the types of oratory as outlined in the *Rhetoric*, thus combining two distinctions of his master. It would seem most logical for this discussion to have been a part of propriety, but there is no proof that Theophrastus did not allude to the kinds of oratory at more than one place in the work.

Theophrastus further instanced certain authors as examples of certain styles of diction. According to Dionysius of Halicarnassus (*Demosthenes* 3), he gave Thrasymachus as an example of a *mixed* style. Different styles are based on diction in Dionysius' discussion, but are associated with kinds of oratory, and the examples given, Gorgias, Lysias, and Thucydides in chapter two, Plato and Isocrates in chapter three, might well have been those chosen by Theophrastus.[27] We know (Cicero, *Orator* 39) that Theophrastus discussed the style of Thucydides and also of Herodotus. It seems quite possible that Theophrastus illustrated his

[27] Dionysius of Halicarnassus' discussion in *Lysias* 6, as Grube has shown, "Thrasymachus, Theophrastus . . ." *cit.* supra n. 25, 255 ff., is not concerned with composition, but with the subjects of different kinds of oratory. It is thus related to the contents of the twelfth chapter of the third book of the *Rhetoric* (esp. 1414a11 ff.) and was probably discussed by Theophrastus under the topic of the appropriate.

remarks on literary style with the styles of artists in which both Cicero (*De oratore* 3.26) and Quintilian (12.10.3 ff.) follow him.[28]

The references indicate that Theophrastus' theory of the three styles was based on diction and associated with genre. The middle style was essentially a mixed one, that is, something half-way between the grand and the plain. In adapting this system to their own purposes, later rhetoricians did not preserve the pure categories nor did they agree on standardized models of each style. Demosthenes, Isocrates, and Lysias are often instanced, but there is a tendency to see an illustration in any triad of speakers, as when Polybius applied the system to the three philosophers Carneades, Critolaus, and Diogenes (Aulus Gellius 6.14.8 ff.). The work *On style* attributed to Demetrius deals with four styles: plain ($\iota\sigma\chi\nu\acute{o}s$), grand ($\mu\epsilon\gamma\alpha\lambda o\pi\rho\epsilon\pi\acute{\eta}s$), elegant ($\gamma\lambda\alpha\phi\nu\rho\acute{o}s$), and forceful ($\delta\epsilon\iota\nu\acute{o}s$). These are all based on diction and subject, which is roughly similar to genre, but also each has a characteristic composition, and the styles can be mixed, so that a single author may use them all or even use more than one at the same time. Each style has a corresponding faulty version. Clearly such a system is not based directly on Theophrastus but is probably a product of the same kind of desire to describe and categorize varieties of style. The *Ad Herennium* reverts to three styles, grand, middle, and plain (4.11), and though the author speaks of composition, he seems to regard the diction, or the diction and the figures (4.16), as the basic difference. A modern reader of his examples would probably stress the difference in subject matter. We are told to vary and interchange the types of style (16). Cicero's account in *De oratore* is brief and associated with the kinds of oratory; in the *Orator* he gives a fuller account, differentiating the styles on the basis of diction, composition, and subject (20 f.). His discussion of specific orators, which follows,

[28] Cf. Kennedy, *op.cit.* supra n. 25, 99 ff.

is complicated by his desire to refute the extreme Atticists who preferred Lysias to Demosthenes. Dionysius of Halicarnassus' *On composition* (21) distinguishes an austere, intermediate, and smooth style of composition, his essay on Demosthenes notes three styles of diction. As Grube points out Isocrates is an example of the smooth style in composition, of the middle style in diction.[29] Quintilian (12.10.58) conflates these two schemes into the plain (ἰσχνός), the grand and forcible (ἁδρός), and a third which some call middle, others florid (ἀνθηρός). He does not find any set of three categories satisfactory (11.10.66). A set of types found in some late rhetoricians is austere (Thucydides, Antiphon), middle (Demosthenes, Hyperides), plain (Lysias, Isocrates).[30]

It seems safe to say, then, that no one system of stylistic classifications was standardized, probably because rhetoricians found it convenient to apply the terms to writers of various periods and to approach the subject from different points of view, depending on whether they wanted to stress diction, composition, or thought. The categories were also applied to delivery. What the rhetoricians do generally agree about, though there are exceptions even to this, is that there should be three categories and that one should be a mean between the others and that they may be exemplified by certain, but varying, authors.

Theophrastus' second most influential rhetorical work was in the field of delivery.[31] Aristotle (*Rhetoric* 1403b20

[29] G. M. A. Grube, *A Greek critic: Demetrius on style*, Toronto, 1961, 24.

[30] Trypho in Spengel 3.201, cf. Mayer, *op.cit.* supra n. 16, 5 f. In general the names of styles reflect body types, cf. Quadlbauer, *op.cit.* supra n. 25, 65 ff.

[31] On Theophrastus' discussion of delivery cf. F. Striller, "De Stoicorum studiis rhetoricis," *Breslauer philologische Abhandlung* 1 (1886) 35; Armin Krumbacher, *Die Stimmbildung der Redner im Altertum bis auf die Zeit Quintilians*, Paderborn, 1920, 32 ff.; Kroll 1075 f.; Solmsen, *op.cit.* supra n. 4, 45 f.; Caplan, *op.cit.* supra n. 3, 189 ff. with notes; see also Robert P. Sonkowsky, "An aspect of

ff.) had pointed out the need for the study of delivery and said that it was a matter of management of the voice to express the emotions. These he, of course, regarded as an integral part of rhetoric, though the subject of delivery itself he labels vulgar because it was the business of actors. As subdivisions of delivery he suggests the three qualities of volume, pitch, and rhythm. Theophrastus wrote a work in one book entitled Περὶ ὑποκρίσεως (Diogenes Laertius 5.48), which could be translated *On delivery*, and he may have discussed the subject in his handbook or elsewhere.[32] Athanasius,[33] after telling the famous story that Demosthenes said delivery was the first, the second, and the third thing in rhetoric, continues:

"Theophrastus the philosopher says that delivery is the greatest factor an orator has for persuasion, referring delivery to first principles and the passions of the soul and the knowledge of these so that the movement of the body and the tone of the voice may be in accordance with the whole science of delivery."

The passage suggests that Theophrastus related the subject to the psychological perception which Plato demanded of rhetoric and which Aristotle tried to attain in his treatment of proof and of such parts of style as metaphor. Second, it indicates a division of the subject into the topics of voice, which we may guess to have been treated according to Aristotle's three categories, and action or gesture. Cicero (*De oratore* 3.221) quotes a story from Theophrastus about

---

delivery in ancient rhetorical theory," TAPA 90 (1959) 256 ff., who discusses especially the organic relation between delivery and composition involved in associating delivery with the ethical and emotional aspects of a speech.

[32] I. Kayser, "Theophrast und Eustathios περὶ ὑποκρίσεως," *Philologus* 69 (1910) 327 ff. casts some doubt on whether this work was really concerned with rhetoric.

[33] Cf. Hugo Rabe, *Prolegomenon sylloge*, Leipzig, 1931, 177, also Walz 6.35 f.

an actor whose fixed gaze was equivalent to turning his back on the audience. Third, it implies that a high degree of accuracy is attainable in fitting the correct tone and gesture to the word and content.

The treatment of delivery in the extant first-century B.C. writings shows the same general categories. Cicero (*De oratore* 3.213 ff. and *Orator* 55 ff.) divides the subject into voice and gesture and says that each emotion has its own facial expression, sound, and gesture. The *Ad Herennium* has the most systematic version (3.19 ff.). It divides delivery into the figure of the voice and the movement of the body. The former has three subdivisions: *magnitudo, firmitudo, mollitudo.* Despite the terminology these present Aristotle's three categories. *Magnitudo* is volume, *firmitudo* means rhythm (for there are objections to sudden piercing exclamations and approval of long unbroken periods), and *mollitudo* refers to the tone of the voice. Tone is of three types: *sermo* or conversation, *contentio* or debate, *amplificatio* or amplification. There is a resemblance in the descriptions to the doctrine of the three styles, plain, middle, and grand. Gesture is discussed in terms of subdivisions of the three types of tone. The whole subject of delivery received very detailed attention in the late Hellenistic period and, as in other areas of rhetoric, rules took on the force of law. Our fullest account is in Quintilian, who demands four qualities (11.3.30) that are identical to the four virtues of style established by Theophrastus. This does not mean that Theophrastus made the same requirement, but it shows how delivery was stamped with Theophrastus' attitude toward rhetoric.

Demetrius (c. 350-c. 280 B.C.)

A second distinguished early Peripatetic and a pupil of Theophrastus (Diogenes Laertius 5.75) was Demetrius of Phaleron. He was a statesman, orator, man of letters, and teacher at least in the sense of having an entourage of followers (e.g. Dinarchus?) at some periods in his life. Cicero (*Brutus* 37 f.) describes his oratorical style as academic rather than practical, the first clear product of rhetorical education and the new functions of rhetoric:

"He delighted the Athenians rather than inflamed them. He set forth into the sun and dust (of the battlefield) not from a soldier's tent, but from the shady groves of the learned Theophrastus. He first made oratory pliable, soft, and tender, and he preferred by his nature to be charming rather than forceful. . . ."

Although Demetrius published works on rhetoric we know relatively little about them.[34] He criticized the composition of Isocrates and the delivery of Demosthenes,[35] and he divided oratory into deliberative, forensic, and ἐντευκτικός, "that which could address and win the favor of all hearers."[36] This is perhaps the beginning of the movement to extend epideictic to include a greater variety of genres, even some not specifically oratorical.

Demetrius is of special interest because of the existence of the work *On style* (Περὶ ἑρμηνείας), which seems to bear his name. The authorship has long been in doubt with suggestions for date ranging from the third century B.C. to the first century A.D. Grube has recently much clarified the matter: the work is probably not by Demetrius of Phaleron, for the language is not quite what he ought to write and there are references a little too late for Demetrius

[34] For the fragments cf. Fritz Wehrli, *Die Schule des Aristoteles iv: Demetrios von Phaleron*, Basel, 1949, 34 ff. For discussion of the rhetorical fragments, cf. G. M. A. Grube, *op.cit.* supra n. 29, 52 ff.

[35] Cf. Philodemus, *Rhetoric* 4 col.15a-16a, i.p.197f. Sudhaus, fr. 169 in Wehrli, *op.cit.* supra n. 34.

[36] Cf. Philodemus, *Rhetoric* 4, col.41a, i.p.222 Sudhaus, fr. 157 in Wehrli. Demetrius was identified by Karl Fuhr, "Zu griechischen Prosaikern," RhM 57 (1902) 433 f.

if, as has usually been believed, he died in the 280's. Demetrius of Phaleron is quoted by name once (289), but
this cannot be taken as disproof of authorship since classical
Greek writers often refer to themselves in the third person.
On the other hand, the author's familiarity with fourth-
century orators, including Demades, who left no written
works, some of his rhetorical categories, the lack of great
enthusiasm for Demosthenes, who becomes such an idol
of later rhetoricians, and the close similarity to concerns
of Theophrastus seem to point to composition before the
middle of the third century B.C.[37] This makes *On style* the
only surviving critical work in a period of over two hundred
years and thus a source of valuable information about the
relation of rhetorical theory to literary criticism.

For *On style* is a work of criticism rather than a rhetorical
treatise. It deals predominantly with prose although in some
passages the author views all literature (e.g. 37 and 132).
He is clearly as interested in philosophical and historical
writing as in oratory and devotes a famous section to the
style of letter-writing (223-235). At the same time, the
basis of the work is the theory of style taught in the rhetorical schools. It begins with a discussion of periodicity
which might almost be described as a commentary on
Aristotle's account. The body of the treatise consists of a
discussion of four styles, the plain, the grand, the elegant,
and the forceful, each in terms of diction, composition,
and subject and each with its corresponding fault. Subject
is briefly treated. The presence of discussions of diction and
composition, including rhythm and figures, is reminiscent
of what we saw in Theophrastus, who is indeed mentioned
four times (41, 114, 173, 222). It has been suggested[38]
that Demetrius' four styles, which except for the grand
and plain are not incompatible with each other, are really
based on Theophrastus' four virtues, but such a violent

[37] Cf. Grube, *op.cit.* supra n. 29, 39 ff.
[38] Cf. Solmsen, *op.cit.* supra n. 20.

286

stretching of categories seems unnecessary in view of the efforts of critics in the fourth century to describe styles. As a matter of fact, the author says as much (36 f.), objecting to systems of two principal classifications with an intervening "mixed" style. Since this is much what Theophrastus had described we should probably not press too hard the connexion of the author with the Peripatetics.[39] In the third century it was difficult to work in many areas of scholarship without showing Peripatetic influence. The total impression is of a man of letters with a more or less typical rhetorical education who has written a treatise, perceptive but not very elegantly put together, applying his knowledge of rhetoric to the larger world of letters. The rhetorical theory which he knows is one much concerned with kinds of style, with diction and composition, with rhythm, periodicity, and figures.

These last two topics show some interesting developments. Aristotle's account of a period is based largely on antithesis, a feature seen also in the account in the *Rhetorica ad Alexandrum* (1435a4 ff. and 1435b25 ff.). Though the antithetical style was no doubt the beginning of Greek periodicity, and the "rounding" demanded of a period was most clearly seen in an antithesis, a great deal of fourth-century writing made Aristotle's treatment seem bald, while his implication that a period had only two parts was especially difficult if a teacher or critic had to apply it to the compositions of Isocrates. Probably the matter was much discussed and increasing attention given to the cola, or clauses, which constitute the unit of delivery (*On style* 1).[40] One Archedemus, otherwise unknown, had redefined a clause as a simple period or part of a compound period (*On style* 34), not setting any particular limit on the number of clauses. The author of *On style* thinks that four is the proper limit. We should remember, of course, that

[39] Cf. Grube, *op.cit.* supra n. 29, 32 ff.
[40] *Ibid.* 34.

grammar was not yet a fully developed science and that grammatical completeness perhaps did not always mean what it does to us. Certainly our notion of a great complex sentence or period with many independent clauses separated by colons, semicolons, and commas as marks of punctuation is foreign to ancient thought. The first time the thought was an entity the period ended; comprehensible phrases or clauses into which the period could be divided were cola. There is in Aristotle and persists in *On style* (2 and 17) some obscurity about single clause sentences. It is assumed that they can be periods, but the nature of their "rounding" is not explained.

Another novel feature of *On style* is the distinction of three kinds of periods (19 ff.): historical, conversational, and rhetorical. These distinctions are not found elsewhere, but it is possible they are the basis of the three types of composition described by Dionysius of Halicarnassus (*On composition* 21 ff.). The historical period has simplicity and dignity; it is "unmolded." The opening of the *Anabasis* is quoted as an example and likened to a solid and secure halting. Dionysius compares austere composition to unworked blocks of stone in a structure; among prose writers the best example is Thucydides. The principal differences between the two accounts are the fact that Dionysius' austere style is historically early and now regarded as old fashioned and that it has a harshness of sound which the historical period lacks. The smooth or florid style of composition described by Dionysius is that of Isocrates. The example in *On style* is from Demosthenes, but the description of elaborate periodicity in the modern sense is most reminiscent of Isocrates. The conversational period is the loosest and least periodic. Plato furnishes the example of this and is similarly the example to Dionysius of the blended style, though Demosthenes is another and so is Herodotus. The latter name suggests the possibility that this category evolved from a nonperiodic style. Dionysius'

blended style is regarded as a mean. In *On style* the mean
is apparently the historical period, but it does not make
a very good one since its distinctive feature is the relationship of its parts: they are more clearly separated than in
any other style. This points very tentatively to the conclusion that Dionysius may have revised the theory of three
periods into a somewhat more logical structure of three
styles of composition based on more extensive criteria. At
the beginning of his work he criticizes earlier writers on composition on the ground that they have treated the subject
inadequately.

In the surviving fourth-century handbooks the treatment
of figures of speech is not very extensive. The word σχῆμα
is common enough generally of any kind of form or con-
figuration. Isocrates describes his *Antidosis* (8) as in the
figure of an apology, and Aristotle (*Rhetoric* 1401a7 and
1408b21) uses the word of style in a general sense.[41] Without calling them figures or tropes or anything else, he discusses similes, proverbs, and hyperbole (1412a34 ff.) as
subdivisions of metaphor, and what were later called
Gorgianic figures he touches upon in discussing the period
(1410a24 ff.). Anaximenes uses the word similarly (1436a2,
where the context is concerned with the figure *parisôsis*)
and also (1439a35) in what is apparently the technical
sense of "figure of speech" referring to such things as anticipation, demands, recapitulation, and irony, which were discussed in earlier chapters (cf. also 1444b34).[42] The earliest
known definition of a figure was made about the same
time by Zoilus—"to pretend one thing and say another."[43]

[41] Cf. H. Schrader, "Σχῆμα und τρόπος in den Homerscholien,"
Hermes 39 (1904) 585, and Karl Barwick, "Probleme der stoischen
Sprachlehre und Rhetorik," *Abhandlungen der sächsischen Akademie der Wissenschaften zu Leipzig* 49.3 (1957) 101.
[42] Cf. Willy Barczat, *De figurarum disciplina atque auctoribus,*
Göttingen, 1904, 17, and Barwick, *loc.cit.* supra n. 41.
[43] Cf. Phoebammon, *On figures* in Walz 8.493, and Quintilian
9.1.14. Cf. also Barczat, *op.cit.* supra n. 42, 21; Mayer, *op.cit.* supra

This looks like Anaximenes' "irony" (1434a17). Theophrastus included figures as one of the parts of ornamentation. The author of *On style* is familiar with a couple of dozen figures with the technical names which they often retained for centuries: *aposiôpêsis, prosôpopoiia, anadiplôsis, klimax* are all good examples. It is difficult to compose a complete list because names sometimes vary slightly from section to section. Is there any difference between *epanaphora* (61) and *anaphora* (141)? The most orderly discussion is in connexion with the forceful style (263 ff.), where appear first figures of thought (263-266), then figures of speech (267-271). The reader is presumed to understand the difference between them, so the distinction cannot be new. A figure of speech is described (59) simply as a form of composition. After the discussion of figures in the forceful style there follows a discussion of diction, which includes the simile (273), also treated as something other than a figure in 146. Indeed, from the point of view of a later rhetorician there is much confusion, in part because the author is not drawing up a list of figures for a handbook, but describing the origins of stylistic effects. He is apparently unfamiliar with the nature or name of a trope, though he does treat metaphors as something apart from figures of thought or diction.

The Stoics

The Peripatetics contributed more to rhetoric than did any of the other philosophical schools. The Stoics were probably second,[44] though they are viewed by less austere

---

n. 16, 212 ff.; Kroll 1109; Radermacher B.xxxv.2-3; W. Buechner, "Ueber den Begriff der *Eironeia*," *Hermes* 76 (1941) 339 ff.

[44] Cf. in general Striller, *op.cit.* supra n. 31; Arnim, 77 ff. and *Stoicorum veterum fragmenta*, 3 vols., Leipzig, 1903-1905; E. Vernon Arnold, *Roman Stoicism*, Cambridge, Eng., 1911, 144 ff.; R. H. Tukey, "The Stoic use of λέξις and φράσις," CP 6 (1911) 444 ff.; Kroll 1081. As Kroll says, there has been a tendency to ascribe

students of the art with some contempt. In his conversation with Cato in *De finibus* Cicero praises the rhetorical exercises of the Peripatetics and Academics, including their use of *theses* and *hypotheses*. Zeno the Stoic left this area untouched. Cicero continues (4.7):

"Cleanthes and Chrysippus too wrote an *Art of rhetoric*, but of such a sort that it is the one book to read if anyone should wish to keep quiet.[45] You see how they speak, coining new words, abandoning those in use. But, you will say, they undertake great themes, for example that this whole universe is our home town (a *thesis*). . . . Therefore the Stoic orator inflames his audience. What? He inflame it? Rather he would quickly extinguish it if he found it burning. As for those epigrams of yours, spoken so neatly and roundly, that the wise man is king, dictator, tycoon, those you have learned from rhetoricians. How bald are the Stoics' own maxims on the force of virtue! Although they believe it to be so great that it is by itself able to make a man happy. They point the argument with their puny little syllogisms, like thorns. People may assent, but they are not convinced in their hearts and go away much as they came. What the Stoics have to say may be true, it is certainly important, but they treat the subject much more off-hand than they should."

Quintilian (10.1.84) describes Stoic oratory thus:

"The old Stoics indulged eloquence rather little. But they pleaded honorable causes and had great success in composing and proving whatever they had undertaken. They were shrewd in handling the subject and did not at all affect to be flowery in speech."

---

much to the Stoics without proof. The treatise on rhetoric by Fortunatianus, though it may have some Stoic concepts in it, is not an example of Stoic rhetoric, cf. Münscher in R-E 7 col.44 ff.

[45] Cicero may have in mind the fact that the Stoics sometimes enjoined silence, cf. *Academics* 2.93.

In fact, Stoic oratory, like Stoic ethics, belonged in an ideal world; their treatment[46] is reminiscent of Socrates' attitude to his oratorical task as expressed in the *Apology*. The best Stoic example of its application was the speech of Rutilius Rufus in his own defense on a charge of extortion. He refused to become a suppliant to his judges or to plead more elaborately than the simple truth demanded (Cicero, *De oratore* 1.229 and *Brutus* 114 ff.). Though patently innocent, he was convicted and went to live in honor among those he was alleged to have fleeced. Quintilian gives a glimpse of the Stoic theory, though he does not mention the Stoics, when he says (5.pr.1) that some have thought the sole duty of the orator (*oratoris officium*) is to teach, and they have excluded all appeals to the emotions on the grounds that perturbation of mind is a fault, that the judge ought not to be distracted from the truth, and that it is unworthy of a man to seek to charm his audience in pursuit of a rhetorical victory. We know that Chrysippus' handbook limited the function of an epilogue to recapitulation (Anonymous in Spengel-Hammer 389). The concept of a single function was accepted by Hermagoras (Sextus Empiricus, *Against the professors* 2.62) and is found in the *Ad Herennium* (1.2). Cicero (*Brutus* 185 and *Orator* 69, cf. Quintilian 3.5.2) revived a set of three functions—to teach, to charm, and to move—which are basically the three forms of proof accepted by Aristotle—logical, ethical, and pathetical. In justifying the latter of the three Cicero introduced the notion that the orator must sincerely feel the emotions he is trying to awaken in his listeners (*De oratore* 2.189 ff.). The Stoic concept made unnecessary any distinction between a good statesman

---

[46] Could it be called the plain style? Perhaps, though the Stoics did not recognize a variety of styles. Although the main thesis is wrong, there is much that is useful in Hendrickson's "Origin and meaning. . . ." *cit.* supra n. 25.

and philosopher on the one hand and a good orator on the other, for to the Stoics the thought of the speech *was* the speech and would produce its own natural and good expression. *Rem tene, verba sequentur,* "hold to the subject, the words will follow," was Cato's expression of it (Julius Victor in Halm 374). The wise man or Stoic sage, who was regarded as the one true king, could also be called the one true orator, and oratory was a "virtue" of the good man (Cicero, *De oratore* 1.83 and 3.65).[47]

From what has been said it should be expected that Stoic rhetoric would be closely interwoven with Stoic dialectic.[48] Zeno compared dialectic to a closed fist, rhetoric to an open hand (Cicero, *De finibus* 2.7, *Orator* 113, and Sextus Empiricus, *Against the professors* 2.7). The materials are the same, and rhetoric allows no more adornment, but it is expansive and thus the tension and attitude of the two are different. Rhetoric was useful and good as long as it was controlled by a responsible, moral orator. Whether or not they originated the phrase, most Stoics would have agreed with Cato's definition of an orator as *vir bonus dicendi peritus,* "a good man skilled in speaking" (Seneca, *Controversiae* 1.pr.9 and Quintilian 12.1.1).[49]

The outlines of the rhetorical system taught by the Stoics were substantially the same as the system of Theophrastus and others. This is clear from the little account of Stoic rhetoric given by Diogenes Laertius (7.42 f.):

[47] Cf. Diogenes of Babylon, fr. 117 von Arnim (supra n. 44) from Philodemus, *Hypomnematicon* col. viii, i. p. 211 Sudhaus and Plutarch, *On the contradictions of the Stoics* 5.1034b.

[48] Cf. Hermann Throm, *Die Thesis,* Paderborn, 1932, 11 ff. and 183 ff.

[49] On its possible Stoic origin cf. L. Radermacher, "Eine Schrift über den Redner als Quelle Ciceros und Quintilians," RhM 54 (1899) 283 ff.; Fritz Schöll, "Vir bonus dicendi peritus," RhM 57 (1902) 312 ff.; J. Morr, "Posidonios von Rhodos über Dichtung und Redekunst," WS 45 (1926) 47 ff.

"They regard rhetoric as the science ($\epsilon\pi\iota\sigma\tau\dot{\eta}\mu\eta$)[50] of speaking well in exposition and dialectic as the science of discussing correctly in question and answer, whence they (e.g. Posidonius, cf. 7.62) also define dialectic as the science of what is true, what is false, and what is neither. Rhetoric itself they say to be threefold: one part is deliberative, one judicial, one concerned with encomia. Its divisions are invention, expression ($\phi\rho\dot{\alpha}\sigma\iota\varsigma$), arrangement, and delivery (cf. Plutarch, *On the contradictions of the Stoics* 28.1047a-b). A formal speech is divided into prooemium, narration, the part against the opponents,[51] and epilogue."

Diogenes' summary of Stoicism continues with a division of dialectic into two parts, one concerned with the subjects of argument and the other with language and grammar. The latter contains a number of features which are also found in the discussion of style in later rhetorical handbooks. Thus (7.59):

"The virtues of speech are five: hellenism, clarity, brevity, propriety, *kataskeuê*. Hellenism is expression without mistake in grammar and with no careless usage. Clarity is style expounding the thought intelligibly. Brevity is style employing only what is strictly necessary for making the matter clear. Propriety is style suitable to the subject. *Kataskeuê* is style avoiding vulgarity. Of the faults of style barbarism is style contrary to the usage of well-bred Greeks and

---

[50] It is part of the one great science of philosophy, incapable of inconsistency with any other part, and thus scientifically true, cf. Arnold, *op.cit.* supra n. 44, 140 f. An origin of the definition might be sought in Plato's *Phaedrus* 259e4 f., taken up by Xenocrates (Sextus Empiricus, *Against the professors* 2.6), cf. R. E. Witt, *Albinus and the history of middle Platonism*, Cambridge, Eng., 1937, 15. Quintilian, who himself adopts the definition *bene dicendi scientia* (2.15.38), attributes (2.15.34) *scientia recte dicendi* to Chrysippus and Cleanthes.

[51] The term is an old one, cf. supra chapter three, n. 36.

solecism is a statement in which the grammatical categories are not in proper agreement."

Here we appear to have an expansion of Theophrastus (Quintilian 3.1.15). Brevity had been to earlier authors a desirable quality of the narration, though Aristotle did not believe it necessary (1416b30).[52] The Stoics' requirement is part of their desire for an extremely straightforward style. In the same way they have adapted Theophrastus' fourth virtue, ornamentation, into a more austere quality. According to Plutarch (*On the contradictions of the Stoics* 28.1047a-b) Chrysippus, in the first book of his work on rhetoric, required a "liberal and simple adornment of the words," while rejecting such niceties of style as avoidance of hiatus; but for a Stoic Chrysippus was somewhat liberal about rhetorical treatment (Fronto, *De eloquentia* 1.15 f.).

The Stoics were especially interested in the virtue known as hellenism, or purity.[53] Aristotle, Theophrastus, and Demetrius had all dealt with faults of style to some extent, but the clear differentiation of a fault in the choice of word, or barbarism, from a fault in the grammatical use of a word, solecism, has not previously been made. Hereafter it is a commonplace (e.g. *Rhetorica ad Herennium* 4.17). The Stoics believed that everything should be called by its proper name (Cicero, *Ad familiares* 9.22.1) and carried this to the extreme of denying that any word was obscene. The wise man should call a spade a spade; anything else might be regarded as a form of ornamentation or dishonesty or hypocrisy.

The development of a science of grammar came just at the time when the separate Greek dialects were giving way

---

[52] Brevity continues to be a virtue of the narration, cf. e.g. *Rhetorica ad Herennium* 1.14, but occasionally crops up in other lists, cf. Cicero, *Partitiones oratoriae* 19, and Dionysius of Halicarnassus, *To Pompeius* 3.775.

[53] Cf. Charles N. Smiley, "*Latinitas* and ἑλληνισμός," *Bulletin of the University of Wisconsin* 3 (1906) 211 ff.

to a single common language (κοινή). Such a process may well have accentuated the problem of defining the proper form of words. Chrysippus, the third of the early Stoics after Zeno and Cleanthes, wrote four books on *anomaly* (Diogenes Laertius 7.192), the doctrine that usage, not consistency, should determine inflexional systems. In this he was followed by Crates, the famous Stoic head of the school of grammarians grouped around the library at Pergamum (Varro, *De lingua Latina* 9.1).[54] Grammarians like Aristarchus at the other great Hellenistic library, at Alexandria, which had Peripatetic connexions, took the opposite view and supported the doctrine of *analogy*,[55] that insofar as possible consistency ought to be imposed upon grammatical categories (Varro, *ibid.*). Crates lectured in Rome "about the time that Ennius died" (169 B.C.) (Suetonius, *De grammaticis* 2), and subsequently other Stoics visited the capital, including Diogenes of Babylon in 155 (Plutarch, *Cato the elder* 22) and Panaetius, who became a member of the Scipionic circle. It was thus, no doubt, that a concern for proper diction as well as an interest in grammar grew up in Rome; it probably produced the purity of language for which Terence is so famous.[56] The corresponding fault of solecism was discussed and a hundred examples enumerated by Lucilius.[57] Work of grammarians must always be envisioned as going on behind rhetorical theory, though it only rarely is expressly discussed: glimpses of the

[54] Cf. John Edwin Sandys, *A history of classical scholarship* 1, Cambridge, Eng., 1921, 46 ff., esp. 156 ff.

[55] Cf. Detler Fehling, "Varro und die grammatische Lehre von der Analogie und der Flexion," *Glotta* 35 (1956) 214 ff. and 36 (1957) 48 ff.

[56] Cf. Hendrickson, *op.cit.* supra n. 16, 101, and G. C. Fiske, "The plain style in the Scipionic circle," *University of Wisconsin studies in language and literature* 3 (1919) 62 ff.

[57] Line 1100 Marx, from Pompeius, *Grammatici Latini* 5.289 Keil. Cf. R. Reitzenstein, "Scipio Aemilianus und die stoische Rhetorik," *Strassburger Festschrift zur xlvi Versammlung deutscher Philologen und Schulmänner*, Strassburg, 1901, 143 ff.

anomaly-analogy controversy can be caught in Cicero's *De oratore*,[58] and the Atticism controversy of the first century is based on proper diction as well as on proper models for imitation. Quintilian's *Institutes* contain an extensive treatment of grammar,[59] but that is a work on education as well as rhetoric and covers the whole span from cradle to retirement.

Stoic grammatical studies also produced the theory of tropes, which is first expressly mentioned in a rhetorical treatise by Cicero (*Brutus* 69). A trope is a single word used in a novel way either because the idea to be expressed has no name of its own (no "proper" word) or for the sake of embellishment. The difference between a trope and a figure is parallel to the difference between barbarism and solecism: a figure, like a solecism, involves at least two words; a trope, like a barbarism, consists of only a single word: a metaphor is a trope, a simile is a figure. Cicero (*Orator* 93) speaks of metonymy (a trope) as a term borrowed from the grammarians, and it seems probable that they developed the concept first. Grammatical treatises display a basic set of eight tropes: *onomatopoiia, katachrêsis, metaphora, metalêpsis, synekdochê, metonymia, antonomasia,* and *antiphrasis,* a list which is somewhat enlarged by rhetoricians (e.g. Quintilian 8.6).[60] The earliest known study of tropes by a grammarian was the work of Crates' pupil Tàuriscus (Sextus Empiricus, *Against the professors* 1.249).[61] Subsequently Dionysius Thrax of the rival Alexandrian school included exegesis of poetical tropes as a

[58] Cf. Hendrickson, *op.cit.* supra n. 16, 113.

[59] Cf. F. H. Colson, "The grammatical chapters in Quintilian," cq 8 (1914) 33 ff., and his commentary to book one, Cambridge, Eng., 1924, and Kurt von Fritz, "Ancient instruction in grammar according to Quintilian," AJP 70 (1949) 337 ff.

[60] Cf. Barwick, *op.cit.* supra n. 41, 90.

[61] Presuming with Striller, *op.cit.* supra n. 44, 10, and Barwick, *op.cit.* supra n. 41, 110, that the work *On tropes* by Cleanthes (Diogenes Laertius 7.76) was devoted to dialectic.

part of grammar. The origin of tropes can be further traced to Stoic theories about the origin of words. They distinguished three bases: similarity of sound or meaning, vicinity (the part for the whole or cause for effect, for example), and contrariety or formation of a word from its opposite.[62] Similarity of sound is onomatopoiia (e.g. "cackle"). Strictly speaking this differs from other tropes in being the coinage of a new word rather than the transference of some other word to a new meaning. The passage from Cicero's *De finibus* quoted above shows that the Stoics approved of word coinage. *Katachrêsis*, metaphor, and *metalêpsis* are all tropes arising from similarity of meaning: metaphor is a wide term for any word transferred from one meaning to another; *katachrêsis* is used when the object or act has no proper word of own ("manufacture" when applied to the product of a machine rather than the hand); *metalêpsis* is used when a partial synonym is substituted ("chant" for "say"). *Synekdochê, metonymia*, and *antonomasia* are all based on vicinity: *synekdochê* is use of the whole for a part or a part for the whole ("poop"); *metonymia* is a wider term, where a word associated with an object in almost any way is used for the object ("Venus" for love); *antonomasia* is the use of an epithet for the proper name ("Tydides," or "son of Tydeus," for Diomedes). *Antiphrasis* is based on contrariety and is often a litotes ("not unmoved"). The Stoics, with their dislike of ornamentation, thought of tropes as ways of expressing concepts which had no proper names. The rhetoricians thought of them as categories of ornamentation to be used for emphasis, variety, or other effects. Many did not clearly distinguish tropes from figures (Quintilian 9.1.1 f.). The author of the *Ad Herennium*, for example, appends tropes to his list of figures as additional

[62] Cf. Barwick, *op.cit.* supra n. 41, 80 ff. Cf. also the logical categories in Diogenes Laertius 7.52 discussed by R. Reitzenstein, *M. Terentius Varro und Johannes Mauropus von Eucharta*, Leipzig, 1901, 77 ff.

exornationes in a class by themselves (4.42 ff.). The Peripatetics may have developed a parallel concept, avoiding the term trope but distinguishing different kinds of metaphor on the basis of Aristotle's account (*Poetics* 1457b7 ff. and *Rhetoric* 1411a1 ff.).[63]

Stoic grammar probably contributed to the theory of figures, though the ground for that had already been laid. Fronto (*De eloquentia* 1.15 f.) quotes a list of figures of thought from Chrysippus. Quintilian (9.3.2) distinguishes figures of diction into two categories, grammatical and rhetorical, the latter in turn subdivided into figures of addition (28-57) and figures of omission (58-65). Subsequently he adds a third heading (66-86) of figures involving a play upon words. His account is based in general upon that of the Augustan rhetorician Caecilius, who wrote the most influential work on figures[64] and seems to have employed divisions into addition, omission, alteration, and interpellation, which are identical to the sources of barbarism as outlined by grammarians under Stoic influence.[65]

[63] Cf. Barwick, *op.cit.* supra n. 41, 95 ff.
[64] *Ibid.* 105 and H. Gomoll, "Caecilius' Stellung zu den σχήματα διανοίας," RhM 82 (1933) 59 ff. For Caecilius' fragments cf. Ernestus Ofenloch, *Caecili Calactini fragmenta*, Leipzig, 1907.
[65] Cf. Barwick, *op.cit.* supra n. 41, 98 f. and 103 ff. The bibliography on ancient grammar, Stoic and other, is extensive. Among the studies which would be useful to one wishing to work in this area would be: E. Jullien, *Les professeurs de littérature dans l'ancienne Rome*, Paris, 1885; H. Nettleship, "The study of Latin grammar among the Romans," JP 15 (1886) 189 ff.; C. Steinthal, *Geschichte der Sprachwissenschaft*, Berlin, 1890; Reitzenstein, *op.cit.* supra n. 57 and 62; Schrader, *op.cit.* supra n. 41; Gudeman in R-E 7, col. 1780 ff. s.v. "Grammatik"; Karl Barwick, "Remmius Palaemon und die römische Ars grammatica," *Philologus Supplementband* 15.2 (1922); J. H. Dahlmann, "Varro und die hellenistische Sprachtheories," *Problemata* 5 (1932); J. Collart, "Palémon et l'Ars grammatica," *Revue de philologie* 12 (1938) 228 ff.; J. H. Dahlmann, "Varro: De lingua Latina Buch viii," *Hermes Einzelschriften* 7 (1940); Fehling, *op.cit.* supra n. 55; Barwick, *op.cit.* supra n. 41; Albrecht Dihle, "Analogie und Attizismus," *Hermes* 85 (1957) 170 ff.; Hermann Koller, "Die Anfänge der griechische Grammatik," *Glotta* 37 (1958) 5 ff.

Other Philosophical Schools

The Academics did not play an important part in the history of rhetoric during the early Hellenistic period. Heraclides Ponticus, not a thorough-going Academic, wrote a work on rhetoric (Diogenes Laertius 5.88); however, his work on poetics was more important.[66] Arcesilaus introduced declamation on either side of an issue about the middle of the third century (Cicero, *De oratore* 3.80). Carneades, Philo, and Antiochus can be more conveniently dealt with below.

The Epicureans were consistently hostile to most rhetorical studies (Dionysius of Halicarnassus, *On composition* 24, Quintilian 2.17.15 and 12.2.24).[67] We have one[68] Epicurean rhetorical treatise, that of Philodemus, written sometime about the middle of the first century B.C. and preserved, albeit badly, on papyri found at Herculaneum.[69] According to Philodemus (1. col.vii, i.pp.11 f. Sudhaus) Epicurus and his orthodox followers accepted an art of sophistic rhetoric, though this statement may involve some exaggera-

[66] Cf. Radermacher B.xxvii and Barwick 57 ff. For a discussion of the work in poetics, cf. Jensen, "Heracleides von Pontos . . ." *cit.* supra n. 25, 292 ff.

[67] Cf. Arnim 73 ff. and Phillip H. De Lacy, "The Epicurean analysis of language," AJP 60 (1939) 85 ff. esp. 89 ff.

[68] There may be some influence of Epicurean thought on other treatises e.g. *Rhetorica ad Herennium*, cf. Caplan, *op.cit.* supra n. 3, index, s.v. "Epicurean doctrine."

[69] The Greek text is available in the Teubner vol. of Siegfried Sudhaus, *Philodemi volumina rhetorica*, 2 vols. Leipzig 1892-1894, with a *Supplementum* containing a revision of part, Leipzig, 1895. Sudhaus' arrangement is not altogether satisfactory. There is a very useful English paraphrase of the work by Harry M. Hubbell, "The *Rhetorica* of Philodemus," *Transactions of the Connecticut academy of arts and sciences* 23 (1920) 246 ff. Philodemus also wrote on poetics, cf. Jensen, *Philodemus . . .*, *cit.* supra n. 25, and Nathan A. Greenberg, "The use of *poiema* and *poiesis*," HSCP 45 (1961) 263 ff.; and on euphony, cf. Francesco Sbordone, "Filodemo e la teoria dell' eufonia," *Rendiconti dell' accademia di archeologia, lettere, e belle arti di Napoli* 30 (1956) 25 ff.

tion and certainly was not believed by all Epicureans.[70] Statements of Epicurus from which it might be deduced are quoted by Philodemus in the *Rhetoric* (2.col.44, i.p.78 Sudhaus) as well as in the shorter and earlier statement of his thesis, the *Hypomnematicon* (col.3a,ii.p.256 Sudhaus). Epicurus apparently did write a work *On rhetoric* (2.col.10, i.p.32) and, according to Philodemus (2.col.24,i.p.50), showed that sophistic is an art of composing speeches and making epideictic orations but that there is no art of judicial or deliberative oratory. Epideictic alone is based on knowledge of rules; judicial and deliberative are solely the result of practice (2.col.13,i.p.107). Philodemus defines sophistic (2.col.22, i.p.122) as an art concerned with *epideixis* and the arrangement of speeches. His examples indicate that by *epideixis* he means the kind of oratory practiced by Isocrates,[71] including the *Panegyricus*, the *Panathenaicus*, the *Busiris*, the *Helen*, and the *Peace* (2.col.27,i.p.127), all of which he thinks of as purely rhetorical documents lacking practical political significance (2.col.32,i.p.137). After this discussion in book two, Philodemus ignores sophistic oratory and attacks the claims of the rhetoricians that their subject is an art and capable of training a statesman. Since most of his arguments are taken from earlier writers the treatise is important for reconstruction of the dispute between rhetoric and philosophy which broke out in the second century, a subject to be discussed presently.

Asianism

Although their contributions were great, the philosophers usually regarded rhetoric as of incidental interest, a subdivision of the more important study of logic. There were professional teachers of rhetoric, but apparently only at the secondary school level, for the notion of rhetoric as an alter-

[70] Cf. Arnim 74 ff. and Hubbell, *op.cit.* supra n. 69, 279.
[71] Cf. Harry M. Hubbell, "Isocrates and the Epicureans," CP 11 (1916) 404 ff.

native to philosophy in higher education disappears at the death of Isocrates and does not reappear until the second century B.C. According to the critics of the first century B.C. the most important development in early Hellenistic rhetoric was what they labeled Asianism.[72] It would be a mistake, however, to think that Asianism was a conscious movement or that the Asianists constituted a school or had some kind of theory peculiar to themselves. In the third century, Greek prose style continued to develop naturally with marked changes in diction and rhythm from those of the fourth century. The nature of rhetorical education, the conditions of actual oratory, and the development of the Greek language into a world tongue tended to produce a bizarre product with distinct loss of any standard of pure diction. No doubt this was especially true outside of Greece proper. According to Cicero (*Brutus* 51), after the decline of oratory in Athens there followed a period when oratory was still in flower in the cities of Asia Minor, though the style was much affected by foreign ways of thought and speech. Another center was the island of Rhodes, whose style retained more similarity to fourth-century oratory. In the *Orator* (25) Cicero speaks of the cities in Caria, Phrygia, and Mysia as the scene of a popular oratory which adopted a "fat and greasy" style of diction. Elsewhere (*Brutus* 325) he distinguishes two kinds of Asianism, at least as seen among his contemporaries: one, which sounds very much like the Silver Latin style of Seneca, is described as sententious and pointed; the other is swift and impetuous with ornate words. Hegesias of Magnesia was the best known of Asian orators in the third century, which is probably much the same as saying that he was the best known orator of the period. He regarded his style as perfectly Attic

[72] For the history and nature of Asianism cf. Norden 126 ff. and U. von Wilamowitz-Moellendorf, "Asianismus und Attizismus," *Hermes* 35 (1900) 1 ff. On the period in general cf. Blass, *op.cit.* supra n. 1.

302

(Cicero, *Brutus* 286). Second-century examples of Asianism, and also the best known orators of their day, were the brothers Hierocles and Menecles of Alabanda in Caria (Cicero, *Brutus* 325 f. and *Orator* 231). In the mid-first century B.C. there was a reaction against stylistic excesses which labeled itself Atticism, since it chose its models from the Attic orators of the classical period. Atticists, as part of their polemic against the literary fashion of the Hellenistic age, fixed upon "Asianists" as an especially suitable term for those they criticized since some, though by no means all, of the oratory to which they objected had flourished in Asia and because the term made such a good antithesis with Attic. Asianism is thus descriptive of a style of oratory in much the way that nineteenth-century Southern oratory might be if used by a twentieth-century northern professor of speech.

Hermagoras

The first distinguished professional teacher of rhetoric after Isocrates was Hermagoras of Temnos, who lived about the middle of the second century B.C.[73] Presumably, that is, he was a teacher of rhetoric somewhere. At least he developed a complicated system and expounded it in a handbook. His work is lost, but his system can be reconstructed

[73] The two basic works have been Georg Thiele, *Hermagoras: ein Beitrag zur Geschichte der Rhetorik*, Strassburg, 1893, and W. Jaeneke, *De statuum doctrina ab Hermogene tradita*, Leipzig, 1904, but both have now been largely superseded by the thorough study with extensive documentation and bibliography of Dieter Matthes, "Hermagoras von Temnos 1904-1955," *Lustrum* 3 (1958) 58-214. The subject has been worked upon mostly by the Germans, but the English reader may consult O. A. L. Dieter, "Stasis," SM 17 (1940) 345 ff., concerned primarily with the definition of the term *stasis*, which the author connects with Aristotle's physics, and Ray Nadeau, "Classical systems of *stases* in Greek: Hermagoras to Hermogenes," *Greek, Roman, and Byzantine studies* 2 (1959) 53 ff., unfortunately written before the appearance of Matthes. Hermagoras' dates cannot be fixed with any exactitude.

in some detail from a few specific quotations in later authors and from the wide influence which these quotations show the work to have had on subsequent Greek and Latin rhetorical treatises.[74] Cicero's *De inventione* and Quintilian provide the most information. Some influence of Stoic logic can be found in his work,[75] and he knew the teachings of Aristotle and Theophrastus, but by and large he cannot be associated with any philosophical school.

The structure of Hermagoras' book was a modification of the system which was common since Aristotle, the parts of rhetoric. The discussion of invention was the most important section of the work and came first; arrangement and style were grouped together under the second heading, *oikonomia*, which was subdivided into judgment, division, order, and style (Quintilian 3.3.9); memory and delivery perhaps followed.[76] The task of the orator was "to treat the proposed political question as persuasively as possible" (Sextus Empiricus, *Against the professors* 2.62, cf. Cicero, *De inventione* 1.6). As among the Stoics, to charm and to move were not regarded as functions, and the ethical and pathetical proofs discussed by Aristotle were largely neglected.[77] By "political question" Hermagoras seems to have meant anything which involved the citizen. It would thus embrace all the traditional kinds of oratory and oratorical exercises, including whatever ethical or political matters

[74] Cf. Matthes, *op.cit.* supra n. 73, 81 ff., and Karl Barwick, "Augustins Schrift *De rhetorica* und Hermagoras von Temnos," *Philologus* 105 (1961) 97 ff.

[75] Cf. Kroll, 1090 and Matthes, *op.cit.* supra n. 73, 121 ff. and esp. 135 f. Striller, *op.cit.* supra n. 44, made constant, but excessive use of Hermagoras in reconstructing Stoic rhetoric.

[76] Cf. Matthes, *op.cit.* supra n. 73, 107 ff.

[77] Cf. Solmsen, *op.cit.* supra n. 4, 178. But Hermagoras should not be assumed to have rejected all emotionalism, as the Stoics did. It should be evident from the discussion of the third *stasis* and of the digression and the conclusion of a speech that Hermagoras expected the orator to pull out all the stops in attacking his opponent and arousing the audience.

might be involved in such speeches, but it would not include discussion of metaphysics or abstract philosophical subjects not somehow related to political life.

Political questions were divided by Hermagoras into two classes, unlimited and limited, or *theses* and *hypotheses*.[78] A *thesis* is a controversy that does not involve definite individuals: Quintilian (3.5.8) gives as examples "Should one marry?" "Should one participate in public life?" The discussion of *theses* is one of a number of indications that Hermagoras was writing a book for students rather than for prospective litigants. Cicero's teacher (*De inventione* 1.8) may have misrepresented Hermagoras by including such nonpolitical *theses* as "What is the shape of the world?" and "What is the magnitude of the sun?"[79] although other rhetoricians may have extended the scope of rhetoric in this way. The philosophical schools had used *theses* as exercises for some time, but Hermagoras may have been the first to assign them to students of rhetoric (Plutarch, *Pompey* 42). *Hypotheses* were specific controversies involving named persons and definite occasions: "Should Cato marry?" More often they took the form of judicial questions, "Did Orestes murder his mother?" Seven specific attributes (μόρια περιστάσεως, Augustine, *De rhetorica* in Halm 141) were named: actor, action, time, place, cause, manner, starting point.[80] *Hypotheses* as a whole were subdivided into questions of fact or justice (λογικὰ ζητήματα, *quaestiones rationales*) and questions of law (νομικὰ ζητήματα, *quaestiones legales*) (Quintilian 3.5.4). Sophistic specimen speeches like Gorgias' *Helen* and *Palamedes* were actually *hypotheses*, even though that term was not yet

---

[78] Cf. Matthes, *op.cit.* supra n. 73, 121 ff. On their subsequent history cf. M. L. Clarke, "The *thesis* in the Roman rhetorical schools of the republic," CQ 1 (1951) 159 ff.

[79] Cf. Matthes, *op.cit.* supra n. 73, 131 ff., but cf. also Arnim 94 ff.

[80] Cf. Matthes, *op.cit.* supra n. 73, 125 ff. Striller, *op.cit.* supra n. 44, 27 ff. regarded *peristasis* as especially a Stoic concept.

used of them. It was not until the late fourth century that original composition of *hypotheses* became a regular exercise for young students of rhetoric (Quintilian 2.4.41 f.). Subsequently they were the most popular exercise and helped to retain the judicial emphasis of rhetorical theory.

In any litigation there are several possible points which could be the significant point at issue between the disputants and the real basis of the court's decision. Thus, when charged with theft a defendant may deny the fact of having taken the property, or he may admit the act but deny the definition of that act as stealing (perhaps the property was his own), or he may admit the fact of theft but allege some justification (he stole a dagger from the hands of a mad man), or finally, he may deny the right of the opponent to prosecute him or the competence of the court (perhaps, as Aeschines alleged of Timarchus, the prosecutor has lost his civil rights). Generally speaking each defense is stronger than the one which follows. All can be found in the Attic orators, and their possibilities were hardly unappreciated by logographers. Aristotle (*Rhetoric* 1417b21 ff.) says that there are four possible disputed points: the fact, the injury, the importance, the justice. Elsewhere (*Rhetoric* 1374a1 ff.) he distinguishes between questions of fact and questions of legal definition. The discussion in the *Rhetorica ad Alexandrum* (1442b33 ff.) is similar, though somewhat more detailed, and introduces the matter of how to treat the laws bearing on a crime (1443a11 ff.): the defendant may try to override the law as unjust, or unbinding, or ambiguous, while the prosecutor will insist upon the letter of the law and demand that only the act of the transgressor be discussed. According to Quintilian (3.6.3) the Greeks called the crucial point at issue the *stasis*. . . .

"a name which they say was not first employed by Hermagoras, but according to some by Naucrates, the pupil of Isocrates, according to others by Zopyrus of Clazomene, although Aeschines seems to use this term in his speech *Against Ctesiphon* (206) when he demands of the jurors that they not permit Demosthenes to wander from the subject, but force him to speak about the real *stasis* of the case."

In Aeschines the word is not used technically, but in a metaphor comparing the treatment of the case by the orator to the *stance* of a boxer. However, it certainly was in technical use before Hermagoras, and other authors of his time discussed the subject, for example Archedemus (Quintilian 3.6.31), who accepted only fact and definition.[81] In addition to these precedents for the discussion of the basis of litigation and for use of the word *stasis,* Quintilian (3.6.23 ff.) saw in the concept of *stasis* the influence of Aristotle's categories as discussed in the work of that name: substance, quantity, relation, and quality. These, he says, constitute *staseis,* other categories constitute topics for argument.

Hermagoras was probably familiar with logic and dialectic as taught by more than one philosophical school and drew up his own categories on what seemed to him to be the most satisfactory grounds without consciously adapting any particular precedent. No earlier writer seems to have included as a separate *stasis* the question of the right of the opponent to speak or of the court to decide (Cicero, *De inventione* 1.16), though as *paragraphê* it was a familiar feature of Greek law. The teacher of the author of *Ad Herennium* objected (1.18) to this fourth category and made it part of the legal *stasis, legitima constitutio,* which is his term for the *stasis* of definition.

The names of the four *staseis* as used by Hermagoras appear to have been:

1. στοχασμός (Augustine, *De rhetorica* in Halm 142), Latin *coniectura.* Both Greek and Latin terms refer to conjecturing about a fact.

[81] Cf. Matthes, *op.cit.* supra n. 73, 71 and 138.

2. ὅρος, "definition," Latin *definitiva* (*De inventione* 1.10) or *proprietas* (Quintilian 3.6.56).

3. κατὰ συμβεβηκός (Quintilian 3.5.14), "contingent," or ποιότης, "quality," Latin *generalis* (*De inventione* 1.10) or *qualitas* (Quintilian 3.1.56).

4. μετάληψις (Augustine, *De rhetorica* in Halm 143), "objection," Latin *translativa* (*De inventione* 1.10) or *translatio* (Quintilian 3.1.56).[82]

In determining the *stasis* of a suit Hermagoras spoke of the κατάφασις or charge of the prosecutor, which defined the αἴτιον or cause of action. This was answered by the ἀπόφασις or denial by the defendant, which provided the συνέχον or containment of the issue and focused the basic conflict. Out of this process appeared the ζήτημα, question, or κρινόμενον, the matter under judgment, which then could be classified as one of the four *staseis*.[83] The process could be viewed as one of elimination of each *stasis* successively, for the defendant's *apophasis* will ordinarily contain the issue at the question of fact if possible ("you did"; "I didn't"), if not, at that of definition ("you did"; "but it wasn't theft"), and only failing those at one of quality ("you did"; "but I had to"). Actually the fourth *stasis* can be a very strong one, but in putting it last Hermagoras seems to have regarded it as a last resort and a kind of petty legalism. Thus he shows that he has rhetorical exercises rather than actual oratory in mind, for in declamation it is not an effective base of argument. Some cases were ἀσύστατα, lacking *stasis*, and should not come to trial, either because the evidence was insufficient or equally balanced on both sides or too one sided or the subject presented some kind of contradiction or difficulty which made decision impossible (Fortunatianus, *Ars rhetorica* 1 in Halm 82).

Each of the four *staseis* was discussed in considerable

[82] *Ibid.* 133 ff.
[83] *Ibid.* 166 ff.

detail by Hermagoras and subdivisions were made. In the *stasis* of fact it is necessary to prove or disprove motive, ability, and desire.[84] Further, the defendant's person and character furnish evidence to indicate the probability or improbability of the alleged action: Cicero (*De inventione* 2.28 ff.) lists name, nature, way of life, fortune, habits (subdivided into six headings), zeal, and purpose. Finally, the act itself furnishes evidence, for the orator should consider its necessary attributes, its performance (place, time, and occasion), its adjuncts, and its result (*De inventione* 2.38 ff.). All of these topics would not be proper in any one speech, but Hermagoras furnished the orator and his scholastic critics with a kind of check list of what might offer grist to the mill. So complete and logical is the system that it seems to afford no alternative and the student of rhetoric could clearly be criticized specifically and severely for failure to follow it (Cicero, *Brutus* 263). The chief faculty allowed to the orator is a subtlety in constructing arguments on the various topics listed, but in that task he had commonplaces and examples of classic orators to imitate.

The *stasis* of definition was almost as detailed.[85] According to Cicero (*De inventione* 2.53 ff.) the speaker must define the crime, prove the definition, compare it with the act of the person accused, introduce commonplaces on the enormity and wickedness of the crime or, in the case of the defendant, on the utility and honorable nature of the act performed, attack the definition of the opponent, compare similar cases with the one in hand, and finally attack the opponent himself. Though the orator might make use of a law in establishing a definition, this topic did not deal with the validity or justice of the laws involved, which was the province of the νομικὰ ζητήματα, a quite separate heading.

The most difficult *stasis* to reconstruct and apparently

[84] *Ibid.* 138 ff.
[85] *Ibid.* 145 ff.

the most complicated was that of quality.[86] It was to be employed when the parties involved agreed about what had been done and about the name which should describe the action, but disagreed about the quality of the action, including its importance, justice, or utility—in other words, when the defense claimed that there were mitigating circumstances. Hermagoras divided the *stasis* of quality into four parts: deliberative, demonstrative, judicial, and pragmatic (πραγματικός, *negotialis*) (Cicero, *De inventione* 1.12, amplified and corrected by Quintilian 3.6.56 ff.). The words suggest the three kinds of oratory with a peculiar addition, though it seems strange to meet such categories here, and Cicero protests against the names. In fact, they were probably not intended to indicate kinds of oratory, but rather topics which could be introduced into a discussion of quality to justify an action admittedly in itself a crime. The topic of expediency, what must be sought and what avoided by a man (Quintilian's *adpetenda et fugienda*), is one and might be described as deliberative; a second is the topic of that which is laudable or blameworthy in an individual (Quintilian's *de persona*), the usual materials of epideictic; the third topic is the just and the unjust; the fourth, which is the least clearly understood,[87] is perhaps to be explained by Cicero's reference to utility (*De inventione* 1.12), the topic of what is practicable and what is not. Hermagoras' contemporary Polybius uses πραγματικός in this sense (3.116.7 and 36.5.1). One could imagine a defendant arguing that he had committed the act alleged,

[86] Cf. Nadeau, *op.cit.* supra n. 73, 55 f., and Matthes, *op.cit.* supra n. 73, 147 ff.

[87] The references to it in Cicero (*De inventione* 1.14) suggest that it refers to legal precedent. Quintilian 3.6.18 makes it into a kind of *thesis*. For a review of interpretations cf. Matthes, *op.cit.* supra n. 73, 150 ff. He would make the discussion an excursus more properly belonging under *thesis*. Nadeau, *op.cit.* supra n. 73, 60, suggests that it related to specific facts, laws, and customs. It is hard to see how any of these suggestions relate to an issue of *quality*.

but that there was nothing else which was expedient, honorable, just, or practicable at the time. Demosthenes' defense of his policy in *On the crown* involves the question, "What else could I do?" A judicial speech can include sections which are deliberative or epideictic in essence, so that the use of the terms is understandable, though it has caused much confusion. So far as we know Hermagoras did not discuss the kinds of oratory as such,[88] but all three traditional kinds are implied under his term "political questions." Ordinary deliberative and epideictic do not exhibit *stasis* in the strict sense, since they do not necessarily imply an opponent. If an opponent is imagined taking the opposite side of the argument, a dispute could be hypothesized in which the quality of a proposed action or the virtue of an individual is under debate and the materials for discussion are then sought in the subdivisions of the *stasis* of quality. In this case deliberative oratory would deal largely with deliberative qualities, epideictic with demonstrative qualities. But all this is hypothetical, and there is no evidence that Hermagoras developed any such argument. As usual he was thinking of judicial *hypotheses* or what the Romans called *controversiae*, practiced in schools of rhetoric.

Clearly the most important quality would be the justice or injustice of the action, and this Hermagoras further divided. The defendant could claim that his action was an appropriate one: it might, for example, be in accordance with custom. This was κατ' ἀντίληψιν (Quintilian 7.4.4), or what Cicero calls "absolute" since it involves the justice of an action quite specifically (*De inventione* 1.15 and 2.60). If this could not be substantiated, the defendant had no choice but to admit that he had done wrong and look for some mitigation outside of the deed. This was κατ' ἀντίθεσιν (Quintilian 7.4.7), what Cicero (*De inven-*

---

[88] The reference in Sopater, Walz 4.63, is probably to a different Hermagoras, often confused with our author.

311

tione 1.15 and 2.69) calls "assumptive."[89] Hermagoras divided this assumptive branch of the judicial part of the *stasis* of quality (to remind the reader where we are) into four subdivisions (Quintilian 7.4.8 ff.): 1. ἀντέγκλημα, 2. ἀντίστασις, 3. μετάστασις, and 4. συγγνώμη. The first form is where the defendant brings countercharges against the persons injured: "He was killed, but he was a robber." The second refers to the defendant's claim that some advantage to somebody resulted from his act or that the act prevented something worse from happening. The third is where the blame for the act is shifted to some other person, for example to a soldier's commander, or to a thing. Quintilian's example of the latter is a law prohibiting an administrator of a will from performing something ordered by a testator. Cicero (*De inventione* 2.91 f.) adds another type of *metastasis*, where not only the blame for an action but the essential part of the action itself is shifted to someone else. In the first type a defendant admits that he ought to have performed an act, but says he was prevented, or he admits that he ought not to have performed an act, but was forced to. In the third type the defendant claims that the alleged act, at which he assisted in some way, was essentially not *his* act or any part of his concern. Cicero's example is that of the boy who held a sacrificial pig in a treaty subsequently disavowed by the Senate and was then charged with responsibility for the treaty. He may claim that the act of sacrifice was not his, but that of his commander. The final form of "assumptive" is a plea for forgiveness on the basis of ignorance, either of some fact or of the law, or accident or overriding necessity (act of God).

The fourth and last *stasis* is μετάληψις, where the defendant argues that the prosecutor has no right to prosecute him or that the court has no right to hear the case, or when he in some way objects to the legal process.[90] Though

[89] Cf. Matthes, *op.cit.* supra n. 73, 152 ff.
[90] Cf. Matthes, *op.cit.* supra n. 73, 165 ff.

common in Greek law, this *stasis* was not well adapted to
Roman procedure, where the question of jurisdiction had
usually been settled before the beginning of the suit
(Cicero, *De inventione* 2.57 f.). Perhaps as a result, we
have relatively little detail about Hermagoras' discussion of
this *stasis*.

Parallel to the four *staseis* of rational questions were the
four legal questions (Quintilian 3.6.61 f.), apparently not
called *staseis*.[91] Κατὰ ῥητὸν καὶ ὑπεξαίρεσιν occurs when a
defendant demands a decision in accordance with the intent
of the lawgiver rather than under the strict letter of the law.
An example in the *Ad Herennium* (1.19) concerns a law
which provides that anyone remaining aboard an otherwise
abandoned ship shall gain possession of it and its cargo.
Yet, if one man is too ill to abandon the ship in a storm,
but unexpectedly both he and the ship survive, can he
claim possession? This was not the intention of the makers
of the law, but it is in accordance with its letter. The case
is one of ἀντινομία when two contrary laws can be in-
voked, of ἀμφιβολία when the law is ambiguous, and of
συλλογισμός when the specific action is not covered in a
law, but some analogous or less serious act is covered and
the question arises "may one argue from the written to the
unwritten?"

The *stasis* theory as outlined above constituted most if
not all of Hermagoras' discussion of invention (Cicero,
Brutus 263).[92] The parts of an oration probably had not
yet intruded into that topic, though this development would
come soon. Steps in the process can be seen by comparing
Cicero's *De inventione* with the *Rhetorica ad Herennium*.
In the former, two-thirds of the discussion is devoted to
the three kinds of speeches and the *stasis* theory. Seven
parts of an oration are somewhat abruptly inserted into
book one. In the *Rhetorica ad Herennium* the discussions

[91] Cf. Matthes, *op.cit.* supra n. 73, 182 ff.
[92] Cf. Matthes, *op.cit.* supra n. 73, 107 ff.

are much more thoroughly assimilated. The parts of an oration are the basic categories, and *stasis* is treated as a subtopic of the part known as the confirmation or proof.

After invention Hermagoras discussed economy (οἰκονο-μία), divided into judgment, division, order, and style. Quintilian (3.3.9) seems to regard this arrangement as peculiar to Hermagoras. Dionysius of Halicarnassus (*Demosthenes* 51) uses "economy" of arrangement on the authority of the "ancients" and that meaning is not uncommon (e.g. *On the sublime* 1.4 and *Excerpta codicis Parisini* 3032 in Rabe's *Prolegomenon syllogê* p. 299). The need for a judgment (κρίσις) to choose some of the possible material and reject some is echoed by most rhetoricians (e.g. *De inventione* 2.16, where it is mentioned in connexion with *stasis*), though Quintilian (3.5.5) thinks that it should not be regarded as a part of arrangement (3.9.2). Dionysius of Halicarnassus (*Thucydides* 9) distinguishes division (διαίρεσις) from arrangement (τάξις) and applies the former to the geographical or chronological method followed by an historian. Arrangement (τάξις) must have included discussion of the parts of the oration, since it is unlikely that these were a part of the discussion of invention. Hermagoras may be responsible for expanding the number of parts of the oration. Up until about his time the usual number was four, with an occasional aberration as in the system of Theodorus; after his time the number is normally greater. Both *De inventione* (1.19) and the *Ad Herennium* (1.4) list six parts: exordium, narration, partition, confirmation, refutation, conclusion. Tacitus (*Dialogus* 19) seems to confirm exordium, narration, partition, and confirmation as Hermagorean, and Cicero (*De inventione* 1.97) specifically attributes to Hermagoras digression, or the insertion of a passage of amplification after the proof, and conclusion. There is no specific testimony

314

that Hermagoras regarded refutation as separate from confirmation.[93]

Hermagoras' discussion of the separate parts can be partially reconstructed and seems to have been a model for discussions in later writers. He formalized the logical basis of the prooemium by distinguishing four kinds of cases, σχήματα ὑποθέσεων (his love of *four* categories is again evident): ἔνδοξον or honorable, παράδοξον or unexpected, ἀμφίδοξον or doubtful, ἄδοξον or disreputable (Augustine, *De rhetorica* in Halm 147 ff.). These appear in *Ad Herennium* (1.5) *as honestum, turpe, dubium,* and *humile.* Other authors add a fifth, the obscure (*De inventione* 1.20), or a sixth, the scandalous (Quintilian 4.1.40). Specific rules like those in *De inventione* or *Ad Herennium* were surely given for each. Both of these authors, and probably Hermagoras too, distinguished a direct introduction and a more subtle approach or "insinuation" (ἔφοδος) to be used when the case is discreditable, when the jury seems convinced by the opponent, or when the jury is tired.

The discussion of the narration probably contained some of the divisions made in *De inventione* (1.27) and *Ad Herennium* (1.12).[94] It is noteworthy that both works discuss the rhetorical exercise known as a narration as well as the treatment of the narration in a legal suit. Doubtless Hermagoras, like most ancient rhetoricians, described the virtues of the narration as brevity, clarity, and plausibility (*De inventione* 1.28 and *Ad Herennium* 1.14).

Partition in the *De inventione* (1.31) and *Ad Herennium* (1.17) is divided into two parts. The first deals with what is agreed to and what contested by the litigants, which is

[93] *De inventione* 1.97 might seem to imply it, but cf. Matthes, *op.cit.* supra n. 73, 203 ff.

[94] Cf. Karl Barwick, "Die Gliederung der *narratio* in der rhetorischen Theorie und ihre Bedeutung für die Geschichte des antiken Romans," *Hermes* 63 (1928) 261 ff. and Matthes, *op.cit.* supra n. 73, 196 ff.

so clearly the statement of *stasis* that there is no need to doubt Hermagoras' influence. The second part is an outline of what is going to be said and may also be Hermagorean, though the restriction of the number of headings to three (*Ad Herennium* 1.17) is hardly his.

The discussion of proof, since it did not involve *stasis*, which had already been discussed, must have concerned primarily the form of rhetorical arguments. As already noticed Hermagoras ignored proof by ethos or pathos. Rhetorical arguments in Aristotle were of two forms, the enthymeme, or rhetorical syllogism, and the example, or inductive proof. Since both induction and syllogistic reasoning are included in *De inventione* (1.51 ff. and 57 ff.) we may guess that they were found in some form in Hermagoras. Induction is lacking in *Ad Herennium*, but, as in the arrangement of invention or in the listing of three rather than four *staseis*, here also its source may not have been Hermagoras. It does, however, use the common Hellenistic and Roman name for a syllogistic rhetorical argument, namely epicheireme (2.2). Aristotle's enthymeme was a syllogism whose two premises and conclusion are probable rather than certain; but Aristotle did not make any specific distinction between the forms of rhetorical and logical arguments, though it was clear that the former are often less systematically expressed or have one part suppressed.[95] The term epicheireme is usually applied to a rhetorical argument based on probability whose parts are fully expressed, though both terms were used by different authors in different ways (Quintilian 5.10.1 ff.). The argument discussed in both *De inventione* (1.57 ff.) and *Ad Herennium* (2.28 ff.) has five parts, and generally speaking it differs from the old Aristotelian enthymeme in that reasons are introduced to support each of the premises, though the form is somewhat different in the two treatises. Cicero says (*De inventione* 1.61) that this concept of an epichei-

[95] Cf. supra, chapter 3, pp. 97 f.

reme as having five parts was taught by the followers of Aristotle and Theophrastus, that is the Peripatetics, and by the most elegant and accomplished rhetoricians. We have seen that Theophrastus used the term epicheireme, though exactly in what sense is not certain. The theory that there were only three parts, the reason supporting each premise being regarded as part of the premise, is mentioned and rejected by Cicero (1.60). Possibly it was the view of the Stoics, who would constitute the other chief group: we know that they taught the syllogism of three parts (Diogenes Laertius 7.76). Hermagoras' love of classification would suggest that he preferred the five parts, and this is supported by Cicero's failure to attribute the three-part system to him. Usually Cicero is happy to make it clear when he and his teacher disagree with the distinguished authority (e.g. 1.8, 1.12, 1.97) who provoked much envy (1.16).

The digression, as has been said, offered an opportunity for amplification. The conclusion or epilogue in both *De inventione* (1.98 ff.) and *Ad Herennium* (2.47 ff.) is divided into three parts: recapitulation, amplification to arouse the indignation of the jurors against the opponent, and emotional appeal on behalf of the speaker or his client. Cicero lists ten commonplaces of amplification; the *Ad Herennium* gives fifteen.

We know nothing about Hermagoras' discussion of style except that one existed (Quintilian 3.3.9). It was not his strong point (Cicero, *Brutus* 263 and 271). By its silence, Quintilian's passage might be taken to imply that Hermagoras also discussed memory and delivery, which he says (3.3.1) most authorities regarded as parts of rhetoric. Delivery was studied by Theophrastus and by the Stoics, so its appearance is not unexpected. *Ad Herennium* 3.38 indicates that there were many Greek discussions of memory systems and that the basic technique described was the association of words with visual images which could be re-

317

membered against some familiar background. Simonides of Ceos is the legendary discoverer of this method (Cicero, *De oratore* 2.352 ff., cf. also 2.299), which was certainly known by the time of Aristotle (*On the soul* 427b18 ff.). In the second century B.C. it was practiced by Charmades and Metrodorus (*De oratore* 2.360). Pliny (*Natural history* 7.89) says that the latter brought the system to perfection, and he is, therefore, perhaps the source of the discussion in Roman handbooks. The oldest extant discussion of memory is that in the *Rhetorica ad Herennium* (3.28 ff.).[96]

This is the system of Hermagoras. Its systematic quality and its detail are immediately evident: rhetoric is regarded as an art in which the rules can be learned, and Hermagoras had discovered virtually all the rules. With him the rhetorical handbook and the traditional system of ancient rhetoric achieved almost its full development. The dullness and sterility of the system were recognized by such men as Cicero (*Brutus* 263 and 271) and Tacitus (*Dialogus* 19), but the system was not rejected for that reason, for the rhetorical mind, of which Hermagoras' was an exceedingly neat example, had been fond of categories from the start. In fact, Hermagoras was very influential, certainly on the rhetoricians and perhaps also on Roman law.[97] He could well be accused of classifying for the sake of classifying: his beloved sets of four are patently artificial, though per-

---

[96] Cf. L. A. Post, "Ancient memory systems," CW 25 (1932) 105 ff.; Helga Hajdu, *Das mnemotechnische Schriftum des Mittelalters*, Vienna, 1936, 11 ff.; Caplan, *op.cit.* supra n. 3, 204 f. Philodemus (*Rhetoric* 2. col.44, i.p.79 Sudhaus, corrected in *Supplementum* 40) attributes to Alexinus (4th cent. B.C.), if Sudhaus' restoration is correct, a criticism of rhetorical sophists who waste their time on such subjects as diction and memory, but the examples may be those of Philodemus rather than Alexinus, and in any event the criticism can refer to practical exercises rather than written discussion.

[97] Cf. Johannes Stroux, *Römische Rechtswissenschaft und Rhetorik*, Potsdam, 1949, 23 ff. For further bibliography cf. Caplan, *op.cit.* supra n. 3, 90 f. and Charles S. Rayment, "A current survey of ancient rhetoric," CW 52 (1958) 90 ff.

haps intended to be easy to remember; while again and again the fact that he has in mind *controversiae* in schools of rhetoric becomes evident. Moreover, his examples show a tendency toward preferring lurid cases of criminal law, mythological examples, or impractical situations rather than usable precedents of actual and significant cases. His system was disciplinary rather than practical.

Hermagoras' system was not intended for young schoolboys, but for advanced students who had completed the *progymnasmata* and wanted further training. After his time advanced rhetorical studies became commonplace. Who were the students, or to phrase the question in another way, what moved Hermagoras to develop an advanced rhetorical education? The answer appears to be "the Romans." The second century is the time when the Romans first became aware of Greek culture on a large scale. Cicero's description of the movement is as follows (*De oratore* 1.14):

"When our empire over all the races had been established and enduring peace made leisure possible, there was hardly an ambitious young man who did not think he should strive with all zeal for the ability to speak. At first, ignorant of the whole study, since they did not realize the existence of any course or exercises or rules of art, they did what they could with their own native ability and reflection. Afterwards, when they had heard the Greek orators and become acquainted with Greek literature and had studied with learned Greeks, our countrymen took fire with an incredible zeal for speaking."

We know the names of some of the teachers of illustrious Romans. Diophanes of Mytilene, for example, taught Tiberius Gracchus (Cicero, *Brutus* 104), Menelaus of Marathus was the preceptor of Gaius Gracchus (*Brutus* 100), and Metrodorus of Scepsis left the Academy in Athens to go as a teacher of rhetoric to Asia with Crassus

319

when the latter was quaestor about 109 B.C.[98] (*De oratore* 3.75). His abandonment of philosophy was permanent (Strabo 13.609). Among the nationalists there was opposition to the new Greek influence: in 161 B.C. both rhetoricians and philosophers were expelled from the city of Rome, but by 91 the teaching of rhetoric was so popular that it had begun in Latin and attempts were made to stop that (Suetonius, *De rhetoribus* 1). Cato the elder is said (Quintilian 3.1.19) to have composed a rhetorical handbook, perhaps a private one addressed to his son (Seneca, *Controversiae* 1.pr.9). A handbook by Antonius was certainly in circulation before the end of the first decade of the first century (*De oratore* 1.94). Cicero's own *De inventione*, not much later, is a product of rhetorical studies in his late teens. He continued to practice declamation in Greek until he became praetor (Suetonius, *De rhetoribus* 1).

Roman interest in philosophy was not nearly so great, though it existed in the Scipionic circle, for example, and Cicero sometimes exaggerated its appeal (e.g. *De oratore* 2.154). In general, philosophy seemed impractical and suspect to the Romans (Tacitus, *Agricola* 4 is the *locus classicus*), rhetoric was useful and systematic. The academic sterility of the latter was obscured by its claims to train for political life. Hermagoras provided an exceedingly systematic approach, and this was clearly the source of his influence for several hundred years. Quintilian says (3.1.16) that he "made as it were a path of his own, which many have followed." We may conclude that Hermagoras was the actual innovator of advanced instruction, but that the demand was so great that numerous other rhetoricians soon imitated him.

Hermagoras' nearest equal and rival, according to the same passage in Quintilian, was Athenaeus about whose

[98] On the studies of Crassus and other Romans in the East cf. Ll. W. Daly, "Roman study abroad," AJP 71 (1950) 40 ff.

teachings we do not know so much as about those of Hermagoras. We have his definition of rhetoric (Sextus Empiricus, *Against the professors* 2.62) as "a power of words aiming at the persuasion of the hearers."[99] Often he seems to have differed with Hermagoras about details: he discussed *theses* and *hypotheses*, but regarded the former as a part of the latter, presumably believing that every *hypothesis* had a general question inherent in it (Quintilian 3.5.5). He recognized four kinds of *stasis* (Quintilian 3.6.47 f.), but the names are not those used by Hermagoras; Quintilian thought that the fourth of Hermagoras' *staseis* was not in Athenaeus' system and that he had substituted a protreptic or hortatory *stasis* suitable for *suasoriae*, but Quintilian had not read the original work and admitted that scholars differed about what Athenaeus' terms meant.[100] A figure was defined as a change leading the hearing to a sense of pleasure (Phoebammon, *On figures* in Spengel 3.44); delivery was labeled the most important part of rhetoric (Philodemus, *Rhetoric* 4.col.11a,1.p.193 Sudhaus). There is nothing to indicate that Athenaeus' system was any more practical or profound than that of Hermagoras.

The Quarrel between Rhetoric and Philosophy

The increasing connexion between Greek rhetoricians and Romans, both at Rome and in the East, disturbed the philosophers whose position at the apex of the educational system was being threatened by the unaccountable preference shown by the Romans for the dreary and trivial in-

[99] The definition *ars fallendi* attributed to Athenaeus in Quintilian 2.15.23 is not necessarily inconsistent with this, though the context is discussing opponents of rhetoric and thus a different Athenaeus may be meant.

[100] It has been claimed, but not persuasively, that Athenaeus' *stasis* system was the basis of that in the early Latin handbook of Antonius, cf. Friedrich Marx, rev. of Thiele, BPW 10 (1890) 1005. On Athenaeus in general cf. Brzoska in R-E 2. col. 2025 f. s.v. "Athenaeus."

struction of the rhetoricians. As a result, during the course of the second century the schools undertook an attack upon the educational claims of the rhetoricians. The philosophers most associated with this attack are Critolaus the Peripatetic and Carneades the Academic. Together with Diogenes of Babylon the Stoic they were sent as ambassadors by the Athenians to Rome in 155 (Cicero, *De oratore* 2.155), which indicates an approximate date for the dispute. Since they were contemporaries and since they represented schools which in varying degrees had accepted rhetoric, their about-face must not have been purely a matter of personal whim. Furthermore, they were able speakers (Aulus Gellius 6.14.8) who much impressed the Romans and must have been aware of the practical utility of oratory. In no case does their rejection of rhetoric seem to have been a necessary consequence of their other philosophical views. Carneades[101] brought a new vigor to the languishing Peripatetic school and a return to some of the serious concerns of Aristotle (Cicero, *De finibus* 5.14), but rhetoric he labeled a κακοτεχνία or false artifice (Sextus Empiricus, *Against the professors* 2.12 and 20, cf. also Quintilian 2.17.15). Carneades, and his disciples Clitomachus and Charmadas, insisted that there was no *art* of speaking, though there might be an innate knack of flattery (Cicero, *De oratore* 1.45 f. and 89 ff. and Sextus Empiricus, *Against the professors* 2.20 ff.). Yet Carneades had imparted a strongly skeptical character to the Academy and had developed a theory of probability which might seem to suggest the epistemology of the sophists (Sextus Empiricus, *Pyrrhonism* 1.220 and 230 ff.). Diogenes' view of rhetoric did not represent any fundamental change from that of earlier Stoics (*De oratore* 2.157 ff.). Like them he believed that a philosopher could be the only true orator, but he shared

[101] Cf. Ludwig Radermacher, "Critolaus und die Rhetorik," in Sudhaus' *Supplementum, op.cit.* supra n. 69, ix ff.; Arnim 87 ff.; Hubbell, *op.cit.* supra n. 69, 364 ff.; Kroll 1083 f.

with his colleagues on the embassy a thoroughness in rejecting any utility from the study of traditional rhetoric and in objecting to its claim to be systematic (Philodemus, *Hypomnematicon* col.1-24,ii.p.202 ff. Sudhaus).

As it is preserved in Cicero (*De oratore* 1.89 ff.), Philodemus (*Rhetoric* 2), Quintilian (2.17), and Sextus (*Against the professors* 2), the challenge to rhetoric was clearly based on the denial that rhetoric was an art. If it were not an art, it was not systematic and thus was incapable of being imparted by a teacher. Parts of the discussion also touched on the utility and morality of rhetoric. Among the arguments advanced to prove that rhetoric could not be an art were the existence of good orators, including those found in the Homeric poems,[102] before the alleged discovery of the art by Corax and Tisias; the generally bad writing of rhetoricians; the existence of able orators like Demades and Aeschines without formal training; the absence of any subject matter which is the peculiar material of rhetoric; the uncertainty of rhetorical techniques; the possibility of using rhetoric for false ends, which ought not to be possible of a true art; and the objections that rhetoric dealt only with opinion, that it had no goal or if it did failed to attain it, and that states had often expelled orators because of the damage they did. Most of the arguments are adaptations of points made by Plato.

We must be careful not to exaggerate the attack on rhetoric by the philosophers. Our sources indicate a rejection of the claim that rhetoric was an art and a contempt for rhetorical theory as taught at the time by rhetoricians. They should not be pressed to mean that the philosophical schools ceased all rhetorical exercises, for we know that Carneades, at least, did not (Cicero, *De oratore* 3.80), or that they entirely rejected oratory as a literary genre. The achievement of orators who lacked technical training was

[102] Cf. George A. Kennedy, "The ancient dispute over rhetoric in Homer," AJP 78 (1957) 23 ff.

appreciated, for example. Sextus Empiricus' account (*Against the professors* 2.20 ff.), which is anti-oratorical as well as anti-rhetorical, perhaps puts a peculiar Cynic slant on the whole subject. Otherwise, rhetoric was criticized because of its limitations and its dullness and because the study of rhetorical rules alone simply did not prepare one to be an effective orator; rhetoricians could not produce eloquence and therefore rhetoric was not an art; perhaps it was an innate knack, perhaps it could be picked up by practice, perhaps, some thought, it could be taught if a really philosophic base were laid for it. The practical threat to the position of the teachers of philosophy was not openly discussed, but it is clearly implied that philosophy is the only worthwhile base of liberal studies.

Our best picture of the true nature of the dispute between philosophers and rhetoricians is the account given by Crassus and Antonius in Cicero's *De oratore* of debates they heard in Athens in the late second century. The principal philosopher quoted is Charmadas the Academic, a pupil of Carneades. He is represented as feeling very strongly on the subject and in his excitement denying that rhetoric is an art (1.90), but it is clear that his objections are not to oratory, but to the contemporary rhetoricians with their dry rules and lack of depth. He admires Demosthenes (1.89) and suggests that his greatness was a result of studies with Plato, much as Plato had attributed Pericles' eloquence to his studies with Anaxagoras (*Phaedrus* 269e4 ff.). Finally (1.93) he concludes not that eloquence is insignificant or nonexistent, but that it is so difficult and lofty that it can be reached only through mastery of philosophy. His position throughout is reminiscent of Plato's attempt in the *Phaedrus* to outline a philosophical rhetoric and of the desire of the Stoics to make rhetoric one of the virtues of the philosopher.

The reply to Charmadas is made by the rhetorician Menedemus, who claims that there is a certain kind of restricted knowledge relating to political matters which can be taught by the rhetoricians (1.85). Menedemus' real weakness was his superficiality: he had many rhetorical examples, but no real ability at argumentation (1.88). The same kind of objection was made against the anti-philosophical strictures of Apollonius of Alabanda (1.75).

The objections of the philosophers were strengthened by the insistence of rhetoricians to include some discussion of *theses*. Such general questions demanded knowledge and training far beyond that which the rhetoricians customarily gave. Charmadas immediately jumped upon the implications of Menedemus' claim that politics belongs to the orator and said that successful discussion of politics implies knowledge of philosophy. On the other hand, if the rhetoricians dropped the *theses* they could equally be accused of superficiality in ignoring the general implications of a case.

Cicero appears to have agreed with some of the complaints of the philosophers—that rhetoric as taught by the Greeks in the second century was a dull routine of technicalities which could not produce a real orator Not only rules but broad general knowledge, natural fitness, and practice are required. The system of Hermagoras is a perfect example of what was objected to.[103] Cicero's own view of rhetoric is considerably more profound than anything to be

[103] Hermagoras was the most famous rhetorician of the second century; he may have originated advanced instruction in rhetoric and in any event was one of the first to offer it; Posidonius may have regarded him as the first rhetorician to discuss *theses* (Plutarch, *Pompey* 42). Beyond these points we have no evidence that Hermagoras precipitated the objections of the rhetoricians. Unfortunately dates cannot be definitely fixed: it is possible that Critolaus' attack on rhetoric anteceded Hermagoras, in which case the philosopher must be regarded as alarmed at the general situation and at the influence the Romans were beginning to have. Some distrust of non-philosophic education had been shown earlier, e.g. by Ariston (Stobaeus 4.110). J. F. D'Alton, *Roman literary theory and criticism*, London, 1931, 216 appears to have regarded Hermagoras as in part reacting *against* the philosopher's hostility, but D'Alton was apparently confused about the nature of Hermagoras' work.

found in Hermagoras, and it has acquired this depth in answer to philosophic objections. It is noteworthy that the arguments of Charmadas and Menedemus correspond roughly to the arguments of Crassus and Antonius in *De oratore*, with the important difference that the Romans speak from the point of view of the orator and Roman men of affairs. Crassus, with whom Cicero agrees (1.17), claims that the orator must be a philosopher and have a very wide general knowledge. He will not specifically agree with all Charmadas has said (1.47), but he is willing to abandon the claim that rhetoric is an art in a technical sense (1.107). His demands like those of Charmadas are so great as to make the quality of an excellent orator almost unattainable. Antonius, on the other hand, in book one argues for a more limited and attainable goal (1.213) which is reminiscent of the point of view of Menedemus. Later he gives this up and admits that a need for a wide knowledge is implied in any discussion of *theses* (2.65). If the resulting pictures of a philosophical rhetoric and a rhetorical philosophy are juxtaposed, it seems that the two groups are not very far apart. Naturally great disagreement could have developed over definitions, especially the word "art," but by the first century B.C. there seems to have been a tacit understanding among everyone except Epicureans like Philodemus that such disputes were not profitable.

The pertinent question at this point is whether Cicero's broad view of rhetoric and the orator was shared with or derived from any Hellenistic Greek rhetorician. There is no clear evidence that it was: its Greek sources were either remote in time or philosophical. The Greek rhetorician who most directly influenced Cicero was Apollonius, the son of Molon, himself sometimes called Molon. Cicero studied with him both in Rome (*Brutus* 307 and 312), where he came on an embassy, and later on Rhodes (*Brutus* 316), but what he learned was entirely related to the practical side of oratory, especially style and delivery. Apollonius is described as a good orator and effective teacher. Other sources (Diogenes Laertius 3.34 and *Scholia* to Aristophanes' *Clouds* 144) indicate that he wasted no affection on philosophy. On the other hand we have already noted that the discussion of style in the third book of *De oratore* is unusually close to Theophrastus. Discussing the work as a whole in a letter (*Ad familiares* 1.9.23) Cicero claims that it departs from common precepts and is based on the teaching of the ancients, including Aristotle (cf. also *De oratore* 2.160) and Isocrates. The similarity between the concept of the orator as a philosopher and the sophistic ideal, best seen in Isocrates, is striking and hardly accidental (*De oratore* 3.126 ff.).[104] Undoubtedly the practical possibilities for the orator in Rome are largely responsible for Cicero's turning back to the concept of the orator as a man of public affairs in Athens. It is the first of a series of influences which Roman civilization was to have on the history of rhetoric.

Apart from this, Cicero was able to draw on the philosophical rhetoric which gradually prevailed at Athens and Rhodes and replaced the bitter opposition to rhetoric of the second century philosophers. This rhetoric, not unlike that of Charmadas, was more or less inspired by Plato's *Phaedrus*. The earliest of the new group of thinkers was Charmadas' friend [?] (Sextus Empiricus, *Pyrrhonism* 1.220) Philo, head of the Academy, who fled to Rome during the first Mithridatic war and whose lectures were enthusiastically attended by Cicero (*Brutus* 306). He taught "the precepts of the rhetoricians at one time, of the philosophers at another" (*Tusculan disputations* 2.9), and he made his students practice *hypotheses* as well as *theses* (*De oratore* 3.110). Since Cicero attributes his own rhetorical

---

[104] Cf. Harry M. Hubbell, *The influence of Isocrates on Cicero, Dionysius, and Aristides*, New Haven, 1913, 16 ff. and S. E. Smethurst, "Cicero and Isocrates," TAPA 84 (1953) 262 ff. On the continuity of sophistry cf. Wilamowitz, *op.cit.* supra n. 72, 13 ff.

327

training[105] to the Academics rather than to the rhetoricians (*Orator* 12), von Arnim thought it very likely that Philo was responsible for the general conception of the orator on which Cicero based *De oratore*.[106] Kroll pointed out disagreement between part of book three and views of Philo; he thought it more likely that Philo's successor Antiochus of Ascalon was Cicero's major influence.[107] Cicero says (*Brutus* 315) that he studied philosophy with Antiochus in Athens in 79-78 B.C. and coincidently worked on rhetoric under Demetrius the Syrian. It seems possible that Philo and Antiochus may have been in general agreement about the need for philosophical training for the orator.[108] A third philosopher who much influenced Cicero was Posidonius the Stoic.[109] He regarded philosophy as the inventor of the arts of civilization (Seneca, *Epistles* 90.7), which may be understood to include rhetoric. The view is essentially the Stoic notion of the philosopher as the only orator. Cicero probably drew on him in the introduction to *De inventione* and perhaps elsewhere.[110] Posidonius' interests included the theory of *stasis* (Plutarch, *Pompey* 42 and Quintilian 3.6.37).

Among the works of Cicero is one which purports (139) to contain the rhetorical precepts of the Academy: this is the *Partitiones oratoriae*, a series of questions by Cicero's son answered by Cicero himself.[111] The two of them had

[105] Subsequent to that embodied in *De inventione* which he repudiated in *De oratore* 1.5.

[106] Cf. *op.cit.* supra n. 1, 100 ff.

[107] Cf. W. Kroll, "Studien über Ciceros Schrift *de oratore*," RhM 58 (1903) 552 ff. His views are somewhat modified in his R-E article 1087.

[108] Cf. Witt, *op.cit.* supra n. 50, 30.

[109] Cf. Kroll 1084 ff.

[110] Cf. R. Philippson, "Ciceroniana 1: *De inventione*," *Neue Jahrbücher für Philologie* 113 (1886) 417 ff. The whole subject is reviewed by Michel, *op.cit.* supra n. 16, 80 ff.

[111] Cf. Paul Sternkopf, *De M. Tulli Ciceronis Partitionibus oratoriis*, Münster, 1914; Kroll 1088; Brady B. Gilleland, "The date

discussed the subject in Greek before (1); thus this work is intended to put the younger Cicero straight about the Latin terminology. It is divided into three parts, avoiding the conflation of systems which the rhetoricians had adopted: in the first the *vis oratoris* or faculty of the orator is discussed (1-26), the second relates to the parts of an oration (27-60), the third to the question (60-138). Although the terminology is sometimes strange (the three kinds of style recognized are called *probabile, illustre,* and *suave*), the material is basically that of traditional rhetorical theory. The faculty of the orator consists of invention, arrangement, style, delivery, and memory; the parts of the oration are four in number, a reversion to the system of Aristotle and the early Hellenistic period; the question refers to a division into limited and unlimited (*hypotheses* and *theses* are meant) and *stasis*. Yet there are a number of distinctive features. First, the use of the term *vis* suggests Aristotle's δύναμις or faculty, a definition acceptable to the Academics (*De oratore* 2.30). The term "art" is not used in the treatise. Second, brevity is included as a virtue of style (19), which suggests some Stoic influence, perfectly possible in the Academy, though it should be noted that stirring the emotions is regarded as quite acceptable (e.g. 8). Third, endless lists of figures of speech are omitted, nor is much said about prose rhythm (18). Fourth, Aristotle's division of the audience into judges or hearers and subjects into things past or things future is reintroduced (10) as the basis of the three kinds of oratory, and epideictic (70-82) and deliberative (83-97) are given unusually extensive treatments. Partly because of these features, the

---

of Cicero's *Partitiones oratoriae*," CP 56 (1961) 29 ff. The work seems to have been composed in the late 50's as a result of Cicero's promise (*Ad Quintum fratrem* 3.3.4) to give his son and nephew some rhetorical training. Its elementary nature suggests that they were still quite young and there is no mention of Atticism, which bulked so large in Cicero's later rhetorical thought.

tone of the whole seems somewhat more practical than was that of Hermagoras. Most important of all is the statement at the end (139 f.) that there can be no understanding or effective use of rhetoric unless the orator has a grasp of philosophy, by which Cicero appears to mean mostly logic and ethics, and especially the philosophy of the Academics.

The ideal orator of the first century B.C. is primarily a Roman concept, although it was influenced by both Plato and Isocrates. Greek philosophers of the time limited themselves to imagining one of their kind who commanded the knack of oratory. Dionysius of Halicarnassus, under Roman influence, admires the philosophical orator (cf. Appendix), but most professional Greek rhetoricians persisted in taking a narrow and traditional view of their task which emphasized the rules of rhetorical theory and the conventions of rhetorical exercises. One is reminded of more recent educators who could see only the disciplinary advantages of the study of Latin grammar. The artificiality of the schools of the Greek rhetoricians is equally evident in the two rhetorical controversies which marked the first century B.C., that between the Atticists and the Asianists and that between the Apollodoreans and the Theodoreans.

Atticism

Atticism is the reaction against the excesses of Hellenistic prose style, but instead of creating good standards of contemporary usage, the new movement demanded an archaic return to the language, rhythms, and style of the classical period.[112] Thus it is inextricably intertwined with classicism, the view that the great literary achievement of the Greeks was past. The practical effects of Atticism were in many cases satisfactory, but its view of artistic creativity reflected

[112] The chief general sources are Cicero, *Brutus* 284 ff. and *Orator* 23 ff. Cf. Kroll 1105 ff.

and contributed to the pessimism of later Greek intellectual history.

We know relatively little about the beginnings of the Atticist movement. Three influences upon it are often recognized, perhaps rightly. The first would be that of the grammarians, who were intent upon establishing purity of diction and language.[113] They were concerned with the texts of individual authors and also with the cataloging of texts for the libraries at Alexandria and Pergamum, which suggests that they may have contributed to the notion of certain authors as "classics" and the establishment of canons in various genres, but there is no proof of this. Teaching grammarians had to draw up a curriculum of reading in their schools, but their choice fell largely on Homer and the poets. We have already noticed the effect of study of grammar on Latin style in the second century.

A second and related influence is that of the philosophers.[114] Certainly Stoic notions of style were a restraining influence. Furthermore, classicism is implicit in Theophrastus' use of Gorgias, Thrasymachus, Thucydides, Plato, and others as models of style. By choosing primarily writers considerably before his own time Theophrastus suggests that literary standards have decayed. Demetrius' *On style* also quotes predominantly classical models. The revival of the Platonic concept of a philosophical rhetoric in the very early first century B.C., the increased interest in or rediscovery of Aristotle's writings, and in Rome the revitalization of the sophistic ideal as seen, for example, in the influence of Isocrates, all contributed to the impression that the greatest writers and thinkers had lived in the fifth and fourth centuries.

It is less clear what part the professional rhetorical schools

[113] Cf. Norden 149 ff.; Wilamowitz, *op.cit.* supra n. 72, 41 ff.; D'Alton, *op.cit.* supra n. 103, 215 f.
[114] Cf. Wilamowitz, *op.cit.* supra n. 72, 43 ff.

played in encouraging the new movement.[115] Oratorical
ability was generally regarded as a result of nature, study of
the rules, and practice, and in this triad most Hellenistic
rhetoricians seem to have emphasized the rules. But rhetorical exercises, if not so popular as they became in Rome,
clearly were practiced, and examples or models for them
must have been suggested. Quintilian (2.4.3) says that
Greek rhetoricians read and commented on the texts of
historians and orators. In many schools the rhetorician
himself was probably the principal model, but rhetoricians
had their favorite among the Attic orators. Hyperides is
said to have been the favorite model of Rhodian rhetors,
including Molon; in other places Plato was preferred or
Thucydides or Isocrates or Demosthenes (Dionysius of
Halicarnassus, *Dinarchus* 8).[116] This rhetorical *mimêsis* or
imitation, in which one studied an author and tried to reproduce his style, became such a major interest of teachers
of rhetoric that in later Hellenistic times it tended to overshadow everything else. In a very general way we may
reckon three periods in the Greek attitude toward literary
creativity. In the first, lasting down until about the time
of Plato, inspiration was regarded as most important,
though naïve imitation played an educational role (Cicero,
De oratore 2.91 ff.). In the fourth century, as seen for
example in the *Poetics* of Aristotle, perhaps under the influence of the rhetorical handbooks, an attempt was made to
formulate rules of composition in comparison with which
inspiration became less influential. Finally it was replaced

[115] Cf. Blass, *op.cit.* supra n. 1, 77 and D'Alton, *op.cit.* supra
n. 103, 215 f.

[116] Isocrates is, of course, quoted frequently as a model of style
by Aristotle. Cleochares, in the third century, wrote a comparison
of the style of Demosthenes and Isocrates (and his pupils), cf.
Photius, *Library* 121b9 Bekker. On the study of Demosthenes cf.
Engelbert Drerup, *Demosthenes im Urteile des Altertums*, Würzburg, 1923, 89 ff. He regarded (p. 97 ff.) Hieronymus of Rhodes as
founder of the worship of Demosthenes as an orator.

by the new concept of imitation, which of course must be carefully distinguished from "imitation" as used by Plato and Aristotle.[117] They meant imitation of reality or of nature, whereas the rhetoricians meant imitation or emulation of a classical literary model. We have portions of a work on imitation by Dionysius and a discussion of the subject by Quintilian (10.2, though the doctrine is implied throughout the account of Greek and Latin literature in 10.1). Quintilian tries to counteract the sterile influence that imitation and nothing but imitation would have when he urges a student to imitate more than one author (10.2.25 f.) or to recognize and correct faults in the one author he does imitate (10.2.28).[118] He established Cicero as the touchstone, but the choice was not so easy for Romans in the first century B.C. They did not have a great classical literature in some golden past to furnish them models. Horace objects strenuously (e.g. *Epistulae* 2.1) to those who tried to make Plautus, Ennius, and other early Latin poets into classics, while Brutus' attempt to label Cato the Roman Lysias was howled down by Atticus (Cicero, *Brutus* 63 f. and 293 f.).

Among Roman Atticists Lysias was commonly regarded as the most suitable object of imitation. Cicero's *Brutus* and *Orator* are both addressed to Lysias' admirer Brutus, and both were intended to show that Lysias is not the only "Attic" orator.[119] Cicero himself preferred Demosthenes,

[117] Cf. Richard McKean, "Literary criticism and the concept of imitation in antiquity," *Modern philology* 34 (1936) 1 ff., and D. L. Clark, "Imitation: theory and practice in Roman rhetoric," QJS 37 (1951) 11 ff.

[118] Cf. George A. Kennedy, "An estimate of Quintilian," AJP 83 (1962) 130 ff.

[119] Cf. Sebastian Schlittenbauer, "Die Tendenz von Cicero's *Orator*," JKP Suppl. 28 (1903) 181 ff.; Edward J. Filbey, "Concerning the oratory of Brutus," CP 6 (1911) 325 ff., who shows that Cicero misrepresents Brutus' position; G. L. Hendrickson, "Cicero's correspondence with Brutus and Calvus on oratorical style," AJP 47 (1926) 234 ff.

whom he regarded as equally Attic (e.g. *Orator* 30). Greek critics and rhetoricians who taught in Rome in the Augustan age all seem to have been Atticists. Caecilius, the most celebrated, favored Lysias over Plato and is rebuked therefore by the author of *On the sublime* (32.8). The tastes of Dionysius of Halicarnassus, though clearly Attic, were more catholic. Dionysius is our major source on Atticism as discussed among the Greeks; in the introduction to his Attic orators, translated below in the Appendix, he stresses the tie between philosophy and Atticism and attributes the success of the movement to the influence of the Romans.[120] Dionysius is not above flattery, but the claim may be true in substance, in which case we have a second indication that what was most vital about rhetoric was not coming from the Greek rhetoricians, but from Rome. Convinced that the future lay in Rome, Dionysius established himself there almost immediately after the battle of Actium (*Roman antiquities* 1.7.2). Caecilius, Apollodorus, and Theodorus, the other great rhetoricians of the age, are all associated with Rome or Roman pupils.

Dionysius, who took an unusually broad view of his subject, was himself an historian as well as a critic of poetry, history, rhetoric, and philosophy. Caecilius was more specialized, but in addition to writing his influential work on figures and his attack on the style of Plato he composed a treatise on fine writing to which the extant work known as Longinus' *On the sublime* is a reply.[121] More typical of

---

[120] The movement did succeed in that diction in literary Greek continued to adhere more or less to Attic standards, or claim to, for several hundred years. The attempts of the extreme Atticists to canonize the simple style were, however, much less successful. Quintilian (12.10.16 ff.) speaks of Asianism entirely as a thing of the past. The latest rhetorician to show clear Asian sympathies is Gorgias, teacher of Cicero's son and author of a work *On figures* which we have in the Latin version of Rutilius Lupus (Quintilian 9.2.102).

[121] Longinus criticizes the work as trivial (1.1) and esp. for its omission of discussion of pathos (8.1).

the pedestrian work of professional rhetoricians was that of Apollodorus of Pergamum, who taught public speaking to Augustus (Strabo 13.625), and Theodorus of Gadara, who taught Tiberius (Suetonius, *Tiberius* 57).[122] Their followers engaged in acrimonious dispute throughout most of the first century A.D. to the contempt of Quintilian (5.13.59). He says that both of them laid down rules without any experience in actual speaking so that their systems were naturally unworkable in the law courts. Although there were numerous minor differences between the two groups, the biggest contention seems to have been over the parts of the oration. The Apollodoreans insisted that every judicial speech, the only kind of oratory in which they were interested (Quintilian 3.1.1), should *always* include the four major parts of prooemium, narration, proof, and epilogue and in the some order (Seneca, *Controversiae* 2.1.36 and *Anonymous Seguerianus* 26, 113, and 124 in Spengel-Hammer 357 ff.). The Theodoreans denied the universality of the need (Seneca, *ibid.*). Scholars have been tempted to generalize the dispute into a rhetorical parallel to the analogy-anomaly dispute of the grammarians or a philosophical distinction between rhetoric as science and rhetoric as art, but the *Anonymous Seguerianus* (30 ff. in Spengel-Hammer 358) makes it clear that the two groups did not perceive the deeper significance of their differences. Theodorus was equally dogmatic about some other points (Quintilian 5.13.59).

This kind of quarrel over academic trivia with an insistence on the absolute value of impractical rules is the state to which Greek rhetoric was reduced at the end of the first century B.C. It is a logical extension of the increasing detail of rhetorical rules found in handbooks from Tisias to An-

---

[122] The basic account was that of Martin Schanz, "Die Apollodoreer und die Theodoreer," *Hermes* 25 (1890) 36 ff. It and subsequent studies are now largely replaced by G. M. A. Grube, "Theodorus of Gadara," AJP 80 (1959) 337 ff.

aximenes to Hermagoras. By the first century it was already evident that rhetorical studies were as much at home in Rome as in Athens and that conditions of Roman oratory, the attitudes of Roman students, and the problems of adapting Greek rhetoric to the Latin language were the most potent factors in contemporary rhetoric. Thus, the limit of this book has thus been reached. There were subsequent significant developments in Greek rhetoric and oratory, the so-called second sophistic is the most important, but all such movements are part of the wider intellectual history of the Roman empire.

Introduction to "On the ancient orators" by Dionysius of Halicarnassus

1. We ought in all justice to feel very grateful, my honorable Ammaeus, to the age in which we live, for many of the arts are flourishing now as they did not in the recent past. Not the least improvement may be noticed in the attention paid to speech. In the period before our own the ancient philosophic eloquence, scorned and subjected to outrageous insult, had been in a state of decay. It began to lose its spirit about the time of the death of Alexander of Macedon. Little by little its flame burned lower, until, at the beginning of our time, it was all but quenched. Another mistress had come to take its place in the house, a mistress of unbearable theatrical impudence, lacking in all breeding, and ignorant of philosophy and the liberal arts. Secretly she worked upon the ignorance of the masses. With the aid of wealth, sophistication, and allure greater than her rivals she not only led the life of a dilettante herself, but acquired the honors and governorship of cities which ought to have belonged to philosophy. She was vulgar in all respects and importunate and in the end she made Greece resemble the houses of profligates and unfortunates. For just as in those houses the freeborn and chaste wife sits mistress of none of her own possessions, while some stupid wench, intent on the ruin of the master's substance, tries to run the whole estate while treading upon and intimidating the other, similarly in every city and not least in those famous for their culture (a fact which is worst of all) the ancient native eloquence of Attica came to hold a position of dishonor and lost the right to her own property, while some Mysian or Phrygian or Carian nonsense, arrived but yesterday or the day before from some hole in Asia, ignorant of philosophy and driven into a rage at the very name of

charity, took upon herself to lord it over the cities of Greece and drive her predecessor from participation in public affairs.

2. However, as Pindar says, "time is the best saviour of just men," and not only of men, but fortunately also of arts and pursuits and all other serious business. Our own age is an example of this, whether because some god intervened or because the cycle of nature is restoring the former condition or because of some human impulse to bring many things into balance. In any event, it has given an opportunity to the old chaste form of rhetoric to take back its rightful place of honor and has ordered the young ignorant hussy to cease plucking at a dignity which does not belong to her and to desist from wasting other people's goods for her own pleasure. Nor should we praise the present age and those contemporaries who are conscious of philosophy only because they began to prefer the better rhetoric to the worse (although it is a true saying that the beginning is half of the whole), but because they have caused the change of fashion to be swift and the improvement of the arts to be great. Except in a few cities of Asia, where perception of artistic excellence is slow because of the ignorance of the inhabitants, everywhere enthusiasm for vulgar, frigid, and insensitive discourse has ceased. Those who were impressed in the past with that fashion are already ashamed of it and are little by little deserting to the other style (except for a few that are altogether incurable) and those who recently began studies are despising it and making any enthusiasm for it seem laughable.

3. It seems to me that the cause and source of this change has been the world-wide authority of Rome who has forced whole cities to look to her. Her rulers are models of virtue and administer the world with a due sense of responsibility. They are exceedingly well educated and exhibit the judgment associated with noble birth. It is their commendation which has encouraged still more the intel-

lectual element in every city and has forced the ignorant to learn sense. It is a direct result of this that many worthwhile histories are being written by our contemporaries, that many charming discourses are produced, and philosophical treatises which certainly ought not to be held in contempt, while many other fine studies have been published, with still more in all probability to come, the result of the zealous labors of both Greeks and Romans. Since there has been so great a change in this short period of time, I would not be surprised if enthusiasm for the ignorant rhetoric did not cease within one generation. For what has been reduced from omnipotence to insignificance is easily brought to the vanishing point.

4. My object in this work is not to give thanks to the age which has brought about this change, nor to praise those who have chosen the best style nor to speculate about future developments on the basis of the past nor any such task, which anyone might do, but to try to point out how this best form of eloquence may become still stronger, having chosen a subject of general interest, humane, and capable of the greatest advantage. The questions I propose to discuss are these: which of the ancient orators and historians are most worthy of study? what were their characteristics of life and speech? what ought to be imitated and what rejected in each? These I think are good subjects of research and very useful to persons practicing political philosophy, nor indeed, as it seems, are they well known, nor worn out by former authors. I at least have not happened on any such writing, although making diligent search. I will not, however, positively assert that none exists as though I knew it for a fact, for possibly there are some such writings which have escaped my attention. It is over-confidence and near insanity to make oneself the standard of knowledge of all things and to deny the existence of what is possible. Therefore, on this subject, as I said, I make no positive claim. Since the orators and historians, who are the subjects of

this study, are both very numerous and excellent I have despaired of writing about them all, for I see that there would be need of a long work to do so, but I have selected the most elegant of them and propose to speak about each of these in chronological order, in this work about the orators and if there is an opportunity in the future about the historians. There will be three comparative accounts of older orators, Lysias, Isocrates, and Isaeus, and three of orators who flourished after them, Demosthenes, Hyperides, and Aeschines, all of whom I think are better than the others. My work will be divided into two parts and will start with what I have written about the three older orators. Now that this much has been said in introduction the time has come to turn to the real matter at hand.

Index

341

69220